900

D0459148

Concise Encyclopedia of Jewish Music

Concise
Encyclopedia
of Jewish
Music

Macy
Nulman

McGRAW-HILL BOOK COMPANY
NEW YORK   ST. LOUIS   SAN FRANCISCO

AUCKLAND   NEW DELHI
DÜSSELDORF   PANAMA
JOHANNESBURG   PARIS
KUALA LUMPUR   SÃO PAULO
LONDON   SINGAPORE
MEXICO   SYDNEY
MONTREAL   TOKYO
TORONTO

Library of Congress Cataloging in Publication Data

Nulman, Macy, date.
    Concise encyclopedia of Jewish music.

    Includes bibliographical references.
    1. Music, Jewish—Dictionaries.   2. Music,
Jewish—Bio-bibliography.   I. Title.
ML106.J49N84   781.7'2'924   74-5053
ISBN 0-07-047546-6

1234567890   HDMM   784321098765

The editors for this book were Leonard Josephson and
Tobia L. Worth, the designer was Richard A. Roth, and
the production supervisor was Stephen J. Boldish. It was
set in Baskerville by University Graphics, Inc., and
Black Dot, Inc.

It was printed by Halliday Lithograph Corporation
and bound by The Maple Press Company.

To
My Wife

TABLE OF CONTENTS

INTRODUCTION

The CONCISE ENCYCLOPEDIA OF JEWISH MUSIC was conceived for the great and long-felt need of the inquiring layman as well as for the professional. It endeavors to make easily accessible in succinct form detailed information concerning the manifold aspects of Jewish music. The 500-odd entries listed alphabetically include definitions of Jewish musical terms and vocabulary, the origin and structure of Biblical and post-Biblical instruments, histories and descriptions of Jewish musical organizations and movements, biographies of representative composers and musicians, descriptive musical works, and principal published collections.

In compiling this encyclopedia I was faced with the problem of selection and deletion of items, titles, and names. For example, composers' names and their works that have been selected are those most likely to be encountered. The book includes historical data but is in no sense intended as a history of Jewish music. Articles should be read in conjunction with other entries that are indicated by cross-references printed in small capitals. The student of Jewish music should also consult the footnotes, in which references are made not only to books and articles of Jewish music but to rabbinic sources of the Talmud, responsa literature, liturgic works, and the like, as well as to a variety of modern European, American, and Israeli sources. Whenever possible, musical figures and photographs have been included in order to illustrate and give meaning to the specific point under discussion. I have constantly kept in sight the main goal: to impart information on what constitutes the Jewish musical heritage with a fresh examination of that heritage in the light of recent research and discoveries.

I am deeply indebted to many people for inspiration, guidance, and assistance in the development of this book. I want to extend my warm appreciation to Dr. Samuel Belkin, president of Yeshiva University, whose personal warmth, inspiration, and friendship have motivated me in my endeavors. I am equally grateful to the late Dr. Karl Adler for his enthusiastic and inspiring encouragement as well as for his helpful suggestions in the early stages of this volume. I want to thank and give credit to Dr. Sidney B. Hoenig for his copious advice and for his suggestions, criticisms, and corrections of many of the articles. A sincere word of thanks is also due Dr. Emanuel Rackman, who has given me the benefit of his specialized knowledge. Finally, but first and foremost, I thank my wife, who read the entire manuscript countless times and whose editorial hand is discernible on every page. Without her endurance, patient listening, and involvement in planning the proportions, tone, and focus of this book, this publication might never have become a reality.

MACY NULMAN
January 1975

LIST OF ABBREVIATIONS

A.V. – Authorized Version
abbrev. – abbreviation
ad loc. – at the place
Ar. – Arakhin (Talmud)
b. – ben (son of)
B.B. – Baba Batra (Talmud)
B.C.E. – Before the Common Era
B.K. – Baba Kamma (Talmud)
B.M. – Baba Mezi'a (Talmud)
Ber. – Berakhot (Talmud)
Bez. – Bezah (Talmud)
c. – *circa* (about)
C.E. – Common Era
cf. – *confer* (compare, refer to)
chap. – chapter
Chron. – Chronicles, Book of
comp. – compare
d. – died
D.W. – *deutsche Weise* (German manner)
Dan. – Daniel, Book of
Deut. – Deuteronomy, Book of
e.g. – *exempli gratia* (for example)
Eccl. – Ecclesiastes, Book of
ed. – edited, edition
Eng. – English
Erub. – Erubin (Talmud)
etc. – *et cetera* (and others, and so forth)
Ex. – Exodus, Book of
Ezek. – Ezekiel, Book of
ff. – and the following pages
Fig. – Figure
fl. – flourished
fol. – folio
Fr. – French
Gen. – Genesis, Book of
Ger. – German
Git. – Gittin (Talmud)
Gr. – Greek
Hab. – Habakkuk, Book of
Heb. – Hebrew
Hos. – Hosea, Book of
Hul. – Hullin (Talmud)
i.e. – *id est* (that is)
ibid. – *ibidem* (in the same place)
Inc. – Incorporated
Isa. – Isaiah, Book of
It. – Italian
Jer. – Jeremiah, Book of; Jerusalem Talmud
Jos. – Joshua, Book of
Judg. – Judges, Book of
K.J.V. – King James Version

Kel. – Kelim (Talmud)
Ket. – Ketubot (Talmud)
Kid. – Kiddushin (Talmud)
Kin. – Kinnim (Talmud)
Lam. – Lamentations, Book of
Lat. – Latin
Lev. – Leviticus
lit. – literally
loc. cit. – *loco citato* (in the place cited)
M.K. – Mo'ed Katan (Talmud)
Meg. – Megillah (Talmud)
Men. – Menahot (Talmud)
Mish. – Mishnah
N.W. – *neue Weise* (new melody)
Naz. – Nazir (Talmud)
Nah. – Nahum, Book of
Ned. – Nedarim (Talmud)
Neh. – Nehemiah, Book of
no., nos. – number, numbers
Numb. – Numbers, Book of
op. – *opus* (a work)
op. cit. – *opus citatum* (the work cited)
p., pp. – page, pages; softly, more softly
P.W. – *polnische Weise* (Polish or Eastern European manner)
Pes. – Pesahim (Talmud)
pl. – plural
Prov. – Proverbs, Book of
ps., pss. – psalm, psalms
R. – Rab, Rabban, Rabbenu, Rabbi, Reb
R.H. – Rosh Hashanah (Talmud)
rev. – revised
S.o.S. – Song of Songs
s.v. – *sub verbo* (under the entry)
Sam. – Samuel, Book of
Sanh. – Sanhedrin (Talmud)
sec. – section
Shab. – Shabbat (Talmud)
Shek. – Shekalim (Talmud)
sing. – singular
Sof. – Soferim
Sot. – Sotah (Talmud)
Suk. – Sukkah (Talmud)
Ta'an. – Ta'anit (Talmud)
Tam. – Tamid (Talmud)
Tos. – Tosefta
tr. – translated, translation
viz. – *videlicet* (namely)
vol., vols. – volume, volumes
W. – *Weise* (melody, tune, or manner)
Yeb. – Yebamot (Talmud)

Yidd. - Yiddish
YIVO - Yiddisher Visenshaftlikher Institut
    (Institute for Jewish Research)
YMHA - Young Men's Hebrew
    Association

Yom. - Yoma (Talmud)
Zeb. - Zebahim (Talmud)
Zech. - Zechariah, Book of
Zeph. - Zephaniah, Book of

AARON BEN ASHER (c. 900–c. 960). Tiberian scholar and Masorete credited with finally fixing the punctuation of the Bible. Ben Asher, as he is sometimes called, was the last of a distinguished family of Masoretes going back to the latter half of the eighth century. His setting of vowel signs and accents for the Biblical texts (*see* ACCENTS, BIBLICAL) is probably the culmination of a period in which distinguished punctuators, including his father Moses, were busily engaged (c. 750–c. 920). His Masoretic work *Dikduke ha-Te'amim* (Grammatical Rules of the Accents)[1] contains the oldest study on the subject. The Academy of the Hebrew Language in Jerusalem published a critical edition of the original text from manuscripts by Aron Dotan called *The Diqduqé Hatte'amim of Aharon ben Mose ben Aser* (1967).

[1]First published in 1517; ed. by S. Baer and H. L. Strack, Leipzig, 1879.

AB HORAHAMIM MODE. *See* MI SHEBERAH MODE.

ABRAHAM AND ISAAC. Work by Igor Stravinsky, subtitled *A Sacred Ballad for Baritone and Chamber Orchestra.* Composed in 1962–1963, it is dedicated to the people of the State of Israel. The text, known as the *Akedah* (The Binding of Isaac), is in the original Hebrew and is taken from Genesis 22:1–19.

ABRASS, JOSHUA (OSIAS) (1820–1884). Eastern European cantor-composer. Abrass, a *singerel* (singer), gained fame in Odessa as a WUNDERKIND (child prodigy) and was nicknamed *pitzsche,* from the Yiddish *pitzele* (little one). From his early youth he showed unusual musical talent. When Bezalel SCHULSINGER came to Berdichev, the city in which Abrass was born, he heard young Joshua sing. He was so deeply impressed with the boy's talent that he insisted that his parents permit him to join his choir in Odessa. The boy sang with Schulsinger and was widely acclaimed for his sweet voice and manner of singing. For a short time he studied with Salomon SULZER in Vienna and then began his professional career as a cantor–choir leader in Tarnopol (Ternopol, 1840–1842). From there he left for Lemberg (Lvov, 1842–1858) and subsequently was engaged in Odessa (1858–1884). Abrass became known throughout Russia and Poland for creating an individual style in rendering the liturgical RECITATIVE with his mellow baritone voice. As a composer he is noted for *Zimrat Yah* (1874), a work for cantor and choir.

ABUB. Syriac word meaning "pierced" or "bored." (1) A musical instrument translated as "a pipe." According to the Talmud, it is identical with the HALIL.[1] The Mishnah describes one pipe of bronze and one of reed; the latter produces a sweeter sound.[2] In Scriptural writings the terms *abuba* and *abubin* are renderings for UGAB.[3] (2) In modern Hebrew the term is used for "oboe."[4]

[1]Ar. 10b.
[2]Ar. 10a.
[3]Targum Onkeles and Targum Jonathan in Gen. 4:21 and ps. 150:4.
[4]David Ettinger, *Hebrew Pictorial Dictionary*, Dvir Publishers, Tel Aviv, 1953, pp. 164, 166, no. 17.

ACCENTS, BIBLICAL. Group of graphic signs accompanying the printed text of the Hebrew Scriptures. Each accent mark is associated with a ready-made melody, forming a melismatic phrase in the intonation of the Scriptures called CANTILLATION. In addition, the accents are used to show stress in the words in which they occur and to show the grammatical or syntactical relationship between the words of a sentence, thus indicating the logical pauses in a verse. According to William Wickes, "The Hebrew accentuation is essentially a musical system." The objective was first to arrange the musical declamation to give meaning to the text by pausal melodies. "The syntactical relation of the words to one another and to the whole clause was indicated by suitable melodies—partly pausal, partly conjunctive. . . .[1] The date of the introduction of the accents into the Hebrew text has not been ascertained. It is possible that they were first used for the instruction of schoolchildren.[2]

See also AARON BEN ASHER; BA'AL KOREI; CONJUNCTIVES; DISJUNCTIVES; NEGGINOT; TE'AMIM; TROP.

[1]*A Treatise on the Accentuation of the Prose Books of the Old Testament,* Clarendon Press, Oxford, 1887, pp. 1, 2.
[2]Meg. 22a.

ACHRON, JOSEPH (1886–1943). Virtuoso violinist, composer, and teacher. Achron was born in Lazdijai, Lithuania. He toured Russia as a child prodigy and in 1899 enrolled at the St. Petersburg Conservatory, from which he graduated in 1904 with high honors. At the conservatory he studied violin under Leopold Auer and composition with Anatol Liadov. He was a co-founder of the SOCIETY FOR JEWISH FOLK MUSIC. From 1913 to 1916 he was head of the violin and chamber music department at the Kharkov Conservatory. In 1918, after serving in the Russian Army during World War I, he became head of the violin and chamber music department of the Petrograd Artists' Union. From 1922 to 1924 he gave concerts throughout Europe, Egypt, and Palestine. Settling in the United States in 1925, he continued to teach, give concerts, and compose.

Joseph Achron.

Achron's HEBREW MELODY and numerous other works written in the Jewish idiom established him as a major representative of the trend toward a national Jewish music. Among his outstanding compositions is his *Evening Service for the Sabbath* (1932), commissioned by Temple Emanu-El in New York. Achron wrote concerti, quartets, sonatas, suites, songs, theatrical scores, and works for solo instruments.

ADLER, ISRAEL (1925–   ). Israeli musicologist and teacher. Born in Berlin, he emigrated to Palestine in 1937 and served in the armies of the Haganah (1943–1948) and the Palmah (1948–1949). He received his musical education in Paris, where he studied harmony and counterpoint at the Conservatoire National de Musique and the École Normale de Musique (1949–1953). He continued his studies at the Sorbonne, where he received his doctorate in musicology in 1963. While in Paris he headed the Judaica section of the Bibliothèque Nationale (1950–1963).

In Jerusalem Adler became director of the music department and National Sound Archives in the Jewish National and University Library (1963–1969), founder and director of the Jewish Music Research Centre at the Hebrew University (1964–1969), and director of the Jewish National and University Library (1969–1971). From 1971 on he served as director of the Jewish Music Research Centre and associate professor of musicology at Tel Aviv University. From 1967 to 1969 he was chairman of the Israeli Musicological Association, and he is a member of the music committee of the Israel Broadcasting Authority.

Among Adler's studies, undertaken in collaboration with other musicologists, are inventories registering the relevant sources of Jewish musical traditions, the place of music in Jewish life, Jewish musicians and their works, and writings by Jews on the philosophy and theory of music and on matters of musical interest. In collaboration with Hanoch AVENARY and Bathja BAYER he served as editor of *Yuval: Studies of the Jewish Music Research Centre* (1968).

ADMON (GOROCHOV), YEDIDYAH (1894–   ). Israeli composer known for creating works rooted in the CANTILLATION of the Bible and in Hassidic and Oriental Jewish song (*see* HASSIDIC SONG). Born in Yekaterinoslav (Dnepropetrovsk), Ukraine, he settled in Palestine in 1906. There he directed his energies toward a musical education, studying with Abraham Zvi IDELSOHN at the Teachers Seminary in Jerusalem and singing in his choir. From 1923 to 1927 he pursued his musical studies at Johns Hopkins University in Baltimore, and in 1930 with Nadia Boulanger at the École Normale de Musique in Paris. His musical works include a cantata, an oratorio, piano solos, songs, music for films, and incidental theater music. His popular song "Shir Hagamal" is performed throughout the world.

ADON OLAM. Initial words, meaning "Lord of the Universe," of a metrical HYMN attributed by some to Solomon ibn-Gabirol (1021–1058) of Spain. Incorporated into the SIDDUR since the fifteenth century, it serves as an introduction to the daily morning service, as part of the night prayer, as a closing hymn for the evening service on the Sabbath and holidays, and as a reading at the deathbed. According to Moroccan tradition, it is recited at the wedding prior to leading the bride to the *huppah* (canopy).

Numerous congregational and choral settings have been written by composers of the nineteenth and early twentieth centuries. A recent setting for *Adon Olam* was made by the contemporary American composer Lukas Foss. It is written for full chorus of mixed voices and cantor with organ accompaniment.[1] Figure 1a is in widespread use for the Sabbath and festivals; it is ascribed to Eliezer Mordecai GEROVITSCH[2] as well as to tradition[3] and to a

Figure 1.

folk tune.[4] Figure 1b is the Eastern European tradition, and Fig. 1c is Western European; both are sung on the High Holy Days. Figure 1d represents the Yemenite tradition, and Fig. 1e the Amsterdam tradition for the Sabbath. In Frankfurt am Main each holiday had its particular theme for *Adon Olam;* on Hanukkah, for example, the text was adapted to the popular MAOZ TZUR melody. While most Ashkenazic communities chanted the prayers on Hoshanah Rabba to the High Holy Day themes and motives, the Frankfurt community used these melodies only for *Adon Olam* and KADDISH.[5] In certain places *Adom Olam* was recited silently when a death occurred, so that the people need not report this bad tiding aloud but still could perform the necessary ritual of honoring the dead. On Sabbaths and holidays, however, this practice did not prevail.[6] Because of the beauty of its form, the simplicity of its language, and the sublimity of its religious thought, the *Adon Olam* prayer remains a favorite and is often set to tunes in folk style as well as to choral composition.

[1]Cf. *Synagogue Music by Contemporary Composers,* G. Schirmer, Inc., New York, pp. 345–354.

[2]Cf. E. M. Gerovitsch, *Schirej Simroh,* 1904, p. 28, no. 17. It is possible that Gerovitsch merely adapted the tune, since he heads it "A.W." (*alte Weise,* meaning "old melody"). See also *Manginot Shabbat,* ed. by Harry Coopersmith, Behrman House, Inc., New York, 1948, p. 44, no. 43A.

[3]I. Goldfarb and I. H. Levinthal, *Zemirot Vetishbahot Leleyl Shabbat,* Brooklyn, N.Y., 1938, p. 63.

[4]Abraham Z. Idelsohn, *The Jewish Song Book,* ed. by B. J. Cohon, Publications for Judaism, Cincinnati, 1951, p. 346.

[5]Rabbi Moses b. Abraham of Przemyśl, *Matte Moshe,* ed. by Rabbi M. Knoblowicz, London, 1958, pp. 290, 291.

[6]Rabbi G. Felder, *Yesodei Yeshurun,* Toronto, 1954, p. 126.

ADOSHEM MALAKH MODE. Mode whose name is derived from the prayer *Adoshem Malakh,* which is chanted in the Friday evening service. This prayer mode is a modified form of the mixolydian scale; that is, its main section consists of the following succession of notes: C D E F G A B♭ C. However, the seventh below the tonic (subtonic) is natural, and the tenth is flat, producing (AB) C D E F G A B♭ C (D E♭). While the subtonic (B) and the third (E) are both natural and create a major quality, the seventh (B♭) and the tenth (E♭) bring about a minor quality.

The probable reason for the current usage of other synagogal modes when chanting the *Adoshem Malakh* prayer is that before 1600 the Friday evening service began with psalm 93, followed by psalm 92. These two psalms no doubt were chanted in the *Adoshem Malakh* mode, but when psalms 95 to 99 and other poetical insertions were added as opening prayers to the service, precentors fused several modes together (*see* PRECENTOR). Thenceforth psalms 93 and 92 were no longer chanted in the pure *Adoshem Malakh* mode but in other modes as well.[1] *See also* MODES, SYNAGOGAL.

[1]Cf. Abraham Baer, *Baal T'fillah,* Göteborg, 1877, p. 96, no. 372.

AGUILAR, EMANUEL ABRAHAM (1824–1904). Composer and pianist. Aguilar was born in Clapham, London. As a pianist he gave concerts in Germany and London, and in London he became well known as a teacher and composer. He is noted for harmonizing a collection of melodies under the title *The Ancient Melodies of the Liturgy of the Spanish and Portuguese Jews* (1857), which Rev. D. A. de Sola prefaced with a historical essay on the poets, poetry, and melodies of the Sephardic liturgy. Aguilar also composed operas, cantatas, symphonies, overtures, chamber music, and songs.

AHAVAH RABBAH MODE. Mode named for a prayer of SHAHARIT with which the READER introduces the mode into the Sabbath service. It is constructed as follows: E F G♯ A B C D(♯) E. Whereas the mode retains a major third, it inserts a minor second, thus forming an augmented second between the second and third degrees of the scale. The heightened seventh (D♯) is identical with the so-called Hedjaz mode. The sixth below the tonic is C♯ (*see* Fig. 2 for a typical succession). In cantorial jargon this mode is often called *phrygush* (sometimes spelled *fregish*), a corruption of the Gregorian Phrygian mode minus the heightened third step (E F G A B C D E). *See also* MODES, SYNAGOGAL.

Figure 2.

AKDAMUT. Aramaic poem of ninety verses. According to the Ashkenazic rite, *Akdamut* (lit. "Before") is chanted responsively on the first day of Shavuot (Pentecost) prior to the reading of the Torah. Attributed to the PRECENTOR Rabbi Meir (Nehorai) ben Isaac of Orléans (eleventh century), the poem eulogizes the Jewish people and its love of God and His Law. Although the melody is not chanted to any system of accents employed in Biblical CANTILLATION, it has become universally known (*see* Fig. 3). The tune in the ADOSHEM MALAKH MODE serves as thematic material for synagogue song (for example, *Kiddush* of the three festivals)[1] and Yiddish folk song (*see* FOLK SONG, YIDDISH; for example, "Gei Mein Kind in Heder").[2]

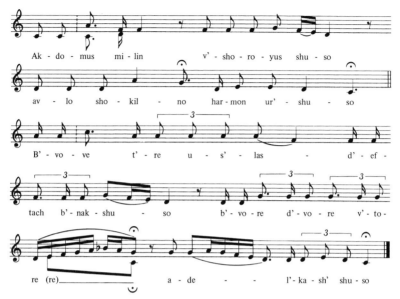

Ak - do - mus mi - lin v' - sho - ro - yus shu - so

av - lo sho - kil - no har - mon ur' - shu - so

B' - vo - ve t' - re u - s' - las d' - ef -

tach b' - nak - shu - so b' - vo - re d' - vo - re v' - to -

re (re)_____ a - de - - l' - ka - sh' shu - so

Figure 3.

[1]Gershon Ephros, *Cantorial Anthology,* Bloch Publishing Company, Inc., New York, 1948, vol. 3, pp. 59–65.

[2]Susman Kisselgof, *Lieder Zamelbuch,* 4th ed., Juwal, Berlin, 1923, pp. 12, 28.

AL-ALAMOT. Expression, meaning "on *alamot,* that appears in the heading of psalm 46:1. (1) The word is generally translated as a musical instrument.[1] Perhaps it indicates an instrument of high soprano pitch, from the noun *almah,* meaning "maiden." Thus the phrase "with psalteries set to *alamot*" (I Chron. 15:20) would mean "with psalteries in the range of the female singing voice." (2) It may signify a kind of lute originally from Elam (Persia). (3) Since *alam* means "hidden" or "to conceal," the word may denote a kind of lyre with a mute attached for the purpose of subduing or deadening the sound. It may also refer to the inner ecstasy of song, a fervor or hidden inwardness of expression not apparent in the musical notes.[2] (4) The word may signify a double flute having a soprano register similar to the Greek *elymos.*[3] (5) It may also denote a melody to which the psalm is to be chanted.[4]

[1]Cf. Rashi; David Kimchi; *Metzudat Tziyon,* loc. cit.

[2]R. Samson Raphael Hirsch, *The Psalms,* New York, 1960.

[3]Abraham Z. Idelsohn, *Jewish Music,* Tudor Publishing Company, New York, 1944, pp. 13, 496, no. 39.

[4]According to Moses Mendelssohn, J. N. Forkel, Wilhelm Gesenius, and others.

AL-AYELET HASHAHAR. Expression in psalm 22:1, translated literally as "upon the hind of the morning" or "upon the morning star." It may refer to (1) a folk melody to which the chief musician was directed to set the psalm, (2) a musical instrument,[1] or (3) a "morning flute."[2]

[1]Rashi; *Metzudat Tziyon;* David Kimchi; Ibn-Ezra.

[2]J. D. Michaelis; Moses Mendelssohn; Albert Knapp.

AL-HAGITTIT. Instruction, meaning "upon the *Gittit,*" superscribed on psalms 8:1, 81:1, and 84:1. Possible explanations include (1) a tune connected with "vintage songs," derived from the term *gat* (winepress);[1] (2) a musical instrument from the Philistine city of Gath,[2] where such instruments were made, introduced by DAVID in Palestine;[3] (3) some connection with Gath-rimmon, a dwelling place of Levite minstrels;[4] (4) a hollow instrument, from *gattat* (to deepen), synonymous with HALIL.[5]

[1] Midrash.
[2] Cf. I Sam. 27:2.
[3] Targum.
[4] Cf. Jos. 21:24, 19:45; I Chron. 6:54.
[5] Julius Fürst, *Concordance.*

AL-HASHMINIT. Expression, meaning "upon the eighth," found in psalms 6:1 and 12:1 as well as in I Chronicles 15:21. (1) It signifies an instrument having eight strings, probably a KINNOR.[1] (2) The expression may refer to the interval, the octave. In I Chronicles 15:20, *nebalim* AL-ALAMOT (after the manner of maidens) can only mean the high voice of women, while in the next verse (15:21) the phrase *kinnorot al-hashminit* (the deeper voice of men) signifies an octave lower.[2]

[1] Cf. Rashi; David Kimchi; Ibn-Ezra; *Metzudat Tziyon,* loc. cit.
[2] Carl Heinrich Cornill, *Music in the Old Testament,* The Open Court Publishing Company, Chicago, 1909, pp. 18, 19.

AL-MAHALAT. Expression, meaning "upon sickness," found in the titles of psalms 53 and 88. Biblical scholars are divided as to its meaning. Some interpretations are (1) a musical instrument;[1] (2) the initial word of a well-known tune to the melody of which the psalm was set;[2] (3) a flutelike instrument (*see* EL-HANEHILOT; HALIL); (4) a soothing tune fitting for the sick; (5) a dance or instrument, derived from the noun MAHOL, thus alluding to the fact that these psalms were meant to be performed with an accompanying dance or an instrument such as the *mahol;* (6) a stylistic direction indicating the manner in which the choir was to sing the psalm, similar to the Italian term *mesto,* meaning "sad" or "mournful";[3] (7) a word having a connection with *Abel-Meholah,*[4] a dwelling place[5] occupied by a musical group.[6]

Psalm 88 adds the word *le'annot* in the title. This may be a connection with the Hebrew verb *anay* (to respond) and hence indicates that the psalm was sung antiphonally (*see* ANTIPHONAL SINGING).

[1] Cf. Rashi; *Metzudat Tziyon,* loc. cit.
[2] Ibn-Ezra, loc. cit.
[3] Franz Delitzsch, *Biblical Commentary on the Psalms,* tr. by Francis Bolton, 3 vols., Edinburgh, 1892.
[4] Cf. *The Jewish Encyclopedia,* vol. I, p. 50.
[5] I Kings 4:12, 19:16.
[6] Julius Fürst, *Hebräisches und chaldäisches Handwörterbuch über das Alte Testament,* Leipzig, 1857–1861.

AL-MUT LABEYN. Expression, found in psalm 9:1 and translated literally as "upon the death to the son." This title has given rise to infinite conjecture. Among the explanations are the following: (1) The word *al-mut* is similar to *alamot,*[1] referring to instruments. *Labeyn* may be interpreted to mean *lehavin* or *levoneyn* (to instruct), possibly being addressed to the chief musician to instruct upon instruments called *alamot.*[2] (2) The expression may be a direction to the Levite minstrel Beyn, whose name appears among the Temple choir in I Chronicles 15:18 and whose brethren played "with psalteries on *alamot.*"[3] (3) It may also be a well-known poem or tune to which the chief musician was directed to adapt the psalm.[4]

[1]*See* AL-ALAMOT.
[2]Menahem ibn-Saruk; cf. Rashi, loc. cit.
[3]Cf. David Kimchi, loc. cit.
[4]J. A. Alexander, *The Psalms Translated and Explained,* Breslau, 1855, p. 64.

AL-SHOSHANIM. Expression, meaning "upon lilies," found in psalm 45:1, to be compared with the titles of psalms 60:1, 69:1, and 80:1. Different meanings given are (1) a musical instrument resembling a lily, whose name is *shoshanah;*[1] (2) perhaps the name of a popular air to which the psalm was sung;[2] (3) a hexachord, an instrument with six strings, from the Hebrew root *shesh,* meaning "six."[3]

[1]Ps. 45:1; David Kimchi; *Metzudat Tziyon.*
[2]Ps. 80:1; David Kimchi.
[3]Cf. William Smith, *Dictionary of the Bible,* Boston, 1883, vol. IV, p. 3020.

AL-TASHHET. Expression, meaning "destroy not," found in psalms 57:1, 58:1, 59:1, and 75:1. Divergent opinions of Biblical commentators are (1) perhaps an indication to the choir director that the psalm was to be sung to a tune utilized by grape treaders, based on a verse in Isaiah 65:8, "As the new wine is found in the cluster of grapes and one saith, destroy it not [*al-tashhitehu*] for a blessing is in it"; (2) the title or beginning of a song or poem to the melody of which these four psalms were chanted.[1]

[1]Ibn-Ezra, loc. cit.; also according to Wilhelm Gesenius and Franz Delitzsch.

AL-YONAT EYLEM REHOKIM. Phrase, meaning "upon the silent dove of them that are distant," that appears as a heading to psalm 56. There is much diversity of opinion as to its meaning. Among the musical interpretations given are (1) a title of a song to the melody of which the psalm was sung;[1] (2) a musical instrument that produced dull, mournful sounds (like those of a dove).[2]

[1]Ibn-Ezra, loc. cit.
[2]Cf. Preface to Moses Mendelssohn's translation of the Psalms.

ALEXANDER, HAIM (HEINZ) (1915–   ). Israeli teacher and composer. Born in Berlin, he attended the Stern Conservatory. In 1936 he emigrated to Palestine. After his graduation from the Israel Academy of Music in Jerusalem, he was invited to join its faculty to teach piano and composition. Alexander's many awards include the Engel Prize of the municipality of Tel Aviv for *Six Israeli Dances* (1951) for piano. He has written for orchestra and for various combinations of instruments. Among recent works are *Ben-Kol uVat-Kol* (1971), for narrator and symphony orchestra (text by Dan Pagis), and *Ahuv Libi Ssameach* (1971), for piano duet. The Israel Composers' Fund, in cooperation with the Ministry of Education and Culture, has commissioned him to decipher the numerous melodies from the collection of phonographic archives of the Hebrew University so that they can be utilized by aspiring music students and Israeli composers.

ALGAZI, LEON (1890–1971). French choirmaster, composer, and writer. Born in Romania, he was graduated from the École Rabbinique de France and received a general musical training in Vienna and France. His interest in Jewish music was aroused when he studied with Abraham Zvi IDELSOHN. Algazi's varied activities caught the attention of forward-looking musicians and educators in France when he was appointed instructor at the École de Liturgie et de Pédagogie of Paris. He began a weekly radio program featuring Jewish music in 1929, and he was appointed choirmaster at the Temple de la Rue de la Victoire in Paris in 1937. From 1936 to 1940 he taught Jewish music at the Schola Cantorum, and in 1961 he became head of the music department of the Association Consistoriale Israélite de Paris. With V. Dick he was active in directing the Mizmor division of the Salabert publishing company.

Algazi is well known for his *Service sacré pour le samedi matin et pour le vendredi soir* (1955) and his *Chants séphardis* (1958). He also wrote music for psalms, suites, folk and art song harmonizations, incidental theater music, and numerous articles on Jewish music.

ALIYAH. Term (lit. "going up") used in the synagogue service for the honor extended to a worshiper who is called up to the *bimah* (reading desk) for a portion of the Torah reading. Prior to the twelfth century every person called

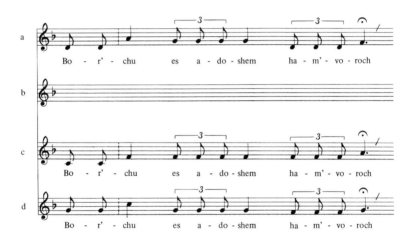

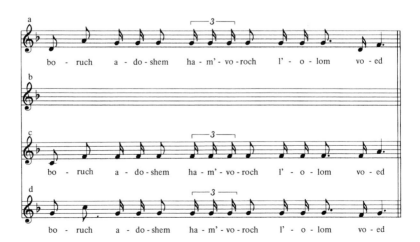

Figure 4a–d.

Figure 4e.

up read his own portion. The reading was prepared well in advance with proper accentuation and CANTILLATION.[1] Between the twelfth and the fourteenth century it became the established custom for the SHELIAH TZIBBUR to prompt the words as well as the accentuation and cantillation for worshipers not proficient in reading.[2] In the fourteenth century a special reader was appointed to read all portions so as not to humiliate any person who was unable to read properly. The person having the *aliyah* then chanted only the benedictions before and after the reading of his portion, a custom that still prevails. Various traditions guide the intonation of these blessings. Figure 4, showing four examples, demonstrates this point. Figures 4*a* and *b* are of the Eastern European tradition; *c* is of the Western European tradition; and *d* is utilized for the High Holy Days. The *a* melody, which utilizes the same intonation for both blessings, was most likely introduced for the *bar mitzvah* (a boy who reaches his thirteenth birthday) in order to make it easier for him to learn the chant.

It was customary in different localities to sell the *aliyot* (pl.) and Torah honors[3] so that the worshipers might pay for the upkeep of the synagogue and for the poor.[4] A special method and melody were employed in the sale of these *mitzvot* (good deeds). Figure 4*e* illustrates the method of sale and its intonation. This chantlike melody possibly dates back to antiquity, when pulpit proclamations were intoned in this manner.[5] *See also* BA'AL KOREI.

[1] Tos. Shab. 1, 6; *Tanhuma, Yitro* 15; Ber. 55a.
[2] Men. 30a, *Tosafot-Shenonah;* Tos. Meg. 3, 6; *The Jewish Encyclopedia,* vol. I, p. 400; Israel Abrahams, *Jewish Life in the Middle Ages,* Atheneum Publishers, New York, 1969, p. 18.
[3] *Magen Avraham, Orah Hayyim* 136.
[4] J.D. Eisenstein, *Ozar Dinim u-Minhagin,* New York, 1938, p. 374.
[5] Israel Rabinovitch, *Of Jewish Music,* The Book Center, Montreal, 1952, pp, 120, 121.

ALMAN, SAMUEL (1877–1947). Choir director and composer responsible for introducing the Eastern European synagogue style into the English service. He was born in Podolia, Russia, and in 1895 began his musical studies at the Odessa Conservatory of Music. Subsequently he served for four years as a musician in the Russian Army. Because of numerous pogroms he emigrated in 1905 to London, where he continued his musical studies at the Royal College of Music. In London he served as choirmaster of the Daltan, Great, Duke's Place, and Hampstead Synagogues, the Halevi Choral Society, and the London Hazzanim Choir. He was the editor of the Supplement to the *Voice of Prayer and Praise* (1933) and contributed articles on Jewish music to the *Jewish Music Journal* in New York.

Among Alman's compositions are an opera, *Melech Ehad* (1912), a string quartet, choral works, pieces for piano and organ, and songs on religious texts. Works in which he presents liturgical compositions and recitatives in the Eastern European style are *Shire Bet Hakeneset* (part 1, 1925; part 2, 1938) and *Shirei Rozumni* (ed. 1930).

ALTE MELODIE. Phrase meaning "old melody," conspicuous because of its use at the head of numerous liturgical choral settings in Hirsch WEINTRAUB's *Schire Beth Hashem* (Königsberg, 1895; e.g., nos. 16–20). Some settings (e.g., nos. 34, 38, and 39) are headed *uralte Melodie* or *uralte Weise* ("very old melody"). Weintraub, in his foreword, states that it is not known how old these melodies are, but he designates melodies in the Phrygian, mixolydian, and aeolian modes with *uralte Melodie* and the rest with *alte Melodie.* The term *alte Melodie* is used also by other synagogue composers.

ALTSHUL (ALTSHULER), JOSEPH (1839–1908). Cantor-composer, teacher, and Talmudic scholar. He was nicknamed Yoshe (Yossi) Slonimer because from about 1870 to 1888 he served as *stadt hazzan* (*see* HAZZAN, STADT) in Slonim, Russia, and exerted a strong influence upon students who apprenticed themselves to him.

Born in Vilna, Altshul left the city for the village of Pikeln, in Courland (Latvia), where he became engrossed in Talmudic study while also showing great talent as a singer. He studied with Cantor Hayyim WASSERZUG and received *kabbalah* as a *shohet* (ritual slaughterer). For a short period he was employed as a *hazzan-shohet* in a small town. Unable to tolerate life in a small place, he left for Berdichev to study and sing as a chorister with Yeruchom BLINDMAN. After serving in Slonim for eighteen years, he was appointed to a post in Grodno, where he remained for the rest of his life.

Altshul was known for his powerful bass voice and his tuneful compositions. He is remembered particularly for his dramatic setting of the HINENI HEANI recitation for the High Holy Days.

AMEN. Solemn response of affirmation or agreement to a preceding statement, meaning "so be it" or "so shall it be." The congregational response "amen" generally corresponds to the modal structure of the preceding prayer or benediction (*see* Fig. 5).

Figure 5.

Great significance and spiritual value are attached to this congregational response throughout Jewish history. In the middle of the basilicasynagogue of Alexandria the HAZZAN *ha-kenesset* (beadle) stood with a flag in his hand, which he waved after the conclusion of a benediction as a signal for the congregation to answer "amen."[1] Of importance are the laws that prescribe its utterance with proper direction of heart,[2] enunciation,[3] dynamics,[4] and duration.[5] Furthermore, *hazzanim* (cantors) who prolong the amen with melismatic chant, thus distorting the word, should be rebuked.[6] Examples of Biblical verses in which the word occurs are Numbers 5:22, Deuteronomy 27:15–26, I Kings 1:36, psalms 41:14 and 72:19, and I Chronicles 16:36.

[1]Suk. 51b.
[2]Sanh. llla.
[3]Ber. 47a.
[4]Ibid., 45b.
[5]Rabbi Isaiah Horowitz, *Shnei Luhot ha-Brit,* Amsterdam, 1698, sec. on *tefilah,* p. 257.
[6]Ibid.

AMIRAN (POUGATCHOV), EMANUEL (1909–   ). Israeli educator, lecturer, and composer. Amiran was born in Warsaw. Soon thereafter his family moved to Russia and from there, in 1924, emigrated to Palestine. His early musical education began in Russia under the tutelage of Joel ENGEL and Professor David Shor. He reached musical maturity under the aegis of Solomon ROSOWSKY in Jerusalem and of Sir Granville Bantock and Alec Roley in London (1934–1936). Together with Leo Kestenberg he founded the Music Teachers Seminary in Tel Aviv, and in 1948 he was appointed an officer and instructor of musical activities in the Israel Defense Army. In 1949 he became the Directing Supervisor of Music Education in the Ministry of Education and Culture.

Amiran's music has been widely performed in Israel and other countries. His compositions include symphonic works, a cantata, chamber music, incidental music, folk songs, children's songs, and music for films. Among his songs that reflect the Israeli folk style are "Mayim Mayim," "Emek Avodah," and "Ki Mitziyon."

ANENU. Outcry or petition, meaning "Answer us," in a congregational refrain, similar to AMEN, HALLELUYAH, and HOSHA NA.[1] On fast days the prayer *Anenu* ("Answer us, O Lord, answer us on this day of the fast of our humiliation") is inserted in the *Amidah.*[2] Its mode of recitation generally follows that of the

Figure 6a, opening and closing (above); **b** (below).

weekday *Amidah* (*see* Fig. 6a).[3] The *Anenu* was also arranged as a prayer in alphabetical acrostic for the SELIHOT service by the Geonim and Rav Amram Gaon (821–875). Polish or Eastern European Jewry employs the *Selihah* mode (P.W. = *polnische Weise*), whereas the German version utilizes the major (D.W. = *deutsche Weise*). *See* Fig. 6b.[4]

[1]Ta'an, 11b, 13b, 14a.
[2]Jer. Ta'an. II, 2.
[3]From Aaron Friedmann's *Schir Lisch'laumau*, Berlin, 1901, pp. 49, 50, no. 68.
[4]From Abraham Baer's *Baal T'fillah*, Göteborg, 1877, p. 315, no. 1360.

ANTIPHONAL SINGING. Response made by one choir to another. For this purpose the choir or congregation is divided into two parts that sing alternately. An early example of this form of singing occurred when David returned in triumph over the Philistines and the women sang one to another in balanced responsive phrases.[1] *See also* RESPONSORIAL.

[1]I Sam. 18:7. For other examples of antiphonal singing, *see* Deut. 27:21–26; Neh. 12:27–42; Sot. 7:5.

ARVIT (also called *Ma'ariv*). The evening prayer. According to tradition this prayer was instituted by the patriarch Jacob.[1] The order of the service is BAREKHU, *Shema* and its benedictions, the *Amidah*, the *Alenu*, and KADDISH. Except for the *Amidah*, the text is basically the same for the entire yearly cycle. Of the three daily services, *Arvit* is the only one in which the *Amidah* is not repeated by the READER. In Tannaitic days[2] a debate developed as to whether the evening service was obligatory or optional, since it did not correspond to any daily sacrifice brought to the Temple. Later generations assumed the evening prayer as a duty.[3]

The prayer chants and melodies vary for weekdays, Sabbath, and holidays, each having its own representative modes and themes.[4] On the Sabbath and holidays *hazzanim* (cantors; *see* HAZZAN) express jubilation generally by intoning the prayers in melismatic chant (*see* MELISMA) with higher pitch levels and embellishments. On weekdays the service is chanted with narrower intervals. Nevertheless, from the early 1900s until recently cantors appeared in "*Ma'ariv* Concerts" or "Grand *Ma'ariv* Concerts" on weekday evenings for fund raising or other worthy causes. This practice gave the cantor and choir free rein in their musical tastes, and thus the texts of the liturgy were set to elaborate musical arrangements. The prolonged "*Arvit* Service-Concert" was usually followed, with the cantor and choir singing liturgical and Yiddish or operatic selections, or both. *See also* CONCERT.

[1]Gen. 28:11.
[2]Ber. 27b.
[3]Rambam, *Yad, Tefilah*, i6.
[4]*See* Jacob L. Wasilkowsky, *Ma'ariv Chants*, ed. by Macy Nulman, Yeshiva University, New York, 1965.

ASAPH. Levite, son of Berekhyahu. He was famous for his skill as a musician and as a leader of King DAVID's choir.[1] Scripture refers to him as a *hozeh* (seer) and as a composer equal to David.[2] Twelve psalms bear his name in the title.[3] The name Asaph refers also to the family that inherited his office or to a school of poets and musical composers who were named after him, "the sons of Asaph."[4]

[1]I Chron. 6:24, 15:17.
[2]II Chron. 29:30; Neh. 12:46.
[3]Pss. 50, 73–83.
[4]I Chron. 25:1; II Chron. 24:14; Ezra 2:41.

ASOR. Word occuring in psalms 33:2, 92:4, and 144:9, generally accepted as being derived from the Hebrew *asarah*, meaning "ten." There are several interpretations: (1) Since the word is always mentioned in connection with the NEBEL, it is considered an adjective, and the phrase is translated as "ten-

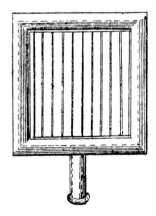

Nebel asor. [Shaul Shaffer, **Hashir Shebamikdash,** Yefey Nof, Jerusalem]

נבל עשור

stringed *nebel.*" (2) Psalm 92:4 reads "on the *asor* and on the *nebel.*" The conjunction "and" seems to indicate a feature separate from the *nebel,* and the phrase possibly alludes to two different instruments.[1] (3) The word may also refer to a ten-stringed zither that the children of Israel adopted from their most civilized neighbors, the Phoenicians.[2]

[1]Cf. David Kimchi's and Ibn-Ezra's comments on ps. 33:2.
[2]Curt Sachs, *The History of Musical Instruments,* W. W. Norton & Company, Inc., New York, 1940, pp. 117, 118.

ATZE BEROSHIM. Expression used in II Samuel 6:15. Various interpretations are (1) instruments made of cypress wood;[1] (2) a generalization referring to the specification of the two instruments that immediately follow it—"and with harps, and with psalteries";[2] (3) a type of clapper instrument made of two sticks of cypress wood.[3]

[1]Rashi; *Metzudat David,* loc. cit. *See also* I Chron. 13:8.
[2]David Kimchi, loc. cit.
[3]Abraham Portaleone, *Shilte ha-Gibborim,* Mantua, 1612, chap. 5.

AVENARY, HANOCH (HERBERT LOEWENSTEIN) (1908–   ). Israeli musicologist and teacher. Born and educated in Germany, Avenary went in 1936 to Palestine, where he devoted his energies to research. He earned the degree of research fellow at the Hebrew University and became a member of the Jewish Music Research Centre in Jerusalem. He serves on the faculty of the department of musicology of Tel Aviv University and is vice-chairman of the Israeli Musicological Association.

Avenary's papers and other writings cover a wide field of research. They include "Formal Structure of Psalms and Canticles in Early Jewish and Christian Chant" (1953), "The Musical Vocabulary of Ashkenazic Hazanim" (1960), *Studies in the Hebrew, Syrian and Greek Liturgical Recitative* (1963), and "The Cantorial Fantasia of the Eighteenth and Nineteenth Centuries" (1968).

AVIDOM (MAHLER-KALKSTEIN), MENAHEM (1908–   ). Israeli composer and teacher. Born in Stanislav, Galicia, he emigrated to Palestine in 1925 and later studied in Paris. His musical activities multiplied as he became a music educator in Tel Aviv (1935–1946), general secretary of the ISRAEL

Menahem Avidom. [Israel Music Institute, Tel Aviv]

PHILHARMONIC ORCHESTRA (1945–1952), adviser on the arts to the Ministry of Tourism (1952–1955), director general of the Israel Performing Rights Society (ACUM), and chairman of the LEAGUE OF COMPOSERS IN ISRAEL. He is also a fellow of the International Institute of Arts and Letters and a member of the Israel National Arts Council. Avidom has written symphonies, operas, string quartets, and works for various intrumental combinations. In 1961 he received the Israel State Prize for his opera *Alexandra.*

AVNI, TZVI (1927–   ). Israeli composer. Born in Germany, he emigrated to Palestine as a child. After graduating from the Israel Academy of Music in Tel Aviv, he continued his studies in the United States. Avni has written chamber music, ballets, choral works, and songs. Among his recent works are *By the Rivers of Babylon* (1972), a prelude for symphony orchestra; and DE PROFUNDIS (1972), for strings.

AVODATH HAKODESH (SACRED SERVICE). Title of Ernest BLOCH's music for the Sabbath morning ritual for baritone (cantor), mixed choir, and organ or full orchestra. Written to a Hebrew text according to the Union Prayer Book, the service was composed in five parts and published in 1933.

AZ YASHIR. *See* SHIRAH, THE.

AZLA (⌐   ). Accent sign placed above the word in the printed text of the Bible. It literally means "going on," that is, not pausing in the melody and referring to the previous sign, the KADMA. When the *kadma* precedes the *azla,* the unit is called *kadma-ve'azla.* [1] The *azla* in this combination always appears on the last syllable of the word *(milra),* and the melody is described as an ascending one. [2]

    See also GERESH; TE'AMIM.

[1] Gen. 1:29.
[2] Aaron ben Asher, *Dikduke ha-Te'amim,* ed. by S. Baer and H. L. Strack, Leipzig, 1879, p. 19.

B

BA'AL KOREI (properly *ba'al keriah*). Officiant who reads the Torah (Law) from the scroll in the synagogue with proper accentuation and CANTILLATION. Prior to the twelfth century it was customary for each person called up to the Torah to read his own portion. In order not to embarrass those unable to read properly a *ba'al korei* was appointed to chant the Torah selection for each of the worshipers honored with an ALIYAH. In the fourteenth century it was also customary for the *ba'al korei* "to recite a prayer on behalf of those called to the Torah so that they may offer a contribution in honor of the Torah."[1] In German communities the appelation *Vorleser* was popularly used for *ba'al korei*.[2]

[1] Israel Elfenbein (ed.), *Sefer Minhagim debay Maharam bereb Baruh mi-Rothenburg*, New York, 1938, p. 14.
[2] Abraham Baer, *Baal T'fillah*, Göteborg, 1877, p. 29, no. 104b.

BA'AL MUSAF. Officiant who leads the congregation in the MUSAF service on the Sabbath and holidays. Because the *Musaf* of the High Holy Days is of exceptional importance, the term *ba'al Musaf* is applied mainly to the officiant of this service, and his rendition is therefore regarded as superior to that of the BA'AL SHAHARIT.[1] The significance[2] and length[3] of the *Musaf Amidah* (standing prayer) require the *ba'al Musaf* to possess sincere devotional qualities and enduring vocal skill. Rabbinic literature is stringent as to the selection of an officiant for this service as well as for other services during the Days of Awe.[4]

[1] Maimonides, *Hilkhot Tefilah*, viii.
[2] R.H. 32a, b; Ber. 29.
[3] R.H. 34b, 35a; Tos. Ber. 1:6.
[4] Ramah, *Orah Hayyim* 581:1.

BA'AL SHAHARIT. Officiant who chants the morning service (SHAHARIT). Although this service is recited daily, the name *ba'al Shaharit* is applied mainly to the READER on the High Holy Days. The melodies and liturgic texts of the High Holy Days differ from those of the rest of the year and hence demand a person with knowledge of the special texts, prayer chants, and pulpit procedures. Of special significance is the first word, *Hamelekh* (the King), with which the *ba'al Shaharit* begins the service *(see* Fig. 7). The chant in its melismatic form *(see* MELISMA) was introduced by the Ashkenazic authority of the thirteenth century, Rabbi Meir of Rothenburg. It was popularized by Rabbi Jacob MOLIN (MaHaRIL), who served as a SHELIAH TZIBBUR for the *Shaharit* service on Rosh Hashanah. He began in a hushed, plaintive manner and gradually increased the volume until he reached a majestic climax.[1] The reader still

Figure 7.

begins the chant softly and raises his voice as he approaches the prayer desk. Customarily, the *ba'al Shaharit* does not chant the MUSAF service, since no one is permitted to stand in prayer for more than three hours at a time.[2]

[1]Abraham Z. Idelsohn, *Jewish Music*, Tudor Publishing Company, New York, 1944, pp. 157, 158; S. Y. Agnon, *Days of Awe*, Schocken Books, Inc., New York, 1948, pp. 57, 58.
[2]Ramban, Ex. 16; Rabbenu Nissim on R.H. 4:7.

BAAL SHEM. Suite for violin and piano composed in 1923 by Ernest BLOCH and subtitled *Three Pictures of Chassidic Life.* The work, which was named after and inspired by Rabbi Israel Baal Shem Tov (1700–1760), portrays three different pictures of Hassidic life: "Vidui" (Confession), expressing moods of repentance; "Niggun" (Melody), in a free improvisational style reflecting the chanting of the Hassid; and "Simchat Torah" (Rejoicing of the Law), named after the most joyous Jewish holiday in the yearly cycle.

BA'AL TEFILAH. Leader in prayer. (1) Term (lit. "master of prayer") generally used in contrast to HAZZAN to designate a person who leads the prayers with a

Title page of an edition of Abraham Baer's *Baal T'fillah* published in Frankfurt am Main.

pleasing voice, knows the traditional prayer chants, and sings them in a simple style without particular variations, embellishments, or COLORATURA. In modern times the term is sometimes translated "associate cantor" or "assistant cantor." (2) Title of a work, spelled *Baal T'fillah,* with a subtitle, *Der practische Vorbeter,* which was first published by Abraham BAER in 1877, with a second edition in 1883; it was revised and enlarged in 1901. A new edition was published in 1930 and again in 1953. The work contains 1,511 chants and directions for all the texts of the prayer book and MAHZOR for the entire year. This work is the most extensive collection ever to be published with instructions for liturgical customs and procedures as well as the ritual of reading the Torah. The volume is notated in various musical traditions such as the Eastern European or Polish rite, marked P.W. *(polnische Weise)* or M.P. *(minhag Poland);* the German rite, marked D.W. *(deutsche Weise)* or M.A. *(minhag Ashkenaz);* and Portuguese chants, marked Port.W. or *minhag Sepharad.* New melodies are appended and marked N.W. *(neue Weise),* and melodies of older *hazzanim* (cantors) are marked A.W. *(alte Weise).* (3) Title of a two-volume handbook of recitatives for the cantor *(see* RECITATIVE) written by Joshua Samuel WEISSER. Volume I is for the Sabbath and the three festivals (1936); Volume II, for the High Holy Days (1940).

BA'AL TOKE'AH (also *toke'ah*). Person officially designated to blow the SHOFAR in the synagogue during the services on the New Year Day. The Talmud describes the sounding of the *shofar* as an art,[1] and great emphasis is placed on the *ba'al toke'ah*'s concentration of thought *(kavanah)* and knowledge of the mode of performance.[2] In addition, the *ba'al toke'ah* recites two benedictions in traditional chant *(see* Fig. 8). The theme of this chant is utilized also for the *Shehekheyanu* blessing on Yom Kippur Eve, as well as for the benedictions prior to reading the *Megillah* on Purim *(see* MEGILLOT, THE FIVE).

All these occasions deal or have dealt with the fate of man. On Rosh Hashanah the *shofar* reminds us of the Day of Judgment,[3] on Yom Kippur each person's lot is determined, and on Purim Haman cast lots to determine the most favorable month and day for the execution of his evil plan to

Figure 8.

exterminate the Jews of Persia.[4] It is possible that the same theme was used for all these occasions in order to direct the worshipers' attention to this sentiment. *See also* MAKRI.

[1]R.H. 29b.
[2]*Orah Hayyim* 589.
[3]This is the eighth of Saadiah Gaon's ten reasons for sounding the *shofar* on Rosh Hashanah.
[4]C. 510 B.C.E.

BACHMANN, JACOB (1846–1905). Russian cantor-composer. Born in Berdichev, he received a Jewish education in a yeshivah while also studying secular subjects. He acquired his musical training by singing in the local synagogue choir of Moses Pasternak. On his eighteenth birthday he enrolled in the St. Petersburg Conservatory, where he studied musicianship and voice under its director, Anton Rubenstein. Bachmann, who became known for his heroic tenor voice, sang successfully in concerts with Rubenstein but chose the cantorate as his career. He held positions in Berdichev, Rostov, and Constantinople. He achieved his greatest fame as chief cantor in Lemberg (LVOV, 1868–1884); Odessa (1884–1885), where he succeeded Joshua ABRASS; and Budapest (1885–1905), at the Rombach Temple.

Jacob Bachmann. [*The History of Hazanuth,* Jewish Ministers Cantors Association of America, New York]

Bachmann is known for his collections of synagogue compositions *Schirath Jacob* (1884) and *Yom Kippur Katan* (1892). In 1879, in honor of the silver anniversary of Emperor Francis Joseph I and Empress Elizabeth, he composed a cantata (psalm 45) for which he was highly praised. He also wrote numerous articles on Jewish and general music.

BADHAN (pl. *badhanim*). Term derived from the Aramaic *badah* (to make merry),[1] designating a comedian, jester, buffoon, or entertainer. Similar terms are *letz* (pl. *leitzim*), MARSCHALLIK (pl. *marschalliks*), and folk singer. Rashi, the Biblical and Talmudic commentator, refers to the *amora* Bar Kappara as a *badhan.*[2] Rabbinic scholars through the ages participated in Jewish life as *badhanim.* As late as the mid-nineteenth century a report was made of an Eastern European *badhan,* Rabbi Eliezer Sislevitch, who interspersed his rhymes with quotations from the Midrash and the Talmud.[3]

The *badhan's* task was to act as singer and master of ceremonies at weddings and circumcisions and on Purim and other happy occasions, sometimes performing in costume. One of his important roles was to put the bride in a proper mood prior to the wedding ceremony. This function was called *kalah bazetzen, kalah badeken,* or *kalah bazingen* (*see* Fig. 9a). The *badhan* also announced, in musical declamation, the donation of wedding gifts (Fig. 9b). Both words and melody were improvised, usually in verse, and had a humor-

ערב החופה

כסוי הכלה

מנגינה זאת המכונה „כלה באדעקנס" וגם „כלה באזעצן" ו„כלה באזינגען" משמיע הבדחן בנכחותן
של נשי הקרובים, חברות הכלה ואורחות.

רשום מפי משה רויטמז הי"ד

מתנת דרשה

נוסח הקריאה של „דרשה געשאנק" עם ה„וויוואט", המכונה בלשון הכליזמרים גם „טוש".

Figure 9a (above) and b (below). [Haifa Music Museum and Amli Library]

Badhan (center) with ***klezmorim*** in Byelorussia (late nineteeth century). [Joachim Stutschewsky, ***Haklezmorim,*** Bialik Institute, Jerusalem]

ous and melancholy quality. The tunes were adapted from and based on the synagogue modes and melodies (*see* MODES, SYNAGOGAL). The *badhan*'s influence on musical folk literature was far-reaching. His songs and folk comedies were the beginning of the Yiddish theater (*see* YIDDISH THEATER MUSIC), and he kept alive a large body of folk melodies, many of which are still current. The most celebrated *badhan* of modern times was Eliakum ZUNSER (1836–1913). The institution of the *badhan* disappeared in Central Europe after the middle of the nineteenth century, but it survived in Eastern Europe until about 1939.

[1] The Targum translates the phrase *veyaltzu vekha* (ps. 5:12) by *veyivdehun bakh.* The phrase *milta debedihuta* (something humorous) can be found in Shab. 30b.

[2] Ned. 50b.

[3] Jacob Zizmor, "Fun mayne Zikhronot vegn Badhanim," in *Pinkes,* ed. by Zalman Reyzen, Vilna, 1923, p. 875.

BAER, ABRAHAM (1834–1894). Cantor and earliest collector of liturgical melodies. Born in Filehne (Wieleń), Posen Province, Prussia, he left his birthplace at an early age to prepare himself for the cantorate. His career as a cantor began in Pakosch (Pakość) and Schwetz (Świecie), West Prussia. In 1857 he was invited to Göteborg, Sweden, by the Jewish community, and he remained there as chief cantor and singing teacher for thirty-seven years. It was in Göteborg, too, that Baer acquired a secular and scientific knowledge of music, which he put to use in collecting and notating, from both oral and written traditions, a great number of musical variations for almost every liturgical text. The fruits of his research appeared in 1877, when he published his monumental opus *Baal T'fillah* (See BA'AL TEFILAH), which he prefaced with an essay on Jewish music.

BAREKHU. Formal call to prayer, meaning "Bless ye," as formulated in the SHAHARIT and ARVIT services.[1] The response of the congregation, "Blessed be the Lord who is to be blessed for ever and ever," which is repeated by the READER, is based on the text "When I call on the name of the Lord, ascribe ye greatness unto our God."[2] For each service of the yearly cycle a special melody

Bor'chu

Kel Chai

Figure 10*a*.

Figure 10*b*.

type is utilized and adapted to that of adjacent prayers (*see* Fig. 10*a*). The reader prolongs the melody of this invocation in order to allow the congregation ample time to recite silently the passage *yitbarakh veyishtabah* (Blessed, praised, etc.).[3] The law states that the congregation must be careful to recite the passage only when the reader is using a melismatic chant (Fig. 10*b; see* MELISMA).[4] If he pronounces the words without a melismatic chant, the congregation remains silent.[5] In the evening service at the conclusion of the Sabbath, the *barekhu* is to be chanted slowly with a melodious intonation as if it were a farewell to the departing Sabbath.[6]

[1]Neh. 9:5; Ber. 49b.
[2]*Sifri;* Deut. 32:3.
[3]*The Authorized Daily Prayer Book,* ed. by Dr. Joseph H. Hertz, Bloch Publishing Company, Inc., New York, 1948, pp. 108, 109.
[4]Example from Abraham Baer, *Baal T'fillah,* Göteborg, 1877, p. 164, no. 719.
[5]*Magen Avraham, Orah Hayyim* 57.
[6]*Orah Hayyim* 293, 3.

BARUKH SHE'AMAR. Initial words, meaning "Blessed be he who spoke," of a prayer in the daily SHAHARIT service that serves as the introductory benediction to the *Pesukay Dezimrah* (Verses of Song) section.[1] Its composition is attributed to the "Men of the Great Assembly,"[2] and it was in common usage in the Geonic period. Some believe that the form of its recitation was RESPONSORIAL: after each clause recited by the READER the congregation repeated the responsive refrain *barukh hu* (Blessed be He).[3] Others dispute this theory, stating that the recitation was responsorial only when the prayer was sung as a hymm at the installation ceremony of the *Resh Galuta* (Exilarch, or Prince of the Captivity) in Babylon. In the service proper the phrase *barukh hu* was part of the prayer.[4] In the Middle Ages it was customary for the reader to chant the entire *barukh she'amar* passage.[5] Rabbi Shimshon ben Rabbi Eliezer (14th century), author of the work *Barukh She'amar*, sang the entire passage with a sweet voice every morning in the synagogue. At an early age he was nicknamed Baruch She'amar, an appellation that clung to him for the rest of his life.[6] In Prague every synagogue had a singing society called Mezamray Barukh She'amar, and the tombstones of de-

Figure 11.

ceased members were marked "Mezamray B'sh."[7] In the late seventeenth and early eighteenth centuries this society played instrumental music on Friday afternoons to welcome the Sabbath in a joyous mood. Abraham BAER notated *barukh she'amar* for weekdays, the Sabbath, festivals, and High Holy Days. Figure 11, according to Eastern European tradition, is excerpted from his volume *Baal T'fillah* (*see* BA'AL TEFILAH) and is sung on the High Holy Days.

[1] Cf. Rif, Ber. 32a.
[2] Cf. *Ture Zahab, Orah Hayyim* 51, 1.
[3] Cf. R. Nathan Hababli, *Sefer ha-Yuhasin;* Solomon Judah Löb Rapoport, *Bikhure ha-Ittim,* x, 117.
[4] S. Baer, *Siddur Avodath Israel,* Rödelheim, 1868, p. 58; *Kol Bo,* 4.
[5] *Tur Orah Hayyim* 51.
[6] R. Hayyim Joseph David Azulai, *Shem ha-Gedolim,* 1852, no. 2.
[7] Simon Hock, *Die Familien Prags nach den Epitaphien des alten jüdischen Friedhofes in Prag,* ed. by David Kaufman, Pressburg, 1892.

BAT KOL. (1) Term used throughout Hebrew literature to refer to a reverberating sound or a voice descending from heaven to offer guidance in human affairs.[1] It is not actually a heavenly voice that is heard, but the reverberation caused by the voice from heaven (a secondary sound), similar to the reverberations caused by the striking of an object. Thus the term *bat kol* (lit. "daughter of a voice" or "daughter of a sound") is used to designate a small voice and distinguishes it from the normal voice.[2] It is recorded that the *tanna* Rabbi Yosi heard a *bat kol* cooing like a dove in the ruins of Jerusalem.[3] (2) Special being who leads the song of the celestial beings in praise of the Most High around His throne.[4] (3) Illustrated musical periodical issued in Israel in 1955, containing historical material (four numbers).

[1]Dan. 4:28.
[2]Cf. *Tosafot*, Sanh. 11a, s.v. *Bat Kol*.
[3]Ber. 3a.
[4]Ludwig Blau quoting Adolf Jellinek in *The Jewish Encyclopedia*, vol. II, p. 592.

BAUER, JACOB (1852–1926). Cantor and teacher. He received a Jewish education in his birthplace, a village near Szenice (Senica), Slovakia, Hungary. Later he studied at the *Realschule* in Vienna and served an apprenticeship with the Polish cantor Pesah Feinsinger and with Professor Franz Vogl for voice. Bauer held positions as a cantor in Szigetvár (1875–1878), Graz (1878–1881), and the Turkish-Israelite Temple in Vienna (1881–1926). He is known for founding the *Österreichisch-Ungarische Cantoren-Zeitung* and cofounding a cantors' association in Austria-Hungary (1881). He served as the association's president and was on the faculty for training prospective cantors. In collaboration with the choirmaster Isidor Löwit, Bauer composed *Shir-ha-Kabod* (1889), a work for the Sephardic ritual.

BAYER, BATHJA (1928–   ). Israeli musicologist. Born in Bingen, Germany, she was taken in 1936 to Palestine, where she graduated from the Israel Academy of Music in Tel Aviv and the Oranim Teachers Seminary. In 1959 she obtained her doctorate in Zurich. She taught at Oranim, served as secretary of the Israeli Musicological Association (1963–1964), and subsequently joined the staff of the Jewish Music Research Centre of the Hebrew University of Jerusalem and the music department of the Jewish National and University Library.

Jewish musicology has been enriched by Bathja Bayer's numerous writings. Her studies *The Material Relics of Music in Ancient Palestine and Its Environs: An Archeological Inventory* (1963) and "The Biblical Nebel" (1968) have shed much light on Biblical instruments.

BEER, AARON (1738–1821). Cantor. Born in Bamberg, Bavaria, Beer began his career as a cantor in Paderborn in 1759. In 1765 he was appointed chief cantor of the Jewish Congregation of Berlin, where he served for fifty-six years. He attained great fame, and worshipers gathered from far and wide to hear him. Beer was the first cantor to obtain rudimentary musical knowledge, and in 1791 he notated, in his own handwriting, a book containing more than 1,200 tunes from the liturgy in the Jewish yearly cycle. The melodies for single voice and those indicated "singer" or "bass" are marked with dates and names of the "composers." Beer's melodies were included in the THESAURUS OF HEBREW-ORIENTAL MELODIES (vol. VI, sec. 1) and in *Jewish Music* by Abraham Zvi IDELSOHN.

BEIMEL, JACOB (1880–1944). Cantor, conductor, teacher, and writer who was a pioneer in the advancement of Jewish music and musicology in Europe and the United States. He received his early musical education by singing in his father's choir in his birthplace, Parichi, Minsk Province, Russia, and with Nisson SPIVAK of Berdichev. His formal musical education was obtained at the Meisterschule für Musikalische Komposition of the Königliche Akademie der Kunst in Berlin. His career was diversified: in Berlin he held a position as cantor while serving as conductor of the Mendelssohn Choir, and later in Copenhagen he held a cantorial post while conducting the Hazomir Choir.

Jacob Beimel. [*The History of Hazanuth*, Jewish Ministers Cantors Association of America, New York]

Beimel continued in the same vein after emigrating to the United States about 1916, serving as cantor at the Jewish Center in New York and as conductor of the Paterson Singing Society. In 1920 he was appointed cantor of Temple Adath Jeshurun in Philadelphia. As a teacher he imparted his knowledge of liturgical music to aspiring students of the cantorate.

Beimel's literary contributions include numerous articles in Hebrew, Yiddish, English, and German on many phases of Jewish music. In addition, he was the founder and editor of the journal *Jewish Music* (1934–1935), in which many musicians expressed their views and ideas. He composed an *Oriental Suite* for symphony orchestra, music for the Sabbath and NE'ILAH services, organ music, and hymns and wrote folk song arrangements and children's songs.

BELLISON, SIMEON (SIMON) (1883–1953). Virtuoso clarinetist and teacher, noted for organizing in Russia and the United States ensembles devoted to the performance of Jewish music. He learned to play the clarinet from his father in his native Moscow, and for ten years after graduating from the Moscow Conservatory he was solo clarinetist of the Moscow Opera House Orchestra as well as a member of the Moscow Symphony Orchestra. In 1910 he became a member of the symphony orchestra founded and directed by Serge Koussevitzky, and in 1915 he was appointed clarinetist of the Imperial Opera Orchestra in St. Petersburg. In 1902 he founded the Moscow Quintet for National Jewish Music, which gave concerts throughout Russia, Poland, and Latvia. In 1918 he organized in St. Petersburg the Zimro group, in which he played the clarinet with G. Mistechkin (first violin), G. Besrodney (second violin), K. Moldavan (viola), I. Cherniavski (cello), and L. Berdichevski (piano). The group toured Siberia, China, Japan, Canada, the United States, and Palestine in programs devoted exclusively to Jewish music.

Upon settling in the United States in 1920, Bellison became solo clarinetist with the New York Philharmonic, a position he held until 1948. He gave clarinet instruction to students throughout the world. In 1925 he organized in New York a string wood ensemble whose programs were devoted to Jewish music; the group's concerts stimulated the development of serious

Jewish music. Bellison is also credited with helping establish a conservatory of music in Palestine. He collected, edited, and arranged a considerable amount of Jewish music, arranged and published pieces for clarinet and piano and for chamber music combinations, and wrote a novel. His archives and a collection of his instruments are housed in the Rubin Academy of Music in Jerusalem.

BELLS. In Scripture two words are translated "bells": *pa'amonim*, from *pa'am*, meaning "to strike"; and *metzilot*, from *tzalal*, meaning "to tinkle" or "to clang." *Pa'amonim* were part of the High Priest's garment;[1] according to the rabbis, seventy-two bells were attached to the hem of his robe so that "the sound thereof shall be heard when he goeth into the holy place before the Lord, and when he cometh out, that he die not."[2] As he moved, the bells would strike against each other and produce a jingling sound. The noun *metzilot* as used in Zecharia 14:20 is translated in the Authorized Version as "bells," but in the margin the word "bridles" is given. According to numerous scholars[3] the *metzilot* were probably flat or concave pieces (or plates) of brass attached to the bridles of horses as ornaments and were similar to the *saharonim* (crescent-shaped ornaments) found in Isaiah 3:18 and Judges 8:21. In Talmudic days, too, it is evident that bells were suspended from the necks of domestic animals. The Talmud describes such a bell as having a ZOG (hood) and an INBAL (inner part, clapper).[4]

Conical bronze bell from Jerusalem (third century C.E.). [Israel Department of Antiquities and Museums]

Breastplate for the Torah with bells, Musée de Cluny, Paris. [*The Jewish Encyclopedia,* Funk and Wagnalls Company]

Crown for the Torah with bells, Temple Shearith Israel, New York. [*The Jewish Encyclopedia,* Funk and Wagnalls Company]

Today bells are attached to the breastplate and crown of the Torah so that their jingling when the Torah is in a raised position summons the congregation.[5] The jingling of the silver bells fringing the mantles of the scrolls of the Law was sometimes a signal for schooltime.[6]

[1] Ex. 28:33, 34; 39:25, 26.
[2] Ex. 28:35.
[3] David Kimchi; Moses Mendelssohn; E. F. K. Rosenmüller; J. Lewis; J. N. Forkel.
[4] Naz. 34b; cf. Shab. 54b.
[5] *Orah Hayyim* 338; *Sha'aray Efrayim,* sec. 10:3.
[6] Cf. Rashi, Shab. 58b, s.v. *Ulemitpahot Sefarim.*

BEN-HAIM (FRANKENBURGER), PAUL (1897–   ). Israeli composer, teacher, and conductor. Educated in Munich, Germany, under Friedrich Klose, Walter Courvoisier, and Berthold Kellermann, he devoted his talents first to conducting and later to composition. He served as assistant to Bruno Walter and as conductor of the Augsburg Opera and Symphony Orchestra.

Paul Ben-Haim. [A. Berger, photographer, Tel Aviv]

In 1933 he went to Palestine, where he changed his surname from Franken-burger to Ben-Haim and began teaching in conservatories in Tel Aviv and Jerusalem. His contact with the artistic Yemenite folk singer and folklore collector Bracha Zefira in 1939 aroused his interest in Jewish-Oriental music. This music exerted a profound influence on his stylistic development, and his compositions soon began to reflect a synthesis of East and West, combining the Oriental flavor of the new environment and spirit with Western musical tradition.

Ben-Haim's works include a piano concerto, chamber music, settings of Biblical and liturgical texts, songs, and arrangements of Oriental melodies. He is widely known for his two symphonies (*see* FIRST SYMPHONY; SECOND SYMPHONY).

BENDIGAMOS. Initial word of a Spanish-language table HYMN, "Bendigamos al altisimo" (O Let Us Bless the Lord Most High). It is chanted on Sukkot (Feast of Tabernacles) after *Birkhat Hamazon* (Grace after Meals) to the melody of the *Shirah* (*see* SHIRAH, THE), which is sung on Sabbath and festival mornings[1] (*see* Fig. 12).

Ben - di - ga - mos al Al - tí - si - mo Al Señ -
or que nos cri - ó Dé - mos - le___ a - gra - de - ci -
mien - to por los bien___ es que nos Di - ó

Figure 12.

[1]H. P. Salomon, "The Strange Odyssey of *Bendigamos*," *American Sephardi*, Yeshiva University, vol. III, 1969, pp. 69–78.

BERNSTEIN, ABRAHAM MOSHE (1866–1932). Russian-born cantor-composer and teacher. Bernstein embarked on a musical career in his late teens after studying the Bible and Talmud in his native town of Shatsk, in Minsk Province, Russia, and subsequently in the yeshivot of Minsk and Mir. He also acquired some musical experience by singing as a chorister. In 1884 he arrived in Kaunas (Kovno), where he began to study seriously with Cantor Refael Yehudah Rabinowitz and made rapid progress in his general and musical education. He served as *hazzan sheni* (associate cantor; *see* HAZZAN) and choir leader to Cantor Rabinowitz, and in 1888 he was appointed cantor of Adath Jeshurun in Białystok. The next year Cantor Boruch Leib ROSOWSKY of Riga invited him to become his choir leader. There, too, Bernstein continued his studies and produced a steady stream of musical and literary works that soon became recognized throughout the world. In 1893 he became chief cantor of the Taharat Hakodesh Synagogue of Vilna, a position he held for thirty years. From 1923 on he continued only as a composer, collector of folk songs, and teacher of music in the Hebrew schools of Vilna.

Of the many liturgical compositions Bernstein wrote, the principal one

Abraham Moshe Bernstein.

is the three-volume *Avodat Haborei* (Service of the Creator; vols. 1 and 2, 1914; vol. 3, 1931). His *Musikalisher Pinkas* (1927) will remain a lasting reference anthology of Eastern European folk melodies. Bernstein is probably known to a wider audience for his setting of *Adoshem Adoshem,* made popular and recorded by Cantor Gershon Sirota. His great success in composing to texts of Hebrew and Yiddish poets established him as an outstanding writer of songs, of which he wrote 205. His settings of "Zamd un Shtern" by S. Frug and "Hemerl, Hemerl Klap" by A. Reisin have had many performances all over the world.

BEROIGEZ TANZ. Improvised dance (lit. "angry dance" or "sulking dance") in duple meter usually performed by *mehutanim* (relatives by marriage) at a wedding. Since there was hardly a wedding at which an argument did not arise, this dance became popular in Eastern Europe. Consequently, its true objective was to dance and forgive. It is characteristically played first at a moderate speed as the people dance away from each other, and then the melody is repeated in a faster and livelier tempo after they forgive and embrace. The *beroigez tanz* is popular today among folk dancers.[1]

[1]*Kammen International Dance Folio No. 1,* New York, 1924, p. 55, no. 50; Dvora Lapson, *Dances of the Jewish People,* Jewish Education Committee Press, New York, 1954, pp. 25–27.

BIBLIOGRAPHY, JEWISH MUSIC. Science of classifying and describing Jewish books and manuscripts according to literature and music. Although there are remote references to Jewish music in such early biographical compilations as *Bibliotheca universalis* (1545–1555) by Konrad von Gesner (1516–1565), it was Giulio Bartolocci (1613–1687) who, in addition to giving the earliest account of Hebrew literature in its rabbinic phases, described Jewish music literature and the music itself in his *Bibliotheca Magna Rabbinica* (1675–1694). The first Jewish bibliographer to list some Jewish musical writings was Shabbethai Bass (1641–1718) in his *Sifte Yeshenim* (1680). The attempts by Bartolocci and Bass were superseded by Johann Nikolaus Forkel (1749–1818), who in his two musicological publications, *Allgemeine Geschichte der Musik* (2 vols., 1788–1801) and *Allgemeine Litteratur der Musik* (1792), brought together and systematized all previous information relating to Jewish music, giving such items as place and year of publication, the name of the publisher, the size and number of pages of the volume, and some biographical data.

Jewish music bibliography remained dormant until the late nineteenth century, when Eduard BIRNBAUM collected and classified several thousand musical items, paying special attention to liturgical music (this collection is housed in the Hebrew Union College in Cincinnati). Credit for attempting a Jewish music bibliography in this period can also be given to the non-Jew Carl Engel (1818–1882) for his listings in *The Music of the Most Ancient Nations* (1864) and *The Literature of National Music* (1879). However, these items had previously been listed. At the turn of the twentieth century Cyrus Adler (1863–1940) wrote "Important Literature on Jewish Music" in the *American Hebrew* (1892), in which he included a listing of some Jewish works. The next name of importance is that of William SPARGER, who wrote *Literature on the Music of the Jews: An Attempt at a Bibliography* (1892), which actually was the first pioneering endeavor in this field.

With the rise of Jewish musicology under Abraham Zvi IDELSOHN, bibliography entered a new era. Idelsohn's numerous writings were appended with bibliographical notes, and his "Collection of and Literature on Synagogue Songs," published in *Studies in Jewish Bibliography: Freidus Memorial Volume* (1929),[1] kept scholars aware of listings of all branches of Jewish musical research. Thus, he influenced future scholars in the field of Jewish musical research to give their literary sources in bibliographic form.

The present phase of Jewish music bibliography has seen its fruition in such works as *Bibliography of Jewish Music* (1951) by Alfred SENDREY. As the most comprehensive work in this field, with listings of almost 10,000 titles, this work provides the first historical survey of the bibliography of Jewish music as well as an account of the aesthetic and sociological aspects. More recent publications are *Bibliography of Publications and Other Resources on Jewish Music* (1969) by Albert WEISSER, based in part upon "The Bibliography of Books and Articles on Jewish Music" (1955) prepared by Joseph YASSER; and *A Bibliography of Instrumental Music of Jewish Interest* (Part 1, *Orchestra and Band,* 1970; Part 2, *Ensemble and Solo,* 1970; Part 3, *Voice with Instruments,* 1971), compiled by Ira S. Goldberg. The latter editions were issued by the NATIONAL JEWISH MUSIC COUNCIL. Important contributions to Jewish music bibliography in Israel are *Bibliography of Jewish Bibliographies* (2d ed., 1965) by Shlomo Shunami; and *Amli Studies in Music Bibliography* (1970, vols. 1–4), edited by Moshe Gorali and published by the Haifa Music Museum and Amli Library.

[1] The Alexander Kohut Memorial Foundation, New York, pp. 388–403. Reprinted in his *Jewish Music in Its Historical Development,* New York, 1929.

BINDER, ABRAHAM WOLF (1895–1967). American-born pedagogue, conductor, writer, lecturer, and composer who pioneered in the propagation of Jewish music in the United States. A native New Yorker and the son of a cantor, Binder received his first musical experience by singing as a chorister with Abraham Frachtenberg. At fourteen he led a choir for Cantor Abraham Singer at the Kamenetzer Synagogue on the lower East Side. He attended the Settlement Music School and Columbia University (1917–1920) and received a bachelor of music degree from the New York College of Music in 1920. Meanwhile, in 1911, his career as a choral director began at Temple Beth El in Brooklyn, and in 1913 he assumed a similar position at Temple Adath Israel in the Bronx. In 1917 he was appointed musical director of the Young Men's and Young Women's Hebrew Association, where he taught music and organized a choral society and a symphony orchestra.

Abraham Wolf Binder.

As instructor of liturgical music at the Hebrew Union College–Jewish Institute of Religion (appointed in 1921) and musical director of the Stephen Wise Free Synagogue (appointed in 1924), he strove to revive the ancient Jewish melos and train students and laymen to become knowledgeable in Jewish music. Visits to Palestine in 1924 and 1931 and to Israel in 1952 had great influence on his musical composition. He is credited with being the founder and first president of the JEWISH MUSIC FORUM and an organizer and officer of the Jewish Music Council. In 1953 the Hebrew Union College–Jewish Institute of Religion awarded him the degree of doctor of Hebrew letters. From 1954 to 1958 he lectured at the Union Theological Seminary in New York.

Binder contributed numerous articles and monographs to encyclopedias and periodicals, wrote the book *Biblical Chant* (1959), and served as the editor of the third edition of the *Union Hymnal* (1946). His musical works include liturgical choral compositions, hymns, orchestral pieces, suites, an overture, a rhapsody, a cantata, an operetta, and folk song arrangements. He is best known for an oratorio for children, *Judas Maccabeus* (1919), and for *New Palestinian Folk Songs* (2 vols., 1926, 1933). A volume called *Studies in Jewish Music: Collected Writings of A. W. Binder* was edited by Irene Heskes and published posthumously in 1971.

BIRNBAUM, ABRAHAM BER (1865–1922). Cantor-composer, *shohet* (ritual slaughterer), writer, and teacher. Born into a Hassidic family in the Russian-Polish city of Pułtusk, Birnbaum was imbued with HASSIDIC SONG at an early age when his father, Reb Moshe Leib, took him along on his visits to the courts of the Kotzker and Gerer Rebbes. Abraham often sang and played the violin at Hassidic gatherings and at *Melaveh Malkah,* the celebration bidding farewell to the Sabbath. In 1886 he apprenticed himself to a *shohet,* and in 1888 he was appointed HAZZAN-*shohet* in a small Hungarian village, where he also furthered his studies in the theory of music and the German language. Subsequently, in 1890, he accepted a post in Prossnitz (Prostějov), Moravia, and in 1893 was appointed OBERKANTOR of the newly erected CHOR-SCHUL in Częstochowa, a position he held until 1913. He then settled in Łódź, where he devoted himself to writing and to teaching *hazzanim* and students of music in Jewish schools. Birnbaum was encouraged to enter into a variety of Jewish musical pursuits under the influence of Haim Haikel Janowsky, a well-known benefactor of gifted Jewish musicians. He edited a monthly cantorial publication,

Abraham Ber Birnbaum.

Yarhon Lehazzanim (four numbers, 1897); wrote a work on the general theory of music in Yiddish and Hebrew, *Torat Hazimrah Hakelalit* (1902); founded a cantorial school (1906); and provided a correspondence course in liturgical and general music. In 1907 he was appointed chairman of the Cantorial Conference, held in Warsaw, which later developed into the Hazzanim-Farband of Poland.

    As a composer Birnbaum wrote numerous settings for the synagogue liturgy and folk and art songs. He is best known for his two-volume opus for the Sabbath, festivals, and High Holy Days, *Amanut Hahazzanut* (The Cantorial Art; vol. I, 1908; vol. II, 1912). His essays and articles, which appeared in various journals, especially the Hebrew daily *Hatzfirah* (1890) and the Hebrew weekly *Haolam* (1908), shed great light on Jewish music.

BIRNBAUM, EDUARD (ASHER ANSHEL) (1855–1920). Cantor, musicologist, and bibliographer of Jewish music. Birnbaum began his Jewish and musical studies in Cracow, his native city, and continued them with Salomon SULZER of Vienna, Moritz DEUTSCH of Breslau, and the historian Heinrich Graetz. He frequently visited Samuel NAUMBOURG in Paris and Hirsch WEINTRAUB in Königsberg, acquiring much knowledge from them. In 1872 he was appointed cantor in Magdeburg, and in 1874 he was called to Beuthen, Upper Silesia. The year 1879 was significant in his life, because he was then recommended by Weintraub to be his successor as chief cantor in Königsberg.

Eduard Birnbaum. [*The History of Hazanuth,* **Jewish Ministers Cantors Association of America, New York**]

Many of Weintraub's compositions and manuscripts, as well as those of other sources dating from about 1620 to about 1910, subsequently came into Birnbaum's possession. He systematically copied and indexed this material, and after his death it was incorporated into the library of the Hebrew Union College in Cincinnati.

Birnbaum's scores, which are predominantly in manuscript form, include a variety of choral settings for the liturgy of the entire yearly cycle. A printed example of one of his popular compositions may be found in the *Cantorial Anthology* of Gershon EPHROS.[1] Birnbaum's many articles enriched Jewish musical literature. They include "Musikalische Traditionen bei der Vorlesung der Megilla" (1891), "Jüdische Musiker am Hofe von Mantua von 1542 bis 1628" (1893), "Franz Schubert als Synagogen-Komponist" (1897), and "Liturgische Übungen" (1900, 1902).

[1]*Hashkivenu, Sholosh R'golim*, vol. 3, no. 4, Bloch Publishing Company, Inc., New York, 1948, p. 42.

BLINDMAN, YERUCHOM (c. 1798–1891). Eastern European cantor-composer and scholar, popularly referred to as Yeruchom Hakaton (the Little One) because of his small physical stature. A child prodigy born in Bessarabia or possibly Galicia, Blindman sang as a chorister with Bezalel SCHULSINGER. Later he studied with Nissan BLUMENTHAL and Wolf SHESTAPOL,

Yeruchom Blindman.
**[*The History of Hazanuth,*
Jewish Ministers Cantors
Association of America,
New York]**

and by 1834 he had become known as an itinerant cantor, creating a sensation wherever he appeared. With his lyric tenor voice and limitless FALSETTO he introduced variations and embellishments into the traditional CHANT and surpassed many of his contemporaries with his improvisations (*see* IMPROVISATION). Despite his rudimentary knowledge of music he conducted his own choir without the aid of a choir leader and held full-time posts in Kishinev (prior to 1860), Berdichev (1861–1872), and Tarnopol (Ternopol, 1877–1886). His choral compositions in folk song style, some showing signs of four-part settings, have remained in manuscript form.

BLOCH, ERNEST (1880–1959). Composer noted for creating art music reflecting Jewish elements and Hebraic spirit. Born in Geneva, Switzerland, Bloch began studying the violin at an early age with Louis Rey and composition with Émile Jaques-Dalcroze. In 1896 he left for Brussels, where he furthered his musical studies under F. Schorg, Eugène Ysäye, and François Rasse. Later he went to Germany and studied with Iwan Knorr in Frankfurt and Ludwig Thuille in Munich. Returning to Geneva, he divided his time between business, lecturing, conducting, and composing. In 1916 Bloch went to the United

Ernest Bloch.
[ASCAP]

States, where he taught composition at the David Mannes Music School in New York and served as director of the Cleveland Institute of Music (1920–1925) and the San Francisco Conservatory (1925–1930). In 1940 he was appointed professor of music at the University of California. Among his many noted pupils were Isadore FREED, Frederick JACOBI, Douglas Moore, Randall Thompson, and Roger Sessions.

The "Hebrew idiom" inherent in Bloch's music is no doubt a result of generations of Jewish ancestry. His paternal grandfather was active in the Jewish community in Lengnau, Canton Aargau; and his father, a clock merchant, was a Biblical scholar who knew the Hebrew language well. The list of compositions known as Bloch's *Jewish Cycle* includes THREE PSALMS (pss. 22, 114, and 137; 1912–1914), THREE JEWISH POEMS (1913), ISRAEL SYMPHONY (1912–1915), SCHELOMO (1916), BAAL SHEM (1923), *From Jewish Life* (1925), MÉDITATION HÉBRAÏQUE (1925), AVODATH HAKODESH (1933), and VOICE IN THE WILDERNESS (1936). Bloch wrote of his *Jewish Cycle* in 1938: "It was this Jewish heritage as a whole which stirred me, and music was the result. To what extent such music is Jewish—to what extent it is just Ernest Bloch—of that I know nothing. The future alone will decide." Among other works are an opera, *Macbeth;* a rhapsody, *America;* and string quartets, a VIOLIN CONCERTO, a concerto grosso, a quintet for piano and strings, and a piano sonata. Bloch was the first truly Jewish composer in the modern world whose music came to be performed regularly on the concert stage.

BLUMENTHAL, NISSAN (1805–1903). First *chor hazzan* in Russia (*see* HAZZAN, CHOR). Born in Berdichev, Blumenthal spent his early years in Iaşi, Romania. He revealed an interest in music as a child and was self-taught. In 1826 he accepted his first position as cantor in Berdichev and later was invited to lead the services in Yekaterinoslav (Dnepropetrovsk). Jewish settlers from Brody, Galicia, organized a CHOR-SCHUL, called the Broder-Schul, in Odessa in 1840 and engaged Blumenthal as their first chief cantor. He held this position with great distinction for about fifty years, until old age forced him to retire.

Blumenthal's introduction of four-part systematic singing and his simplification of the CHANT, in which he emphasized inspirational and emotional qualities of devotion rather than ostentatious vocal display, were among the contributions that raised the standards of synagogue song in Russia. His collaboration with David NOWAKOWSKY, his choir director, spread his in-

Nissan Blumenthal. [*The History of Hazanuth,* **Jewish Ministers Cantors Association of America, New York**]

fluence throughout Europe. Blumenthal left many liturgical choral compositions in manuscript form. Of the compositions in print, several are included in the collection *Avodat Habore* of Vilna and in the *Cantorial Anthology* of Gershon EPHROS.

BOSCOVICH, ALEXANDER URIA (1907–1964). Israeli composer, educator, and critic. Born in Kolozvár, Hungary (now Cluj, Romania), he began his musical studies at the Budapest Academy and continued them in Vienna. Later he enrolled in the Schola Cantorum and the École Normale de Musique in Paris, where he studied with Nadia Boulanger and Paul Dukas. In 1938 he went to Palestine and taught at the Conservatory of Music in Tel Aviv and at the Israel Academy of Music. He served as the music critic of the newspaper *Ha'Aretz* and with H. Shmueli translated Paul Hindemith's *Traditional Harmony and Counterpoint.*

Boscovich was known as an innovator of the Eastern-Mediterranean school of composition, a collector of Eastern European folk melodies, and a dedicated educator of a generation of young Israeli composers. He wrote orchestral works, chamber music, concerti, suites, a cantata, piano pieces, songs, and incidental music for the theater. Among his outstanding compositions are *The Golden Chain* (1937), *Semitic Suite* (1946), *Shir Hama'alot* (1960–1961), *Daughter of Israel* (1961), and *Concerto da Camera* (1962). His compositions have been performed under the baton of leading conductors, including Charles Munch and Gary Bertini, and won him several awards (Engel Prize, 1946 and 1954; Israel Philharmonic First Prize, 1960 and 1961).

Alexander Uria Boscovich. [Israel Music Institute, Tel Aviv]

BOTNON. Word, mentioned in Mishnah Kelim XV:6, having various meanings: (1) a large musical instrument called *zithra* that rests on the player's abdomen *(beten);*[1] (2) "a sort of bagpipe" or "cittern fastened around the body";[2] (3) a lute;[3] (4) a belly-shaped instrument;[4] (5) in modern Hebrew, a double bass or contrabass *(bitnon).*[5]

[1] R. Obadiah Bertinoro, loc. cit.
[2] Marcus Jastrow, *Dictionary*, London, 1903, vol. I, p. 158.
[3] *The Mishnahs, Kelim,* chap. XV:6, The Soncino Press, London, p. 76.
[4] Samuel Krauss, *Talmudische Archäologie,* Leipzig, 1910–1912, vol. III, p. 87.
[5] David Ettinger, *Hebrew Pictorial Dictionary,* Dvir Publishers, Tel Aviv, 1953, p. 164, no. 4.

BRAUN, YEHEZKIEL (1922–   ). Israeli composer and teacher. Born in Breslau, Germany, Braun was taken in 1924 to Palestine, where he studied at the Kibbutzim Teachers College and the Israel Academy of Music in Tel Aviv. He was later appointed an instructor at the Israel Academy of Music and the Music Teachers College. Among his many works inspired by Jewish subject matter are *Psalm for Strings* (1960), *Sabbath Eve Service* (1965) for orchestra, and *Illuminations to the Book of Ruth* (1966) for orchestra.

BRESLAUR, EMIL (1836–1899). German choirmaster, teacher, critic, and author. Breslaur first held the office of preacher and religious instructor of the Jewish Congregation of Cottbus, his native city. After studying music at the Stern Conservatory in Berlin, he embarked on a musical career. He became active as a teacher of piano and in 1883 was appointed choirmaster of the Reformed Synagogue of Berlin. Besides founding and directing a piano teachers seminary, he formed an organization of music teachers in Berlin (1879), which later developed into the Deutscher Musiklehrer-Verband (1886), and served as music critic of several newspapers. In addition to numerous pedagogical works on piano playing, techniques, and study, he wrote *Sind originale Synagogen- und Volks-Melodien bei den Juden geschichtlich nachweisbar?* (1898), a pamphlet devoted to the discussion of the melodies of the Jewish liturgy; *Geistliche Gesänge für Synagoge, Schule und Haus* (1863), for voice and organ accompaniment; and choral and piano pieces.

BRETTEL. Term (lit. "board" or "plank") referring to the board or plank that sometimes is placed on the floor in front of the prayer desk in a synagogue for acoustical purposes. The Yiddish saying *Er loift tzum brettel* (He runs to the board or plank) is directed at an officiant who is anxious to act as READER but is not qualified.

BROADCASTING, JEWISH MUSIC. Transmission by radio and television of programs featuring Jewish music. Jewish music was first heard on radio when Station WEVD in New York began broadcasting in 1932. Other stations that included Jewish music in their programming were WHN, WMCA, and WLIB. Frequent programs are currently heard over Station WEVD and also on stations in large cities such as Chicago and Philadelphia. In 1933 Nicholas L. Zaslavsky became music director of WEVD, and under his leadership an ensemble of eleven musicians was employed. A regular weekly feature, "The Forward Hour," still heard today, was instituted by the *Jewish Daily Forward;* it included a choral group, an ensemble, and guest singers. Joseph Garnett followed Zaslavsky as director, and since 1969 William Gunther has headed the station's music department. Four instrumentalists are employed, and a record and Jewish music library is maintained. A great deal of broadcasting time is devoted to the performance of liturgical music, Israeli and Jewish folk music, and Jewish art music. Many television networks feature programs with Jewish music content before Jewish holidays.

On March 30, 1936, the first network in Palestine, the Palestine Broadcasting Service in Jerusalem, came into existence. Under the British Mandate the network included a music section headed by Karl Salomon. Programs featured Jewish music and presented a picture of Jewish musical culture in Palestine and of the Jewish people in general. The network employed a studio ensemble of six to eight members that gave weekly concerts. The Shem Choir, established by the National Council of Palestine Jews, also gave regular concerts. Oriental music received a warm reception under the aegis of Ezra Aharon, who presented concerts with a choir and a small Oriental orchestra. In addition, a Jewish Music Month featured local talent.

In 1948, with the establishment of the State of Israel, the Kol Yisrael (Voice of Israel) Broadcasting Service came into being. It has its own sixty-two-member Kol Yisrael Orchestra and chamber orchestras that promote music by Israeli composers and encourage young talent. Programs featuring both Ashkenazic and Sephardic HAZZANUT have large followings. There is also a radio station of the Israel Defense Forces, and regular television broadcasting was introduced in 1967. One of the early programs to be televised was a concert given by the ISRAEL PHILHARMONIC ORCHESTRA under the baton of Leonard Bernstein. Both radio and television programming in Israel include Jewish liturgical, folk, and art music.

BROD, MAX (1884–1967). Critic, author, and composer. A native of Prague, Brod attended the Piaristen Volksschule and the Stefan Gymnasium and graduated from the German University of Prague, where he studied composition and violin with Adolf Schrieber. In 1914 he became the music critic of the *Prager Tageblatt,* and in 1918 he was instrumental in forming the Jewish National Council of Prague. He journeyed to Palestine in 1928, made his permanent residence in Tel Aviv in 1939, and became the dramatic consultant of the Habima Theater. Brod became known for his novels, opera and oratorio libretti, and the popular HAGGADAH (1936) with music by Paul DESSAU. His work *Israel's Music* (1951) is an important contribution to Jewish musicology and history. As a composer he wrote a sonata for violin and piano, two suites for piano, orchestral works, songs, and the *Requiem Hebraicus* for baritone and small orchestra in memory of his wife.

BROUNOFF, PLATON G. *See* BRUNOFF, PLATON G.

BRUMMEN. German word meaning "to hum." Since instruments may not be used in the synagogue, it has become customary for choristers to supply supporting tones as a special effect of vocal accompaniment. Usually this is

Figure 13.

done by humming a tone in unison at the end of a phrase. The choristers may also hum the tonic triad while the cantor chants the RECITATIVE, thereby furnishing indefinite sustaining tones similar to those of the ORGAN (*see* Fig. 13). *See also* CHOIR.

BRUNOFF (BROUNOFF), PLATON G. (1863?–1924). Composer, teacher, conductor, and music critic who pioneered in collecting and arranging Jewish folk and art songs. Born in Yelisavetgrad (Kirovograd), Russia, he first studied at the Warsaw Conservatory and later became a pupil of Anton Rubinstein and Nikolai Rimski-Korsakov at the St. Petersburg Conservatory. After graduating in 1891 he emigrated to the United States and finally settled in New York. His varied activities included lecturing on Russian music, teaching operatic classes at the Institute of Musical Art, conducting symphonic orchestras, teaching piano, and serving as music critic for the New York *Jewish Daily Forward.* He also founded and conducted the first Jewish secular choir, the Poale Zion Singing Society.

Brunoff collected more that 300 folk melodies. He published *Jewish Folk Songs* (1911), which includes fifty melodies with piano accompaniment, as well as other songs for solo voice and piano and for chorus and piano. He wrote four symphonies, an overture, and a book, *Stolen Correspondence from the Dead Letter Office between Musical Celebrities* (1901).

Samuel Bugatch.

BUGATCH, SAMUEL (1898–   ). Composer and conductor. Bugatch grew up in a musical environment and sang as a chorister in his native Rogachev, White Russia. At the age of thirteen he went to the United States and settled in Baltimore, where he conducted choruses while still a boy. Later he enrolled at the Peabody Conservatory of Music and received a teacher's certificate in harmony and composition. Bugatch has conducted synagogue and secular choruses in many large centers. He was music director of the Beth Tfiloh Synagogue in Baltimore and of Temple Adath Israel in the Bronx. He has written numerous liturgical and secular works for chorus, voice and piano, organ, and songs. His major compositions are *Judea* (1943), a cantata for tenor, baritone, mixed chorus, and piano or orchestra, or both (text by Lord Byron); and *Israel, a Dream Realized* (1950), a cantata for unison chorus and piano. Bugatch has also contributed articles to various periodicals.

BUSCHEL, BEN-ZION. *See* ORGAD, BEN-ZION.

C

CANTILLATION. Term originally applied to the mode of chanting or intonation used in the public recital of prayers and Holy Scripture. Since the beginning of the twentieth century the term has been used mainly to describe the musical interpretation of the TE'AMIM that accompany the printed text of the Hebrew Scriptures. This combination of reading with singing the scroll of the Law in the synagogue is called among Yiddish-speaking Jews Torah *Leinen* and among German Jewry *Vorlesen der Thorah*.

Biblical cantillation, the oldest source of Jewish music, is required, for anyone who reads the Scriptures without a tune shows a disregard for them and their laws.[1] Moreover, the chanting must adhere to the traditional modes and tunes, for "whoever intones Holy Scriptures in the manner of secular song abuses the Torah."[2] The READER is also required to chant the words of the Scriptures in all their beauty. Rabbi Levi said: "Whoever reads the Bible with its delightful tone and tune, of him is said, honey and milk under his tongue."[3] Such importance is attributed to public reading of Scripture that the verse "And they that forsake the Lord shall be consumed"[4] is interpreted to mean persons who leave the scroll while it is being read and go out from the synagogue.[5] The practice of public reading of the Torah for the Sabbath, festivals, intermediate days, and Rosh Hodesh (New Moon) was introduced by Moses.[6] In Ezra's time (500 B.C.E.) the Torah was read also on Monday and Thursday mornings,[7] and he introduced its reading at the MINHAH service on Sabbath.[8] The custom of reading the Prophets dates back to the Second Commonwealth. The Book of Esther has been read since the period of the Maccabees (second century B.C.E.), Lamentations since the destruction of the Second Temple (C.E. 70), and the Song of Songs, Ruth, and Ecclesiastes since the first century.[9] In some communities Psalms and Job are cantillated. However, Proverbs, Ezra, Nehemiah, and Chronicles have no system of cantillation because they are not recited at public services.

Simhah ben Samuel, a pupil of Rashi, states: "The [method of] chanting the accents was revealed to Moses: when one should draw out [the tune], raise [one's voice], dwell [on a syllable], stand, raise, lower, and when to rest." However, the actual symbols for the accents are post-Talmudic.[10] Although Jews of Germany, Lithuania, Yemen, Iraq, Syria, Morocco, Egypt, and Baghdad utilize musical variants in the interpretation of the Biblical accents (*see* ACCENTS, BIBLICAL), there are similarities in mode construction, melodic contour and direction, and character of expression, proving that they share a common and ancient ancestry. Although identical signs serve the chanting of all the books, the mode of the cantillations varies with each book.[11]

[1]Meg. 32a.
[2]Sanh. 101a.
[3]*Song of Songs Rabbah* 4:11.
[4]Isa. 1:28.
[5]Ber. 8a.
[6]Ex. 24:7; Deut. 31:12; Meg. 31a.
[7]Jer. Meg. 4, 1.
[8]B.K. 82a.
[9]Sof. XIV:18.
[10]*Mahzor Vitry*, Berlin, 1893, p. 91.
[11]Abraham Z. Idelsohn, *The Jewish Song Book,* ed. by B. J. Cohon, Publications for Judaism, Cincinnati, 1951, pp. 488–510.

CANTIQUES DE SOLOMON ROSSI. *See* HASHIRIM ASHER LISHLOMO.

CANTOR. Word of Latin origin meaning "singer," designating the solo singer of the synagogue who leads the congregation in prayer. The title was most probably adapted from the church.[1] It was used at the beginning of the eighteenth century in lands where any of the Romance languages were spoken. According to Abraham Zvi IDELSOHN, Salomon SULZER of Vienna, a HAZZAN of high artistic and social standing, demanded to be called cantor.[2] However, Eric Mandell says that the reverse was true: Sulzer preferred to be called *hazzan* or SHELIAH TZIBBUR.[3] *See also* PRECENTOR.

[1]Abraham Z. Idelsohn, *Jewish Music,* Tudor Publishing Company, New York, 1944, pp. 109, 512, note 11.
[2]Loc. cit., p. 259.
[3]"Salomon Sulzer," *The Jews of Austria: Essays on Their Life, History and Destruction,* ed. by Josef Fraenkel, London, 1967, p. 228.

CANTORIAL ORGANIZATIONS. Bodies whose membership is devoted to the interests of the cantorate in all its aspects. They set standards and qualifications for cantors, publish Jewish music and music literature, secure support for cantorial schools, obtain tenure and economic security for their members, and foster a spirit of fellowship. An early group in Austria-Hungary was the Österreich-Ungarischer Kantorenverein, organized by Salomon SULZER in 1881. It founded a cantorial school and issued a newspaper, the *Österreichisch-Ungarische Cantoren-Zeitung.* Another early group was the Agudat haHazzanim of Poland, which had a membership of about 600 cantors. It was instrumental in publishing *Die Hazzanim-Welt* (later *Die Shul un Hazzanim-Welt*), a significant monthly journal that appeared for three consecutive years.

The earliest cantorial organization in the United States was the Jewish Ministers Cantors Association of America (Hazzanim Varband), established in New York in 1894. Other groups were the Board of American Hazzan Ministers, an association of Reform cantors formed in 1925, and the Cantors Cultural Organization (1930), devoted solely to education. Since the inception of schools for cantors in the United States their associates and alumni have maintained cantorial organizations. The Cantors Assembly of America, affiliated with the Cantors Institute and the College of Jewish Music of the Jewish Theological Seminary in New York, was founded in 1947. The American Conference of Certified Cantors, affiliated with the School of Sacred Music, Hebrew Union College–Jewish Institute of Religion, was organized in 1953. The Cantorial Council of America, affiliated with the Cantorial Training Institute of the Rabbi Isaac Elchanan Theological Seminary of Yeshiva University, was established in 1960. Local cantorial groups exist in major cities

Members of the Jewish Ministers Cantors Association of America.

such as Philadelphia, Boston, and Chicago. The Jewish Liturgical Music Society of America, founded in New York in 1962 and renamed in 1974 the American Society for Jewish Music, serves cantors and musicians through educational activities.

In England the Association of Ministers Chazanim of Great Britain was founded by Marcus HAST. La Sociedad de Cantores Liturgicos Israelitas de la Argentina (Agudat he-Hazzanim be-Argentina) was established in Argentina in 1932. In Israel the professional organization is the Irgun Hahazzanim Beyisrael (Association of Cantors of Israel).

Mario Castelnuovo-Tedesco.

CASTELNUOVO-TEDESCO, MARIO (1895–1968). Italian composer. Born in Florence to a Sephardic family, he received his musical education at the Cherubini Royal Institute and later studied with Ildebrando Pizzetti. When Jews were banned from Italian cultural life in 1938, he left his native land and, in 1939, emigrated to the United States. Among the leading modern Italian composers, Castelnuovo-Tedesco wrote numerous works. The wellspring of his works of Jewish content is found in his childhood. His grandfather instilled in him both an inclination for music and deep religious feeling. Castelnuovo-Tedesco was inspired to compose Jewish music when he found a notebook with Hebrew prayers set to music in his grandfather's handwriting. This paved the way for such compositions in Hebraic spirit as *Le danze del re David* (*see* DANZE DEL RE DAVID, LE), *Tre corali su melodie ebraiche*, *The Prophets* (*see* PROPHETS, THE), SACRED SERVICE FOR THE SABBATH EVE, and *Lecho Dodi* (*see* LEKHA DODI).

CHAJES, JULIUS (1910–   ). Composer, pianist, conductor, and teacher recognized for making a contribution to Jewish music in the twentieth century in Palestine and the United States. Born in Lemberg (Lvov), Galicia, he gave his first piano recital at the age of nine and composed a string quartet when he was eleven. At fifteen he played his own piano concerto with the Vienna Symphony Orchestra, and in 1933 he won a prize at an international contest for pianists in Vienna. He studied piano with Richard Robert and Hedwig Rosenthal, conducting with Rudolf Nilius, composition with Hugo Kauder, and musicology at the University of Vienna. From 1934 to 1936 he taught piano in Tel Aviv, conducted the Jerusalem Male Chorus, and did research in Jewish music.

Chajes went to the United States in 1937 and taught at the New York College of Music (1939–1940). Later he served as music director of Temple Beth El in Detroit and taught composition at the Institute of Musical Art of the University of Detroit (1941–1945). He assumed the post of musical director at the Jewish Community Center of Detroit, conducted the Cleveland Jewish Singing Society, and joined the faculty of the music department of Wayne State University. As a propagandist of Jewish music he cofounded and served as chairman of Hashofar, a society for the advancement of Jewish music in Detroit established in 1945.

Chajes's compositions include works for the piano, cantatas, chamber music, a concerto, an opera, a Sabbath evening service (1946), choral works, and arrangements of Israeli folk songs. His songs "Adarim," "Palestinian Nights," and "Galil" are often performed on the concert stage.

CHANT. Freely flowing vocal line sung in the synagogue service. It is modal, monophonic, melismatic (*see* MELISMA), nonmetric, and of limited range. Numerous motives of synagogue prayer chant can be traced to the CANTILLATION of the Bible.[1] Features of Hebrew chant were adopted in the musical practices of the early Christians.[2] For a study of the chant of the Ashkenazic tradition, *see* Baruch Joseph Cohon, "The Structure of the Synagogue Prayer-Chant," *Journal of the American Musicological Society*, vol. III, no. 1, 1950, pp. 17–32.

[1]Abraham Z. Idelsohn, *Jewish Music*, Tudor Publishing Company, New York, 1944, chap. IV.

[2]*Grove's Dictionary of Music and Musicians*, 5th ed., London, 1954, vol. IV, p. 628, vol. VI, p. 815.

CHANT OF THE DEAD, THE. Medieval German melody actually having nothing to do with the dead. However, since it was sung when the priests mounted the platform to bless the congregation (*dukhenen*) during the concluding days of the festivals when the *Yizkor* (memorial service) was recited, it was associated with the remembrance of departed relatives (*Hazkarat Neshamot*) and hence was called "Niggun Metim" (The Chant of the Dead). Arranged for instruments by Samuel NAUMBOURG of Paris,[1] the melody attracted the attention of Queen Victoria and was played at several memorial services of the British royal family. Figure 14 shows the chant in its original simple form.

[1]Cf. E. Pauer and F. L. Cohen, *Traditional Hebrew Melodies*, London, 1896.

BIRKAT KOHANIM

Figure 14. [*The Jewish Encyclopedia*, Funk and Wagnalls Company]

CHANTS POPULAIRES. Seven songs for voice and piano accompaniment written by Maurice Ravel (1875–1937) in 1910. Song No. 4, the most frequently performed, is "Chanson hébraïque," known as "Mejerke." Retaining the Yiddish text, Ravel harmonized an Eastern European song attributed to the Hassidic rabbi Levi Yitzhak of Berdichev (1740-1809). These songs were brought to Ravel's attention by a competition organized by the Maison du Lied in Moscow.

See also DEUX MÉLODIES HÉBRAÏQUES.

CHIRONOMY. Ancient system of manual signs used by teachers or by a *tomekh* (helper) to indicate to the student or READER of Scripture the melodic rise and fall of the voice (the word is derived from the Greek *cheir*, "the hand," and *nemein*, "to manage" or "wield"). An ascending tone was probably indicated by the lowering of the finger and a sustained tone by keeping the hand uplifted. The nomenclature of some of the accent marks (*see* ACCENTS, BIBLICAL) alludes to this fact. For example, *zakef* (upright; *see* ZAKEF GADOL; ZAKEF KATAN), TIPKHA (hand breadth), PASHTA (stretching), and SHALSHELET (chain) all indicate a swaying movement or gesture of the fingers and hands. Rashi refers to the movements made with the right hand when the Biblical intonations are chanted and concludes that this was the custom of Palestinians in his day.[1] In the twelfth century Pethahiah of Regensburg found that the hand movements were still being practiced in Baghdad synagogues. According to Yaakov Saphir, in countries like Yemen the custom was still employed in the nineteenth century. In 1966 a film, *The Traditional Chironomy of the Hebrew Scriptures*, was documented in Jerusalem by Saul Levin of the State University of New York at Binghamton. *See also* AARON BEN ASHER; BA'AL KOREI; CANTILLATION; TE'AMIM.

[1]Ber. 62a.

CHOIR (Heb. *makhelah*). Group of singers specializing mainly in the singing of sacred music, probably on the basis of the Biblical phrase "Bless ye God in full assemblies."[1] In Temple worship the Levite choir consisted of a minimum of twelve adult male singers.[2] Singers were admitted to the choir at the age of thirty after having been trained for five years.[3] After the destruction of the Second Temple in C.E. 70 the Levite choir ceased to function, and the rabbis decreed that both vocal and instrumental music be banned as a sign of national mourning. Subsequently this regulation was modified when Maimonides permitted the choir to sing at synagogue services and at all religious feasts.[4] Instrumental music has continued to be forbidden, and choirs sing *a cappella*. Female choristers are prohibited, for "to listen to the voice of women is invitation to lust."[5]

There were several stages in the development of the modern-day choir. In the early centuries TOMEKHIM assisted the PRECENTOR as prompters and musical assistants. As time went on, the "bass" and the "singer" in the Ashkenazic synagogue served as *Unterhalter* (supporters) to the precentor and supplied harmonic accompaniment in an improvisatory manner. The institution of the HAZZAN-BASS-SINGER lasted as late as the early nineteenth century. In Adrianople (Edirne), Turkey, a choral group called the Maftirim Choir flourished from the seventeenth century on. It sang *piyyutim* (religious poetry; *see* PIYYUT) every Sabbath morning at dawn and was known for nurturing a great number of cantors and assistant singers (*maftirim*, or *mezammrim*). *Hazzanim* such as Isaac B. Solomon Algazi (1882–1964) often sang as choristers in the Maftirim Choir, a circumstance that also made Adrianople a center for HYMN writing. Other flourishing singing societies were the Shomerim Laboker (Watchmen of the Morning), in Italy, and Mezamre Barukh She'amar (Singers of BARUKH SHE'AMAR), in Prague.

With the encouragement of the Chief Rabbi of the Republic of Venice, Leone da Modena, Solomon ROSSI (c. 1570–c. 1630) organized a choir that sang arrangements of psalms in three to eight voices. Although Israel LOVY (1773–1832) is credited with being the first to institute four-part choir singing, it was Salomon SULZER (1804–1890) of Vienna whose choir practices and musical service met with real success. Franz Liszt described a service at which Sulzer and a choir officiated in a Vienna temple: "Once, and once only, has it happened to us, as it were, to catch a glimpse and overhear what a Jewish art *might* become if the Israelite were to display, within forms invented by their own Asiatic genius, all the pomp of their imagination and dreams. . . . Rarely has it happened to us to be attacked by so lively an emotion. . . . "[6] Among those who followed Sulzer were Louis LEWANDOWSKI, in Berlin; Samuel NAUMBOURG, in Paris; Hirsch WEINTRAUB, in Königsberg; Israel Lazarus MOMBACH, in London; Eliezer Mordecai GEROVITSCH, in Rostov; David NOWAKOWSKY, in Odessa; and Boruch SCHORR, in Lemberg (Lvov). In the United States four-part choir singing was introduced by Jacob Samuel MARAGOWSKY and Abraham Frachtenberg. In the early twentieth century this practice was perpetuated by Herman Wohl, Jacob Margulies, and Meyer Machtenberg and in Poland by David Eisenstadt, Yitzhak Schlossberg, and Avraham Zvi Davidovitz.

Since the middle of the twentieth century there has been a decline in the use of professional choirs. The lengthened service required for choral singing provoked resistance, and congregational participation through active singing rather than passive listening has become the vogue. Interest in synagogue musicianship as a vocation or avocation has decreased. Nonetheless, numerous synagogues throughout the world still engage volunteer choir singers for the High Holy Days.

See also CHORUS; LEVITES; MESHORERIM; ORGAN.

[1]Ps. 68:27.
[2]Ar. II:6.
[3]Hul. 24a.
[4]*Yad, Ta'aniyot,* V:14; *Shulhan Arukh, Orah Hayyim* 560, 3.
[5]Ber. 24a; *Shulhan Arukh, Orah Hayyim* 75, 3.
[6]Franz Liszt, *The Gipsy in Music,* tr. by Edwin Evans, William Reeves, London, 1926, vol. 1, pp. 52–54.

CHOR-SCHUL. Choir (lit. "choir-synagogue") that sang music arranged for four voices in the modern synagogue of Eastern Europe. Specifically, it was a choir school for the study and preparation of the repertoire of the Sabbath and holiday services. Beginning in about 1840 many Eastern European synagogues were modeled after the Viennese Seitenstettengasse Temple, where Salomon SULZER was employed as cantor. Although they adapted Sulzer's musical service and choir practices or introduced new choral settings into the service, they did not use the ORGAN. Among *hazzanim* (cantors; *see* HAZZAN) who were employed in a *chor-schul* were Nissan BLUMENTHAL, in Odessa, and Wolf SHESTAPOL, in Kherson.

CHORUS. Group of singers that generally performs Jewish secular music with Yiddish or Hebrew texts. Originally a distinction was made between a chorus and a CHOIR, which was restricted to sacred music, but the terms are now used interchangeably. Joseph RUMSHINSKY, who pioneered with Jewish choral groups in Łódź, Poland, organized a group called the Hazomir Choral Society in 1899. He was succeeded in 1903 by Zavel ZILBERTS; in Warsaw Leo LOW was the director of the society. In the United States Platon G. BRUNOFF organized the Poale Zion Singing Society; Henry Lefkowitz succeeded him . Other early choruses were the Hadassah Choral Union (1916) and the New York 92d Street Y Choral Society (1917), directed by Abraham Wolf BINDER; the Paterson Singing Society (1918), conducted by Henry Lefkowitz; and the Freiheit Singing Society (1923) and the Workmen's Circle Choir (1925), directed by

FIRST MUSIC FESTIVAL
THE CHORUS OF UNITED HEBREW CHORAL SOCIETIES
OF UNITED STATES AND CANADA.

Members of Jewish choral societies who participated in a joint concert at the Hippodrome, New York, on April 15, 1923.

Lazar WEINER. Additional flourishing groups were the Yiddish Culture Chorus, the Farband–Labor Zionist Order Chorus, the Jewish Music Alliance Choruses, the Zilberts Choral Society, and the Vinaver Choir.

Among other musicians and conductors who exerted a strong influence on Jewish choral singing were Jacob BEIMEL, Samuel BUGATCH, Vladimir Heifetz, Max HELFMAN, and Jacob Posner in the United States and Yaakov Gerstein, Yitzhak Zaks, Avraham Slep, Yisrael Feivishes, and M. Shneyur in Poland. Israel's larger choruses were organized by Shlomo Kaplan, conducting the United Choruses, and Israel Brandman, conducting the Workers Chorus. Numerous choruses also exist in the kibbutzim under the auspices of the Histadrut. The choral movement was stimulated with the establishment in 1952 of the triennial Zimriyah (Choir Festival) for choruses from the Diaspora and Israel.

COHEN, FRANCIS LYON (1862–1934). Rabbi and writer on Jewish music. Born in Aldershot and educated at Jews' College and University College, London, Cohen held posts as minister in South Hackney (1883–1885), Dublin (1885–1886), London (1886–1904), and Sydney, Australia (1905–1934). He acted as editor to the choir committee of the United Synagogue, lectured at Oxford, and served as music editor of *The Jewish Encyclopedia* (1901–1905).

Cohen is best known for compiling (with B. L. Mosely) *The Handbook of Synagogue Music* (1889) and reediting and rearranging it (with D. M. Davis) as *The Voice of Prayer and Praise* (1899; 2d ed., 1914). He wrote numerous articles and pamphlets including "Synagogue Music: Its History and Character,"[1] *The Rise and Development of Jewish Music*,[2] "Synagogue Plain-Song,"[3] *La revue de chant grégorien*,[4] and "Song in the Synagogue."[5]

[1] *Jewish Chronicle*, 1883.
[2] Pamphlet, London, 1888.
[3] *Organist and Choirmaster*, 1897.
[4] Marseille, 1899.
[5] *Musical Times*, London, 1899.

COLORATURA. Term of Italian origin meaning "coloring," used to designate a melodic style in Jewish liturgical music characterized by vocal embellishments, generally executed with free IMPROVISATION by the Eastern European and Oriental VIRTUOSO HAZZAN. With the pious *hazzan* it is part of his expression and not mere vocal gymnastics exhibiting virtuosity. The use of coloratura among Eastern European–oriented *hazzanim* can be attributed to Oriental and operatic influences. The earliest Jews to settle in Eastern Europe were Oriental Jews, and before the fourteenth-century German immigration the music of the synagogue service was probably Oriental in character. Later the *hazzanim* Orientalized the German synagogue song and developed cantorial improvisation with its unique coloratura.

In general musical history the year 1600 marks the appearance of opera and also the growing passion for virtuosity in all fields of musical performance. Leopold Löw comments that the coloratura and ornamentation of the Eastern European *hazzan* grew from the seventeenth century onward. This style has been called "pilpul set to music" (in Talmudic studies pilpul denotes a type of hairsplitting gymnastics). The *hazzanim* of Poland, Germany, and Austria called their solos *seborot* (hypotheses), also an expression borrowed from the Talmudists.[1] Abraham Zvi IDELSOHN found no basis for applying the term pilpul to the use of coloratura because the pilpulistic period, which flourished in southwestern Germany, produced a simple chant in contrast to the intricate Eastern European song. Furthermore, the Talmud was unknown among the Arabs, Turks, Ukrainians, and gypsies, from whom the Eastern European ornamental style was taken.[2]

Recently there has been a deemphasis of the virtuoso *hazzan*. Thus coloratura embellishments are slowly disappearing from the Ashkenazic synagogue service. Replacing them is a syllabic and melismatic treatment of the text, resulting in a simpler chant style. Meanwhile, the Oriental-Sephardic *hazzan* continues to adorn the melodic line with coloratura and ornamental embellishments. *See also* MELISMA.

[1]*Die Lebensalter in der jüdischen Literatur*, 1875, p. 314.
[2]Abraham Z. Idelsohn, *Jewish Music*, Tudor Publishing Company, New York, 1944, p. 184.

CONCERT. Public performance of vocal or instrumental music, or both. Until the end of the nineteenth century the synagogue and the home were virtually the only places where Jewish music was heard. Concerts featuring Jewish music were first given in 1899 in Łódź, Poland, by Joseph RUM-SHINSKY and his Hazomir Choral Society. There followed the concerts of Simeon BELLISON with his Moscow Quintet for National Jewish Music in 1902 and with his Zimrah Ensemble in the United States in 1921. The growth of concert activity was greatly stimulated by the founding of the SOCIETY FOR JEWISH FOLK MUSIC in 1908.

The first step toward the public performance of classical music peculiarly Hebraic in character was taken at Carnegie Hall in New York in 1917, when a program that included Ernest BLOCH'S THREE PSALMS and THREE JEWISH POEMS and the first movement of his ISRAEL SYMPHONY was presented. In addition, concerts of liturgical music were popularized in the synagogue and the concert hall. The earliest public performances of this music were those of the Jewish Ministers Cantors Association of America at Madison Square Garden in New York (February 3, 1923) and the Association of Jewish Choirs at the Hippodrome in New York (April 15, 1923), in which ten choirs participated with Cantor Joseph ROSENBLATT as soloist. Cantors Mordecai Hershman (1886–1940) and Zavel Kwartin (1874–1952) also gained their reputation and popularity as performers of sacred song at such concerts. Cantorial concert giving often included a service (MINHAH, ARVIT, *Sefirah*, YOM KIPPUR KATAN), and on such occasions as Hanukkah an orchestra would be added to the choir.

Since about 1950 concerts featuring synagogue song have declined, and they are no longer used for fund raising. Jews frequent the opera and are patrons of symphony orchestras, and other kinds of entertainment are available to them. Moreover, many Jews are unable to read Hebrew fluently and so lack interest in and appreciation for cantorial selections or even synagogue song. Nonetheless, concerts including Jewish instrumental and choral music continue. In Israel the ISRAEL PHILHARMONIC ORCHESTRA alone presents some 180 concerts a year. Other Israeli orchestras include those of Haifa, Ramat Gan, the Defense Forces, and the Gadna Youth Corps, and there are also about 120 choirs. The Israel Festival of Music and Drama, Israel Music Weeks, and the En Gev Music Festival are held annually. In the United States encouragement and guidance for concert activities are provided by the NATIONAL JEWISH MUSIC COUNCIL of the National Jewish Welfare Board.

Y. M. H. A. FELIX FULD AUDITORIUM
HIGH and WEST KINNEY STREETS — NEWARK, N. J.

זונטאג אבענד, 20טען דעצעמבער, 1931

וועט שטאטפינדען א

גראנדיעזער תהלים קאנצערט

פון דעם גרעסטען אידישען מוזיק פערפאסער און קאנצערט מייסטער

הר' זײדעל ראָװנער

מיט א נרויסען מחיק ארקעסטער און א גרויסען מענער כאהר

מיט די גרעסטע סאליסטען, אויך דאם קלענסטע חזנד'ל

שלמה'לע מאנדעל

אלס סאליסט

אין דעם גרויסען קאנצערטס וועלען אויך אנטהייל נעהמען די פאלגענדע בעריהמטע חזנים:

נואיקער חזנים: הר' בערעלע חני, הר' משה זאיעטץ, הר' ישראל בריה

ניו-קער חזנים: הר' יאסעלע ראזענבלאטט, הר' דיד רייסמאן, הר' אהרן קאטשקע

A GRAND PSALM CONCERT

given by the greatest composer of Jewish Music

CANTOR Seidel Rovner

with a big orchestra and choir will take place

on Sunday December 20th, 1931

at 8 p. m.

the greatest Cantors will participate, also the little

Cantor Slomele Mandel

will be the soloist

..פראגראם..

1. ד' מלך ירגזו עמים (תהלים 99)
   כאהר, ארקעסטער, אויך סאליסטען

2. די חזנים סאליסטען וועלען זיך אויסצייכענען מיט
   קאנצערטס נומערען מיט פיאנא בעגלייטונג.
   אינטערמישאן 15 מינוט

3. לדוד מזמור (תהלים 24) כאהר, ארקעסטער
   אויך סאליסטען

4. חזנים סאליסטען אויך דאס קלײן חזנד'ל שלמה'לע
   מאנדעל וועלען זיך אויסצייכענען מיט גרויסארטיגע
   קאנצערטסנע נומערען מיט פיאנא בעגלייטונג.
   אינטערמישאן 15 מינוט

5. מזמור שיר חנוכת הבית (תהלים 30)
   כאהר, ארקעסטער, אויך סאליסטען

6. הללו את ד' כל גוים (תהלים 117) כאהר, ארקעסטער

און כדי צו נעכען יעדען א מעגליכקיים צו הערען אזא קאנצערט וועלכען מען קען ניט הערען פון קיין חזן
דער וועלם, איז פרייזען פיר טיקעטס נאר בילינ $1.00 און 75 סענט.
טיקעטס צו בעקומען אין אדמיניום, און אויך אין באאציכענטע פלעצער.

Flyer advertising a concert of Jewish music held in Newark, New Jersey, in 1931.

CONGREGATIONAL SINGING. Public participation in singing at religious services. Its origin can be traced to Moses and the children of Israel, who alternated as solo and chorus in the "Song of the Red Sea" (*see* SHIRAH, THE). In Temple services worshipers were known to respond with such refrains as AMEN, ANENU, HALLELUYAH, and HOSHA NA. In medieval times the introduction of the PIYYUT in prayer enabled the congregation to participate musically in the service. A twelfth-century observer reported that as soon as the leader in prayer started his *hazzanya* (the *piyyut* and its music), the congregation joined in fortissimo singing.[1] A strong influence in the developemtp of congregational singing was the eighteenth-century Hassidic movement. From its inception the Hassidic service appreciated the importance of song to induce fervor and enthusiasm in worship.

From the latter part of the eighteenth century to the beginning of the twentieth century the solo rendition of the CANTOR dominated the service in the Ashkenazic synagogue, and congregational singing was therefore minimal. Among the reasons leading to the subsequent restoration of congregational singing were resistance to the elongated service with the cantor's solo and choir, a desire for decorum based on active singing rather than passive listening, the fact that worshipers uninitiated in Hebrew reading found the service more stirring and meaningful with congregational singing, and a lack of funds to engage professional choirs. The deemphasis of cantorial virtuosity, which has been replaced by simplicity of chant, has also drawn the congregation into active participation with the cantor. Congregational participation, with the HAZZAN serving as the leader, has always been the practice in Sephardic synagogues.

In general, congregational melodies are monodic, metric, predominantly syllabic, lyrical in quality with a songlike style, simple and limited in range, and strophic. Recent research has found some rudimentary forms of polyphony in the musical liturgy of the Yemen Jews, the Samaritans, and the Corfu Jews.[2]

[1]Ismar Elbogen, *Der jüdische Gottesdienst in seiner geschichtlichen Entwicklung,* J. Kauffmann Verlag, Frankfurt am Main, 1924, pp. 283, 284.
[2]Edith Gerson Kiwi, "Vocal Folk Polyphonies of the Western Orient in Jewish Tradition," *Yuval,* Magnes Press, Hebrew University, Jerusalem, 1968, pp. 169–193.

CONJUNCTIVES. Masoretic accents (*see* ACCENTS, BIBLICAL) that serve as binding motives, both grammatically and musically. They are called *servi*[1] and, in Hebrew, *meshartim* or *mehubarim* (servants or connectors).[2] Conjunctives precede and connect themselves with the accents called DISJUNCTIVES and serve as links in connecting words within a phrase. In all, there are eight conjunctive accents (TELISHA-KETANAH, MAPAKH, YERAH-BEN-YOMO, MUNAH, MERKHA, KADMA, DARGA, and MERKHA-KEFULAH), designated by a mnemonic device contained in the words *Te'aMIM-MuKDaM*.

[1]Wilhelm Gesenius, *Hebrew Grammar,* rev. by E. Roediger and tr. by T. J. Conant, 14th ed., New York, 1846, p. 54.
[2]Aaron ben Asher, *Dikduke ha-Te'amim,* ed. by S. Baer and H. L. Strack, Leipzig, 1879, p. 180.

CONSOLO, FEDERICO (YEHIEL NAHMANI SEFARDI) (1841–1906). Virtuoso violinist, scholar, and transcriber of synagogue music. Born in Ancona, Italy, he studied violin with Giorgetti in Florence and Henri Vieuxtemps in Brussels and composition with François Fétis and Franz

Liszt. In 1858 he embarked on a career as violinist, giving concerts throughout Europe and the Orient until 1884, when a nervous affliction compelled him to abandon the concert stage. He then moved to Florence and devoted himself to the study of ancient synagogal song and composition. He also undertook archaeological studies.

Consolo is best known for his *Sefer Shire Yisrael (Libro dei canti d'Israel,* 1891), a work containing the traditional tunes of the Italian Jews, who had preserved the ancient Sephardic music. He also published traditional tunes arranged for four voices or solo with piano or organ accompaniment. His literary studies resulted in a historical survey of Jewish music and the music of the Bible.

CONTRAFACTUM. Adaptation of a text to a melody already used with another text. This practice probably originated in psalm singing (*see* AL-HAGITTIT; AL-MAHALAT). In Spain it was customary in the twelfth century for poets to write above the first line of a poem an indication of a preexisting melody to be sung to their new text.[1] In the sixteenth century Israel NAJARA used numerous *contrafacta* for his DIWAN (songster). This method of adaptation may have developed because existing folk tunes appealed to the masses who knew them and because text writing progressed faster than tune writing. Furthermore, in the eighteenth and nineteenth centuries Hassidim considered it their duty to replace secular texts by sacred ones. One such *contrafactum* is "Shekhinah, Shekhinah," the famous shepherd love song sung by Reb Yitzhak of Nagykálló (Kalov), Hungary.[2]

[1] Ps. 7:1; Ibn-Ezra's comment on *al divre khush.*
[2] Abraham Z. Idelsohn, *Jewish Music,* Tudor Publishing Company, New York, 1944, pp. 417, 418, 421, no. 4.

COOPERSMITH, HARRY (1902–   ). Jewish music educator. Coopersmith was taken from Russia to the United Stated when he was nine years old. He studied at the Institute of Musical Arts and received his B.S. and M.A. degrees in music from Columbia University. In 1921 he graduated from the Teachers Institute of the Jewish Theological Seminary of New York, and from 1930 to 1932 he continued his musical studies in Vienna. Coopersmith began to pioneer in Jewish music education as an instructor in the Hebrew schools in Brooklyn (1920–1926). He organized the music department of the Board of Jewish Education of Chicago in 1926 and served as its director until 1930. From 1933 to 1940 he was music director of the Anshe Emet Synagogue in Chicago, and in 1940 he was appointed music director of the Jewish Education Committee of New York (later the Board of Jewish Education of New York).

Coopersmith was instrumental in improving the quality of teaching in the various schools by instituting in-service courses, giving guidance to the teaching staff, and lecturing on music education in the Jewish schools of New York.[1] To stimulate teachers and students he compiled and edited numerous volumes of songs and two- and three-part choral settings for school and home use. He also wrote several liturgical choral works and operettas.

[1] Cf. *Jewish Music Forum Bulletin,* vol. VI, no. 1, December 1945, pp. 7, 8.

CYMBALS. In Scripture cymbals (Heb. *tziltzelim* or *metziltayim,* onomatopoeic words derived from the verb *tzalah,* meaning to "tinkle," "clash," or "clatter") are mentioned as being used to accompany the Levite singers on

צלצלי תרועה

צלצלי שמע

Bronze cymbals of the Byzantine period. [Haifa Music Museum and Amli Library]

Tziltzelay teruah (above) and *tziltzelay shama* (below). [Shaul Shaffer, *Hashir Shebamikdash*, Yefey Nof, Jerusalem]

sacred occasions.[1] In Second Temple days, under the priest-official Ben Arza,[2] cymbals gave the signal to the Levite choir to begin chanting the psalm.[3]

A distinction is made in psalm 150:5 between two kinds of cymbals, the *tziltzelay shama* and the *tziltzelay teruah*. According to numerous Bible critics, the difference between these two types is unknown, but some scholars believe that the *tziltzelay shama* were constructed to produce a loud noise and the *tziltzelay teruah* a high-sounding tone.[4] Curt Sachs is of the opinion that the former term refers to a clear sound and the latter to a harsh, noisy sound and that the shape of the instrument and the manner in which it was held while being struck (that is, horizontally or vertically) determined its sound.[5]

[1] Chron. 15:19, 16:5.
[2] Shek. 5, 1.
[3] Tam. 7, 3.
[4] *The Jewish Encyclopedia*, vol. IV, s.v. "Cymbals"; William Smith, *Dictionary of the Bible*, Boston, 1883, vol. I, p. 522.
[5] Curt Sachs, *The History of Musical Instruments*, W. W. Norton & Company, Inc., New York, 1940, pp. 121–123.

D

DAHAVON. Obscure Aramaic expression in Daniel 6:19 whose uncertainty has led to contradictory interpretations. Some Biblical commentators render the word by "food."[1] Others interpret the word in a musical sense, possibly derived from *deha* (to be merry) or *hedvah* (joy or rejoicing). Saadiah Gaon, in explaining the term, said that it was customary to entertain the King with stringed instruments (KINNOR; NEBEL) and young maidens playing before him.[2] Ibn-Ezra rendered the word by NEGGINOT (stringed instruments) and *shirot* (songs; *see* SHIR).[3] According to *Metzudat Tziyon*, it is the rejoicing produced by instrument playing.[4] Jastrow was of the opinion that the word is the plural of *dahava*, meaning "jesters" or "dancers."[5]

[1] E.g., Septuagint; Theodotion; Vulgate.
[2] Ad loc.
[3] Ad loc.
[4] Ad loc.
[5] Marcus Jastrow, *Dictionary,* London, 1903, vol. I, p. 291.

DANCE. Universal human expression that embraces all movements of the limbs and body and almost invariably is accompanied by vocal or instrumental music, or both. In Biblical days dance was combined with song and

Oriental dance performed in the amphitheater of the Hebrew University, Mount Scopus, Jerusalem. [Central Zionist Archives, Jerusalem]

Hassidic dance performed on Lag BaOmer in Meron, Israel. [Central Zionist Archives, Jerusalem]

instrument playing: "And Miriam the prophetess, the sister of Aaron, took a timbrel in her hand; and all the women went out after her with timbrels and with dances."[1] Although there are many Hebraic names for dance,[2] the term RIKKUD is most popularly used. Throughout Jewish history dancing, accompanied by music, has been practiced at weddings, on Purim and Simhat Torah (Rejoicing of the Law), and at Hassidic gatherings. Hassidim have attributed great importance to the dance. Dances by men and women combined are never permitted, a prohibition based on the Scriptural text "Hand to hand shall not go unpunished."[3]

Folk dancing made great strides in the United States and Palestine in the early 1900s. In the first quarter of the century artistic dancing gained a place in the education and art of the people. Dance instruction in the United States is fostered by the Board of Jewish Education, the 92d Street Young Men's and Young Women's Hebrew Association, and the Zionist Youth Foundation in New York, the University of Judaism in Los Angeles, and Gratz College in Philadelphia.

In Israel dance instruction began in the 1920s with the Israel National Ballet and continued with the Yemenite Inbal Dance Theater, the Batsheva Dance Company, the Bat-Dor Dance Company, the dance department of the Rubin Academy of Music in Jerusalem, the Institute for the Art of Dance in Haifa, and dance studios in various kibbutzim. The internationally famed Inbal Dance Theater, founded in 1949 by Sarah Levy-Tannai, gave as its first program pantomimes set to music relating the Biblical story of Ruth the Moabite, the "Song of Deborah," and scenes from everyday life in Yemen. In 1964 the Batsheva Dance Company made its debut at the Habima Theater in Tel Aviv. Israeli composers have been inspired by the traditional Near Eastern dances and have written scores for ballet and dance scenes.

See also BEROIGEZ TANZ; FRAILACH; HOPKE; HORA; KARAHOD; MITZVAH TANZ; PATCH TANZ; SHER; TANZHAUS.

[1]Ex. 15:20-21.
[2]*Mahol* (Judg. 21:21); *sahak* (II Sam. 6:15); *karar* (II Sam. 6:14); *pazaz* (II Sam. 6:16); *hagag* (ps. 42:5); *dalag* and *kafatz* (S.o.S. 2:8); *savav* (ps. 48:13).
[3]Prov. 11:21.

DANZE DEL RE DAVID, LE. Piano suite in seven episodes based on seven different themes, composed in 1925 by Mario CASTELNUOVO-TEDESCO and first performed in 1926 by Walter Gieseking at the International Festival of Contemporary Music in Frankfurt, Germany. The work, which bears the subtitle *Hebrew Rhapsody on Traditional Themes,* is dedicated to the memory of the composer's grandfather, whom he remembers singing these themes. Bitonality and a variety of rhythms are utilized to portray King David's religious ecstasy.

DARGA ($\overline{}$s   ). Accent sign, meaning "stepwise," placed below the word in the text of sacred literature. It is almost always followed by the symbol called TEVIR.[1] The graphic form of the *darga* seems to resemble the SHAL-SHELET, and according to several treatises on Biblical accentuation (*see* ACCENTS, BIBLICAL), the *darga* was also termed *shalshelet* and *shishla.* Its musical rendition was a trill or quaver, but to a lesser extent than the *shalshelet.*[2] Its current musical form is a descending melody.

[1]E.g., Gen. 1:22.
[2]William Wickes, *A Treatise on the Accentuation of the Prose Books of the Old Testament,* Clarendon Press, Oxford, 1887, p. 25.

DAVENEN (DAVNEN). Term, meaning "to pray," utilized by Eastern European Jews. Reference is made to the leader in prayer as *einer vos davent faren amud* (one who intones the prayers at the prayer desk) while the worshipers respond in a musical monotone. Several etymologies are given for the derivation of the term: (1) from the Aramaic word *de'avinun* (of our fathers), since it is believed that the patriarchs Abraham, Isaac, and Jacob instituted the recitation of the three daily prayers; (2) from the Latin *divinus* (divine) or *devovere* (to exercise devotion); (3) from the English *dawn,* referring especially to the prayer of the early morning;[1] (4) from the Arabic *da'a* (to pray), an altered form taken from the speech of Turkish Jews, *du'a* or *da'wa*; and (5) from the Arabic *diwan,* a collection of poems (in Arabic-speaking lands the prayer book is called a *diwan*). Jews of Germany utilize the term *oren* (from the Latin *ora,* meaning "pray") for reciting prayers. In Spanish and Portuguese communities *rezar* (from the Latin *recitare,* meaning "to recite") means "to pray." Thus the various prayer books used in the services are called *reza*-books. The act of praying is called "reading" (*rezar*) or "saying *tefilla.*"[2]

[1]Cf. Solomon ibn-Gabirol's poetic plea beginning with the words *Shahar avakeshkha* (At dawn I seek thee), in S. Baer, *Siddur Avodath Israel,* Rödelheim, 1868.
[2]H. P. Salomon, "Sephardi Terminology," *American Sephardi,* Yeshiva University, vol. V, 1971, pp. 63, 64.

DAVID (1034-965 B.C.E). Second King of Israel, son of Jesse the Bethlehem-ite. The reign of King David, his life, and accomplishments are given in I Samuel (beginning with Chapter 15), II Samuel, I Kings (first two chapters), parts of I Chronicles, and Ruth. His life was filled with greatness and splendor, and messianic hope is attached to his descendants. He is often referred to as the Sweet Singer of Israel[1] and is noted for playing the

KINNOR.[2] Under David's rule music became identified with Jewish religious life.[3] With the appointment of HEMAN, ASAPH, and JEDUTHUN as the chief Levitical musicians (*see* LEVITES), music and singing were brought into the Sanctuary.[4] According to tradition, King David was the author of the Psalms: "David wrote the Book of Psalms, including in it the works of the [ten] elders."[5]

[1]II Sam. 23:1.
[2]I Sam. 16:23.
[3]II Sam. 6:5.
[4]I Chron. 25:1–6.
[5]B.B. 14b.

DAVNEN. *See* DAVENEN.

DE PROFUNDIS. (1) Work by Jacques Halévy for three voices to psalm 130 (in Hebrew), composed on the death of the Duc de Berry and dedicated to Luigi Cherubini. It was performed at a memorial service held on March 24, 1820, at the synagogue in the Rue Sainte-Avoye. *See also* JUIVE, LA; MIN HAMMETZAR. (2) Setting (op. 50B) by Arnold Schönberg (1874–1951) for a six-voice chorus (*a cappella*) with the subtitle *A Song of Ascents—Out of the Depths* (ps. 130). The work, composed in 1950 to the original Hebrew text and based on traditional prayer patterns utilized on the High Holy Days, was written at the request of Chemjo VINAVER, in whose *Anthology of Jewish Music* it is included.[1] It has been recorded by the Gregg Smith Singers for the Everest Records Production (3182) in Los Angeles, Calif. *See also* KOL NIDRE; SURVIVOR FROM WARSAW, A. (3) Work written for strings by Tzvi AVNI in 1972 and first performed by the Israel Broadcasting Symphony Orchestra under the baton of Y. Aharonowitch at the Twelfth Israel Festival of Music and Drama.

[1]E. B. Marks Music Corporation, New York, 1955, pp. 201–214.

ישיבת רבנו יצחק אלחנן—מכון להדרכת חזנים
RABBI ISAAC ELCHANAN THEOLOGICAL SEMINARY

This is to certify that

having completed the program prescribed by the faculty of our
CANTORIAL TRAINING INSTITUTE
is hereby awarded this

Cantorial Diploma

with all the rights, privileges and honors thereunto pertaining. In testimony whereof this document is granted in the City of New York
on the   day of   corresponding to

DIRECTOR OF THE SEMINARY   DIRECTOR OF THE INSTITUTE

Diploma issued by the Cantorial Training Institute, an affiliate of Yeshiva University.

DEGREE, JEWISH MUSIC. Academic degree bestowed upon students fulfilling certain requirements. The Jewish music degrees usually conferred are associate cantor's certificate, cantorial diploma, bachelor of sacred music, master of sacred music, doctor of sacred music, and master of arts in sacred music. The concept of granting a degree, which began about 1950, grew out of the need to discipline and train students to be well versed in the scholarly domain of Jewish music and qualified in the practical skills and techniques of the cantorate. An important factor also was keeping pace with other educational fields of endeavor and professions. The requirements for the various degrees differ in different institutions. *See also* EDUCATION, JEWISH MUSIC.

DESPIDIDA TUNE. Melody (lit. "farewell tune") associated with Sephardim as a last-day theme for the Pilgrim Festivals (Shalosh Regalim). It represents parting with the joyousness of the holiday and is adapted to various texts of the liturgy in different services (for example, KADDISH, *Kedushah, Hallel,* EN KELOHENU). See Fig. 15.

KADDISH (La Despidida)

Figure 15. [*The Jewish Encyclopedia,* Funk and Wagnalls Company]

DESSAU, PAUL (1894–   ). Composer, conductor, and educator. Born in Hamburg, Germany, Dessau gained an early knowledge of the Jewish musical heritage from his father, Cantor Moses Dessau. He served as an operatic coach at the Hamburg Opera and conducted orchestras in Cologne (1919–1923), Mainz (1924), and Berlin (1925–1933). After the Nazis came to power, he was compelled to leave Germany and traveled in Europe and Palestine. In 1939 he arrived in the United States, where he taught composition for a time in New York. In 1948 he returned to Berlin. Dessau's works embodying Jewish content as well as fragments of Jewish melody are his oratorio HAGGADAH, *Seven Psalms,* and *Friday Evening Service.* He has also written a symphony, chamber music, and songs for chorus and solo voice.

DEUTSCH, MORITZ (MOSHE) (1818–c. 1894). Cantor-composer of the Great Synagogue of Breslau, known for founding a cantorial institute in that city. As a child Deutsch showed a remarkable aptitude for Talmudic learning. His parents gave him the opportunity to advance his Hebraic studies in his native city of Nikolsburg (Mikulov), Moravia, and later in Leipnik (Lipník nad Bečvou), Eisenstadt, and Pressburg (Bratislava). Deutsch did not begin to study music until he was twenty-one years old. He was highly gifted and made rapid progress studying with Salomon

SULZER and at the Vienna Conservatory, from which he graduated with honors as a singer and music teacher. His professional career as a cantor began when he was appointed *hazzan sheni* (associate cantor; *see* HAZZAN) to Sulzer in 1842. In 1844 he was called to the position of cantor–choir director of the Great Synagogue of Breslau, where he served with great distinction for fifty years. In 1854 he was appointed instructor of music at the Jewish Theological Seminary of Breslau, a post he held for more than thirty years.

Deutsch's striving to develop and improve the music of the synagogue service went far beyond the environs of the synagogue. In 1859 he organized a cantorial institute in which more than 130 students received a thorough liturgical music education. He was also instrumental in finding positions for his students. (For some reason the institute closed its doors in 1885.) Deutsch wrote a series of compositions for the synagogue and twelve preludes for the organ or pianoforte called *Breslauer Synagogengesänge* (1880). He is best known for his *Vorbeterschule* (1871), a musical work for the liturgy of the yearly cycle. Based on eastern German tradition and written as a reference book for fledgling cantors, the foreword and addenda (*Der Ritualgesang der Synagoge,* 1890) show the beginnings of Jewish liturgical musicological research. In addition, Deutsch wrote articles on Jewish liturgical music.

DEUX MÉLODIES HÉBRAÏQUES. Two settings based on Eastern European song, written in 1914 by Maurice Ravel (1875–1937) for voice and orchestra. They are "Kaddish," the traditional Hebrew chant before MUSAF for the High Holy Days (*see* KADDISH), and "L'énigme éternelle" (*Alte Kashe*), a Yiddish folk tune.

DEVAYKUT. Stylistic direction in Hebraic music (lit. "clinging unto,"[1] a term signifying spiritual attachment) meaning officiating or performing with extraordinary devotion or devoutness. Hassidim stress the singing of tunes expressing the *devaykut* style, which is characteristically mystic, meditative, couched in nonmetrical free form, and sung in a slow tempo. The branch of the Hassidim that favors this style of melody is the HaBaD movement. Its adherents refer to numerous tunes as *devaykele,* using the endearing diminutive *le. See also* HASSIDIC SONG.

[1]Cf. Deut. 11:22.

DIN TORAH MIT GOTT, A. Classic Hebrew-Yiddish folk song (lit. "A Litigation with God"), subtitled "Reb Levi Yitzhak Berdichev's Kaddish" or "Rebbe's Kaddish." Its origin is attributed to the Hassidic master R. Levi Yitzhak of Berdichev (1740–1809), who on a Rosh Hashanah morning halted the service before the KADDISH and began to chant this personal prayer of adjuration in which he extols *Hamelekh* (the King, referring to God). The popular melody utilizing the NE'ILAH Kaddish theme as well as the concluding motive of the festival *Amidah* has also come down in another version. It appears under the title "Daray Ma'alah im Daray Matah" (Those That Dwell on High with Those That Dwell Down Below on Earth).[1] The version in Fig. 16 has been notated by M. Kipnis in his *140 Folks-Lieder.*

[1]Cf. *Folks-Gezangen,* C. Kotylansky Book Committee, Los Angeles, Calif., and Aveltlicher Yiddisher Kultur-Farband (YCUF), New York, 1944, pp. 21–24.

קַדִּישׁ.

גוּטער מאָרגען דיר, רבּונו של עולם!

איך, לוי יצחק בּן שרה מבּאַרדיטשעוו,

בּין איך געקומען צו דיר מיט אַ דין תורה

פון דיין פאָלק ישראל.

וואָס האָסטו צו דיין פאָלק ישראל?

די עו - לָם - בָּ יֶשׁ מוֹת - אוּ מֶה - כַ, מַעֲל - הי אין סְעַר - זִי ניט - טְע - טֶא

con fuoco

דִי יַם . מְ - דוּ - אַ יַם - לְ - בָּב , יַם - ס - פַּר

Accelando

די .סְעַר - קִי אִז סְעַר - קִי עֶר - זֵי אַז נְגַן - זָא וואָס ,דְער - לֶעֶנ-רוֹס

די אוּן כּוֹת - מַל אִז כּוֹת - מַל עֶר - זֵי אַז נְגַן - זָא וואָס דְער - לֶעֶנ-דֵיטש

אוּן סְעַר - קִי אִז כּוֹת - מַל עֶר - זֵי אַז נְגַן זָא וואָס דְער - לֶעֶנ - עֶנֶג

זָאג טשעוואָ-די-באָר - מַ רְה - שָׁ בֶּן הָק - יֶצ וִי - לְ אִיך

בְּאָ - ר מֶה - שׁ רְשׁ - קִ - יֶת - וּ רָל - נְ - יֶת !

piu mosso   piu a piu mosso.

לֹא זָאנטשעוואָ-די-באָר - מַ רְה - שָׁ בֶּן הַק - יֶצ וִי - לְ אִיך אוּן

וואָס האָסטו זיך אָנגעזעצט צֹאויף דיין פֿאָלק ישׂראל?

אַז וואו נאָר אַ זאָר, צֹאיז אָמוֹר אֶל בְּנֵי ישׂראל,

אַז וואו נאָר אַ זאָך, צֹאיז צוֹ אֶל בְּנֵי ישׂראל,

אַז וואו נאָר אַ זאָך, צֹאיז דבר אֶל בְּנֵי ישׂראל,

טאַטעניו! כמה צֹאומות יש בעולם:

פרסים, בבלים, צֹאדומים.

Figure 16.

DIRIGENT. German term for the conductor or director of an orchestra, chorus, or synagogue choir. The synagogue choir leader of Eastern Europe was often called a *chor-dirigent.*

DISJUNCTIVES. Accent marks in Scriptural texts that indicate, both grammatically and musically, the complete ending of a sentence or the conclusion of a part therein. Referred to as *domini*[1] and, in Hebrew, *herusim,*[2] *meyuhadim,*[3] *sarim,* and *mafsikim,*[4] they possess distinct separating pausal strength and are arranged according to their relative powers. Disjunctives are subdivided into the following five categories:[5] (1) *kesarim* (emperors), very strong disjunctives including SILLUK and ETNAHTA; (2) *melahim* (kings), strong disjunctives including SEGOL, SHALSHELET, ZAKEF KATAN, ZAKEF GADOL, TIPKHA, and REVI'I; (3) *mishnim* (dukes), secondary disjunctives including TEVIR, ZARKA, PASHTA, YETIV, GERESH, GERSHAYIM, and AZLA; (4)

shelishim (counts), third-ranking group including PAZER, TELISHA-GEDOLAH, and KARNE-FARAH; and (5) a *mafsik katan* (petty lord), MUNAH LEGARMEH. *See also* CONJUNCTIVES; TE'AMIM.

[1]Cf. Wilhelm Gesenius, *Hebrew Grammar*, rev. by E. Roediger and tr. by T. J. Conant, 14th ed., New York, 1846, p. 53.
[2]Aaron ben Asher, *Dikduke ha-Te'amim*, ed. by S. Baer and H. L. Strack, Leipzig, 1879, p. 18.
[3]Ibid., p. 16.
[4]*The Jewish Encyclopedia*, vol. I, p. 151.
[5]Solomon Rosowsky, *The Cantillation of the Bible*, The Reconstructionist Press, New York, 1957.

DITTY. Short tune of a light nature and simple character that found its way into the synagogue service of Eastern European Jewry in the late nineteenth century. It was generally inserted in the developed RECITATIVE. Its inclusion was probably due to the abundance of and love for the general folk song (*see* FOLK SONG, YIDDISH), which flourished in the repertory of Eastern European Jews, and to the strong influence of HASSIDIC SONG. To Western Jews who lacked a Yiddish folk music background, it remained alien. The ditty eventually paved the way and served as source material for CONGREGATIONAL SINGING. Among synagogue composers who utilized this form of musical expression were Jacob Rapaport (1890–1943),[1] Eliyahu Shnipelisky (1879–1947),[2] Jacob Leib Wasilkowsky (1882–1942),[3] Joshua Samuel WEISSER (1888–1952),[4] and Simon Zemachson (1870–1928).[5]

[1]Cf. *Hazzanut for the High Holy Days*, ed. by Noah Schall, Cantorial Council of America, New York, 1969, p. 27, no. 18, "Kevakoras."
[2]Cf. *Tefillat Eliyahu*, 1924, p. 22, no. 19, "L'ma'an achay."
[3]Cf. *Ma'ariv Chants*, ed. by Macy Nulman, Yeshiva University, New York, 1965, p. 15, no. 18, "Tov l'hodos."
[4]Cf. *Baal T'filo*, 1940, p. 121, no. 104, "Labris habet."
[5]Cf. *Shire T'fillah*, part 2, 1926, p. 49, no. 35, "Uvyom hashabos."

DIWAN. Songster utilized in Oriental communities and arranged according to recurrent melodic patterns. The earliest *diwan* to be published was *Zemirot Yisrael* (Safed, 1587) by Israel NAJARA, arranged according to twelve *maqamât* (*see* MAQĀM).

DRONG (pl. *dronges*). Term (lit. "log" or "pole") generally used for a fool or an awkward person. In the vocabulary of *hazzanim* (cantors; *see* HAZZAN) the derogatory expression was applied to a cantor or singer whose voice had a wooden quality or whose rendition was unmusical, or both. The following verse was often cited in jest with the appellation *drong*: "Then shall all the trees of the forest sing for joy" (ps. 96:12).

DUDULE (DUDELE), A (also known as *Du-Du*). Popular Hebrew-Yiddish folk song attributed to R. Levi Yitzhak of Berdichev (1740–1809). The title is a play upon the pronoun *Du* (Thou, referring to God); the *le* represents an endearing diminutive. The text, according to Nathan Ausubel,[1] is probably based on a morning prayer, *Kah anah emtza'akha* (Lord, where shall I find thee?) by Judah Ha-Levi (c. 1075–1141).[2] The first part of the song is a RECITATIVE in the LERN-STEIGER. It is followed by a metrical tune in the AHAVAH RABBAH MODE. *See* Fig. 17.

[1]*A Treasury of Jewish Folklore*, Crown Publishers, Inc., New York, 1952, p. 721.
[2]Cf. A. Ben-UR, *Toldot Hashirah Ha'ivrit Bime Habeynayim*, Izreel, Tel Aviv, 1961, vol. II, p. 53.

א דודעלע.

רבּוֹנוֹ שֶׁל עוֹלָם, רבּוֹנוֹ שֶׁל עוֹלָם,
רבּוֹנוֹ שֶׁל עוֹלָם, רבּוֹנוֹ שֶׁל עוֹלָם,
רבּוֹנוֹ שֶׁל עוֹלָם, כ׳חעל דיר א דודעלע זינגעו
דו־די־דו, דו־דו —

נוט צוען־מ־ע – איז .דו דו דו דו

דו , אי – שלעכט לה־לי־חַ ,דו

! דו דו־דו־דו דו דו דו ,דו דו דו דו דו דו אי

.דו רום־דָ .דו פוֹן־צָ .דו רַב־מֶע ,דו רָח־מִז

,דו רְצ־א,דו ים־מ – שָ ,דו דו דו דו דו דו דו דו

דו דו דו דו דו דו דו דו דו דו דו דו ,דו טָה־מַ .דו לָה־מֶע

! דו דו מיך וועדעד איך וואו מיך קעהר איך וואן ,דו דו דו דו דו

שיה אמצאך, ואיה לא אמצאך?

וואו קאָן איך דיך יאָ געפינען,

און וואו קאָן איך דיך נישט געפינען?

דו=דו=דו, דו=דו —

אַז וואו איך גיי — דו!

און וואו איך שטיי — דו!

רק דו, נאָר דו, ווידער דו, אָבֶּר דו=

דו=דו=דו, דו=דוּן

אײַז עמיצען גוט — דו!
חלילה שלעכט — אי דו
אײַ, דו=דו=דו=דו=דו=דו!
דו=דו=דו=דו=דו=דו=דו!

מזרח—דו, מערב—דו
צפון—דו, דרום—דו'
דו=דו=דו,
דו=דו=דו,
דו=דו=דו!

שמים—דו, ארץ—דו,
מעלה—דו, מטה—דו'
דו=דו=דו, דו=דו=דו.

דו=דו=דו, דו=דו=דו, דו דו דו!
וואו איד קער מיד וואו איד וועגד מיד ➤
רי — דו !!!

Figure 17. [M. Kipnis, *140 Folks-Lieder*, Warsaw]

DUKHAN. Platform on which the LEVITES stood while chanting the daily psalm[1] and playing their instruments.[2] In Temple days the priestly blessing, taken from Numbers 6:24−26, was likewise recited by the Kohanim (priests) on a special rostrum or platform (*dukhan*). Hence, the term *dukhenen* is used for the ceremony in which the Kohanim mount the platform to bless the congregation at the end of the *Amidah* prayer.[3] They repeat the priestly blessing in chantlike manner, word for word, after the HAZZAN. In Israel this ritual is a daily occurrence; in the Diaspora it takes place on the three festivals and High Holy Days in the Ashkenazic rite and daily in the Sephardic rite. The chant and melodies vary from community to community and for the different holidays in the yearly cycle.[4]

[1]Meg. 3a.
[2]Ar. II, 6.
[3]Shab. 118b.
[4]Abraham Baer, *Baal T'fillah*, Göteborg, 1877, pp. 198, 199, 287−289.

DUNAJEWSKI, A. (1843−1911). Russian-born synagogue composer and conductor who flourished in Odessa. Little is known about his life. He wrote a two-volume work, *Israelitische Tempel Compositionen* (1887, 1893) for the Sabbath that was reissued by the Sacred Music Press in New York. His melody for *Av Horahamim*,[1] which is sung prior to taking the Torah from the Ark on Sabbaths and holidays, has become popular throughout the world.

[1]Macy Nulman, *Sabbath Chants*, Yeshiva University, New York, 1958, p. 28, no. 40.

DYBBUK, THE. Famous play (the word means a demon or evil spirit that takes possession of a person) in three acts by Solomon Ansky (1863–1920), produced in Moscow (1922) by the Habima Theater. Hayyim Nahman Bialik translated it into Hebrew, and Joel ENGEL wrote the musical score. The incidental music, which contributes greatly to the success of the drama and can be played as a compositional entity, is known as *Suite Ha-Dibuk*. It is scored for string quartet, double bass, clarinet, and percussion (op. 35).[1] Of special significance is the opening Hassidic melody "Mipne mah," which Aaron Copland adapted as the basis for his work VITEBSK.

[1]Juwal, Berlin and Tel Aviv, 1926.

E

EDEL, YITZHAK (1896–   ). Polish-Israeli conductor, pedagogue, and composer. He fostered Jewish music in both Eastern Europe and Israel and is known for creating musical works in Israel with the imprint of Eastern Jewish melos. He was born in Warsaw, Poland, of a Hassidic family that achieved an outstanding reputation in Jewish scholarship. To Edel, music was part of his daily life; he learned to play the violin at an early age. He began formal music studies in Kiev and then in Moscow (1917), and in 1922 he returned to Warsaw to complete his music education. In Warsaw, Edel taught general and Jewish music at Yehudiyah (a school for girls), the Tarbut schools, and the Janusz Korczak Institute (a children's home). He also conducted the Hashomer Hatzair choir. He arrived in Palestine in 1929 and was appointed to the faculty of the Levinsky Women Teachers Seminary in Tel Aviv, a position he held until his retirement in 1965. He is known for helping and befriending fellow musicians (e.g., Solomon ROSOWSKY and Mordecai Golinkin). His monograph *Hashir Ha'aretz-Yisra'eli* (1946) is an important contribution to the understanding of Israeli folk song. Edel's works were performed in Israel and abroad and won numerous prizes and awards. His compositions include cantatas, two string quartets, a suite (in memory of the Polish victims of the Holocaust), chamber music, choral music, piano solos, and songs for mixed chorus and solo voice.

EDUCATION, JEWISH MUSIC. Informal and formal musical education in Jewish cultural life. After Moses, Miriam, and the children of Israel were liberated from the bondage of Egypt, they participated in singing and instrumental playing (*see* SHIRAH, THE), thus demonstrating that everyone practiced some form of music. LEVITES took a five-year course of instruction in order to be admitted into the Levitical choir.[1] Systematic music instruction was also part of the schools of the Prophets.[2] Mention is made in the Talmud of professional teachers who received their fee for giving instruction in teaching punctuation (*pisuk te'amim*),[3] which undoubtedly was a musical system (*see* TE'AMIM). Music is also described in the Talmud as being extremely helpful in aiding the learning process.[4] Musical values and habits were imparted throughout Jewish history in various ways. Joseph ben Judah ibn Aknin, a disciple of Moses Maimonides, wrote that the Jew should study the art of music for its association with the ancient sacrifices, and especially for its spiritual power, for its value in "guiding the mind to clear sight, to keen distinction, and to the faculty of meditation."[5]

From the Middle Ages the family sat around the table after the meal on Friday evenings and Saturday mornings singing table hymns (ZEMIROT).

Musically trained women instructed other women in the singing of the synagogue hymns. They played musical instruments and sang, with musical accompaniment, the verses that their husbands composed.[6] In Venice Rabbi Leone da Modena directed a Jewish academy of music from 1629 to 1639. From about the mid-1800s, the synagogue became an effective force in the musical training for boys, adult male singers, and cantors. Choristers and prospective cantors apprenticed themselves to individual synagogue-composers and participated in the congregational CHOIR or CHOR-SCHUL. Formal liturgical music training began in 1859, when Moritz DEUTSCH organized a cantorial institute in Breslau. A cantorial school was established in 1881 under the auspices of the cantors' association in Austria-Hungary with Jacob BAUER serving on its faculty. In 1906 Abraham Ber BIRNBAUM founded a cantorial school in Częstochowa and provided a correspondence course of liturgical and general music. In England, Israel Lazarus MOMBACH taught HAZZANUT at Jews' College, where a department was established in 1855 as part of the rabbinical faculty department. In Vilna Abraham Moshe BERNSTEIN taught *hazzanut* to individuals and music in the Hebrew schools. In 1910 the Bureau of Jewish Education was the first organization in the United States to give impetus to formal Jewish music education under the directorship of Samuel E. Goldfarb. In 1926 the music department of the Board of Jewish Education of Chicago was organized by Harry COOPERSMITH, who assumed a similar post as director of the music department of the Jewish Education Committee of New York in 1940 (later the Board of Jewish Education of New York).

During the third quarter of the twentieth century the scope of Jewish music education broadened. Yeshivot and Hebrew schools include music instruction as part of the curriculum. Special schools that have been established to train cantors and Jewish musicians are the School of Sacred Music of the Hebrew Union College–Jewish Institute of Religion, established in 1948 under the guidance of Eric WERNER and Abraham Wolf BINDER; the Cantors Institute and Seminary College of Jewish Music, founded at the Jewish Theological Seminary of America in 1952 with Hugo Weisgall as its director; the Hebrew Arts School for Music and Dance, established by the Hebrew Arts Foundation in New York City in 1952 with Tzipora H. Jochsberger as its director; the Cantorial Training Institute of the Rabbi Isaac Elchanan Theological Seminary (an affiliate of Yeshiva University), founded in 1954 and headed by Dr. Karl Adler, who was assisted by Cantor Macy Nulman, its current director; and the music department at Gratz College in Philadelphia, instituted in 1958. Jewish folk music is also part of the curriculum of the Judaic studies program of the University of the City of New York.

In Israel, among the earliest to influence Jewish music education were Abraham Zvi IDELSOHN and Joel ENGEL. Between 1906 and 1921 Idelsohn contributed to Jewish music pedagogy at the Teachers Seminary, Jewish People's School, Institute for Jewish Music, and the Jewish Music School. From 1924 to his death in 1927, Engel introduced special courses for nursery school teachers and taught at the Shulamit Conservatory in Tel Aviv. Jewish musicological study reached fruition under Robert LACHMANN and Edith GERSON-KIWI. Liturgical music was sponsored by the Israel Institute for Sacred Music in Jerusalem, the Selah Seminary in Tel Aviv (Shlomo Ravitz), Shirat Yisrael in Jerusalem (Shlomo Zalman Rivlin), and the Academy for Hazzanut in Tel Aviv (Leib Glantz). In 1933 Emil Hauser founded the Palestine Conservatoire of Music. This developed into the Jerusalem Music Academy and the Israel Academy of Music with independent schools in Jerusalem and Tel Aviv, both now known as the Rubin Academy of Music. Musicology departments exist at the Hebrew University in Jerusalem (established 1965), Tel Aviv University (established 1966), and Bar-Ilan University (established 1970). Currently the Ministry of Education and Culture supervises twenty-nine conservatories with 9,700 students, including the Rubin Academy of Music in Jerusalem and in Tel Aviv.

[1]Hul. 24a.
[2]I Sam. 10:5; 19:19, 20.
[3]Ned. 37a.
[4]Cf. Meg. 32a, *Tosafot-vehashone belo zimrah.*
[5]*Tabb al Nufus,* chap. 27.
[6]Cf. D. Kaufmann, *Jewish Quarterly Review,* vol. III, p. 298.

EHRLICH, ABEL (1915‒   ). Israeli composer and teacher. Born in Kranz, East Prussia, Ehrlich received a general and musical education there until 1934. His serious music study began when he enrolled at the Academy of Music in Zagreb, Yugoslavia. After spending five years at the academy, he went to Palestine in 1939 and studied composition under Solomon ROSOWSKY. After 1940 he was active teaching theory and composition at the Oranim Teachers Seminary and at the Rubin Academy of Music in Tel Aviv. Ehrlich composed orchestral and choral works, string quartets, chamber music, and piano pieces. Among his popular compositions are *Bashrav* for violin solo (1953) and *Symphonic Bashrav* for orchestra (1958), *The Writing of Hezkiah* (1962) for soprano, violin, oboe, and bassoons, and *Be Ye Not as Your Fathers* (1964) for mixed choir, *a cappella.*

EL-HANEHILOT. Caption in psalm 5, the meaning of which has been explained in various ways: (1) *Nehilot* is derived from *halal,* "to bore," "pierce," or "perforate," the allusion being to instruments such as pipes or flutes that accompanied the psalm.[1] (2) The origin of the word possibly is in the phrase *nahil shel devorim,* "a swarm of bees," hence referring to a melody or instruments having the tonal quality of the whistling or buzzing of bees.[2] The phrase *nahil shel devorim* (i.e., the idea of multitude) may also signify that the psalm was chanted by the entire people of Israel. The Arabic *nahala,* "to winnow," suggests that it was sung by a purified portion of the people.[3] (3) *El-hanehilot* is a secular melody, i.e., a folk song to which the psalm was sung.[4]

[1]Wilhelm Gesenius and others; cf. David Kimchi, ps. 87:7, where the word *holalim* is interpreted as "flute players."
[2]R. Hai, quoted by David Kimchi; *Metzudat Tziyon,* ad loc.
[3]William Smith, *Dictionary of the Bible,* Boston, 1883, vol. III, p. 2103.

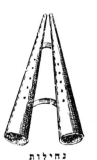

**Nehilot. [Shaul Shaffer,
Hashir Shebamikdash,
Yefey Nof, Jersualem]**

נחילות

[4]Carl Heinrich Cornill, *Music in the Old Testament*, The Open Court Publishing Company, Chicago, 1909, p. 23.

ELEGY (ÉLÉGIE). Mournful or plaintive poem in honor of the dead expressed either vocally or by instrument. Early Biblical elegies are those of King DAVID on the death of Saul and Jonathan[1] and on the death of Abner.[2] In modern times instrumental works of similar intention and mood are *Elegy* (1927) for string quartet, in memory of Joel ENGEL, written by Joseph ACHRON; *Élégie-Trio* for violin, cello, and piano by Alexander Abramovich KREIN; and *Elegy on Ponar* (1943) for orchestra by Wolf Durmashkin. In the early 1920s *Élégie* by Jules Massenet was set to a Hebrew text and recorded[3] and popularized by Joseph ROSENBLATT.[4]

[1]II Sam. 1:17.
[2]Ibid., 3:33.
[3]Columbia Records.
[4]Published by S. Schenker for voice, piano, and violin, New York, 1921.

ELI, ELI. Well-known Hebrew-Yiddish folk song, the title of which means "My God, My God." It opens with a poignant cry of perplexity, "My God, my God, why hast Thou forsaken me" (ps. 22:2), and closes with Israel's confession of faith, "Hear, O Israel, the Lord our God, the Lord is One" (Deut. 6:4). The tune, in the AHAVAH RABBAH MODE, composed in 1896 by Jacob Koppel Sandler, owes its popularity to Cantor Joseph ROSENBLATT, who recorded it as an encore in many of his concerts in the early 1900s. Sophie Braslau, a leading contralto of the Metropolitan Opera Company, included it in her repertoire at her Sunday evening concerts at the Metropolitan Opera House in New York (1920). Numerous arrangements have been written for voice and piano accompaniment.[1] Mischa Elman's violin transcription of the melody has been recorded under the title "Hebraic Melodies."[2]

[1]Alfred Sendrey, *Bibliography of Jewish Music*, Columbia University Press, New York, 1951, nos. 9366–9370. For Jacob Koppel Sandler's suit against Joseph Katz for publishing this song in 1923, *see* Eric Mandell, *A Collector of Jewish Music Speaks: A Kaleidoscopic Look at Collecting*, 1961, p. 18.
[2]Vanguard-Stereolab, VSD-2137.

ELI TZIYON (LAMENT, O ZION). Last of the elegies recited on the morning of Tishah b'Ab (the Ninth of Ab), the anniversary of the destruction of the Temple. Composed by R. Judah Ha-Levi (c. 1075–1141), the alphabetical hymn with its refrain is distinguished mainly by its traditional melody. Francis Lyon COHEN dates the tune to the later Middle Ages, its probable origin being southern Germany.[1] Abraham Zvi IDELSOHN calls the tune a "wandering melody" originating in Spain, in all likelihood spread by pilgrims of the Middle Ages to Central and Eastern European countries.[2] The theme (*see* Fig. 18*a*) has become interwoven with the chants of various holiday texts in order to turn the attention of the congregation to its sentiment (e.g., the *bene veshka kevathilah* phrase in the MUSAF of the

Figure 18*a*.

Figure 18b.

three festivals). The theme is also sung by some as the refrain to the hymn LEKHA DODI during the "Three Weeks" (i.e., the time between the fast of Tammuz and the Ninth of Ab), and by others only on Shabbat Hazon (the Sabbath preceding the Ninth of Ab). Some congregations omit the use of the melody for the last stanza, 'Bo'i Veshalom."[3] The adaptation of "Eli Tziyon" for "Lekha Dodi" on Shabbat was spurned by some rabbis because it aroused feelings of grief and sorrow.[4]

According to Abraham BAER, in the Polish tradition, the first phrase of the melody (note 1 in measure 4) ends on F sharp instead of on F natural.[5] Perhaps Baer was not aware that in Polish tradition, as well as in other Eastern European traditions, "Eli Tziyon" is chanted either in strict accentual rhythm or in RECITATIVE form, with its melismatic (*see* MELISMA) opening ending on D, not on F sharp (*see* Fig. 18b). The tune with its variants has become so associated with Jewish musical tradition that on the morning of the Ninth of Ab the worshiper invariably remains in the synagogue, despite the lengthiness of the service, until its recital has been concluded. It is customary, too, that before the recital of the tune, the congregants who have been sitting on the floor or on upturned book rests or benches rise, and the READER ascends to his desk to chant this hymn, which closes the series of KINOT.

[1]Cf. *The Jewish Encyclopedia*, vol. V, p. 107.
[2]Cf. *Jewish Music*, Tudor Publishing Company, New York, 1944, p. 171.
[3]*The Jewish Encyclopedia*, vol. V, p. 107; A. Rosenfeld, *Kinot*, London, 1965, xxv, xxvi.
[4]Abraham Eliezer Hirshowitz, *Otzar Shalem Leminhagey Yisrael*, 1892, p. 233.
[5]Cf. *Baal T'fillah*, 2d ed., Göteborg, 1883, p. 64, no. 213.

ELLSTEIN, ABRAHAM (1907–1963). Composer and pianist who propagated Jewish music in the United States. Born in New York City, he sang as a chorister in a synagogue choir on the lower East Side. His early general musical training began at the Third Street Settlement House, and later he studied piano with Frederick JACOBI and counterpoint with Charles Haubiel. At the age of seventeen he was awarded a four-year scholarship to the Juilliard Graduate School of Music, where he came under the tutelage of Rubin Goldmark (composition) and Albert Stoessel (conducting). In his early career, Ellstein eked out a living for himself and his family by conducting a choir for High Holy Day services and accompanying concert artists. From 1926 to about 1932 he accompanied Cantor Joseph ROSENBLATT on a world tour. Ellstein wrote for Broadway, radio, and television, conducted "pop" concerts, made recordings, and toured European cities

Abraham Ellstein.

as well as South Africa and South America. His name has become associated with modern Yiddish theater on Second Avenue in New York City because of the incidental music he composed for Yiddish plays and because of his orchestra conducting. His works encompass many phases of composition: liturgical choral music, oratorios, cantatas, operas, works for orchestra and piano, songs, and theater music. Among his works written in a classical vein are a cantata, *Ode to the King of Kings;* an opera, *The Golem;* a piano suite, *Haftorah; Negev Concerto* for piano and orchestra; and an oratorio, *The Redemption.*

EN KELOHENU. Popular hymn (lit. "There is none like our God") chanted on Sabbath and festivals immediately after the conclusion of the MUSAF service. According to Sephardic rite, it is also recited on weekdays and is sometimes employed as one of the table hymns (ZEMIROT) during the third Sabbath meal (Shalosh Seudot). Although the text has been set to numerous tunes, the most popular is that by Julius Freudenthal (Brunswick, Germany, 1805–1874; *see* Fig. 19a). This tune, derived from a German melody, "Grosser Gott wir loben Dich," has been revised several times

Figure 19*a.*

EN KELOHENU

Figure 19b. [*The Jewish Encyclopedia,* Funk and Wagnalls Company]

until its present form.[1] Figure 19b is a traditional melody as employed by the Sephardim.

[1]Abraham Z. Idelsohn, *Jewish Music,* Tudor Publishing Company, New York, 1944, pp. 238, 239.

ENGEL, JOEL (1868–1927). Composer, music critic, lecturer, and teacher, regarded as the "father of Jewish music." Engel was the first to find identity as a musician in Jewish folk and religious sources and to pioneer for the advancement of Jewish music. The son of a well-to-do merchant, he received his education in the Gymnasium (grammar school) in his native city, Berdyansk (Osipenko), Russia. He studied piano while he was a law student at Kharkov University. Following the advice of Pyotr Tchaikovsky, he entered the Imperial Conservatory in Moscow in 1892 and reached musical maturity under the aegis of Taneyev, Arenski, and Ippolitov-Ivanov. After graduation in 1897 he became music critic of *Russkiya Vedomosti* (The Russian Messenger), and when the paper was suspended, he was appointed principal of a school in a suburb of Moscow. During this time he wrote several literary works and translated Hugo Riemann's *Musiklexikon* into Russian. He became recognized as a proponent of Jewish music in 1900, when he delivered a lecture before the Imperial Ethnographic Society in Moscow entitled "The Jewish Folk Song." This event sparked an interest in Jewish musical activity that culminated in the founding of the SOCIETY FOR JEWISH FOLK MUSIC.

In 1922 Engel left for Berlin, where he organized the Juwal Verlag and the Yibneh music press, devoted to publishing music of Jewish content. After a two-year stay in Berlin he departed for Palestine and was appointed instructor in music theory at the Shulamit Conservatory in Tel Aviv. It is probable that Engel realized the importance of Jewish music education for youth when he established special courses for nursery school teachers. He collected and edited numerous folk melodies, and his

Joel Engel. [Albert Weisser, *The Modern Renaissance of Jewish Music,* Bloch Publishing Company, Inc.]

children's songs reflect his fondness for children. His music was the earliest to be sung in Palestine and was popularized at concerts by the Ohel Chorus, which he conducted. Many of his articles on Jewish music appeared in newspapers and periodicals, and he became known as the spokesman for national Jewish music.

Engel was so revered by Jews in Palestine, and throughout the world, that after his death in Tel Aviv the Municipal Council renamed one of its streets Rehov Engel and granted a stipend to his widow. The Engel Prize was established in his honor by the Tel Aviv Municipal Council and is awarded annually to outstanding composers and musicians. In the Soviet Union the Kiev Museum of Jewish Culture established the Engel Room, and in the United States a concert was given in New York featuring Joseph Achron's string quartet *Elegy* (op. 62), dedicated to Engel (*see* ACHRON, Joseph). The JEWISH MUSIC FORUM sponsored a commemoration of the twentieth anniversary of Engel's death on February 17, 1947. His musical works include chamber music, choral works, piano and violin pieces, songs, and theater music. He is best known for his incidental music to Ansky's play *The Dybbuk* (*see* DYBBUK, THE).

EPHROS, GERSHON (1890–   ). Cantor-composer and teacher who compiled and edited the six-volume *Cantorial Anthology* (1929–1969). Born in Serotsk (Serock), Poland, Ephros was reared in the home of his stepfather, Cantor Moses Fromberg. There he received his first musical training and experience by singing in Fromberg's choir. At the age of seventeen he led his own choir in Zgersh (Zgierz). In 1909 he left for Palestine and pursued his studies in HAZZANUT and harmony with Abraham Zvi IDELSOHN, whom he served as choir director. He emigrated to the United States in 1911 and continued his musical studies with Professor Hermann Spielter and Joseph ACHRON. His cantorial career began when he was appointed cantor of Congregational Beth-El in Norfolk, Va., in 1918. He was later called to serve as cantor in Congregation Beth Elokim in the Bronx. From 1927 until his retirement in 1957 he served at Congregation Beth Mordecai of Perth Amboy, N.J. He taught Jewish music in the Hebrew schools under the aegis of the New York Bureau of Jewish Education and served as a member of the faculty of the Hebrew Union College

Gershon Ephros.

School of Sacred Music. Ephros was president of the JEWISH MUSIC FORUM and thereafter a member of the executive board of the NATIONAL JEWISH MUSIC COUNCIL. His *Cantorial Anthology*, the first of its kind in Jewish music, made materials available for the entire yearly cycle that had been unobtainable or had never before been in print. In addition to his many liturgical compositions, he wrote the *Children's Suite* (1936), the *Aeolian String Quartet* (1961), and *Vocalise* (1962), and various vocal and instrumental works. The American Society of Composers, Authors, and Publishers (ASCAP) presented him with an award on his seventy-first birthday.

ERUS. Percussion instrument, its name probably derived from *aras*, "to betroth," and mainly used for weddings.[1] It is evident, too, that it was employed for funerals. R. Judah ruled: "The *erus* is unclean as a seat since the wailing woman sits on it."[2] This instrument probably served as rhythmical accompaniment for the MEKONENET.

This instrument has been defined in various ways: (1) A kind of bell.[3] (2) A *tambour* (Fr. for drum). R. Obadiah Bertinoro describes it as being in the shape of a sieve with rounded sides and a thin skin stretched over the opening; when struck with a stick, it produced a ringing sound.[4] (3) Marcus Jastrow gives "drum" and "tabaret" as its translation.[5] (4) The *erus* may possibly be identified with the TOF.[6]

[1] Sot. 49a, b.
[2] Mish., Kel. XV: 6.
[3] Cf. Rashi's commentary on Sot. 49b.
[4] Kel., loc. cit.
[5] *Dictionary*, London, 1903, p. 60, s.v. *erus.*
[6] Curt Sachs, *The History of Musical Instruments*, W. W. Norton & Company, Inc., New York, 1940, p. 109.

ESTRO POETICO-ARMONICO, PARAFRASI SOPRA LI SALMI. Title (*Harmonic Poetry Transposed above the Psalms*) of the settings by Benedetto Marcello (1686–1739) to fifty psalms, published in Venice between 1724 and 1727 in eight volumes. It is written for one to four voices with occasional solos for violin and violoncello and with figured basses added. Marcello utilized eleven Hebrew themes stemming from Ashkenazic and Sephardic synagogue tunes. He adapted the Hebrew text, which together with the music is read from right to left.

ETHAN. *See* JEDUTHUN.

ETNAHTA ($\overline{\wedge}$ **).** Accent sign, placed below words in the text of sacred literature, meaning "to rest." The second-strongest Masoretic accent, it divides the verse into two parts and is similar to the semicolon or colon in the English language. *See also* DISJUNCTIVES; TE'AMIM.

EVENING TWILIGHT, THE. *See* HAMAARIV AROVIM.

EWEN, DAVID (1907–   ). Writer on secular and Jewish music. Born in Lemberg (Lvov), Galicia, he was taken to the United States in 1911. Ewen wrote approximately fifty books on every facet of music. His many articles, which appeared in nearly all Anglo-Jewish publications, deal with almost every aspect of Jewish music.[1] He served as editor of *Jewish Music Notes*, published by the NATIONAL JEWISH MUSIC COUNCIL (1950), and was a contributor to the *Universal Jewish Encyclopedia*. He is the author of *Hebrew Music—A Study and an Interpretation* (1931).

[1] Cf. Alfred Sendrey, *Bibliography of Jewish Music*, Columbia University Press, New York, 1951, p. 366, for many listings.

FALSETTO (Ger. *Falsett*). Word of Italian origin, referring to singing by the male voice in a register above its natural compass, resulting in an effeminate sound. This kind of singing may have been practiced by male Temple singers as deduced from AL-ALAMOT, an expression that appears in the heading of psalm 46:1 and is generally interpreted as meaning "in the range of the female singing voice." Falsetto singing was no doubt a common feature in Temple days, for women's voices were excluded from the service. It is still in vogue today among Oriental singers. In describing Yemenite singers, Edith GERSON-KIWI compares their thin falsetto registers to "the graceful and delicately formed South-Arabian mountain nomads, with whom they have in common the tense agility of the body which during their singing never ceases to perform dance-like movements."[1] The Oriental Torah reader, too, enhances the melodic line with ornaments, making use of the falsetto voice.[2] Oriental mannerisms in singing styles influenced Eastern European liturgical musical practices (*see* COLORATURA), and *hazzanim* and choristers, in particular, adopted falsetto singing. It is also possible that the falsetto was used as a substitute for instrumental accompaniment, which is forbidden in the synagogue on Sabbath and holidays. The singer whose task it was to accompany the HAZZAN with falsetto singing and to imitate high-pitched instruments (e.g., flute or violin) was called a *fleytel singer,* from the Yiddish *fleyt,* meaning "flute;" or *fistel-singer,* from the Latin *fistula,* meaning "flute." The use of the falsetto furthermore facilitated singing for the *hazzan,* who was thereby able to interpolate intricate embellishments and coloratura into his chant.

The falsetto was completely alien to the music of Western Europe. The vocal music of the oratorio and opera strongly influenced Western *hazzanim.* After Western synagogues introduced the ORGAN and four-part singing, the shrieking falsetto voice was regarded by the Western Jew as a comic effect.

See also KELIM.

[1]*The Legacy of Jewish Music through the Ages,* National Council of Culture and Art, World Zionist Organization, Israel and the Organization Departments, Research Section, Jerusalem, 1963, p. 4.
[2]Hanoch Avenary, *Studies in the Hebrew, Syrian and Greek Liturgical Recitative,* Israel Music Institute, Tel Aviv, 1963, p. 21.

FIRST SYMPHONY. First large-scale work (op. 25) composed in Palestine by Paul BEN-HAIM. A work in three movements, it was composed in 1939–1940. It was the first symphony to be written in Ben-Haim's newly adopted country and was performed by the ISRAEL PHILHARMONIC OR-

CHESTRA. The slow second movement, characteristic of Oriental influence, is based on an ancient traditional chant of Persian Jews.

FOLK SONG, YIDDISH. Abundant collection of songs, distinctive as the people itself and accepted by a substantial part of the population. They are sung by the people, many of whom make changes; thus musical and textual variants occur. Although these songs develop spontaneously, their "composers" being anonymous, sometimes a name lives on with a tune and it can be called a "composed folk song" (e.g., ROZHINKES MIT MANDLEN, by Abraham GOLDFADEN, or "Oifen Pripitshok," by Mark Warshawsky). In any event, the songs, not the composers, became more important to the people who sang them.

Folk song began to develop about the end of the sixteenth century and reached its culmination at the end of the nineteenth century, mainly in Slavic countries, especially Poland, the Ukraine, Lithuania, and southern Russia, as well as Hungary and Romania. The songs can be classified into the following general categories: love songs, cradle songs, children's songs, humorous songs, workers' songs, and soldiers' songs. Notwithstanding their secular character, many of the tunes were governed by the Biblical and prayer modes. In fact, their texts, especially the love songs, reflect Biblical and prayer mode influence, as Ruth RUBIN comments. "No song suggests that the singer is willing to relinquish identification with the Jewish community and the traditions of his Jewish heritage."[1] Nature songs were alien to the Eastern European Jew. He was generally a ghetto dweller living in a large city, forced to occupy himself with commerce and trade, and entirely estranged from nature.

General characteristics of Yiddish folk song are: (1) The themes, on the whole, deal with the spirit and sentiment of Jewish life. (2) The dialect, which is Yiddish, often includes a bilingual (e.g., Yiddish-Hebrew or Yiddish-Ukrainian) or even trilingual (e.g., Ukrainian-Hebrew-Yiddish) text. (3) The tonalities are essentially the Biblical and prayer modes (*see* MODES, SYNAGOGAL) and various forms of minor. The major scale is used only occasionally and is more recent and of German and Slavic adaptation. (4) The free recitative style is often used. When meter is employed, the most common ones are $\frac{2}{4}, \frac{3}{4}, \frac{4}{4}, \frac{6}{8}$. There is also a frequent change of meter within the same song. (5) Types of ornamentation are appoggiaturas that descend in a gliding and stepwise fashion and other embellishments such as trills, mordents, grace notes, strong vibratos, tremolos, and scale segments that in turn are extended and embellished. Some songs resemble folk music in their simplicity and their general appeal and are referred to as *volkstümliche Lieder* (songs in folk style); an archetype is ELI, ELI.

The BADHAN was greatly responsible for creating and popularizing many Yiddish folk songs. His tunes became part of the masses that sang them and in turn passed them on. Early collections of Yiddish folk song were compiled by Saul Ginsburg and Pesach Marek, J. L. Cahan, M. Kipnis, and Susman Kisselgof. Abraham Zvi IDELSOHN presented the first scientific study of Yiddish folk song in volume 9 of his THESAURUS OF HEBREW-ORIENTAL MELODIES. He classified more than a thousand folk tunes according to mode, meter, form, and origin of melodic line.[2]

Yiddish folk music also found its way into art music composition, for example, Maurice Ravel's arrangement for *Alte Kashe*, called *L'énigme éternelle,* and Sergei Prokofiev's OVERTURE ON HEBREW THEMES. On the whole, since the early twentieth century there has been a decline of Yiddish folk song. In isolated parts of the world (e.g., the Soviet Union, Argentina, and parts of Europe) Yiddish folk song is still created and sung. In Israel and in the United States it has been replaced with the Israeli folk song and HASSIDIC SONG.

See also ISRAELI MUSIC; LADINO SONG; YIDDISH THEATER MUSIC.

[1]"East European Yiddish Folk Love Songs," *Studies in Biblical and Jewish Folklore,* Indiana University Press, Bloomington, 1960, p. 220.
[2]Cf. Abraham Z. Idelsohn, *Thesaurus of Hebrew-Oriental Melodies,* Leipzig, 1932, vol. IX; id., *Jewish Music,* Tudor Publishing Company, New York, 1944, pp. 396–400.

FORLEINER (FORZUGERIN). *See* SAGERIN.

FRAILACH (pl. *frailachs*). Circle dance (lit. "joyful") in lively duple meter, also called *Mehutanim Tanz,* performed by relatives and friends at Jewish weddings.

FRANKENBURGER, PAUL. *See* BEN-HAIM, PAUL.

FREDERICK R. MANN AUDITORIUM. Concert hall in Tel Aviv, with a capacity of about 3,000 seats. The auditorium was built with the help of Frederick R. Mann of Philadelphia, the administration of Tel Aviv, and the American-Israel Cultural Foundation. On October 2, 1957, when the concert hall opened, a gala concert was presented by the ISRAEL PHILHARMONIC ORCHESTRA, with Artur Rubinstein, Gregor Piatigorsky, and Isaac Stern as soloists and Leonard Bernstein as conductor. The Mann Auditorium is the home of the Israel Philharmonic Orchestra.

FREED, ISADORE (1900–1960). Composer, conductor, organist, and lecturer. Born in Brest-Litovsk, Russia, Freed was taken to Philadelphia at a very early age. He graduated from the University of Pennsylvania with the degree of bachelor of music, having studied during the same time at the Philadelphia Conservatory of Music. He continued his studies in composition with Ernest BLOCH, piano with George Bayle and Josef Hofmann, and organ with Rollo Maitland. In 1928 after teaching, lecturing, composing, and performing for a number of years, Freed departed for a five-year stay in Paris, where he devoted his time to composing and performing. He studied with Vincent d'Indy and gave a joint concert with Arthur

Isadore Freed.

Honegger. Freed returned to the United States in 1933, taught at the Curtis Institute of Music in Philadelphia, and assumed the post of music director and organist at the Keneseth Israel Temple in Philadelphia. In 1946 he accepted a similar position in Temple Israel, in Lawrence, N.Y. With other Jewish musicians he helped found (1939) the JEWISH MUSIC FORUM, serving as its president from 1942 to 1944, and the NATIONAL JEWISH MUSIC COUNCIL. In 1950 he was appointed professor of sacred music at the School of Sacred Music of the Hebrew Union College. Freed wrote many secular works including symphonies, chamber music, and operas that have been performed under the direction of such conductors as Eugene Ormandy and Pierre Monteux. Among his many compositions in the Hebrew idiom are his six services for the synagogue, anthems, organ pieces, and THREE PSALMS. His last major work was *Prophecy of Micha* (1956). Freed's *Harmonizing the Jewish Modes* (1958) is an important contribution to the study of synagogue song.

Joseph Freudenthal.

FREUDENTHAL, JOSEPH (1903–1964). Composer and publisher, noted for fostering a Jewish music movement in the United States. Born in Geisa, in central Germany, he studied philosophy, music, and law and received the degrees of doctor of philosophy (1923) and doctor of law (1926) from the University of Würzburg. Prior to emigrating to the United States in 1938, he was in charge of the legal department of the Benjamin Verlag, a music publishing concern in Leipzig, and served as its vice-president. When he arrived in the United States, he founded the Transcontinental Music Corporation, which published more than 1,500 works for the synagogue and the Jewish community. A recognized leader in the advancement of Jewish music, he served as president of the JEWISH MUSIC FORUM. He was a member of the governing board of the NATIONAL JEWISH MUSIC COUNCIL, and the advisory council of the School of Sacred Music of the Hebrew Union College, and an officer of the Society for the Advancement of Jewish Liturgical Music. He was also a member of the American Society of Composers, Authors, and Publishers (ASCAP). Freudenthal, who had more than sixty published works to his credit, wrote sacred music and songs and edited and arranged Israeli folk songs.

FRIEDMANN, AARON (1855–1936). Cantor and writer on Jewish music. A native of Sakiai (Shaki, Szaki), Lithuania, he was a pupil of Louis LEWANDOWSKI and a student at the Berlin Academy of Fine Arts. From 1882 to 1923 he served as chief cantor of the Berlin Jewish Community, and in 1907 the state conferred upon him the title of *Königlicher Musikdirektor* (Royal Director of Music) in recognition of his creativity in composition. He is best known for his *Schir Lisch'laumau* (1901), a volume of chants for the entire year cycle; *Der synagogale Gesang* (1st ed., 1904; 2d ed., 1908), a treatise on cantillation and synagogue song; and *Lebensbilder berühmter Cantorin* (vol. I, 1918; vol. II, 1921; vol. III, 1927), a biographical work about cantors. He also issued a collection of essays on Jewish music in memory of Eduard BIRNBAUM (1922).

Herbert Fromm.

FROMM, HERBERT (1905–   ). Composer and conductor. Born in Kitzingen am Main, Bavaria, he received his musical education at the Academy of Music in Munich. From 1930 to 1933 he served as conductor of the opera in Würzburg. After emigrating to the United States in 1937, he was appointed music director and organist at Temple Beth Zion in Buffalo, N.Y. After 1941 he occupied a similar post in Temple Israel in Boston. Fromm's compositions include sacred choral music, orchestral works, chamber music, cantatas, organ pieces, and songs. He is best known for his Friday evening service *Adath Israel* (1943) and for his choral composition *The Song of Miriam,* for which he won the Ernest BLOCH Award in 1945.

G

GEFIL-HAZZANUT. Phrase (Heb. *tefillat-ha-regesh*) implying that the liturgical rendition is freely executed, with much feeling and emotion, and is the result of the immediate inspiration of the HAZZAN, in other words, free IMPROVISATION. Until the second half of the eighteenth century the *hazzan*, lacking any musical training, intoned the prayer chants in a spontaneous manner. These improvisations were a free outpouring of the soul, rather than studied renditions. Since the mid-nineteenth century the READER has utilized the prayer modes systematically and varies the prayer chant in a disciplinary fashion; this type of improvisation is referred to as *tefillat-ha-seder*.[1]

[1]Joseph Yasser, "The Philosophy of Improvisation," *The Cantorial Art*, National Jewish Music Council, New York, 1966, pp. 43, 45.

GELBRUN, ARTUR (1913–   ). Israeli composer and conductor. He received his music education in Warsaw, Poland, his native city, and in Italy. He emigrated to Israel in 1949 and beginning in 1953 taught conducting and composition at the Rubin Academy of Music in Tel Aviv. Gelbrun appeared as guest conductor of orchestras in Israel and Europe and wrote symphonies, chamber music, ballets, suites, piano music, and songs.

GERESH (*r*). Accent mark meaning "drive out" or "expulsion," found above the word in Scriptural text. William Wickes remarks that "this accent was one of the highest notes, and required a strong 'expulsion' of the voice to produce it."[1] Its graphic form is identical to that of the AZLA. Whereas the *azla* appears on the last syllable (*milra*) of the word (e.g., Gen. 1:29), the *geresh* is on the penultimate (*milayl*) syllable (e.g., Gen. 7:14). Readers call the *geresh* by the name *azla-geresh;* when the KADMA precedes the *azla*, the accent mark is called *kadma-ve'azla*. Some authors make a further differentiation: the unit is called *kadma-ve'azla* when the *azla* appears on the *milra* word (e.g., Gen. 1:29) and *kadma-geresh* when the accent is on the *milayl* word (e.g., Gen. 1:9).[2] The musical contours of the *kadma-ve'azla* and *azla-geresh* differ slightly. *See also* TE'AMIM.

[1]*Treatise on the Accentuation of the Prose Books of the Old Testament*, Clarendon Press, Oxford, 1887, p. 20.
[2]Abraham W. Binder, *Biblical Chant*, Philosophical Library, Inc., New York, 1959, pp. 52, 53; P. Spiro, *Haftarah Chanting*, Jewish Education Committee Press, New York, 1964, pp. 24, 25.

GEROVITSCH, ELIEZER MORDECAI (1844–1914). Russian-born cantor-composer. Until 1862 Gerovitsch remained in his native town near Kiev,

Eliezer Mordecai Gerovitsch.

studying Scripture, Talmud, and general subjects with his father and with the local rabbi. Against his father's wishes he journeyed through Berdichev and Odessa and became an apprentice to Cantors Spitzberg (a pupil of Salomon SULZER) and Nissan BLUMENTHAL. With them he studied the repertoire of the classical synagogue composers (e.g., Sulzer, LOUIS LEWANDOWSKI). Dissatisfied with his musical accomplishments, he enrolled at the St. Petersburg Conservatory and received a thorough musical training. His cantorial career began in the city of Nikolayev, and in 1887 he was appointed to the Rostov CHOR-SHUL, a position he held with great distinction for twenty-five years. Gerovitsch's fame rests largely upon his accomplishments in the area of artistic Eastern European synagogue song. In his *Shire Tefillah* (1890) and *Schirej Simroh* (1904) he wrote a complete choral service for the entire yearly cycle, reestablishing the ancient traditional chant, in contradistinction to Sulzer and Lewandowski, whose treatments were Westernized. These collections were reissued in 1953 by the Sacred Music Press.

GERSHAYIM (_ℐℐ_). Accent mark placed above the word in the printed text of the Bible.[1] Its graphic form is two GERESH signs, one inside the other. Thus the *geresh* is technically referred to as *geresh-katan*, and the *gershayim* is called *geresh-gadol* (double *geresh*). Whereas the *geresh* accents the penultimate syllable *(milayl)* of the word and may be preceded by a KADMA, the *gershayim* accents the last syllable *(milra)* and is not preceded by a *kadma*. The musical rendering of the *gershayim* and *geresh* differs. *See also* TE'AMIM.

[1]E.g., Gen. 18:28.

GERSON-KIWI, EDITH (1908–). Israeli musicologist and teacher whose studies center around the music of the Oriental Jewish communities. Born in Berlin, Edith Gerson-Kiwi studied at the Universities of Freiburg. Leipzig, and Bologna and received her doctorate from the University of Heidelberg in 1933. She emigrated to Jerusalem in 1935 and, following in the path of Abraham Zvi IDELSOHN and Robert LACHMANN, continued researching, recording, and transcribing folk and liturgical music of Israel and secluded regions of the Near East. In Israel she became associated with the Archives for Oriental Music at the Hebrew University and was appointed its director in 1947. She lectures at the department of musicology of Tel Aviv University and at the Rubin Academy of Music in Jerusalem and Tel Aviv. Her many activities include the chairmanship of the Israeli Musicological Association; membership in the presidential board of the International Musicological Society; membership in the executive board of the International Folk Music Council; membership in the scientific board of the International Institute of Comparative Music Studies; membership in the editorial boards of *Ethnomusicology* (United States) and *Encyclopedia Hebraica.* Among her many monographs are "Vocal Folk-Polyphonies of the Western Orient in Jewish Tradition," "Women's Songs from the Yemen: Their Tonal Structure and Form," "The Persian Doctrine of Dastga-Composition," "The Bards of the Bible," "The Legacy of Jewish Music through the Ages." She also wrote many articles on Jewish music for various journals and encyclopedias.

GESHURI, MEIR SHIMON (1897–   ). Israeli writer and researcher of Jewish music. Born into a Hassidic family in Upper Silesia, young Meir Shimon accompanied his father to a Hassidic court where he heard Hassidic tunes, dances, and marches and often assisted his father in the synagogue services. Geshuri acquired his Jewish education in the local yeshivah and his general education in the Gymnasium. Later, in Berlin, when he enrolled at the Stern Conservatory, his musical studies became serious. Before long Geshuri became known for organizing Jewish music groups among the students of the universities and for organizing Hassidic singing groups. In 1920 he emigrated to Palestine and entered various fields of endeavor. He was instrumental in collecting thousands of Hassidic melodies and categorizing them according to place of origin, "composer," and Hassidic dynasty. He also investigated and researched the song of the Sephardic and Oriental communities, and together with Mordecai Sandburg he published a periodical, *Hallel* (1930). His works *La-Hassidim Mizmor* (1936), the three-volume *Encyclopedia of Hassidism: The Song and Dance* (1955–1959), *Kol Israel* (vols. I and 2, 1964), and *Jerusalem the Musical City* (1968) paved the way for his deserved recognition.

GNIESSIN (GNESSIN, GNESIN), MICHAEL FABIANOVICH (1883–1957). Russian composer, teacher, and writer whose fame rests largely upon his contribution to the Jewish music renaissance in Russia. Gniessin grew up in an intellectual atmosphere in Rostov; his father was a rabbi, and his mother was musically gifted. His maternal grandfather was the famous BADHAN Shayke Feifer (Isaiah Fleytsinger) of Vilna. Influenced by the noted Cantor Eliezer Mordecai GEROVITSCH, Gniessin was imbued with

Michael Gniessen. [Albert Weisser, *The Modern Renaissance of Jewish Music*, Bloch Publishing Company, Inc.]

Jewish song and furthered his early musical studies with Oscar Fritsche. In 1901 he entered the St. Petersburg Conservatory and studied with Glazunov, Liadov, and Rimski-Korsakov. He became a favorite disciple of Rimski-Korsakov, who later hailed him as the "Jewish Glinka." Gniessin was a moving force in the establishment of the SOCIETY FOR JEWISH FOLK MUSIC. He visited Palestine in 1914 and returned in 1921. Later he left for Germany, where he founded the Yibneh music publishing house. He taught at the Moscow Conservatory (1923–1935) and at the Leningrad Conservatory of Music (1935–1945). He then assumed a post as head of the composition department at the music school that bore his and his sister's name (1945–1951). Gniessin composed two operas utilizing Jewish themes, *The Youth of Abraham* and *The Maccabeans.* Other works embodying the Jewish idiom are his *Variations on a Jewish Folk Theme* for string quartet (1916); *Ora,* variations for piano, four hands (1921); *Jewish Orchestra at the Ball of the Town Bailiff,* a suite for orchestra (1926); and *Hebrew Songs* for voice and piano (1928). In addition to these compositions, he wrote numerous orchestral works, songs, and chamber music bearing Jewish titles. He wrote books on composition and Jewish music, a study of Rimski-Korsakov, and his own memoirs.

Abraham Goldfaden. [*The Jewish Encyclopedia*, Funk and Wagnalls Company]

GOLDFADEN, ABRAHAM (1840–1908). Poet-singer and founder of the Yiddish theater. As a young child he sang in a synagogue choir and composed verses. His father, Hayyim Lippe, a watchmaker by trade, called him Avremele Badhan (*see* BADHAN). Born in Staro-Konstantinov, Russia, Goldfaden began his schooling in 1855 in the Yiddishe Kroin-Shulen. In 1857 he entered the Zhitomir rabbinical school, in which rabbis, teachers, and other communal leaders were trained, and he graduated as a teacher in 1866. A year prior to his graduation he published *Tzitzim Uferahim,* a collection of Hebrew poems dedicated to his father, and a year later *Dos Yiddele,* a collection of Yiddish songs dedicated to his mother. In 1869 he published a collection, *Die Yiddene,* which was so popular that a second printing soon followed. For nine years he served as a schoolteacher in Simferopol and in Odessa, and in 1875 he left for Lemberg (Lvov), where he embarked on a career in journalism. Faced with prohibitions by the Austrian government, he left Lemberg and tried his hand at publishing once again in Czernowitz (Chernovtsy). After a brief existence of his

Bukowiner Israelitisches Volksblatt, he left for Iași, Romania. There he came in contact with the "Broder Singers" and laid the foundation of the Yiddish theater, which later spread to Russia, Poland, France, England, and the United States (*see* YIDDISH THEATER MUSIC). Goldfaden went to the United States for the first time in 1887, but, finding much competition, he returned to Europe. In 1903 he traveled again to the United States and spent his last years in poverty in New York City. He was buried in Washington Cemetery in Brooklyn, with thousands of admirers attending his funeral.

Although Goldfaden had no technical musical knowledge, the appeal of his melodies and texts was universal. Influences of synagogue song, folk song, and Italian and French opera are evident in his twenty-six dramatic productions. His operettas *Shulamit, Bar-Kochba,* and *Akedat Yitzhak* have had a lasting effect upon Jewish folklore. His songs "Shtei oif Mein Folk," "Dos Pintele Yid," "Yankele Geht in Shul Arein," and "Kum Yisrolikel Aheim" have been accepted by the Jewish masses and are regarded as tunes with folk flavor. Goldfaden cannot be credited with musical creativity and style; nonetheless he succeeded in spontaneously molding melodies that reflected the spirit of his people.

Israel Goldfarb.

GOLDFARB, ISRAEL (1879–1956). Rabbi and cantor who contributed greatly to the musical growth of liturgical melody in the synagogue, school, and home in the United States. After his arrival in the United States in 1893 from Sieniawa, Galicia, Poland, his native town, he attended the Jewish Theological Seminary, Columbia University (from which he graduated in 1902), and the Institute of Musical Art. From 1901 to 1905 he served as rabbi and cantor in Staten Island, and from 1905 until his death he was affiliated with Congregation Beth Israel Anshei Emes in Brooklyn. In 1920 Goldfarb was appointed to the faculty of the Jewish Theological Seminary as an instructor in liturgical music, a post he held until 1942. Among his chief contributions to Jewish music were his various books and pamphlets that popularized original and heretofore unpublished congregational and secular Jewish songs and melodies, among which are the following: *Song and Praise for Sabbath Eve* (with I. H. Levinthal, 1920), *Synagogue Melodies for the High Holy Days* (1926), *The Jewish Songster* (in collaboration with Samuel E. Goldfarb, part 1, 1925; part 2, 1929), and *Sabbath in the Home* (1953). Goldfarb is also known for arranging congregational responses and complete services for children and congregational choirs for the yearly cycle. His melody for the ZEMIROT text *Shalom Aleyhem* has become popular throughout the world.[1]

[1] *Sabbath in the Home,* p. 11.

GOROCHOV, YEDIDYAH. *See* ADMON, YEDIDYAH.

GOTT FUN AVRAHAM. Meditation marking the end of the Sabbath, re-
cited by women at dusk in poignant chant style. It is attributed to Reb
Levi Yitzhak of Berdichev (1740–1809), who intoned it after the third
Sabbath meal (Shalosh Seudot). This recital, repeated three times, has
circulated in several textual and musical variants such as that shown in
Fig. 20 and at the top of page 91.

GOTT FUN AVROHOM – גאָט פֿון אברהם

Figure 20. [A. E. Millgram, *Sabbath—the Day of Delight,* Jewish Publication Society of America]

ג-ט פון אברהם און פון יצחק
און פון יעקב

בעהיט דײַן ליב פאָלק ישראל פֿון אלעם בײיזען
אין דײַנעם לויב אז דער ליבער שַׁבָּת קוֹדֶשׁ גייט.
אז די וואָר און דער חוֹדֶשׁ און דער יאָר, זאָל
אונז צו קומען צו אֱמוּנָה שְׁלֵימָה צו אֱמוּנַת חֲכָמִים
צו אַהֲבַת חֲבֵרִים ; צו דְּבֵיקַת הַבּוֹרֵא ב״ה, מַאֲמִין
צו זיין בשלוש עֶשְׂרֵה עִקְרִים שֶׁלְךָ וּבְגְאוּלָה קְרוֹבָה
בִּמְהֵרָה בְיָמֵינוּ, וּבִתְחִיַת הַמֵּתִים, וּבִנְבוּאַת מֹשֶׁה
רַבֵּינוּ, עָלָיו הַשָּׁלוֹם.
רִבּוֹנוֹ שֶׁל עוֹלָם, דו ביזט דאָר הַנוֹתֵן לַעֵף כֹּחַ.
גיב דײַנֶע ליבֶע יודישע קינדערליך אויר כֹּח דיר
צו לויבען. און נאָר דיר צו דינען און קיין אַנדֶערין
חֲלִילָה נישט. און אז די וואָר און דער חוֹדֶשׁ און
דער יאָר זאָל אונז קומען צו געזונד און צו
מַזָל און צו בְּרָכָה וְהַצְלָחָה, און צו חֶסֶד און צו
בְּנֵי חַיֵי אֲרִיכֵי וּמְזוֹנֵי רְוִיחֵי וְסִיַעְתָּא דִשְׁמַיָא לָנוּ.
וּלְכָל יִשְׂרָאֵל, וְנֹאמַר אָמֵן :

G-d of Abraham, Isaac and Jacob

guard Your beloved people from every evil...
now the cherished Sabbath departs. This week,
this month, this year, let us gain in perfect
belief, in faith in our Sages, in love for our
fellow-beings, in devotion to the blessed
Creator — that we may believe in Your 13
principles of faith, in the approaching Redemption (may it come soon, in our days), in the
Resurrection, and in the prophetic words of
our Master Moses.

O, Sovereign Ruler of the world, You give
strength to the weary. Then grant Your beloved
Jewish children strength to praise You, to
serve only You and no other.... And this
week, this month, this year, let us gain in
health, good fortune, blessing, and success —
to be granted kindness, good children, long life,
with bountiful provision and Heaven's help
for us and for all Jewry. And let us say *Amen.*

**Yiddish-Hebrew and English texts of "Gott fun Avraham." [Beth Oloth Home
for Immigrant Girls and Orphans, Jerusalem]**

GRADENWITZ, PETER (EMANUEL) (1910–   ). Israeli musicologist
and composer. Born in Berlin, he obtained his general and musical education at the Universities of Freiburg and Berlin and received his doctorate
from the University of Prague. Prior to 1933 he was active as a lecturer and
critic and was associated with various broadcasting systems. Because of the
Nazi terror he left for Paris (1934) and then London (1935), and in 1936
he finally settled in Tel Aviv. Gradenwitz became active as a writer, lecturer, and organizer of concerts and established the Israeli Music Publications,
Ltd., one of the most noted publishing houses of serious music in Israel.
He also served as president of the Israeli Musicological Association (1964).
He wrote a history of Jewish music in Hebrew, called *Hamuzikah Beyisrael*
(1945), which was later expanded into an English version entitled *The
Music of Israel—Its Rise and Growth through 5000 Years* (1949). The volume
also appeared in Spanish and German editions. His numerous articles
on Israel's music and Israeli musicians appeared in periodicals and ency-

Peter Gradenwitz.

clopedias throughout the world, for example, the *Encyclopedia of Zionism and Israel* (1971). He authored books on chamber and symphonic music, among which his *Olam-Hasimfonia* (eight ed., 1945–1959), a historical concert guide, has been a great aid to Israeli concert goers. Among his compositions are chamber music, a string quartet, various orchestral works, and songs.

GROGGER. Percussion instrument (sometimes spelled *gregar*, from the Polish *grzégarz*, meaning "rattle"; modern Heb. *ra'ashan*; Ger. *Haman-Klopfer* or *Haman-Dreher*; Yidd. *Haman-klepel*) generally sounded fifty-four times during the reading of the *Megillah* (*see* MEGILLOT, THE FIVE) whenever Haman's name is mentioned. The instrument was first used in the thirteenth century in France and Germany. The practice of drowning out the name of Haman goes back to the second century.[1] When Rav came to Haman's name on Purim, he said: "Cursed be Haman and his children," in order to fulfill the obligation of the Scriptural verse, "and the name of the transgressors shall be blotted out."[2] The roaring sound of the *grogger* often disturbed public reading, and the rabbis protested vehemently.[3]

The design of the *grogger* resembles that of two primitive instruments, the bull-roarer and the scraper. The bull-roarer is a long stick to which a cord is attached. At the end of the cord is a thin board. Whirling the stick produces a roaring or wailing sound. The scraper is a notched implement (a stick, shell, bone, or gourd) that the player scrapes with a rigid object. The *grogger* used most often by Jews today is constructed of a wooden handle to which is attached a notched metal disk that is encased in a metal resonating box. A piece of metal is cut to meet the disk. Friction created when the scraper is twirled produces roaring sounds. Similar *groggers* have been made throughout the ages of wood or silver.

[1] Cf. Jer. Meg., chap. 1.
[2] Prov. 10:7.
[3] Rabbi Isaiah Horowitz, *Shnei Luhot ha-Brit*, Amsterdam, 1698, pp. 260a, 261a.

Groggers used in Russia. ["Globus," *The Jewish Encyclopedia*, Funk and Wagnalls Company]

GRUENTHAL, JOSEPH. *See* TAL, JOSEPH.

GURGANA. Aramaic word used to describe the "organ instrument" HY-DRAULIS.[1] Marcus Jastrow interprets the term as being "connected with a wheel work," thus, "a musical instrument [of pipes] worked by the pressure of water."[2]

See also TABLA.

[1]Ar. 10b.
[2]*Dictionary*, London, 1903, vol. I, p. 226.

GUST. Word of French (*goût*), Italian (*gusto*), or Latin (*gustus*) origin, meaning "taste" or "style." It is used by the Ashkenazic *hazzanim* (*see* HAZZAN) in connection with the scales used in CHANT and is thus synonymous with STEIGER and MODE (*see* MODES, SYNAGOGAL). More accurately, it implies the general characteristic style, or "taste," of the chant, for example, *Ahavah Rabbah* gust and *Yekum Purkan* gust (*see* AHAVAH RABBAH MODE; YEKUM PURKAN MODE). In general music of the eighteenth century the terms *goût* and *gusto* were used in Germany as well as in the countries of their origin. For example, the original title of Bach's *Italian Concerto* was *Concerto nach italiaenischer Gusto*, that is, "concerto in Italian style," or "according to Italian taste." The term was probably borrowed by *hazzanim* at this time.

HAGGADAH. (1) Ritual and story of the Exodus from Egypt contained in a special book used at the Passover Seder service. Literally, the term means "telling." from the Biblical injunction (Ex. 13:8) *vehigadeta lebinha,* "And thou shall tell thy son." The Haggadah's varied literature developed from Mishnaic times, from about c.e. 200[1] to approximately the sixteenth century. The book usually includes both pictorial and written instructions on how to set the Seder table. In the introduction is a mnemonic device consisting of fifteen words, each of which stands for a specific ritual in the order to follow. This list of the fifteen subdivisions, dating from the time when the Haggadah was an oral tradition, has been set to numerous tunes in cantillatory and folk character. The chants and melodies sung to the texts that follow have greatly inspired this home service and its liturgical literature throughout the ages. Among the most popular and outstanding texts of the Haggadah are: *Kiddush, Ma Nishtanah, Ha Lahma Anya, Hallel, Ki Lo Na'eh, Addir Hu, Ehad Mi Yode'a,* and *Had Gadyah.* The *Kiddush* is recited in similar manner to that of the other festivals (i.e., Shavuot and Sukkot) utilizing the AKDAMUT theme; *Ma Nishtanah* is chanted in the traditional major LERN-STEIGER; *Ha Lahma Anya* resembles the CANTILLATION mode used for the High Holy Days (*see* STUBEN-TROP); and *Hallel* is chanted in the musical tradition of the synagogue. The latter four poems are generally sung to metrical melodies in folk song style. (2) Oratorio composed in 1936 by Paul DESSAU, based on a libretto by Max BROD, for solo, chorus, children's chorus, and orchestra. The work was translated into Hebrew by Georg Mordecai Langer.

[1]Cf. Pes. X.

HALIL. Perforated wind instrument (from *halal,* "to bore through"), generally translated as "pipe"; a more accurate meaning of the term would be "shawm." It was used for joyous and ceremonial occasions[1] as well as for mourning ceremonies.[2] It was a cylindrical tube originally having two, three, or four holes and made of reed or metal. When describing the official music in the Sanctuary, the Talmud states that reed pipes were favored over metal because the timbre was characterized as pleasant (*arev*) and sweet (*hali*); thus the name *halil.*[3]

Bertinoro[4] and some modern Biblical scholars[5] identify the *halil* with the French *chalumeau,* a type of clarinet, and with the Arabic *muzmar* (*zummara*), a kind of double clarinet (the latter is also the opinion held by Maimonides). Curt Sachs is of the opinion that only modern translators render the word *halil* by flute. He comments that no ancient artist depicted

Bronze Age *halil* made of bird bone. [Haifa Music Museum and Amli Library]

a flute for *halil* and that the Septuagint translates it "exclusively as *aulos*, and the Vulgate as *tibia* [terms associated with the oboe]." Hence he infers that the *halil* must have been a double oboe used "all over the ancient world [by] pipers."[6] Other terms in Scripture and Talmud related to the *halil* family are ABUB, AL-MAHALAT, EL-HANEHILOT, MAHOL, MASHROKITA, NEKABEKHA, SUMPONYAH, and UGAB.

[1]Cf. I *Kings* 1:40; Isa. 5:12, 30:29; B.M. Mish. VI:1.
[2]Cf. Jer. 48:36; Ket. Mish. IV:4; Mish., loc. cit.
[3]Ar. 10b.
[4]Ar. Mish. III:3.
[5]E.g., Carl Heinrich Cornill, *Music in the Old Testament*, The Open Court Publishing Company, Chicago, 1909, p. 12.
[6]*The History of Musical Instruments*, W. W. Norton & Company, Inc., New York, 1940, p. 119.

HALLELUYAH (HALLELUJAH). Term, meaning "praise the Lord," occurring twenty-three times in the Book of Psalms. It first appears in psalm 104:35 and occurs also at the beginnings and ends of psalms and once in the middle, in psalm 135:3. Both the Palestinian[1] and Babylonian Talmud[2] discuss whether the expression is one word or a combination of two words (*hallelu-Yah*). It is regarded as the most exalted form in praise of God.[3]

The Babylonian Talmud asks, "What is the meaning of *halleluyah?*" and concludes, "The Book of Psalms was uttered with ten synonyms of praise . . . the greatest of all is *halleluyah*, because it embraces the [Divine] Name and praise simultaneously."[4] Rab, therefore, considers the proper designation for the Book of Psalms to be *Halleluyah*.[5]

In Temple days, *halleluyah* was already considered a form of acclamation. After the LEVITES concluded their praises, the congregation burst forth, from time to time, with the expression *halleluyah*.[6] According to Talmudic tradition it was also uttered as a refrain after each verse of the *Hallel* (pss. 113–118, recited on certain festive days), adding up to 123 times.[7] According to Heinrich Graetz, it was the term employed by the officiating Levite in the Temple as a signal for the congregation to join in the service.[8] E. G. Hirsch remarks that the word originally prefaced the psalms and did not come at the end.[9] Today, Yemenites sometimes add *wehalleluyah* after each of the PIYYUT recitals called *Shiroth*.[10]

The expression found its way in Gregorian liturgical chant with the Latinized spelling *alleluia*. The term is also used as a text for choruses in cantatas and oratorios. The most popular is the "Hallelujah Chorus" from *The Messiah*, an oratorio by George Frederick Handel, first produced in Dublin in 1742.

[1]Suk. 3:12, 53d; Meg. 1:11, 72a.
[2]Pes. 117a.
[3]Jer. Suk. iii, 54a.
[4]Loc. cit.
[5]*Midrash Tehillim*, chap. i.
[6]Eliezer Levi, *Yesodot Hatefillah*, Bitan Hassefer, Tel Aviv, 1952, p. 24.
[7]Jer. Shab. 16, 11.
[8]A. Cohen (ed), *The Psalms*, The Soncino Press, London, 1960, p. 343, note on ps. 104:35.
[9]Cf. *The Jewish Encyclopedia*, vol. X, p. 247.
[10]Abraham Z. Idelsohn, *Thesaurus of Hebrew-Oriental Melodies*, 1925, vol. I, p. 14.

HAMAARIV AROVIM (THE EVENING TWILIGHT). Work by Morton Gould (1913–   ) scored for full chorus of mixed voices and tenor solo with organ accompaniment. The text is the first benediction preceding the *Shema* in the ARVIT service.[1]

[1]Cf. *Synagogue Music by Contemporary Composers,* G. Schirmer, Inc., New York, pp. 170ff.

HASHIRIM ASHER LISHLOMO (CANTIQUES DE SOLOMON ROSSI). Collection of thirty-three psalms, songs, and hymns by Solomon ROSSI for a three, four, five, six, seven, and eight voice choir. Composed in 1623 in Venice, the work represents the earliest introduction of polyphonic music for the synagogue and the first printed music that appeared with a Hebrew text. The preface was written in Hebrew by Leone da Modena, who also served as editor and proofreader. In 1876 a Naumbourg-D'Indy edition of the work appeared in Paris in modern musical transcription with an addition of Rossi's secular madrigals. In 1967 an edition appeared in the United States, edited by Fritz Rikko and with a preface by Hugo Weisgall.

HASHKIVENU. Composition ("Grant, Lord our God, that we lie down in peace") by Leonard Bernstein (1918–   ), scored for full chorus of mixed voices and cantor with organ accompaniment.[1]

[1]Cf. *Synagogue Music by Contemporary Composers,* G. Schirmer, Inc., New York, pp. 228ff.

HASSIDIC SONG. Folk song originating with the Hassidim (pious ones). Hassidism gave impetus to Jewish music in Poland in the eighteenth century, and two main divisions, the Ukrainian and Galician and the White Russian and Lithuanian branches, evolved. From its inception, Hassidism, founded by R. Israel Baal Shem Tov (known as the BeShT; 1700–1760) of Podolia, ascribed primary importance to music. Heir to the Kabbalistic movement, Hassidism considered song an active force in attaining inspiration, devotion, exaltation, ecstasy, piety, and joy. According to the Zohar (Book of Splendor) the Torah is acquired through song; communion with the *Shekhinah* (Divine Presence) is attained through song; and Israel will emerge from exile through song.[1]

Historically, music in Hassidic life manifested itself in the following manner. After the destruction of the Temple (C.E. 70), music was forbidden as a sign of national mourning. Persecutions, massacres, and expulsions continually lessened musical activity for the Jew. Eastern European Jewry in the eighteenth century was in a depressed state following the Chmielnicki pogroms and massacres in Russia. Internal Jewish life was suffering because of the false messiah Shabbetai Tzevi and because of disregard for the simple people in the community by the learned and rabbinic scholars. The ideas of the Besht, that all are equal before God, that purity of heart is superior to study, and that the attainment of a state of joy or ecstasy is a religious obligation, appealed to the masses and attracted the populace. Music began to occupy an all-important place in Hassidic life. Reb Hillel of Parichi, Byelorussia, a disciple of Hassidism, is reputed as saying, "Whoever has no sense for music has no sense for Hassidism." R. Nahman of Bratslav, a Hassidic leader, remarked, "Music originates from the prophetic spirit, and has the power to elevate one to prophetic inspiration." The spiritual leaders, called *tzadikim* (sing. *tzadik*; "righteous ones"), inspired their "courts" and were also responsible for creating tunes that were honored in Hassidic life. If the *tzadik* lacked creative musical ability, a "court singer" would then be engaged. The court singer was always alert to new tunes, adapting, reshaping, and interpreting them according to the *tzadik's* moods and spirit. Each court had its original style, preferred mode, and favorite tunes.

Musical activity developed side by side in both divisions of Hassidism: "the system of the Besht" (i.e., the Hassidim of Poland, southern Russia, Romania, and Hungary) and the HaBaD, from *hakhma*, "wisdom," *binah*, "insight," and *da'at*, "knowledge" (i.e., the Hassidim of Lithuania and White Russia). The founder of the Habad movement was R. Shneor Zalman of Lyady (1747–1813), and it was centered in the province of Mogilev. The music of both schools can be characterized as follows: (1) The tune itself is called NIGGUN (pl. *niggunim*) and most often is wordless. Tunes are divided into categories: *tish niggunim* ("table songs"), represented by *niggunay hitvadut* ("devotional melodies") and *niggunay ga'aguim* ("melodies of yearning"); dance *niggunim*, comprising *niggunay simha* and RIKKUD (joy and dance tunes), which are melodies of instrumental character; and *shir lekhet* ("march tunes") and waltzes. When a text is utilized, it is either in Hebrew or with Hebrew-Yiddish, Hebrew-Ukrainian, Hebrew-Russian, or White Russian words or phrases interpolated. In the wordless tunes, meaningless syllables such as ay-ay-ay, bay-bay-bay, bam-bam, ya-ba-bam, and ta-ta-da-ri-da are interjected. Hassidim believe that a text limits the time of the tune. With the conclusion of the words, the melody, too, comes to an end. The wordless tune, therefore, can be repeated endlessly. (2) Metrical tunes are usually sung in unison by a group; nonmetrical ones are rendered by a solo voice. The songs are sung exclusively by men and are taught orally, memorized, and carried to the *tzadik*'s followers. (3) The tonality of Hassidic song is generally the same as that of synagogue and Yiddish folk song. (4) Instrumental music sometimes accompanies the singers at joyous gatherings called *farbrang*. An early group of singers and instrumentalists were known as the Mitteler Rebbe's Kapelle (*see* KAPELLE). (5) Most often a tune developed through independent styles of repetitive rendering of parts of the melody.

A comparison between the corresponding elements of style of the two schools shows marked differences in their respective melodies. Whereas the Beshtian school generally utilizes vigorous syncopated rhythmical figurations and tempo vivace, Habad sing in free, nonmetrical form or RECITATIVE called DEVAYKUT. If meter is imposed, the tempo is slow-moving. The Besht sing melodies expressing extreme joyous moods, usually culminating in ecstatic dance and bodily motion; the Habad prefer lyric-sentimental melodies of mystical character voicing yearning and revery. The Beshtian school sing the *Shir Lekhet* or *marsh* (Yidd.) more frequently than the Habad do. Although they are also sung among Habad, these tunes are adaptations, mostly of Polish and other extraction.[2] Melodies in the Beshtian movement are predominantly in major; those of the Habad are derived from the basic MI SHEBERAH MODE and AHAVAH RABBAH MODE, the latter being used most frequently.[3]

Hassidic song exerted an influence on Jewish and general art music. Its strength lies in the fact that "there is an indefinable something in these songs—something which cannot be explained by harmonic laws or musical statutes but which exists nevertheless. It is in emotion that these songs are Hebrew . . . and because of its unadorned emotion these songs come from the very heart of Israel. . . ."[4] Although Hassidism did not nurture HAZZANUT as such, the power of its philosophy and music is recognizable in works and creations of some of the leading *hazzanim* (cantors; *see* HAZZAN) and synagogue composers of the late nineteenth and the early twentieth centuries (e.g., Jacob Samuel MARAGOWSKY). Yiddish folk song grew rapidly as a result of Hassidic musical creation. Many of the songs of adjuration and dialogue by R. Levi Yitzhak of Berdichev (e.g., "A Din Torah mit Gott," "A Dudule") became part of general Yiddish folk song literature (*see* DIN TORAH MIT GOTT, A; DUDULE, A). The *Mitnaggdim*, antagonists of the Hassidim, often imitated and caricatured their songs. By utilizing humorous texts and devices such as change of rhythm, tempo, dynamics, and other musical elements, they developed a body of folk song that became part of Yiddish folk song literature. Jews throughout the world still sing songs of satire or caricature of Hassidic song such as "Sha-Shtil," "Kum Aher du Filazof," and "A Sudenyu." Among the art music works that have been inspired by or have utilized Hassidic motifs or themes are BAAL SHEM by Ernest BLOCH, HEBREW MELODY by Joseph ACHRON, VITEBSK by Aaron Copland, *Chassidic Niggun* by Solomon ROSOWSKY, *Chassidic Suite* by Lazare SAMINSKY, and *Chanson hébraïque* (*Mejerke*) by Maurice Ravel.

Hassidism continues to flourish in many parts of the world. One of the most significant aspects in preserving and popularizing the styles and songs of the various dynasties has been the continually increasing availability of recorded Hassidic music. Furthermore, notated Hassidic song has also brought to life many less familiar tunes heretofore unavailable. Currently, new Hassidic music is being created. Whereas, in the past, "outside" musical influences were synthesized to "the service of the Lord," today the melodies are sometimes separated from the original objective and are merely a vehicle for independent song arrangements.

See also HEKHAL HANEGGINAH.

[1]*Tikkuney Zohar,* chap. 21.
[2]*Sefer Hanigunim,* Nichoach, 1957, vol. II, Introduction, p. 20 (p. 76).
[3]Meir S. Geshuri, *La-Hassidim Mizmor,* Jerusalem, 1936, pp. 15–20.
[4]David Ewen, *Hebrew Music,* Bloch Publishing Company, Inc., New York, 1931, pp. 41, 42.

HAST, MARCUS (1840–1911). Cantor-composer and teacher. His early Talmudic learning and singing in the choir in his native town, Praga (near

Marcus Hast.

Warsaw), resulted in a career that moved forward steadily through the years. After holding positions in Warsaw and in Thorn (Toruń), Germany, where he also spent considerable time studying music, he left in 1864 for Breslau. He was elected cantor of the Orthodox synagogue there and served for six years. In addition he gave instruction to numerous cantorial students, among them the noted Eduard BIRNBAUM. He succeeded Simon Asher in 1871 as chief cantor of the Great Synagogue in Duke's Place in London, a position he held for forty years. There he founded the Association of Ministers Chazanim of Great Britain. Among his works are oratorios, cantatas, hymns, and psalms. His four-volume *Avodat Hakodesh* (1910) placed him in the forefront of English synagogue composers.

HATIKVAH. Hymn (lit. "The Hope") adopted by the First Zionist Congress in Basel, Switzerland, in 1897 at the suggestion of the Zionist leader David Wolffsohn (1856–1914) and formally declared the Zionist anthem in 1933 at the Zionist Congress in Prague. It was the unofficial anthem of Palestine for more than fifty years and was sung at the proclamation of the State of Israel on May 14, 1948. The nine-stanza poem, originally called 'Tikvatenu" ("Our Hope"), was written in 1878 by the itinerant Hebrew poet Naphtali Herz Imber (1856–1909) and appeared in a collection called *Barkai* (The Morning Star) in 1886 in Jerusalem. Its melody has been ascribed by some to Samuel Cohen, of Bohemian descent, who was an early settler of Rishon le-Zion.[1] Much conjecture has been advanced by Jewish musicologists as to the origin of the "Hatikvah" melody (*see* Fig. 21*a*). Most agree that it is a "wandering melody"; that is, its tune and variants are found in folk traditions in widely separated countries. Abraham Zvi IDELSOHN noted eight sources in which a melodic line like that of "Hatikvah" can be found (*see* Fig. 21*b*). Eric WERNER is of the opinion that the "Hatikvah" melody is simply based on the MAGEN AVOT MODE (A B C D E F G A) and is an extended version of the older Sephardic *Hallel* and

Figure 21*a*.

Table of Comparative Folk-songs.

Figure 21b. [Abraham Zvi Idelsohn, *Manual of Musical Illustrations,* Hebrew Union College]

Tal tunes.[2] Joseph Reider voiced a similar opinion earlier, but he refuted David de Sola Pool's contention that the "Hatikvah" was only an adaptation from the old Sephardic tune in *Hallel*.[3] Recent findings are that the melody is a direct quote from a Moldavian-Romanian folk song, "Carul cu boi" (Cart and Oxen), which Samuel Cohen adapted to Imber's poem when he emigrated to Palestine in 1878 from Moldavia. The same

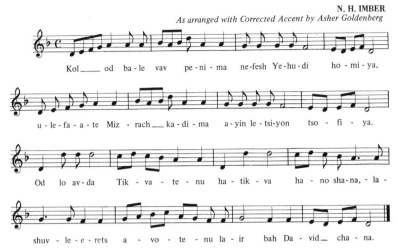

N. H. IMBER
As arranged with Corrected Accent by Asher Goldenberg

Kol___ od ba-le vav pe-ni-ma ne-fesh Ye-hu-di ho-mi-ya,

u-le-fa-a-te Miz-rach___ ka-di-ma a-yin le-tsi-yon tso-fi-ya.

Od lo av-da Tik-va-te-nu ha-tik-va ha-no sha-na, -la-

shuv-le-e-rets a-vo-te-nu la-ir bah Da-vid__ cha-na.

Figure 21c.

theory has been expounded independently by Menashe RAVINA and Eliahu Hacohen.[4] According to Eric Mandell, the earliest printed version of the melody of "Hatikvah" appeared in 1895, probably in the city of Breslau.[5] The first orchestral arrangement by Kurt Weill of "Hatikvah" was recently found (1971); it was first performed in New York City in 1947. Other arrangements were made by Bernardino Molinari, Shalom Riklis (used by the Israel Defense Army Orchestra), Paul BEN-HAIM, and Julius CHAJES.

The musical setting of the "Hatikvah" text shows an inconsistency in accentuation. It is possible that the early settlers in Israel continued to accent their texts, as was their custom in the *Galut* (Diaspora). This arbitrary accentuation was probably also the result of the inspiring melody and its rhythm meaning more than the text itself. Cantor Asher Goldenberg (1885–c. 1957) of New York attempted to arrange the "Hatikvah" anthem with the corrected accentuation but was unsuccessful (*see* Fig. 21c). Since 1948 the refrain, expressing Zionistic hope for Jewish liberation and redemption, has been modified.

Early version:

Od lo avdah tikvatenu	Our hope is not yet lost,
Hatikvah hanoshanah	The ancient hope,
Lashuv le'eretz avotenu	To return to the land of our fathers,
La'ir bah David hanah.	To the city where David dwelt.

Modified version:

Od lo avdah tikvatenu	Our hope is not yet lost,
Hatikvah shenot alpayim	The hope of two millennia,
Lih'yot am hafshi be'artzenu	To be a free people in our land,
Be'eretz tziyon virushalayim.	The land of Zion and Jerusalem.

Manuscripts of the poem in Imber's handwriting are at Yale University and at the Hebrew University of Jerusalem. The original manuscript of Kurt Weill's harmonization of "Hatikvah" is also at the Hebrew University.

[1]Paul Nettl, *National Anthems*, Storm Publishers, New York, 1952, p. 137; *The Universal Jewish Encyclopedia*, vol. 5, p. 249.

[2]"The Jewish Contribution to Music," in Louis Finkelstein (ed.), *The Jews*, New York, 1949, vol. II, chap. 23.

³"Secular Currents in the Synagogal Chant in America," *Jewish Forum*, 1918, p. 11.
⁴Cf. *Encyclopedia Judaica*, 1971, vol. 7, p. 1470, for the melody as it was reproduced from D. Idelovich, ed., *Rishon le-Ziyyon*, 1941.
⁵"A Collector's Random Notes on the Bibliography of Jewish Music," *Journal of Synagogue Music*, vol. I, no. 2, p. 30.

HATZOT (also called *Tikkun Hatzot*). Time of night (from the Hebrew *haytzi*, meaning "half," referring to midnight) when pietists arise to recite psalms and lamentations on Zion and study the Torah. *Hatzot* has its origin in the statement by DAVID: "At midnight I will rise to give thanks unto thee."[1] The Talmud comments that David was satisfied with "sixty breaths of sleep."[2] At midnight the strings of the KINNOR above his bed vibrated, and David awoke and began to study the Torah.[3]

The custom of reciting prayers at midnight possibly existed in Temple days.[4] R. Hai Gaon upheld *Tikkun Hatzot* as a duty for every Jew,[5] and according to R. Israel Baal Shem Tov, this custom is to be followed every night of the year.[6]

¹Ps. 119:62.
²Suk. 26b.
³Ber. 3b; *Pirke de-Rabbi Eliezer*, chap. 21.
⁴Menashe Unger, *Reb Yisroel Baal-Shem-Tov*, Shulsinger Bros., Inc., New York, 1963, p. 346.
⁵*Sefer ha-Eshkol*, ed. by Benjamin Z. Auerbach, Halberstadt, 1867, p. 7.
⁶*Tzava'at ha-Ribash*, 3a, 8a.

HATZOTZERAH. *See* TRUMPET.

HAVAH NAGILAH. Israeli tune ("Come Let Us Rejoice") that, in the course of fifty years, has become popular throughout the world as a traditional HORA melody. Originally, the song was a Hassidic melody sung in the court of Sadgora, Bukovina. It was later taken to Jerusalem.[1] In 1915 Abraham Zvi IDELSOHN notated it, adapting its text, which is attributed to Moshe Nathanson, and in 1918 arranged it for four voices. Its first appearance was in his *Sefer ha-Shirim*.[2] The song, which is in the AHAVAH RABBAH MODE, is sung moderately fast and with much vigor.

¹Abraham Z. Idelsohn, *Thesaurus of Hebrew-Oriental Melodies*, Leipzig, 1932, vol. IX, p. 24, no. 716, and vol. X, no. 155.
²Jüdischer Verlag, Berlin, 1922, pp. 164, 165.

HAZZAN (pl. *hazzanim*). In Temple and Talmudic days, a general communal functionary; since about the sixth and seventh centuries the READER (cantor) who recites aloud the prayers before the congregation. Most scholars have traced the term *hazzan* to the root *hazah*, "to see." Thus *hazzan ha-kenesset*[1] is translated as "overseer of the assembly" or "head of the assembly"; *kenesset* refers to the Pharasaic leaders of the *Anshe Maamad* who were stationed in the Temple as lay participants alongside the Sadducean officiants.[2] Some scholars believe that the word was borrowed from the Assyrian *hazzanu*, also meaning "overseer" or "director." According to Perez Smolenskin (1842–1885), *hazzan* is derived from *harzan*, meaning "versifier" or "rhymester," because early *hazzanim* often supplemented the prayers with their own poems and hymns (*piyyutim* and *haruzzim*). Saadiah Gaon, in his SIDDUR, applies the name *hazzan* to one who sings *piyyutim* (poems). Thus HAZZANUT is often used synonomously with *payyetanut*, that is, the art of liturgical composition (*see* PIYYUT).

In Talmudic days the office of the *hazzan* encompassed diversified tasks. He was a "town guard,"[3] superintendent at prayer meetings,[4] officer at proceedings,[5] town crier or sheriff,[6] and instructor of children.[7] He blew the SHOFAR at the beginning of Sabbaths and holy days from the roof of the synagogue,[8] and he sometimes read aloud from the Torah (Law) with special permission from the congregation.[9] That the *hazzan* also served as PRECENTOR is indicated in the Talmud; in Simoniya Levi b. Sisi, at the recommendation of Yehudah Hannasi, functioned simultaneously as judge, schoolmaster, preacher, and *hazzan*.[10] This was the practice in small communities, where several offices had to be the responsibility of one man.[11]

It is uncertain when the change of the office of the *hazzan* to that of reader occurred; however, it is first recorded in *Pirke de-Rabbi Eliezer*. Apparently, after the fall of the Temple (C.E. 70), there was not enough personnel qualified to act as SHELIAH TZIBBUR (an earlier name applied to the reader), and the *hazzan* eventually was retained as precentor. The Talmud relates "that from the day the Temple was destroyed, the Sages deteriorated [in quality] like school teachers, school teachers like synagogue attendants [*ke-hazzanyah*], synagogue attendants like common people, and the common people became more and more debased."[12] Consequently, the *hazzan*, who had always served the community and synagogue in one way or another and had a basic knowledge of the prayer chants, was by the sixth and seventh centuries able to assume the task of reader.[13] With poetic interpolation (*piyyut*) constantly being added to the service, often by readers themselves, a demand arose for a more professional precentor, the *hazzan*. As late as the Middle Ages, the reader was the only one who possessed a SIDDUR or MAHZOR. The worshipers were completely dependent upon him and had to follow by rote. When prayer books became available with the invention of printing (c. 1456), and each worshiper was able to read for himself, the *hazzan* then stressed even more the musical and vocal aspects of the prayers.[14] In time he became an indispensable synagogue functionary.

The qualifications required of the *hazzan* are manifold. "He should be a man free of transgressions and with a good reputation that has not been soiled even in his youth. He should be of humble and pleasing personality. He should possess a sweet voice, and should be fluent in the reading of the Torah, the Prophets, and the Writings. If such a man is not available, the best man in terms of scholarship and piety is to be chosen."[15] The three letters of the word *HaZaN* have been interpreted playfully as the initials of *hakham* (a man well versed in the Torah), *zakayn* (at least thirty years of age and wearing a flowing beard), and *nasuiy* (married).[16] There have also been mystical interpretations of these three initial letters.[17]

In the nineteenth century the office of *hazzan* was sometimes subdivided into *hazzan rishon*, the principal (first) *hazzan*, and *hazzan sheni*, associate (second) *hazzan*. For example, Moritz DEUTSCH served as *hazzan sheni* to Salomon SULZER in Vienna from 1842 to 1844, and David NOWAKOWSKY was appointed choir leader and *hazzan sheni* in the Broder-Schul in Russia while Nissan BLUMENTHAL served as *hazzan rishon*. The position of *hazzan sheni* evolved because the principal *hazzan* was busy with the CHORSCHUL and needed to be relieved of some of his duties. He composed new music for almost every service and occasion, trained and rehearsed with the four-voice choir, and in addition, was a virtuoso performer. The *hazzan sheni* provided relief by officiating at minor holidays (e.g., Tishah b'Ab) and on one or two Sabbaths in the month.

Rabbis, poets, and *hazzanim* who had an influence on the development of *hazzanut* and established traditions are: (1) Eleazar ben Jacob

Kallir (sixth or seventh century), of Palestine, was the earliest and most prolific of the *payyetanim* (liturgical poets). He is said to have studied *hahmat hahizzun* (the art of *hazzanut*) with Yannai, and many of his poems have been incorporated into the synagogue liturgy. (2) Yehudai (ben Nahman) Gaon served in Sura from 760 to 764. Possibly he occasionally served as a *hazzan;* he was blind and had ruled that blindness would not be a bar to the appointment as *hazzan* of a man otherwise irreproachable.[18] His responsa emphasize the order of prayers and reading from the Scriptures. Early *hazzanim* are said to have received their tradition from R. Yehudai.[19] (3) Jacob MOLIN of Mainz, known as the Maharil, is considered the outstanding Ashkenazic authority. He greatly contributed to the unification of synagogue melodies and their ritual. He served as *hazzan* mainly on the High Holy Days, festivals, and fast days and ruled that "one must not change *minhag* [custom] of a place in any matter even in regard to the introduction of melodies to which the people are not accustomed"[20] and thus gave rise to the MISSINAI TUNES or SCARBOVA melodies. (4) Solomon ROSSI of Italy was the first to introduce choral music into the synagogue service, using from three to eight voices. This innovation aroused much controversy. Rossi not only influenced the rabbis and *hazzanim* of Italy (e.g., Leone da Modena) but indirectly paved the way for choral synagogue music in Germany and Central Europe. (5) Salomon SULZER of Vienna is known for having rejuvenated Jewish music tradition by arranging *nushaot* (see NUSAH), old melodies, and traditional responses and for arranging modern settings for the four-part choir. The criteria he established for the *hazzan* and his musical influence penetrated all of Ashkenazic Jewry (East and West).

See also EDUCATION, JEWISH MUSIC.

[1]Yom. VIII:1.
[2]S. B. Hoenig, "The Supposititious Temple-Synagogue," *Jewish Quarterly Review,* vol. LIV, no. 2, October 1963.
[3]B.M. 93b.
[4]Suk. 51b.
[5]Jer. Ber. IV, 7d.
[6]Shab. 56a.
[7]Ibid., 11a, 12b, 13a.
[8]Tos. Suk. 4.
[9]Tos. Meg. III.
[10]Jer. Yeb. 13a.
[11]*The Jewish Encyclopedia,* vol. VI, p. 284; S. W. Baron, *The Jewish Community,* Jewish Publication Society of America, Philadelphia, 1942, vol. I, pp. 200, 201.
[12]Sot. 49a, b.
[13]Abraham Z. Idelsohn, *Jewish Music,* Tudor Publishing Company, New York, 1944, p. 107.
[14]Abraham Eliezer Hirshowitz, *Otzar Shalem Leminhagey Yisrael,* 1892, p. 52; Elias Zaludkowski, *Kulturträger von der jüdischen Liturgie,* 1930, p. 8.
[15]Cf. *Orah Hayyim,* chap. 53:3–5; *see also* chaps. 579, 581.
[16]Rabbi G. Felder, *Yesodei Yeshurun,* Toronto, 1954, part 1, p. 41.
[17]R. Tzevi Hirsch Kaidanover, *Kab Hayashar,* Lublin, 1909, chap. 41, pp. 75b, 76a.
[18]*Or Zarua* i, 116.
[19]*Sefer ha-Eshkol,* ed. by Benjamin Z. Auerbach, Halberstadt, 1867, vol. l, chap. 25, p. 55.
[20]*Sefer Maharil,* Shklov, 1796, p. 46b; *Orah Hayyim* 619:1.

HAZZAN, CHOR. Cantor employed in a CHOR-SCHUL. The *chor hazzan* of the large Eastern European synagogue utilized a style of singing that differed from that of the BA'AL TEFILAH, to whom the community was accustomed. Because *chor hazzanim* sang long extended tones, introduced German classical compositions into the Jewish religious service, and wore "priestly" attire, they were mockingly called *galahim* (priests of the church). Their style of singing was labeled *galahish.*

HAZZAN, STADT. Cantor (lit. "city cantor") who was employed in a large Eastern European metropolis and whose sole duty was to officiate at services. In smaller communities the HAZZAN generally served in other capacities, for example, as *shohet* (ritual slaughterer), teacher, and *mohel* (circumciser).

HAZZAN, VOICELESS. Cantor whose voice is limited in range and power. Beginning in the early nineteenth century this term applied to Eastern European synagogue composers and choir leaders who functioned as cantors despite a lack of vocal ability (e.g., Nisson SPIVAK). Because of this shortcoming, certain innovations were introduced into the synagogue musical literature: (1) the entire musical service was focused upon the choir, resulting in lengthy choral settings; (2) cantorial solo parts were kept to a minimum; (3) the solo chorister with vocal agility assumed new prominence; and (4) tuneful and rhythmic melody replaced the simple chant.

HAZZAN-BASS-SINGER. Seventeenth-century trio who sang in the synagogue. An itinerant HAZZAN officiated, with a bass *meshorer* (chorister) and a boy singer (*singerel*) assisting him during the service. Singing in unison or in thirds in an improvisatory manner, they either repeated the cantor's last word or words in cadence or answered his rendition with a refrain. Humming (*see* BRUMMEN) as accompaniment to the cantor's singing was extemporized. The group "harmonized" tunes they had created themselves or had obtained from other cantors. The bass singer often assumed the name "Bass" (called Bassista by Christians; Heb., *meshorer*) in lieu of his own name (e.g., Shabbetai ben Joseph Bass of Prague (1641–1718). "Bass" was also appended to the singer's first name as identification, for example, "Yekel Bass" (eighteenth century), "Yossel Bass" (twentieth century). The members of the *hazzan-bass-singer* trio were remunerated by contributions made by various congregants. Because of their unworthy deportment they were frequently called *kele HaMaS* ("tools of lawlessness"), from the first letters of *hazzan*, *meshorer*, *singer*, or *ZeBaH resha'im* (*zinger*, *bass*, *hazzan*), from Proverbs 21:27: "The sacrifice of the wicked

A *hazzan* with two singers, as represented in the fourteenth-century manuscript of a *mahzor*. [*Encyclopedia Judaica*]

is abominable." Rabbi Ephraim Luntschitz of Lublin and Prague spoke derisively of this group as "the three who yell while no one answers." *See also* CHOIR; MESHORERIM.

HAZZANUT. Term described by Saadiah Gaon in his SIDDUR as the art of PIYYUT (poetry); for example, Yannai's poems (c. C.E. 700) were called *Hazzanut Yannai*.[1] Later, the term was applied to the melodies that accompanied the *piyyutim*. Today the term has several other connotations: (1) It is a general term applied to the profession of HAZZAN. (2) It refers to the improvisations (*see* IMPROVISATION) of the professional *hazzan*, based on certain "melody types" and sung in a highly florid style with stirring pathos. (3) It may refer to the styles or melodies utilized in specific locations, for example, Polish *hazzanut* or *hazzanut* of southern Germany.

[1]*Teshuvot Hageonim*, Responsa 59.

HAZZANUT-BRIEF. Written agreement or contract between the community and the cantor as to his obligations, remuneration, and so on.

ח"י הנ"ל ועל הש"ץ השני לקבן מעות מי שבידך וליתן חלק לחזן להש"ץ מהבהכ"נ שמתפלל שם הבעל שמחה תדיר

כנהוג והמותר יחלק חלק הש"ץ הראשון להש"ץ השני מהבהכ"נ הגדולה, וחלילה לשום חזן לעשות בלעדו ח"ו

וזה מחת שכרו הראשונה חלף עבודתו עבודת הקודש

ג) **השו"ץ** ר' ח'ש הנ"ל יקבל שכריות מהגבאים ודבהכ"נ הגדולה בכל שבוע ושבוע סך עשרים רו"כ, היינו

שבא ח"ב מהכנסת הבהכנ"ס הנ"ל, וארבעה עשר רו"כ מהקעפסטיל דפה, וחלילה לשום גבאי שיהיה בזמנו

לקח שכרו של ה"ר ח"י הנ"ל אעולו פ"א מהסך הנ"ל, רק כ"א מחויב להשתדל שיקבל שכרו בשלמות

במועדו ובזמנו, ומהסך הנ"ל יחזיק ליום ח"י הנ"ל מארודים ראוים ונכונים :

ד) **כל** הכתבים הש"ץ להש"ץ מלו ומקדם. בלעדו לא יתם איש את ידו לכתוב אחד מכל הכתבים הנ"ל :

ה) **רחשׁ** להש"ץ כנהוג היו מחה מאשר יתט על הבי'קי"ה . ובעד כתנת הכתבה יקבל א' זה'

ו) **הכנסת** הבית עלמין אין להש"ץ מע"י מטלו ומקדם, ואין לשם אדם ליכן על הצ"ע לאמור אמור מעו"ר

אלול עד אחר יעם הנוראים חוץ מהש"ץ רעיח מבהכ"נ הגדולה מבהכ"ע דיהם, שיש לו חלק שלים מקדם קדמתה :

ז) **כל** המקומות המסודרים לבעל שיתפלל ה"ר ח"י הנ"ל אזה מהתפלות הסכרים למעלה מחויבים לעמוד בשביל

קערה בעיו"כ ולמסר המעות לב"ד ח"י הנ"ל :

(י)

ורשות למו"ה חי בהל למחב את הש"ץ השני

מעשית מי שבידך כנ'ל

ח] **הש"ץ** והמשורדים פטורים מכל עול הנתמות הנהוג פה, חוץ מטואקסע מהבר ועופות

ט) **וכסבדרם** פסרנו בלרוגע הטוב את הש"ץ ה"ר ח"י הנ"ל מלמת על בן זכר בעדר שבת קודם לו הוה ולו משרדריו

בשם מקום :

י) **הש"ץ** ה"ר ח"י הנ"ל אים רשו לנשא אל אחר הצרים להתפלל כמנהג שאר החזים אשר יקבצו בעדים בתי

רשות הגבאים דבהכ"נ הגדולה דעל"י , וקבל עלו באלה ובשבועה לבל למשך את עיר בארדיטשוב להיו צן קבוט

במקום אחר כל ימי חיין :

כל הנ"ל עלה במוקטם כלנו קהל ועדה דפה מרזעו הטוב ונעשה בכל תוקף ועו ובכל אוהי"מ לדתוהי"ק וקאא"ס

ת"ב יפ"מ וכל המשנה יד וע על התתחונה ענוש יענש כפי דיהה"ק :

דּבּרי האלועים רלאב הקהאלה בדירך הגבאים ונגידים יחידי סגולה בשלמות רגונם . וכן יסכימו מן ה שמים

על שלוחנו ומפגיע אשר במדינו ליכותנו בלב טהור ורוח נכון ותיריתנו יערב כאשם וכנחותם וקדב נכה לשעת

עולמים . ויעמד וזן וזעפל לכל החתם פה **בבל וּעשרן** לפרט : אור לים ה' ט' אלול שנת **תארך** לפ"ק

Hazzanut-brief made by the Great Synagogue of Berdichev with Yeruchom Blindman. [*The History of Hazanuth*, Jewish Ministers Cantors Association of America, New York]

HEBRÄISCHE GESÄNGE. Max Bruch's (1838–1920) Hebrew songs written in Leipzig (1888) after Lord Byron's *Hebrew Melodies* (*see* HEBREW MELODY). They are scored for chorus, orchestra, and organ.

HEBREW MELODY (MELODIES). (1) Name of Lord Byron's poems issued in 1815 to which the Jewish musician and composer Isaac Nathan (1791–1864) set the music. The famous Jewish singer John Braham (1774–1856) introduced them to the public.[1] Six of the "Melodies" are tunes used in the synagogue service.[2] (2) Opus 9 for viola and piano composed by Joseph Joachim (1831–1907). (3) Opus 43 for cello and piano written by Alexander Abramovich KREIN. (4) Work for violin and piano (also for violin

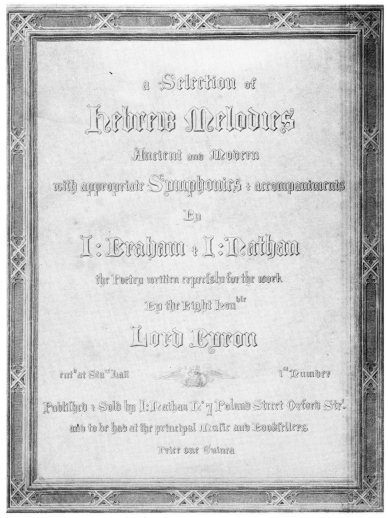

Title page of Lord Byron's *Hebrew Melodies*.

and orchestra) by Joseph ACHRON, written in 1911 and inspired by a NIGGUN sung to him by his grandfather.

[1]T. L. Ashton, *Byron's Hebrew Melodies*, University of Texas Press, Austin, 1972, p. 8.
[2]Cf. *The Jewish Encyclopedia*, vol. IX, p. 179.

HEKHAL HANEGGINAH. According to the Kabbalists, a heavenly palace or temple (lit. "palace" or "temple of song") into which entrance can be gained only through song.[1] Furthermore, it is believed that "all melodies derive from the source of sanctity, from the temple of music,"[2] and that the *hekhal hanegginah* is close to the *hekhal hateshuvah* ("temple of penitence").[3] These mystic ideas follow the doctrines set down by the Zohar (Book of Splendor) "that all that God created sing His praises"[4] and "melody gladdens the heart."[5]

R. Israel Baal Shem Tov (1700–1760) is reputed to have "cleansed" secular tunes by first returning them to the *hekhel hanegginah* and then applying them to sacred texts. The saintly leaders of the Kabbalistic and, later, the Hassidic movements spoke of *tzadikim* (righteous ones) entering the *hekhal hanegginah* and selecting tunes for their specific moods and needs.[6] *See* CONTRAFACTUM; HASSIDIC SONG.

[1]*Tikkuney Zohar*, 45:1.
[2]*Lekkute Moharan*, 1874.
[3]Attributed to R. Pinhas of Korets (1736–1801).
[4]*Parshat Haye Sarah*, 123:1.
[5]*Parshat Yitro*, 93.
[6]R. Yosef Yitzhak Shneerson, *Sefer Hasihot*, 1940.

Max Helfman.

HELFMAN, MAX (1901–1963). Composer, conductor, teacher, and lecturer. He began his Jewish education in his native town, Radzin (Radzyń), Poland, and continued his education, both Jewish and musical, after he emigrated to New York City in 1909. He attended the Rabbi Jacob Joseph School on the lower East Side and various music schools and was awarded a three-year fellowship to the Curtis Institute in Philadelphia. He led the Philharmonic Choral Society, the Bach-Handel Society, the Jewish Music Alliance Chorus in New York, and the Paterson Singing Society. He served as music director at the Sinai Temple of Los Angeles, Temple Israel of Hollywood, Temple B'nai Abraham of Newark, and Temple Emanuel of Paterson. From 1944 to 1961 Helfman served as head of the music department at the Brandeis Arts Institute of the Brandeis Youth Foundation in Santa Susana, Calif. In 1961 he founded the School of Fine Arts at the University of Judaism in Los Angeles and later became the founding dean of the School of Fine Arts at the Jewish Theological Seminary of America in New York City. He is known for writing a Friday evening service, *Shabbat Kodesh* (1942), as well as numerous sacred choral compositions, secular vocal music for solo and chorus, preludes for organ, a violin sonata, chamber music, ballet music, and song arrangements.

HEMAN. Kohathite, the first of the three chief LEVITES,[1] to whom the vocal and instrumental music of the Temple service was entrusted in the reign of DAVID.[2] The son of Joel and grandson of Samuel the Prophet, Heman is surnamed *hameshorer*, "the singer."[3] He is also called "the king's seer [*hozeh*] in the matters of God." He had fourteen sons and three daughters. The sons all assisted their father, and each was the head of one of the twenty-four courses, or wards, into which 288 musicians were divided by King David. Among the tasks assigned to Heman's sons was blowing the horns.[4]

[1]Cf. ASAPH; JEDUTHUN.
[2]I Chron. 15:16–22.
[3]Ibid., 6:19.
[4]Ibid., 25:4–31.

HEMSI, ALBERTO (1898–   ). Composer, teacher, music director, and writer known for gathering and preserving the musical tradition of the Sephardim. Born in Kasaba (Turgutlu), Turkey, young Alberto left for İzmir to study composition with Shem Tov Shikayar and liturgical music with HAZZAN-Rabbi Yitzhak Algaze. He continued his musical studies at the Royal Conservatory of Milan and about 1914 returned to Izmir, where he became active as a composer and pedagogue. He set as his task the collection of Sephardic materials from such areas as Turkey, Greece, and the islands of the Dodecanese and Rhodes. In 1926 he accepted the post of musical director of the Grand Temple de la Communauté Israélite in Egypt and after 1956 was music director at the Bérith Salom Sephardic Synagogue and music instructor at the rabbinical seminary in Paris. Hemsi's numerous articles and essays appeared in various journals and display the great breadth of Sephardic tradition. His work *Coplas séfardies* (*Chansons judéo-espagnoles;* 1932–1938) is an important contribution to Jewish music.

HIGGAYON. Word that occurs three times in the Book of Psalms and has several interpretations: (1) silent meditation or thought;[1] (2) a melody;[2] (3) a type of musical instrument;[3] (4) "to whisper," from the Hebrew *hegeh.* Thus, according to Fürst, *higgayon bekinnor* as used in psalm 92:4 alludes to the vibrations of the harp, and *higgayon selah* in psalm 9:17 denotes a musical interlude. This interpretation is supported by the Septuagint and Symmachus.

[1]Cf. David Kimchi and *Metzudat David,* ps. 19:15; Rashi, ps. 9:17.
[2]Cf. David Kimchi, ps. 92:4; thus Kimchi assigns two distinct meanings.
[3]Cf. Ibn-Ezra, ps. 92:4. He also interprets *higgayon* as the melody of the hymn.

HINENI HEANI. Initial words of a prayer recited by the HAZZAN before the MUSAF service on Rosh Hashanah (New Year) and Yom Kippur (Day of Atonement). Of unknown authorship, the supplication probably dates from medieval times and has, through the ages, inspired *hazzanim* as well as worshipers. The chant that generally accompanies the text does not have a fixed melody or any traditional motives. It is chanted either in the AHAVAH RABBAH MODE, with a modulation to the fourth, or in a minor key. It seems that at one time the entire meditation was recited silently by the *hazzan*. With the passing of time, he raised his voice at those words or phrases that had the power to arouse the emotions of the worshipers, who quietly awaited the conclusion of the prayer.[1] Although today the *hazzan* chants most of the prayer aloud, it is evident that a higher pitch level or forte dynamic level or both are utilized for words and phrases such as *Shadai* ("Almighty") and *vesigar besatan* ("rebuke the adversary"). However, certain parts are still recited in an undertone; for example, from *vena al tafshi'em* to *vesigar besatan*, and from *vihi ratzon* to the end. The various settings originating with *hazzanim* of Eastern Europe in the nineteenth century have added drama to the *Hineni* recitation. The *hazzan* sometimes began the prayer at the entrance to the synagogue and completed it as he reached the *bimah* (prayer desk). Joseph ALTSHUL of Slonim was responsible for one of these innovations. His choir stood at the *bimah* while he waited at the entrance of the synagogue. One of the choristers would then chant, "Where is the *hazzan*?" The *hazzan* would reply, "*Hineni*—Here I am." "Why are you standing at the doorway?" a second chorister would inquire. The *hazzan* would then answer, "*He'ani*—I am poor." "Is he in need of money?" the choir would then ask. And he would reply, "*He'ani mima'as*—I am poor in good deeds." Altshul would then make his way up the aisle to the prayer desk while chanting the rest of the prayer.

[1]Ephraim Zalman Margolies, *Matte Ephraim*, chap. 590, 38.

Artur Holde.

HOLDE, ARTUR (1885‒1962). German-American critic, conductor, and writer. Born in Rendsburg, Schleswig-Holstein, Holde received his musical education studying with Max Friedlaender and Hermann Kretzschmar at the Berlin University and at the Prussian Academy of Arts. From 1910 to 1936 he served as conductor at the Frankfurt synagogue and was active as music critic for various Frankfurt publications. He emigrated to the United States in 1937 and in New York held the post of choirmaster from 1937 to 1943 at the Hebrew Tabernacle and served as music critic of the German newspaper *Aufbau*. He contributed numerous articles to various music publications and lectured on Jewish music before the JEWISH MUSIC

FORUM.[1] His volume *Jews in Music* (1959) concerns the large number of musicians of Jewish descent who have had a lasting influence on the character and form of both general and Jewish culture.

[1]Cf. vols. VII, VIII, 1946–1947, pp. 21–23.

HOPKE. Yiddish term meaning "hop," signifying a lively DANCE in duple or quadruple time that includes leaping, jumping, or skipping. Jewish dances of ancient and medieval times have been characterized as consisting of

Youth Aliyah group dancing the *hora* at the kibbutz En Harod, Israel. [Central Zionist Archives, Jerusalem]

gesticulations, violent leaps and bounds, and hopping in a circle, rather than graceful pose or soft rhythmic movement.[1] The *hopke* is danced by Hassidim at weddings, Simhat Torah (Rejoicing of the Law), and other special occasions.

[1]Wilhelm Nowack, *Lehrbuch der hebräische Archäologie*, 1893, vol. I, p. 279.

HORA. Popular Israeli folk DANCE originating in the Balkans and taking root in the early 1900s. Its Palestinian Jewish version was originated in 1924 by Barukh Agadati, an actor from Romania who settled in Palestine in 1910. The dance was first introduced by the Tel Aviv Ohel Theater into the settlements of the Jezreel Valley and Galilee. A circle dance, in a moderately fast quadruple meter, the *hora* invites public participation. With its gay, dynamic rhythm, it expresses the temperament of *halutzim* (pioneers) and incorporates the spirit and soul of Hassidism. Israel's main dance medium, it has become a symbol of the country, and numerous composers have created *horas* (e.g., Abraham Wolf BINDER, Marc LAVRY, and Baruch Liftman). The *hora* has been retained in passages of suites and finales of symphonies. A folk song that has become closely associated with the *hora* is HAVAH NAGILAH.

HOSHA NA. Phrase, meaning "Save, we beseech Thee" (a contraction from *hoshiah na*, ps. 118:25), which, like AMEN, ANENU, and HALLELUYAH, was chanted as a congregational refrain in Temple days and is still practiced today.[1] Because of the accustomed manner of pronouncing the two words as one, the Sages used the contracted form *Hoshana*.[2] It is generally uttered after each phrase or verse of *Hoshanot* prayer-poems during the Sukkot Festival, when it is customary to take a scroll from the Ark and make a circuit around the prayer desk while each person holds in his hands four plant species: *lulab* (palm branch), *etrog* (citron), *hadassim* (boughs of myrtle), and the *aravot* (willows of the brook). The seventh day of Sukkot is known as Hoshana Rabbah, at which time seven circuits are made.[3] Five willow twigs, which in turn came to be called a *hoshana*,[4] are struck upon the ground or upon a vessel two or three times[5] while the refrain *Kol mevaser, mevaser ve-omer* ("A voice brings news and says") is chanted three times.

[1]Eliezer Levi, *Yesodot Hatefillah*, Tel Aviv, 1952, p. 270.
[2]Cf. *Siddur Otzar Hatefillot*, s.v. *Seder Hoshanot.*
[3]Jer. Suk. 4:5.
[4]Suk. 30b, 31a, 34a, 37a, b, 46b.
[5]*Levush*, chap. 664, 3.

HYDRAULIS. Ancient instrument, known as a "water organ," whose wind pressure was supplied by a water compressor and pistons and not by bellows. The Talmud relates that no such musical instrument (*hirdolim*) was found in the Sanctuary because its sound was heavy and disturbed the music.[1] It interfered with the sweetness of the song, that is, with the sound of the other instruments.

See also GURGANA; MAGREFAH; ORGAN; TABLA; UGAB.

[1]Ar. 10b. Rashi's version reads with a *samakh* at the end; thus, *hirdolis* and not *hirdolim*.

HYMN. Song of praise usually addressed to God. The term is employed freely by the Septuagint in translating the Hebrew names for almost every kind of poetic composition. Throughout Hebrew literature it has been vague in its application and was applied as the occasion arose. In modern prayer books the term is used for such recitals as ADON OLAM, *Yigdal*, and

EN KELOHENU. The title *Zemirot leShabbat* is often translated as Sabbath table hymns.[1] Hymns in the form of PIYYUT interpolations were introduced as early as the fifth century as artfully designed prayers to circumvent decrees against public instruction. General characteristics of the hymn are: the words are specially written, based directly or indirectly upon the Bible; they are in verse and stanza form with a refrain; and they are sung congregationally. Modern hymnody had its origin in the Reform movement in Hamburg, Germany (1818). Its published *Hamburg Songbook* included German texts—modified German Lutheran hymns set to music in the German choral style. Early hymnals in the United States were written by Penina Moise (1797–1880) of Charleston, S.C., Adolph Huebsch (1830–1894) of New York, Simon Hecht of Evansville, Ind., and Otto Loeb of Chicago. A major development in Jewish hymnody came in 1894 with the work of Rabbi Isaac S. Moses, of the Central Synagogue of New York, who, with the assistance of Cantor Theodor Guinsburg and Gideon Froelich (organist), published an elaborate hymnal. Although their aim was to include tunes with the spirit of Jewish melody worship, the hymns still showed German influence. Hymnal writing continued to flourish under the auspices of the Union of American Hebrew Congregations in cooperation with the Conference of American Cantors. They published their first edition of the *Union Hymnal* in 1897. In spite of the many editions, Jewish composers have constantly written and spoken out for publication of a hymnbook that reflects Jewish character, uses traditional material, and is a product of Jewish composers.[2]

[1]"Hymns and Cognate Forms," *The Authorized Daily Prayer Book,* ed. by Dr. Joseph H. Hertz, Bloch Publishing Company, Inc., New York, 1948, pp. 410, 411.

[2]Herbert Fromm, "Jewish Hymnology: Its Past and Future," *Jewish Music Forum Bulletin,* vol. IX, December 1948, pp. 11ff.

IDELSOHN, ABRAHAM ZVI (1882–1938). Foremost musicologist of Jewish music. He was born in Courland (Latvia). The family moved to Libau (Liepāja), where young Idelsohn sang as a chorister for the local cantor, Abraham Mordecai Rabinowitz, and received a rudimentary knowledge of Jewish music. Journeying through Königsberg and later in London, Idelsohn suffered great hardships and was prevented from realizing his desire to further his studies and find a vocation. He returned to Libau, where he rejoined Cantor Rabinowitz's choir. Cantor Rabinowitz introduced him to the hazzanic (*see* HAZZANUT) literature of Salomon SULZER, Louis LEWANDOWSKI, and Hirsch WEINTRAUB, as well as to the compositions of the European classic composers. At this time he learned to recognize authentic Jewish melody and acquired musical taste. In 1901 he went to Berlin and studied at the Stern Conservatory, and in 1902 he left for Leipzig, where he obtained a cantorial position and pursued his musical studies at the Conservatory of Leipzig under Professors Jadassohn, Krehl, Zöllner, and Kretzschmar. Guided by Cantor Zvi Schneider, whose daughter he married, he learned the melodic line of traditional *hazzanut,* which was free from German influence. In 1903 he accepted a position as cantor and *shohet* (ritual slaughterer) in Regensburg, Bavaria. In 1904, at the request of relatives, he moved to Johannesburg, South Africa, where he served as cantor. Inspired by the Zionist ideal, he emigrated to Jerusalem in 1906 to devote his time to the research of Jewish song and to teach at the Teachers Seminary and the Jewish People's School. He organized the

Abraham Zvi Idelsohn.

Institute for Jewish Music (1910) and the Jewish Music School (1919). In 1921 he traveled to Europe to make known his musical research, and in 1922 he gave lectures in the United States. He was invited to catalog the Eduard BIRNBAUM collection at the Hebrew Union College in Cincinnati in 1924. That year the college engaged him to lecture on Jewish music and appointed him professor of Hebrew and liturgy and Jewish music, a post he occupied until his retirement in 1934. In 1933 the degree of doctor of Hebrew law was conferred upon him. Idelsohn's outstanding literary works are his THESAURUS OF HEBREW-ORIENTAL MELODIES (1914–1933), *Jewish Music in Its Historical Development* (1929), *Ceremonies of Judaism* (2d ed., 1930), and *Jewish Liturgy and Its Development* (1932). His musical compositions include *Shire Tefillah* (1911), a liturgical work; *Jiftah* (1922), a musical drama in five acts; *Sefer ha-Shirim* (1912 and 1922), a collection of Hebrew songs for children; and folk songs. Idelsohn was among the earliest to pioneer in and popularize Jewish musicology. His achievements and conclusions have not only shed light on Jewish music but are now part of general music history and musicology.

ILTUR. *See* IMPROVISATION.

IMMORTAL PIANO, THE (KING DAVID'S HARP; SIENA PIANO). According to legend, the sounding board of this piano was constructed from the spruce wood of the original pillars of Solomon's Temple, and it is said that the spirit of "David's harp" entered into it. Built about 1800, the piano was given in 1868 by the city of Siena to Prince Humbert as a wedding gift. It was rediscovered by Avner Carmi, who traveled thousands of miles in its quest. Because the legend of the piano reaches as far back as the roots of ancient Israel, it was renamed "The Immortal Piano" in 1951.[1] A number of Siena Piano recordings have been produced by Counterpoint/Esoteric Records in Hollywood.

[1]Avner and Hannah Carmi, *The Immortal Piano*, Crown Publishers, Inc., New York, 1960.

The Immortal Piano, shown on a record album.
[The Everest Record Group, Los Angeles]

IMPROVISATION. Spontaneous creation of music without prior preparation (Heb. *iltur*, from the Aramaic *le'altar*, meaning "on the spot" or "at once"). HAZZANUT is based on the principle of improvising that occurs in a given mode with traditional motives therein. Sometimes, if the HAZZAN is not bound by any traditional prayer patterns (NUSAH), he renders a wholly improvised selection. Cantor-theorists and musicologists distinguish between two types of improvisational synagogue song: *tefillat-ha-seder*, meaning that the cantorial modes are used in a well-ordered fashion for the ensuing improvisation when rendering the prayers, and *tefillat-ha-regesh*, implying that the musical rendition of the prayers depends almost exclusively on the immediate inspiration of the *hazzan* during his recitation.[1] The latter, sometimes called "free improvisation," originated in the Orient and was the creation of later virtuoso *hazzanim* who developed the simple prayer modes of the BA'AL TEFILAH into this specific art. In the course of time, certain motives and melodic curves, modulations, and COLORATURA passages within given modes became distinctive of the improvisation of the virtuoso hazzan. This free improvisation is sometimes described as a sort of "second tradition" (Mishnah Torah) in liturgical music. It was a spontaneous outpouring of the soul (*hishtaphut hanefesh*), and its effect upon the worshiper was hypnotic and electrifying.[2] It is unthinkable for a *hazzan* to lack the ability to improvise in some manner. Abraham Zvi IDELSOHN outlined the following rudimentary musical theoretical tools: "In order to be able to improvise, the singer has to be permeated with the nature of the modes, and have a thorough training in all their elements and characteristics. He has to know the meaning of the text, and the occasion upon which the prayer is used."[3] The improvisatory elaboration of the prayer modes was cultivated by such early *hazzanim* as Salomon WEINTRAUB, Bezalel SCHULSINGER, and Yeruchom BLINDMAN. In the late nineteenth and early twentieth centuries this art was continued by Alter Yechiel Karniol (1855–1929), David Roitman (1884–1943), Aryeh Leib Rutman (1866–1935), and others.

See also RECITATIVE.

[1]Cf. Jacob Beimel, "Rev. David Roitman, An Artist in the Cantorial Profession," *Jewish Music Forum Bulletin*, vol. V, no. 1, December 1944, pp. 7ff.; Joseph Yasser, "The Philosophy of Improvisation," *The Cantorial Art*, National Jewish Music Council, New York, 1966, pp. 43, 45.
[2]Gershon Ephros, *Cantorial Anthology*, Bloch Publishing Company, Inc., New York, 1953, vol. 4, p. vi.
[3]Abraham Z. Idelsohn, *Thesaurus of Hebrew-Oriental Melodies*, Leipzig, 1932, vol. VIII.

INBAL. Term in Nazir VI:1 meaning "clapper," that is, the clapper (inner part) of a bell. The outer part is called ZOG, and both terms are utilized by Rashi (Ar. 10b) to describe the instrument TABLA.

INSTRUMENTS, MUSICAL. The plural term instruments is used to denote contrivances used specifically in Biblical and post-Biblical days to produce musical sounds. Whereas ancient peoples attributed the origin of music (instrumental) to a national hero or a god, Judaism adheres to Genesis 4:21, which mentions Jubal, a common man, as "the father of all such as handle the lyre [KINNOR] and the pipe [UGAB]." Biblical references indicate an inseparableness of singing and playing, for example, in the phrase "lyres and harps for singers [*lesharim*].[1] According to the Talmud, "the essential feature [of the Temple worship] was vocal music; instrumental music was merely to sweeten the tone."[2]

Hebrew synonyms used for musical instruments are *kele shir*,[3] *kele negginah*,[4] and *kele zemer*.[5] Stringed instruments were, by far, the most im-

Detail from the Arch of Titus, Rome, showing the captured vessels of the Temple in Jerusalem, including the sacred trumpets. [*The Jewish Encyclopedia*, Funk and Wagnalls Company]

portant to ancient Israel. In order to attain the proper mood during prayer, King DAVID accompanied himself on the *kinnor*.[6] A distinction is made between two characteristically different expressions for playing on strings: *zamar*, "to pluck," and *naggan*, "to strike."[7] It is possible that, since stringed instruments were most popular, the two expressions *kele zemer* and *kele negginah* were applied to all musical instruments and were used interchangeably with *kele shir*.

Approximately nineteen instruments can be identified in Scripture and are classified into three divisions; namely, percussion instruments (possibly *mezamrot*),[8] wind instruments (*nehilot*),[9] and string instruments (*negginot*).[10] To the percussion family belong such instruments as BELLS, CYMBALS, MENA'ANE'IM, and TOF. Wind instruments include the HALIL, KEREN, MASHROKITA, SHOFAR, and TRUMPET. To the string family belong ASOR, KATROS, KINNOR, NEBEL, PSANTERIN, and SABKHA. The terms MINNIM, SHALISHIM, SUMPONYAH, and UGAB are not included in these three divisions because of the diversity of their various meanings. Other terms signifying musical instruments and appearing in Biblical, post-Biblical, and general literature are ATZE BEROSHIM, BOTNON, DAHAVON, ERUS, GROGGER, GURGANA, HYDRAULIS, INBAL, MAGREFAH, MAHOL, MARKOF, NEKABEKHA, NIKATMON, REVI'IT, TABLA, TANBURA, TUNING FORK, ZOG. In addition to these terms, words or phrases referring to musical instruments appear in the headings of numerous psalms (they have been treated under their respective titles; e.g., AL-HAGITTIT, AL-HASHMINIT, AL-MAHALAT). Recent archaeological finds and pictorial representations disprove the old notion that no picture of a Palestinian instrument has survived throughout the years. Furthermore, both sources substantiate Biblical descriptions. Among these findings are a mouthpiece of a *halil* near Aqaba, lyres and oboes of Ur, Mesopotamia, and Bar Kokhba coins from 132–135 on which lyres and trumpets are depicted.[11]

After the destruction of the Temple (C.E. 70), instrumental music was banned as a sign of national mourning. The only instrument still used in the ritual, and which still survives, is the ancient horn, the *shofar*, based on the command in Numbers 29:1 and Leviticus 23:23. Decorative

Jewish coin from the Bar Kokhba period (C.E. 132–135), showing trumpets. [Haifa Music Museum and Amli Library]

BELLS (*pa'amonim;* sometimes called *rimonim*) on the curtain that covers the Ark or the breastplate and crown of the Torah (or both) have their place among synagogue ornaments. The practice of using the GROGGER and various noisemaking rattling devices during the reading of the *Megillah* (*see* MEGILLOT, THE FIVE) also became part of the synagogue service. Instrumental music was permitted for wedding feasts and other festive occasions. In Jerusalem today instrumental music, except for drums, is still prohibited at weddings.[12] Playing musical instruments during a religious service on Sabbath and holidays is prohibited.[13] The destruction of the Temple meant so much to the Jews that they took an oath on the shores of Babylon never to play music. This was confirmed by the Levites, who later cut off their thumbs so as to be unable to play again.[14] Responsa literature points out that the synagogue is a miniature Temple, and hence the oath is still binding.[15]

[1] I Kings 10:12; II Chron. 9:11.
[2] Ar. 11a.
[3] Neh. 12:36.
[4] Ps. 68:26.
[5] Midrash, Gen. 23:3.
[6] R. Judah he-Hassid, *Sefer Hassidim,* Jerusalem, 1963, p. 15.
[7] Carl Heinrich Cornill, *Music in the Old Testament,* The Open Court Publishing Company, Chicago, 1909, p. 19.
[8] II Kings 12:14.
[9] Ps. 5:1.
[10] Ps. 4, 6, 54, 55, 67, 76; Hab. 3:19.
[11] Cf. Bathja Bayer, *The Material Relics of Music in Ancient Palestine and Its Environs,* Israel Music Institute, Tel Aviv, 1963.
[12] Ya'akov Geles, *Minhage Eretz Yisrael,* Mosad Harav Kuk, Jerusalem, 1968, *Hilkhot Kiddushin,* p. 337.
[13] *Orah Hayyim* 338; Maimonides, *Yad, Shabbat* 23:4.
[14] *Midrash Bereshit Rabbah.*
[15] *Ketav Sofer, She'eylot u-Teshuvot, Hashmatos,* chap. 192.

ISRAEL PHILHARMONIC ORCHESTRA. Orchestra established in Tel Aviv by the violinist Bronisław Hubermann (1882–1947). Originally called the Palestine Orchestra, it was renamed the Palestine Philharmonic Orchestra in 1936. In 1948, the year of the founding of the State of Israel, the name Israel Philharmonic Orchestra was assumed. Its inaugural concert was given on December 26, 1936, at the Levant Fair Grounds in Tel Aviv, with Arturo Toscanini conducting Weber's *Oberon* Overture as its opening number. The idea of founding an orchestra made up of all Jewish musicians came to Hubermann when the Nazis took over in Germany, expelled all Jewish musicians, and banned music by composers of Jewish descent. Hubermann's task was herculean in that he had to audition member musicians from such places as Berlin, Budapest, Frankfurt, Vienna, and Warsaw, bear the responsibility for organizational work, and do fund raising. The orchestra's first rehearsals were held under the baton of William Steinberg. Among the many guest conductors were Leonard Bernstein, Charles Munch, and Zubin Mehta, who recently was appointed

The Israel Philharmonic Orchestra with Zubin Mehta as conductor. [Hurok Concerts, Inc.]

musical adviser to the orchestra. Israeli conductors of the orchestra have been Moshe Atzman, Gary Bertini, Sergiu Commissiona, Mendi Rodan, and Michael Taube. The establishment of the orchestra attracted outstanding musicians to settle in Israel, raised performing and pedagogic standards of music, gave the Israeli composer an opportunity to have his works performed, and made it possible for audiences to listen to the world's greatest music. The orchestra toured the United States, Canada, Europe, and the Far East and recorded for Columbia and Decca Records. It has about 36,000 subscribers (a world-record percentage of the population). Currently more than 40 percent of its 104 members are Israel-born and Israel-trained.

ISRAEL SYMPHONY. Orchestral work composed between 1912 and 1915 in two movements by Ernest BLOCH and first performed in the United States in 1917 under the baton of Artur Bodanzky. Bloch had intended to name this symphony *Fêtes juives* but, at the suggestion of Romain Rolland, gave it its present name. In the second movement the climax is augmented by a vocal group (two sopranos, two altos, and solo bass) that joins the orchestra in a prayer.

ISRAELI MUSIC. Designation for modern musical activity in Israel, which originated in 1882, when the first *aliyah* (migration), caused by Russian pogroms, was made by Bilu (first modern Zionist pioneering movement). It developed with the successive waves of immigration along two general lines, folk music and art music. Both areas have been exposed to the many traditions, forms, and styles of East and West and constantly blend contemporary influences.

The first immigrants to arrive in Palestine were from Eastern European countries. They sang folk songs based on Slavic tunes that had been previously translated into Hebrew. In addition, they sang Hassidic and synagogue tunes and Arabic and Yemenite melodies that they encountered in Palestine. The second wave of immigration, from Central and Western European countries, brought a high level of general musical culture. Folk tunes embodying strains of German folk song were sung. Blending Eastern European song with Oriental music was more easily achieved than blending the song of Central and Western countries with Oriental song. This was probably because Eastern European melody has an Oriental heritage in that it is ornamental and is expressed greatly through IMPROVISATION. Furthermore, the use of the various minor modes in both traditions makes them generally closer. The songs that developed predominantly in the kibbutz (cooperative settlement) and were sung by the *halutzim* (pioneers) derived their inspiration from the new environment, climate, and language as well as from the agricultural and economic aspirations of the early settlers. As time progressed, each migration developed a song distinguished by content and mood. Whereas the early songs reflect the memories of suffering and longing, those of the later periods echo strength, courage, and triumph. Beginning in the 1940s a homogeneous group of folk song was created and sung by the masses. This large body of song is recognizable not only by its melodic characteristics but by its use of a specific text—the Bible. Among the many such song texts are "Eretz Zavat Halav Udevash" (Deut. 26:15), "Kol Dodi" (S.o.S. 2:8), and "Usheavtem Mayim" (Is. 12:3). Melodic characteristics of these songs are: (1) Use of similar modes, for example, the Dorian, aeolian, and mixolydian. (2) Modulation to a key a fourth above the original key, which is found also in synagogue song. (3)

Small melodic range, believed by some to be the result of the simple, primitive life the *halutzim* chose to live when they left European civilization. Others are of the opinion that this type of melodic range is due to Oriental influence. (4) Change and experimentation in rhythmic design as well as syncopation reflect the spirit of the country. Fighting songs, marches, and tunes that tell of Jewish resistance also emerged.

A new kind of song appeared after the Six-Day War. Leaning heavily on the aspect of entertainment after weeks of tension, Israelis found that European and American "beat music" became attractive. Texts dealing with daily life became important, and the kibbutz was no longer a source for folk song creativity. Instead, commercial and popular tunes became the vogue. Synagogue song lost its influence, and Oriental music is becoming Westernized. Above all, wars, terrorism, and economic stress had a tremendous effect on folk song development in Israel. Among early song writers to exert influences on folk song creativity were Abraham Zvi IDELSOHN and Joel ENGEL. Other pioneers were Yedidyah ADMON, Emanuel AMIRAN, Paul BEN-HAIM, Alexander Uria BOSCOVICH, Moshe Byk, Yitzhak EDEL, Marc LAVRY, Nahum NARDI, Menashe RAVINA, David Sambursky, Mattityahu Shalem, Yehudah Sharett, Sarah Levy-Tannai, David Zahavi, and Mordechai Zeira. More recent folk song writers are Nira Hen, Amitai Ne'eman, Naomi Shemer, and Emanuel Zamir.

Israeli art music represents a diversity of styles, since the majority of the early composers were not native-born and were trained in foreign schools that had their own traditions. Today, with the increased immigration and numerous settlements of Orientals, it is not clear whether Western-oriented music is the right fare for audiences of these cultures.

Joel Engel and Solomon ROSOWSKY, the earliest composers in Palestine, derived their style of composition from their Eastern European Jewish heritage. In the mid-1930s composers such as Paul Ben-Haim, Oedoen PARTOS, Alexander U. Boscovich, Menahem AVIDOM, and Marc Lavry created music in a folkloristic-Mediterranean idiom within a framework of Western musical tradition. When, in the late 1940s and early 1950s, mass immigration brought Jews from North African countries and Yemen, composers such as Mordecai Seter and Partos found a source of inspiration in the peculiar motives and trills of the ancient melos. Partos, like many young Israeli composers, began to develop a serial technique of composition. Although Boscovich was attracted first to the Eastern-Mediterranean way of expression, he later switched to writing music synthesizing dodecaphonic and Oriental Jewish elements. By 1960 Israel began to keep pace with the avant-garde and with the electronic techniques that were appearing abroad. A significant avant-garde composer was Ami Ma'ayani. Joseph TAL was important in the field of electronic music.

Other composers who played an important role in Israel's art music are Aviassof Bernstein, Bernard Bergel, Israel Brandman, Abraham Daus, Yitzhak Edel, Hanoch JACOBY, Joseph KAMINSKI, Karel Salmon, Erich-Walter STERNBERG, and Joachim STUTSCHEWSKY. To the younger generation belong Gary Bertini, Yeheskiel Braun, Abel Ehrlich, Yehoshua Lakner. Ben-Zion ORGAD, Yizhak Sadai, Noam Sheriff, and Habib Touma. In the short history of the country Israeli composers have made a special place for themselves in the musical life of Israel as well as the world over and have created an original Israeli musical culture. *See* EDUCATION, JEWISH MUSIC; ISRAEL PHILHARMONIC ORCHESTRA; LEAGUE OF COMPOSERS IN ISRAEL.

JACOBI, FREDERICK (1891–1952). Composer, conductor, and teacher. Born in San Francisco, he received a musical education with Paolo Gallico and Rafael Joseffy (piano) and Rubin Goldmark (composition). He continued his studies at the Hochschule für Musik in Berlin under Paul Juon and also studied with Ernest BLOCH. During his career he served at the Metropolitan Opera House in New York City as assistant conductor to Alfred Hertz and Artur Bodanzky (1913–1917), lectured and taught at the University of California at Berkeley, the Juilliard School of Music in New York City, and the Julius Hartt School of Music in Hartford. He composed a large number of works that were performed by leading orchestras. Among Jacobi's works regarded as Jewish in content or inspiration are

Frederick Jacobi.

Sabbath Evening Service (1931), *Six Pieces for the Organ for Use in the Synagogue* (1933), *Three Biblical Narratives for String Quartet and Piano* (1938), and *Hymn* (to a text by Saadiah Gaon, 1942). He is also known for his arrangements of Palestinian folk songs.

JACOBY, HANOCH (1909–   ). Composer, violist, teacher, and conductor. Born in Königsberg, Germany, he studied under Paul Hindemith in Berlin and in 1934 emigrated to Palestine, where he taught composition, violin, and viola at the Palestine Conservatoire of Music in Jerusalem. After 1936 he was active as an organizer and conductor of the radio orchestra Kol Yisrael, and during the War of Liberation he organized and conducted an orchestra for the Tzeva Haganah le-Israel. Jacoby is known for his orchestral works and chamber music, notably *King David's Lyre* (1948), a variation for small orchestra based on an ancient Talmudic legend, and *Capriccio Israélien* (1951), a light symphonic work influenced by, but composed independently of, Israeli folklore. In 1971 he composed his *Partita Concertata* for symphony orchestra, commissioned by the Israel National Arts Council; it was first performed in Israel in 1972 by the ISRAEL PHILHARMONIC ORCHESTRA under the baton of Zubin Mehta.

JAKOB MICHAEL COLLECTION OF JEWISH MUSIC. Music library, formerly housed in New York City, presented in the summer of 1966 to the Jewish National and University Library at the Hebrew University in Jerusalem. It is one of the largest such collections in the world. Its founder, Jakob Michael, an American Jewish philanthropist, gathered together about 10,000 printed works and about 15,000 manuscripts of Jewish music as well as literature on Jewish music from about thirty lands. Phonograph records and tapes are also included in the collection.

JAPHET, ISRAEL MEYER (1818–1892). Choir director, teacher, and grammarian. Born in Kassel, Germany, Japhet served as a choral director and religious teacher in Wolfhagen and Gudensberg, and from 1853 to 1892 he held similar positions in the Orthodox Congregation in Frankfurt am Main. His writings include a translation of the SIDDUR and HAGGADAH into German, with musical supplements (1884); *Shire Yeshurin* (two parts, 1856 and 1864); *Methek Sefathayim* (1861), a Hebrew grammar; *More Hakore* (1896), dealing with the accents of the Bible; and various choral arrangements for the synagogue service.

Pinchos Jassinowsky. [*The History of Hazanuth*, Jewish Ministers Cantors Association of America, New York]

JASSINOWSKY, PINCHOS (1886–1954). Cantor-composer, poet, and teacher. Born near Kiev, Russia, young Pinchos sang as a chorister with Pinchos MINKOWSKY in Kherson. In 1906 Jassinowsky, upon the recommendation of César Cui, was admitted to the St. Petersburg Conservatory, where he was a pupil of Aleksandr Glazunov and Nikolai Sokolov. For a while he served as assistant choir conductor at the St. Petersburg Synagogue. After he graduated from the conservatory in 1915, he gave concerts as a singer in the Scandinavian countries and finally settled in the United States in 1916. He embarked upon a cantorial career, holding positions in St. Louis and Tulsa. In 1920 he was invited to serve the Jewish

Center in New York City, a post he held with great distinction for thirty-four years until his death. He was an instructor of Jewish music at the Teachers Institute of the Rabbi Isaac Elchanan Theological Seminary and later taught HAZZANUT at the Cantorial Workshop there. Jassinowsky contributed numerous articles and essays on Jewish music to journals and periodicals, among which are the following: "Vos Darf a Hazzan Zingen beim Amud?" (1924),[1] "Khorgezang bei di Yiddishe Massn in Amerike" (1929),[2] and "Congregational Singing" (1934).[3] His musical works include liturgical and secular choral settings, anthems, and songs. His *Symphonische Gesängen* (1936), section 5 of which gives a poetic description of Beethoven's Third, Fifth, and Seventh Symphonies, shows his ability as a writer of Yiddish poetry.

[1]*The History of Hazanut*, New York, 1924.
[2]*Dos Yiddishe Lid*, vol. VI.
[3]*Jewish Music*, vol. 1, no. 1.

JEDUTHUN (JEDITHUN). Word of several meanings that appears in the headings of psalms 39, 62, and 77: (1) It refers to the name of a singer in charge of the choir in the time of DAVID.[1] As a Levite of the family of Merari, like HEMAN and ASAPH, Jeduthun was responsible for presiding over the music of the Temple.[2] Psalm 39 utilizes the preposition *le* (to), no doubt a direction for Jeduthun the choirmaster, under whose leadership the psalm was to be sung. Psalms 62 and 77 have the preposition *al* ("concerning," "as regards"), probably denoting a group of singers named after Jeduthun and consisting in part, at least, of his sons or descendants.[3] Furthermore, I Chronicles 15:17−19 makes mention of Ethan, one of a group of Levitical singers, who was appointed to play aloud with cymbals of copper. It is possible that the name Ethan is a variation or a corruption of the phrase [*al*] *yede Ethan* ("[upon] the hands of Ethan," i.e., Ethan being a leader) and that Ethan and Jeduthun refer to the same person.[4] (2) The name of an instrument.[5] (3) A direction for the leader that the psalm be sung in the style of Jeduthun.[6]

[1]Cf. Rashi; David Kimchi, ad loc.
[2]Cf. I Chron. 16:41ff., 25:1ff.; II Chron. 5:12, 29:14, 35:15.
[3]Cf. II Chron. 29:14.
[4]William Smith, *Dictionary of the Bible*, Boston, 1883, vol. II, p. 1223, s.v. *Jeduthun*.
[5]Rashi; Metzudat Tziyon, ad loc.
[6]A Cohen (ed.), *The Psalms*, The Soncino Press, London, 1960, p. 120, note 1.

JEREMIAH SYMPHONY. Leonard Bernstein's Symphony No. 1, in three movements ("Prophecy," "Profanation," and "Lamentation"), first performed on January 28, 1944, by the Pittsburgh Symphony Orchestra. The last movement of this work is a setting of text from the Book of Lamentations (1:1, 2, 3, 4; 4:14, 15; 5:20, 21) and introduces a mezzo-soprano solo to the score. Various idioms of Jewish liturgical melody serve as basic elements in the symphony: (1) the first movement is based on the AMEN response as sung in the liturgy of the three festivals; (2) the opening theme of the second movement is the traditional *Haftarah* chant; (3) the third movement contains fragments of the *Ekhah* chant utilized on Tishah b'Ab (Ninth of Ab).

JERUSALEM OF GOLD. *See* YERUSHALAYIM SHEL ZAHAV.

JEWISH MUSIC FORUM. Group of Jewish musicians, composers, and musicologists organized in New York in 1939 to found a "society for the advancement of Jewish musical culture." Its program consisted of public readings of scholarly papers and of original works by contemporary Jewish composers and general discussions on problems pertaining to Jewish music. Synopses of these papers and music programs were published in its yearly bulletins, the final one of which was Volume 9, for 1949–1955. The organization was dissolved in 1962.

JEWS' HARP. Small instrument (correctly, "jaws' harp") made of brass or iron, basically a horseshoe-shaped frame with a protruding strip of metal fixed within it and bent outward at a right angle; the other end is free. The player's jaws grasp the frame, supported by the pressure against the teeth, and the metal strip is plucked with the finger. The vibrations of the metal strip produce a very low sound, but changing the shape of the mouth, with the cavity of the mouth acting as a resonating chamber, causes the sound to change. The force of the tone is controlled by the player.

The Jews' harp, known during the Middle Ages in Europe primarily as a vagabond's instrument, enjoyed great popularity during the 1800s. It is also called *guimbarde* (Fr.), *Maul-Trommel, Mund-Harmonika,* or *Brummeisen* (Ger.), *nebel yehudi* (Heb.)., and *tromp* (Highlands).

JONAS, ÉMILE (1827–1905). Composer, music director, and teacher. Born in Paris, he received his musical training at the Paris Conservatory. During his lifetime he was professor of solfège at the Paris Conservatory, bandmaster in the Garde Nationale, and music director of the Portuguese Synagogue in Paris. He is known for his numerous operettas and a volume, *Schiroth Israël—Recueil des chants hébraïques anciens et modernes exécutés au temple du rit portugais de Paris* (1854).

JOSHUA. Cantata composed in 1874 by Modest Moussorgsky (Musorgski, 1839–1881) for chorus and orchestra. Of significance is his use of a distinct Jewish melody that sings out in the grief of "Amorea's daughters." The melody, which Moussorgsky probably heard in a small Jewish town, was later engraved on his tombstone.

JUDAISM IN MUSIC (DAS JUDENTUM IN DER MUSIK). Vicious pamphlet, published in 1850 by Richard Wagner (1813–1883), in which he maliciously and falsely attacks composers of Jewish descent and their influence in music (e.g., Mendelssohn and Meyerbeer).

JUDAS MACCABAEUS. George Frederick Handel's twelfth oratorio, written between July 9 and August 11, 1746, in honor of the Duke of Cumberland's victories in Scotland and first performed at Covent Garden on April 1, 1747. Handel suggested the subject to Dr. Thomas Morell, who wrote the libretto, which is based on the Maccabean narrative as given in the First Book of Maccabees and the twelfth book of *Antiquities of the Jews* by Flavius Josephus. Handel himself conducted thirty-eight performances of the oratorio, and its success is said to have been due to the support of the Anglo-Jewish community. Its solos and choruses are still part of the repertory of the concert stage. Favorite selections, especially during the Hanukkah holiday, are "See the Conquering Hero" and "Sound and Alarm."

JUDENTUM IN DER MUSIK, DAS. *See* JUDAISM IN MUSIC.

JUIVE, LA. Opera in five acts by Jacques Halévy with a libretto by Eugène Scribe, first performed in Paris on February 23, 1835. The theme centers around the "Jewess" Rachel, who, having been executed by the order of Cardinal Brogni, turns out to be his own daughter.

KABBALAT SHABBAT. (1) First part (lit. "Welcoming the Sabbath") of the Friday evening service, introduced by the Kabbalists in the sixteenth century in Safed. From ancient times the Sabbath was personified as a bride and accordingly welcomed with rejoicing. The Talmud records various song texts for expressing joyousness as the Sabbath hour approached.[1] Every Friday afternoon six blasts were sounded on the SHOFAR: the first to warn field laborers to desist from their work, the second to direct shopkeepers to close their shops, the third to indicate that it was time to kindle the Sabbath lights, and after an interval the last three to commence the Sabbath.[2] In Safed the Kabbalists welcomed the Sabbath by singing psalms and various greetings to the bride—the Sabbath.[3] The six psalms[4] and the hymn LEKHA DODI in the Ashkenazic rite owe their inclusion in the service to Rabbis Moses Cordovero and Solomon Alkabetz, respectively. (2) Work for cantor (tenor), soprano solo, chorus, and organ (or nine instruments) written during 1966 and 1967 by Paul BEN-HAIM. Commissioned by the National Federation of Temple Youth, an affiliate of the Union of American Hebrew Congregations, the work had its premiere at Philharmonic Hall (now Avery Fisher Hall), Lincoln Center, in New York City, with Abraham Kaplan as conductor.

[1]B.K. 32a, b.
[2]Shab. 35b.
[3]*Tikkuney Shabbat,* Venice, 1640, p. 8a.
[4]Pss. 95–99, 29.

KADDISH. (1) Doxology (lit. "sanctification") written in a mixture of Hebrew and Aramaic and often recited in the synagogue service in various forms after principal sections of the liturgy. It was first recited at the close of a rabbinic discourse; later it was incorporated into the liturgy; and about 1200 it became a mourner's recitation. Its origin is ancient, but its present form probably dates back to Talmudic days. Of utmost importance are the congregational responses "May his great name be blessed forever and ever,"[1] around which the Kaddish developed, and the word AMEN. These responses are generally modeled upon the melodic material of the particular Kaddish itself. Each Kaddish in the liturgy has its particular musical mode or fixed melody, which is closely associated with the section that immediately precedes or follows it. The tunes vary according to the occasion or season, but the text remains the same. On certain holidays (e.g., festivals and High Holy Days) the singing of the text is prolonged in order to give the worshiper time to meditate.

Basically, there are thirteen different musical settings for the Kad-

Figure 22.

dish text. Figure 22 demonstrates these settings (*a* and *b* are for weekday; *c* for Friday evening; *d* for *Shaharit* on Sabbath morning; *e* for *Musaf* on Sabbath morning; *f* for *Kaddish Shalem* on Sabbath or festival; *g* for Sabbath *Minhah; h* for *Ma'ariv (Arvit)* on festivals; *i* for *Tal* and *Geshem; j* for *Ma'ariv* on the High Holy Days; *k* for *Shaharit* on the High Holy Days; *l* for *Musaf* on the High Holy Days; *m* for *Ne'ilah*).

These settings do not, however, include special renderings such as the *Yahrkaddish*[2] chanted at ARVIT on Simhat Torah or after *Hazkarat Neshamot* (the Memorial Service) on the festivals[3] to a cento of phrases from melodies in use throughout the year; a Hassidic setting as chanted at the conclusion of the NE'ILAH service;[4] MINHA Kaddish of Yom Kippur;[5] and the numerous settings found in the various cantorial anthologies.[6] Of special significance are the Kaddish tunes called SCARBOVA, chanted before the MUSAF on the High Holy Days (*see* Fig. *22l*) and for the *Tal* (Dew) and *Geshem* (Rain) prayers on the festivals (*see* Fig. *22i*). Created between the eleventh and fifteenth centuries, the *scarbova* tunes were originally identical and later branched out into two separate melodies. They are chanted with much spirit and devotion, rousing the feelings of the worshipers.

(2) Word used in the title of the classic Yiddish folk song "Reb Levi Yitzhak Berdichev's Kaddish" or "Rebbe's Kaddish" (*see* DIN TORAH MIT GOTT, A). The text of this song ends with the opening phrase of the doxology *Yitgadal veyitkadash sheme rabbah* ("Magnified and sanctified be His great name"). (3) Name of one of the DEUX MÉLODIES HÉBRAÏQUES, for voice and orchestra by Maurice Ravel, based on the traditional chant utilized in the synagogue during the High Holy Days. (4) Symphonic cantata composed in 1921–1922 for tenor, mixed chorus, and orchestra by Alexander Abramovich KREIN. (5) Symphony No. 3 for orchestra, mixed chorus, boys' choir, speaker (woman), and soprano solo by Leonard Bernstein in three movements, first performed on December 10, 1963, in Tel Aviv.

[1]Dan. 2:20.
[2]Cf. Fabian Ogutsch, *Der Frankfurter Kantor*, Frankfurt am Main, 1930, p. 39, no. 106; A. J. Weisgal, *Shirei Hayyim Ve-Emunah*, Baltimore, 1950, pp. 113, 114.
[3]Hanoch ben Avraham, *Reshit Bikkurim*, Frankfurt am Main, 1708.
[4]Abraham M. Bernstein, *Musikalisher Pinkas*, Vilna, 1927, p. 92, no. 240.
[5]Abraham Baer, *Baal T'fillah*, Göteborg, 1877, p. 334, no. 1455.
[6]Cf. "Schluss Kaddisch," *Der Frankfurter Kantor*, pp. 44–47, nos. I–V, and pp. 50, 51; "Kaddisch nach dem Lesen der Torah," in Louis Lewandowski, *Rinnah U'Tfillah*, 1871, p. 62; Kaddish for Yamim Noraim and Kaddish for Yom Kippur Katan, in Salomon Sulzer, *Schir Zion*, c. 1840–1866, pp. 255, no. 341, and p. 423, no. 497.

KADMA (־֨). Conjunctive accent sign, meaning "to precede," placed above the word and used in Biblical CANTILLATION. Designated with the same symbol as the PASHTA, it is recognized because it is not placed on the last letter but on the letter with the vowel. For example, in Genesis 33:10, the word *na* appears two times with the same symbol; the first *na* bears a *pashta*, whereas the second has a *kadma*. In ultimate *(milra)* words, when the last syllable consists of only one letter, the *kadma* is found to the right of the letter (e.g., *vehotzesa* in Numb. 20:8), and the *pashta* is placed on the left (e.g., *ushe'elkha* in Gen. 32:18). When the *kadma* is followed by the AZLA, the two accents are called *kadma-ve'azla*, as it were, "the leader and the goer on" with the melody. The melody is an ascending one.

See also CHIRONOMY; GERESH; TE'AMIM.

KAISER, ALOIS (1840–1908). Cantor-composer born in Szabadka, Hungary (now Subotica, Yugoslavia). Kaiser was apprenticed to Salomon SULZER and received a secular education at the *Realschule*. As cantor, he served communities in Vienna (1859–1863) and in Prague (1863–1866). He emigrated to the United States in 1866, and from that year until his death he officiated at Congregation Oheb Shalom in Baltimore. He held the office of president of the Society of American Cantors and was an honorary member of the Central Conference of American Rabbis. His musical and literary output includes *Zimrat Yah* (1871–1886; in collaboration with others), *Confirmation Hymns* (1873), *Memorial Service for the Day of Atonement* (1879), *Cantata for Simhat Torah* (1890; with William SPARGER), *Souvenir of the Jewish Women's Congress at the World's Columbian Exposition* (1893; with Sparger), and *Union Hymnal* (1st ed., 1897; with Sparger).

KAMINSKI, JOSEPH (1903–   ). Israeli composer and violinist. Born in Odessa, Russia, Kaminski is the son of Abraham Yitzhak Kaminski and Esther Rachel Kaminski, of the well-known family of Yiddish actors. Educated in Warsaw and later at the Berlin Hochschule and Vienna Academy, he returned to Warsaw in 1926. He became the first violinist of the Warsaw Radio Symphony Orchestra and organized the Warsaw Quartet. At the request of Bronislaw Hubermann, he emigrated to Palestine in 1937 and became concertmaster of the ISRAEL PHILHARMONIC ORCHESTRA. Kaminski's works include compositions for solo instruments and orchestra and chamber groups. Among his works that reflect Eastern European Jewish flavor and Oriental coloring are *Legend and Dance* (1939), *Ha'aliyah* (1942), *Israeli Sketches*, and *Variations for English Horn and String Orchestra*.

KAMMERTON. *See* TUNING FORK.

KAPELLE ((KAPELLYE). Yiddish term meaning band or orchestra, from the German *Kapelle*. In *Grove's Dictionary of Music and Musicians*[1] the word *kapella* is defined as "a musical establishment, usually orchestral. The word was formerly applied to the private band of a prince or other magnifico but is now used to denote any band." In Hassidic circles, the band of the "court" of the Mitteler Rebbe (Rabbi Dov Ber)[2] was called the Mitteler Rebbe's Kapelle. Its function, according to his son-in-law the Tzemah Tzedek (Rabbi Menahem Mendl), was to prevent the Rebbe from reaching the state of termination of earthly existence.

See also HASSIDIC SONG.

[1]London, 1898, vol. II, p. 47.
[2]One of the three sons of Shneor Zalman (d. Kislev, 1828).

KARAHOD. Yiddish word of Slavic origin designating a circle dance performed generally in a lively duple or quadruple meter. The dancers (men only) grasp hands, hook arms, or place their hands on each others' shoulders. The Hassidic leader R. Tzvi Elimelek Shapiro of Dynów reputedly said that "the reason Hassidim dance in a circle[1] is that in a circle everyone is equal, there is no upper or lower eschelon."[2] The *karahod* is still danced at Hassidic weddings and festal occasions. *See also* HOPKE; HORA.

[1]Heb. *igul;* Yidd. *rod*, meaning "wheel."
[2]Menashe Unger, *Reb Yisroel Baal-Shem-Tov*, Shulsinger Bros., Inc., New York, 1963, p. 292.

KARLINER, BORUCH (c. 1810–1879). Cantor active in White Russia. He studied with Sender POLATSHIK and was known for having a voice of limited power and range (*see* HAZZAN, VOICELESS) and little general musical knowledge. In spite of these deficiencies he rose to be one of the leading cantors of his time. He and his choristers were itinerant singers and traveled from city to city. During his career he held positions as cantor in Karlin, Russia (thus the name Karliner), his native town, and in nearby Pinsk. Upon a signal from Karliner, his chief singer, Nehemia Bass, introduced a vocal prelude called a SHTEL, a practice of early *hazzanim*. Karliner then continued with spontaneous IMPROVISATION. Many singers apprenticed themselves to him, among them Nisson SPIVAK.

KARNA. Instrument, mentioned in Daniel 3:5, 7, 10, 15, meaning "horn" or "TRUMPET." It is identical with the Hebrew KEREN, which in turn is considered to be the same instrument as the SHOFAR.[1]

> [1]Cf. Ibn-Ezra; Saadiah Gaon, ad loc.

KARNE-FARAH (֜֝). Rare accent mark (lit. "cow's horns") occurring sixteen times in the vocalized text of Scripture and always preceded by the graphic sign YERAH-BEN-YOMO. The two publicly read verses utilizing this symbol are Numbers 35:5 and Esther 7:9; the other verses in which it occurs are Joshua 19:51, II Samuel 4:2, II Kings 10:5, Jeremiah 13:13 and 38:25, Ezekiel 48:21, Ezra 6:9, Nehemiah 1:6, 5:13, 13:5, and 13:15, I Chronicles 28:1, and II Chronicles 24:5 and 35:7. The *karne-farah* graphically resembles the TELISHA-KETANAH combined with the TELISHA-GEDOLAH. It is generally cantillated in this order and has the same respective note groups, but with a slight rhythmical change.[1] William Wickes remarks that this graphic form is a misleading representation, since originally *karne-farah* was known as *pazer gadol* ("great PAZER") and *pazer* had no connection with *telisha*.[2] It is thus evident why some readers cantillate *karne-farah* in the same manner as *pazer*.[3] The introduction of this rare accent by the Masoretes is believed to "mark a *midrash halakha*" (interpretation involving a legal point in Jewish law); that is, this rare accent is used on certain words to call to mind a homiletic interpretation.[4] *See also* TE'AMIM.

> [1]Salomon Rosowsky, *The Cantillation of the Bible*, The Reconstructionist Press, New York, 1957, p. 459.
> [2]*A Treatise on the Accentuation of the Prose Books of the Old Testament*, Clarendon Press, Oxford, 1887, p. 114.
> [3]Abraham Z. Idelsohn, *The Jewish Song Book*, ed. by B. J. Cohon, Publications for Judaism, Cincinnati, 1951, p. 488.
> [4]David Weissberg, "The Rare Accents of the Twenty-one Books," *Jewish Quarterly Review*, vols. LVI, LVII, LVIII, 1966.

KATROS. Plucked string instrument mentioned in the Book of Daniel (3:5, 7, 10, 15), corresponding to the Greek *kithara*, that is, a lyrelike instrument from which the guitar and zither are derived. Saadiah Gaon and Ibn-Ezra identify it with the KINNOR. According to most scholars, it is translated as a "lyre" or "guitar."

A *katros*. [Shaul Shaffer, *Hashir Shebamikdash*, Yefey Nof, Jerusalem]

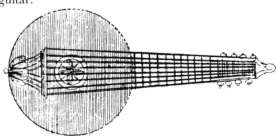

קתרוס

KELIM (sing. *keli*). Idiomatic word (lit. "utensils," "vessels," "instruments") used to describe the sweet, flexible voice of the HAZZAN who chanted the developed RECITATIVE with a distinctly instrumental character. An expression typical of Eastern European Jewry was *der hazzan hot a tei'ere keli* ("the chanter has a splendid organ").[1] Like other Oriental peoples, the Eastern European Jew preferred that the voice of the *hazzan* be a sweet lyric tenor (often with a nasal quality) and that he chant the prayers in a florid manner with characteristically instrumental flourishes. Cantors or singers who attained this lyric quality in their voices were often nicknamed *fidele* (fiddle), *fletele* flute), or *fistelsinger* (Lat. *fistula*, "flute"). They were able to imitate the high-pitched range and flexibility of these instruments, which are so suitable for expressing sweetness, warmth, sentiment, and lyricism, and often moved the heart of the Jew.[2] To the Western Jew this vocal style was alien. One voice placement was desired rather than different ones for each emotional situation. The latter practice prevails currently among Ashkenazic *hazzanim* both in the United States and in Israel. Oriental-Sephardic readers "adorn the melodic line with many delicate turns, inflections of voice, microtonal deviations, and transition into tender falsetto."[3] To the Sephardic Jews of Spanish descent, vocal ability is secondary. Although they sometimes bestow the title of NE'IM ZEMIROT YISRA'EL ("sweet singer of Israel") upon the READER, the stress is upon his pronunciation, enunciation, articulation, and intonation.[4]

Throughout the ages great concern was expressed for the *hazzan*'s voice. Rabbi Jacob MOLIN (known as the Maharil), the forerunner of a whole class of clerical musicians, ruled that *hazzanim* should not remain awake all night in the synagogue on Yom Kippur Eve to read psalms and hymns, for they might thereby weaken their voices.[5] Rabbi Israel Salanter (1810–1883) said: "Rightfully, in accordance with our expression of goodness, the congregation should recite the lengthy *piyyutim* [poems] on High Holy Days so that the Reader can rest briefly."[6] Furthermore, special recitals in which the reader beseeches God to grant him a sweet and strong voice have been included as a preface to the MUSAF service of the High Holy Days and the blessings of *Tal* and *Geshem* of the Pesah and Sukkot festivals.[7] Even in mystical folklore, reference is made to Biblical verses that were chosen to be recited in order to acquire a sweet voice (Ex. 15:1, S.o.S. 1:1) and a strong voice (Gen. 44:18).[8]

[1]Alexander Harkavy, *Complete Dictionary*, Hebrew Publishing Company, New York, 1898, p. 177, s.v. *keli*.

[2]Cf. Rashi, *Ta'an.* 16a, s.v. *neimah.*

[3]Hanoch Avenary, *Studies in the Hebrew, Syrian and Greek Liturgical Recitative*, Israel Music Institute, Tel Aviv, 1963, p. 21.

[4]A. L. Cardoza, *Music of the Sephardim*, Herzl Press, New York, 1960, p. 40.

[5]*Orah Hayyim* 619:6.

[6]*Sefer Hayye Hamusar*, Bnai Berak, 1963, vol. 1, p. 70.

[7]Cf. *Mahzor Kol Bo.*

[8]J. Trachtenberg, *Jewish Magic and Superstition*, Meridian Books, Inc., New York, p. 110.

KEREN. Word, appearing in Joshua 6:5 and I Chronicles 25:5, meaning "horn"; the equivalent is KARNA. R. Yosi considers SHOFAR and *keren* to be one and the same musical instrument.[1] This opinion is shared by modern scholars such as Curt Sachs and Israel Shalita. Joel Brill states that the *shofar* and *hatzotzerah* (*see* TRUMPET) belong to the species of *keren*, a general term for horn.[2]

[1]R.H. 26a.

[2]Preface to Moses Mendelssohn's version of the Psalms.

KEROBAH. (1) Word (from the Hebrew *karob*, "approach") used as the title

Figure 23.

of the person who led the prayers on behalf of the congregation—he would approach the Ark in order to recite the *Amidah* (standing prayer).[1] In the Temple in Jerusalem the priest represented the congregation in offering the sacrifices. When prayer later replaced sacrifices,[2] the duties of the priest were assumed by the lay leader PRECENTOR, who intoned the services and was considered to be the one who approached God and offered a sacrifice. In Midrashic literature the term is synonymous with cantor-poet.[3] (2) Singular form for the series of *piyyutim* (poems) that are inserted during the cantor's repetition of the benedictions of the *Amidah*. The plural form is *kerobot*. According to Bet Joseph 68, the word should be *KeRoBBeTZ*, from the first letters of the words in the verse (ps. 118:15) *kol rinah vi-yeshuah be'ahalay tzadikim*, "the voice of rejoicing and salvation is in the tents of the righteous." Some believe that *kerobbetz* is merely an old French pronunciation of *kerobot*. *Kerobot* insertions became so important in the Ashkenazic rite that sometimes the MAHZOR prayer book was designated *Sefer Kerobot*. The antiquity of the *kerobah* mode was noted by Simeon b. Zemah Duran in the 1400s.[4] Figure 23 gives two examples of the *kerobah* mode (*a* for the Sabbath and festival mornings; *b* for High Holy Days).

[1] Jer. Ber. 3c, bottom; *Midrash Shir Hashirim* 3:10; *Midrash Tehillim*, ps. 19:1.
[2] Hos. 14:3.
[3] Israel Davidson, *Mahzor Yannai*, Bloch Publishing Company, New York, 1919, p. 28, no. 34.
[4] *Magen Avot*, p. 52b.

KING DAVID'S HARP. *See* IMMORTAL PIANO, THE.

KINNOR (pl. *kinnorim, kinnorot*). Lyrelike instrument first mentioned in Genesis 4:21; its invention is ascribed to Jubal, "father" of all musical instruments. In modern Hebrew, *kinnor* means "violin."

In the Septuagint and the Vulgate, the majority of the translations of *kinnor* are, respectively, *kithara* and *cithara* (*see* KATROS), the interpretation probably being a lyre similar to the Greek instrument called *kithara*. The King James Version, as well as numerous other sources, gives "harp" as its meaning, an erroneous translation. According to some scholars *kinnor* is a general term for instruments belonging to the string family.[1] The word *kinnor* may possibly be derived from *kenara* (Syrian) or *kunar* (Arabic-Persian), meaning "lotus," that is, wood from the lotus plant used to make musical instruments. Lake Kinneret in Galilee was named after this instrument because of its lyrelike shape, or perhaps because the inhabitants of the area were proficient in playing or making this instrument.[2] The Talmud inquires, "And why was it called *kinneret*?" The answer is, "Because its fruits are sweet like the music of the *kinnor*."[3] It may thus be deduced that the quality of its tone was sweet and tender.

The strings of the *kinnor*, made of the small intestines of sheep,[4] were drawn across wood, probably cypress[5] or sandalwood.[6] There are

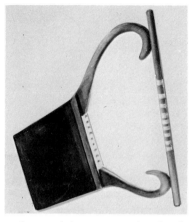

A wooden *kinnor* with nine strings, from an ivory carving (1350–1150 B.C.E.). [Haifa Music Museum and Amli Library]

various opinions concerning its shape and the number of strings: (1) R. Judah states that the *kinnor* in the Sanctuary had seven strings and was identical to the NEBEL.[7] (2) Flavius Josephus asserts that it had ten strings.[8] (3) Ibn-Ezra comments that the *kinnor* had the shape of a candelabrum.[9] (4) Abraham Portaleone describes it as resembling the modern harp and having forty-seven strings. Furthermore, he identifies a phrase in I Chronicles 15:21, *kinnor al-hashminit* (lyre on the eighth), with the octave (*see* AL-HASHMINIT).[10] Others believe that the phrase indicates eight strings. (5) Joel Brill supports the claim of the Vulgate that the shape of the *kinnor* was similar to the Greek letter delta and that the instrument had six strings.[11] (6) Abraham Zvi IDELSOHN asserts that the number of strings of both harps and lyres varied from three to twenty-two.[12]

Producing a sound from stringed instruments with a bow was unknown among ancient civilizations. Josephus records that the *kinnor* was played with a plectrum, a small stick.[13] A modern commentator describes the playing of the *kinnor* in the following manner: the player picks the strings with the fingers of his left hand and strikes them with a so-called plectrum in his right hand.[14] The contradiction in Samuel 16:23, 18:10, 19:9, that DAVID played on the *kinnor* with his hand, is interpreted as meaning that the plectrum was used when the *kinnor* accompanied singing and that plucking with the fingers occurred only when playing did not accompany singing.[15] Others comment that, although the *kinnor* was used for accompaniment, "it could be very eloquent when played alone, with the fingers of both hands sweeping the strings freely."[16]

Since David and the LEVITES were *kinnor* players, it is considered to be the foremost instrument among Jews. It was used in times of joy, in giving praise and thanksgiving to the Almighty.[17] Reference is also made in the Bible to its secular use[18] and to its use in driving away melancholy.[19] The minimum number of *kinnorot* played in the Temple was nine; there was no maximum.[20] During the Babylonian Exile the *kinnor* was silenced as a sign of mourning.[21]

The Talmud relates that a *kinnor* hung over David's bed, and as midnight arrived, a north wind blew upon it and vibrated its strings, thus producing musical sounds. David then awakened and began to study the Torah.[22] *See also* HATZOT.

[1]Marcus M. Kalisch, *An Historical and Critical Commentary on the Old Testament*, Gen., 1858.

[2]Alfred Sendrey and Mildred Norton, *David's Harp*, NAL Books, New York, 1963, pp. 113, 114; *The Babylonian Talmud*, vol. IV, *Megillah*, The Soncino Press, London, 1935–1952, p. 26, no. 2.

[3]Meg. 6a.

[4]Kin, 3:6.

[5]II Sam. 6:5.

[6]I Kings 10:12.

[7]Ar. 13b.

[8]*Antiquities of the Jews*, VII, 12, 3.

[9]Dan. 3:5.

[10]*Shilte ha-Gibborim*, Mantua, 1612, chap. 9.

[11]Preface to Moses Mendelssohn's version of the Psalms.

[12]*Jewish Music*, Tudor Publishing Company, New York, 1944, p. 8.

[13]Ibid.

[14]Carl Heinrich Cornill, *Music in the Old Testament*, The Open Court Publishing Company, Chicago, 1909, p. 10.

[15]Curt Sachs, *The History of Musical Instruments*, W. W. Norton & Company, Inc., New York, 1940, p. 108.

[16]Sendrey and Norton, loc. cit.

[17]Gen. 31:27; I Sam. 16:23; II Chron. 20:28; ps. 33:2.

[18]Isa. 23:16, 5:12.

[19]I Sam. 16:15.

[20]Ar. 13a.

[21]Ps. 137:2.

[22]Ber. 3b.

KINOT (sing. *kinah*). Name given to lamentations, elegies, or dirges chanted over the death of an individual[1] or over a fallen city[2] or land.[3] Rabbinic literature applied the name *kinot* specifically to the Book of Lamentations, ascribed to Jeremiah,[4] the Hebrew title of which is *Megillat Ekhah*.[5] The earliest *kinot* were collected into a separate book about the eighth century. As persecutions and sufferings continued for the Jew, especially in later Middle Ages, the number of *kinot* increased. They are chanted in the syna-

Chanting *kinot* on Tishah b'Ab in a Polish synagogue, from a painting by Leopold Horowitz. [*The Jewish Encyclopedia*, Funk and Wagnalls Company]

Figure 24.

gogue on Tishah b'Ab (Ninth of Ab) in the evening and in the morning after the reading of *Ekhah*. Of special significance are the customs connected with their recitation. The light in the synagogue is dimmed, and the curtain is removed from the Ark. The worshipers remove their shoes and sit like mourners with bowed heads, either on the floor or on upturned book rests or benches. According to the Maharil, the first eighteen *kinot* of the morning, together with the three *kinot* recited in the evening, constitute the nucleus of the lamentations of Tishah b'Ab. Thus these twenty-one lamentations correspond in number to the twenty-one days of mourning (beginning with the Seventeenth Day of Tammuz and ending with the Ninth Day of Ab) and are chanted by the READER; the rest are divided among the prominent members of the congregation. The character of the chant is generally dirgelike and wailing, and the Maharil defined which dynamic levels and modes of mournful expression to use when reciting the different elegies.[6] Figure 24 is the setting by Jacob Samuel MARAGOWSKY for cantor and choir of *Az Bahalokh Yirmiyahu*, an elegy arranged in an alphabetical acrostic by Eleazar Kallir of the seventh century. The last poem, ELI TZIYON, which belongs to the "Zionides" (*Shire Tziyon*), is sung to a fixed traditional tune that has become universal among Ashkenazic Jewry.

[1] II Sam. 1:17.
[2] Ezek. 26:17.
[3] Lamentations.
[4] II Chron. 35:25.
[5] Ber. 57b; B.B. 15a.
[6] *Sefer Maharil, Hilkhot Tishah B'ab*, 49b, 50b.

KIRSCHNER, EMANUEL (1857–1938). Cantor-composer born in Upper Silesia. During his career he was employed in Berlin (1880–1881) and later in Munich (1881–1928). In Munich he was also an instructor of singing at the local academy of music. A devotee of synagogue music, he concentrated on creating compositions utilizing Biblical modes. His magnum opus is his four-volume *Tehilloth Le'el Elyon-Synagogen-Gesänge* for cantor and choir and organ (1897–1926).

KLEZMER (pl. *klezmorim*). Yiddish term, meaning "instrumentalist" (from the Hebrew *kele-zemer*, "musical instruments"). The *klezmer*, an itinerant musician fulfilling the artistic and cultural needs of the Jewish community, appeared in Central, Western, and Eastern Europe toward the end of the

Klezmer bands participating in German Jewish marriage processions in the eighteenth century, from J. C. G. Bodenschatz, *Kirchliche Verfassung*. [*The Jewish Encyclopedia*, Funk and Wagnalls Company]

Figure 25.

Michael Joseph Gusikow.

Middle Ages and continued to function until about the middle of the nineteenth century. His playing was largely improvisatory while accompanying singing (i.e., the BADHAN) and playing dance music at weddings. Musically, he was illiterate, but nevertheless his virtuosity made a strong impact on the musical world. Felix Mendelssohn's letters refer to a distinguished *klezmer*, Michael Joseph Gusikow (1806–1837), a player of the *Strohfiedel* ("straw fiddle").[1]

Although instrumental music was banned from Jewish life after the destruction of the Temple (C.E. 70), it gradually became part of Jewish weddings, special occasions (e.g., dedication of a synagogue or scroll), minor holidays (Hanukkah and Purim), and even KABBALAT SHABBAT (Welcoming the Sabbath) in the synagogue in Prague (between 1594 and 1716). But on Friday evening these musicians ceased to play immediately before the recitation of psalm 92 (*Mizmor Shir Leyom Hashabbat*), at which point the Friday night service officially begins.[2]

Jewish *klezmorim*, instead of non-Jewish musicians, were often preferred at Christian festal occasions because of their artistry, modesty, and sobriety. Eventually governmental authorities imposed heavy taxes and restrictions on them. Nevertheless, *klezmorim* served noblemen and became part of military bands. Their instruments were the *Hackbrett* (dulcimer) and others taken from the cultured tradition: the violin, clarinet, violoncello, flute, trumpet, trombone, and drums. Any combination made up a typical *klezmer* band, which consisted of three to five men. Early "*klezmer* melodies" were notated in Elhanan Henle Kirchhan's *Simhat Hannefesh* (Fürth, 1727; New York, 1926). A typical "*kelzmer* tune" is the notation of the NIGGUN by Abraham Moshe BERNSTEIN entitled "Zeyt Gezund" (*see* Fig. 25).[3]

The appellation *klezmer* was sometimes used in a derogatory manner. Even in Talmudic days the term *letz* ("comedian," "merrymaker") was synonymous with musician.[4] A biography of Leonard Bernstein records that his father did not wish him to become a *klezmer*. Bernstein's father recalled the *klezmer* in Russia as a humble, impoverished person, suffering humiliation, degradation, and poverty.[5] Notwithstanding, *klezmorim* are considered to be the forerunners of numerous Jewish interpretive musicians (viz., violinists and pianists) and as having been important in the development of European art music.

[1] Between 1833 and 1847; Eng. tr. by Lady Wallace, Boston, 1863, pp. 98–99.
[2] David Tzvi Hoffman, *Sefer Melamid Leho'il*, Frankfurt am Main, 1925, pp. 14ff.
[3] Abraham M. Bernstein, *Musikalisher Pinkas*, Vilna, 1927, p. 96, no. 243.
[4] Sanh. 101a.
[5] David Ewen, *Leonard Bernstein*, Bantam Books, Inc., New York, 1960, p. 7.

KOL NIDRE. (1) Aramaic prefatory declaration, meaning "All Vows," recited on Yom Kippur (Day of Atonement) Eve to nullify all vows and oaths. It is difficult to ascertain the date of its composition and its author, but in all probability it existed in the Geonic period (eighth and ninth centuries). Its Ashkenazic musical setting (*see* Fig. 26a), which is an expression of deep

Figure 26a. [Jacob L. Wasilkowsky, *Ma'ariv Chants*, ed. by M. Nulman, Yeshiva University]

religious feeling, became rooted in the people and spread into many countries. The *Kol Nidre* text acquired significance for the Marranos during the Spanish Inquisition, when they recited it secretly on Yom Kippur to renounce their promise to adopt the new religion that had been forced upon them. However, the well-known Ashkenazic melody used today does not date back to the time of the Marranos. It is unknown to Sephardic and Oriental Jews, who recite *Kol Nidre* to a completely different chant (*see* Fig. 26*b*).

The first to mention a fixed *Kol Nidre* tune was Rabbi Mordecai Jaffe (1530–1612). In his rabbinical code, the *Levush* (chap. 619), he approves of the quality of the tune but complains that, in spite of his efforts to correct certain errors in the text, the *hazzanim* (cantors) were "unable to incorporate the changes in the course of their chanting because they are too attached to the old melody which fits the familiar text." Abraham Zvi

IDELSOHN suggests that this "old melody" is the present tune, which developed between the middle of the fifteenth and sixteenth centuries.[1] Furthermore, he states that it was a HAZZAN of southwestern Germany who "voiced the sentiments of the terror-stricken Marranos as they recited the *Kol Nidre*, in a touching tune which expresses the fear, horror, fervent pleading, and stern hope for ultimate salvation."[2] Johanna SPECTOR maintains that the introductory motives of *Kol Nidre* resemble the Babylonian cantillation of *Bereshit bara*. Since it was customary in Babylonia to chant *Bereshit* at the MINHAH service prior to the Day of Atonement and at the NE'ILAH service, its chant was probably adapted for the text of *Kol Nidre*.[3] Other references to a *Kol Nidre* chant or melody are: Yehudai Gaon's introduction of the *Kol Nidre* sung by the *hazzan* in Sura in the eighth century;[4]

Figure 26*b*. [Arno Nadel, *Gemeindeblatt,* Berlin]

method of recitation prescribed by Simhah ben Samuel (d. 1105) in his *Mahzor Vitry:* "The first time he [the *hazzan*] must utter it very softly like one who hesitates to enter the palace of the king to ask a gift of Him whom he fears to approach; the second time he may speak somewhat louder; and the third time more loudly still, as one who is accustomed to dwell at court and to approach his sovereign as a friend"[5] (the cantor and choir usually make it a practice to raise the key and increase the volume of each recital); and the suggestion by Rabbi Jacob MOLIN (the Maharil) that the chanting of the *Kol Nidre* in an improvisatory manner should be prolonged until night in order to enable latecomers to hear it.[6]

The *Kol Nidre* is one of the chants belonging to a corpus of tunes called SCARBOVA or MISSINAI TUNES in the Ashkenazic tradition. The characteristic motives, which are of cantillatory character and of German minnesong origin, permeate the liturgy of the High Holy Days. For example, the well-known introductory motive appears in the *Hamelekh* prayer, and its ending is identical with parts of *Alenu* and *Avot*. It has been suggested that the association of the *Alenu* motive with *Kol Nidre* originated in the twelfth century in Blois, France, where many persecuted Jews died while singing the *Alenu*. Thus the Jews of France and the Rhineland adopted the *Alenu* motive for this most important hour and declaration of the High Festival liturgy—the *Kol Nidre*. Furthermore, its melody, which is triumphant in character, is most fitting as a concluding note.[7]

(2) Concerto (op. 47) for cello and orchestra composed in 1881 by the German composer-conductor Max Bruch (1838–1920). Bruch, in a letter to the musicologist Eduard BIRNBAUM (April 12, 1889), attributes his interest in Jewish traditional tunes (viz., *Kol Nidre*) to his friend Cantor Abraham Jacob Lichtenstein (1806–1880) of Berlin. (3) Opus 39 by Arnold Schönberg (1874–1951), composed in 1938 for speaker, choir, and orchestra. (4) Work for violoncello and piano by Mario CASTELNUOVO-TEDESCO in manuscript form as listed in the *Bibliography of Jewish Music* by Alfred SENDREY.[8] (5) Melody traditionally attached to its rendition, utilized as thematic material by composers who wrote secular art music. In Ludwig van Beethoven's Quartet No. XIV, Opus 131, sixth movement (*Adagio quasi un poco andante*, measures 1–5), there is a remarkable resemblance to the *Kol Nidre* melody. In 1825 Beethoven was asked by the Viennese Hebrew Community to write a cantata on the occasion of the dedication of its house of worship. He did not do it: it was written by Joseph Drechsler. This fact, discovered by Emil BRESLAUR,[9] may be evidence of Beethoven's general acquaintance with Jewish music.[10] The traditional theme is also found in the C Major Symphony by Paul DESSAU.

[1]*Thesaurus of Hebrew-Oriental Melodies*, Leipzig, 1933, vol. VII, p. 34.
[2]*Jewish Liturgy and Its Development*, Henry Holt and Company, Inc., 1932, p. 228.
[3]"The Kol Nidre: At Least 1,200 Years Old," *Jewish Music Notes*, 1955, pp. 3–4.
[4]L. Ginsberg, *Ginse Schechter*, vol. II, p. 120.
[5]Berlin, 1892, p. 388.
[6]*Maharil*, Warsaw, 1874, p. 45b.
[7]B. M. Casper, *Talks on Jewish Prayer*, Jerusalem, 1958, p. 67.
[8]Columbia University Press, New York, 1951, no. 7175.
[9]*Sind originale Synagogen- und Volks-Melodien bei den Juden geschichtlich nachweisbar?*, Leipzig, 1898, p. 35.
[10]Paul Nettl, *Alte jüdische Spielleute und Musiker*, Prague, 1923, p. 43.

KOLAN. *See* TUNING FORK.

KOSAKOFF, REUVEN (1898–   ). Composer, pianist, and teacher. Born into a musical family in New Haven, Conn., he graduated from Yale

Music School and continued his studies at the Juilliard Graduate School in New York. He then went to Berlin, where he furthered his studies in piano with Artur Schnabel. Kosakoff devoted much of his talent and energy to the advancement of Jewish music in the United States. He served on the governing board of the JEWISH MUSIC FORUM and is a member of the executive board of the NATIONAL JEWISH MUSIC COUNCIL. His lecture-papers "Harmony and Jewish Music"[1] and "Problems of the Jewish Instrumental Composer"[2] show his deep concern for Jewish music and the Jewish composer. Included among his compositions in the Jewish idiom are sacred works, works for orchestra, piano pieces, and arrangements of folk songs.

[1]*Jewish Music Forum Bulletin*, December 1946, 1947, pp. 9, 10.
[2]Ibid., December 1943, pp. 25, 26.

Alexander Abramovich Krein.
[Albert Weisser, *The Modern Renaissance of Jewish Music*, Bloch Publishing Company, Inc.]

KREIN, ALEXANDER ABRAMOVICH (1883–1951). Composer and teacher. Krein, a descendant of a musical family, was born in Nizhni Novgorod (Gorki), Russia, where his father, Abraham Krein, was a violinist and known for collecting folk and synagogue melodies. At the age of fourteen, young Alexander was admitted to the Moscow Conservatory, where he took up the violoncello with Glehn, at the same time studying composition privately with Nikolayev and Yavorsky. After graduating in 1908, Krein became an influential musical figure and composer in Russia. His symphonic work *Salome* (1913), performed at the Moscow Symphony concerts, attracted much attention in the Russian musical world. He served as instructor of composition at the Moscow Folk Conservatory (1912–1917) and secretary for modern music in the music section of the Commissariat for Folklore (1918–1920), and in 1922 was appointed a jury member of the State Publishing House. During his friendship with Joel ENGEL he became conscious of a Jewish musical renaissance, and like his contemporaries, he studied and familiarized himself with CANTILLATION and the melodies of the synagogue. Many of his works reflect the structure and ornamental characteristics of these chants and melodies, among the best known being his *Hebrew Sketches* for string quartet and clarinet (op. 12, 1909; op. 13, 1910), KADDISH (1921–1922), and *Ornaments* for voice and piano (1924–1927). His compositions include chamber music, operas, ballets, incidental theater music, pieces for piano, numerous orchestral works, and songs and reflect many different styles and forms.

L

LACHMANN, ISAAK (1838–1900). Cantor-composer, born in Dubno, Russia. He received his early musical training singing as a chorister with Joshua ABRASS and Bezalel SCHULSINGER. Lachmann practiced the profession of cantor in several communities including Berent (Kościerzyna), Stolp (Słupsk), and Lauenburg Lębork). He wrote numerous articles and essays on Jewish music in German periodicals, including, "Die Geschichte, die Rechte und die Pflichten des jüdischen Kantors" (1880),[1] "Unsere synagogale national Musik" (1880),[2] and "Ein Beitrag zur Klärung der Frage über die traditionellen Tonarten" (1888).[3] Constantly striving to uphold and perpetuate the prayer modes and chants, he published a volume for the weekday service entitled *Awaudas Yisroeil* (1899).

[1]*Der Jüdische Kantor,* Bromberg (Bydgoszcz).
[2]Ibid.
[3]*Österreichisch-Ungarische Cantoren Zeitung,* Vienna.

LACHMANN, ROBERT (1892–1939). Berlin-born musicologist known for researching and recording Jewish-Oriental music in Jerusalem. After he received his doctorate at the Berlin University in musicology in 1922, he became librarian of the music division of the Prussian State Library (1927–1933). His research took him to Tripoli, Tunis, and Algiers. In 1935 he emigrated to Palestine and turned to Jewish musicological research, continuing in the tradition of Abraham Zvi IDELSOHN. He soon assumed the role of director of the Archives for Oriental Music in Jerusalem and was instrumental in recording and collecting material from the musical tradition and musical life of the Oriental Jewish communities. He is known for his writings, notably the literary work *Jewish Cantillation and Song on the Isle of Djerba*, published posthumously in Jerusalem (1940).

LADINO SONG. Tunes with Oriental color and adaptations or imitations of Greek-Turkish melodies with a dialect consisting of a mixture of medieval Castilian and Hebrew. Sung by Jews of Judeo-Spanish communities, the songs are of both religious and secular character. They were perpetuated predominantly by women, who sang them to their young children. The earliest texts of Ladino folk song were published by A. Danon in 1896–1897. In 1912 and 1915 Manuel de Lara collected Ladino tunes and texts from the Balkans and North Africa. A popular Ladino song is "La Rosa Enflorese" (The Rose Blooms), the melody of which has also been adapted to the table hymn "Tzur Mishelo" (*see* Fig. 27).

La ro-sa in - flo-re - se en el mez de
mars i mi al - ma se - cu-re -
se de-es-tar en es - te mal es-te-mal.

Figure 27. [Abraham Zvi Idelsohn, *Jewish Music in Its Historical Development*, Holt, Rinehart, and Winston]

LAHAN. Hebrew and Arabic term, meaning "tune," "air," "melody," or "mode," referring to the musical practice, especially among the Sephardim, of adapting a characteristic melodic pattern within a modal scale to other texts. A poem is generally marked *be-lahan;* that is, it is to be sung "to the tune of . . . ," and this principle is sometimes called the *lahan* system. Jewish music theorists of the Middle Ages called it *ne'imah.* Ashkenazic Jews referred to this practice as NIGGUN; Byzantines, as *hirmos;* Syrians, as *rišqolo;* Hindus, as *raga;* Greeks, as *nomos;* Javanese, as *patet.* Adapting a modal tune to a new text goes back to antiquity. *See* AL-HAGITTIT; AL-MAHALAT; CONTRAFACTUM; MAQĀM.

LAMENATZE'AH. Introductory word that appears in the heading of fifty-four psalms and once at the end of Habakkuk 3:19. Various translations are: (1) "for the leader," "to the conductor," or "to the chief musician," that is, instruction regarding the melody or accompaniment of the psalm; (2) "to the conqueror" (from *natze'ah,* meaning "to win"), an interpretation based on the lifelong efforts of King DAVID to conquer evil and establish the ascendancy of virtue through melody and song;[1] (3) "to be performed"; thus the expression *Lamenatze'ah binegginot* (ps. 4:1) means "to be performed on stringed instruments."[2]

[1]R. Menahem Mendel Hager, *Ahavat Shalom, Beshalah.*
[2]Curt Sachs, *The History of Musical Instruments,* W. W. Norton & Company, Inc., New York, 1940, p. 125.

LAVRY, MARC (1903–1967). Composer and conductor. In Israel and musical circles throughout the world, Lavry's name became known for his grasp of all phases of music as well as his prodigious and prolific output of musical works based on Jewish folk material and the folk spirit of Israel. Born into a musical family in Riga, Latvia, he was introduced by his mother to classical music, by his father to HASSIDIC SONG, and by his uncle to CANTILLATION and liturgical music. He studied architecture at the Technical College in Oldenburg and, later, music at the conservatories of Leipzig and Riga. His principal teachers were Aleksandr Glazunov and Hermann Scherchen. Prior to emigrating to Palestine in 1935, he conducted orchestras and groups in Saarbrücken (1927–1928), Munich and Berlin (1927–1932), Riga (1932–1934), and Stockholm (1934–1935). In Israel he conducted the Israel Folk Opera, appeared as guest conductor of the ISRAEL PHILHARMONIC ORCHESTRA and the Haifa Municipal Orchestra, served from 1950 to 1958 as director of the Kol Zion Lagola (the Israeli short-wave station), and organized various musical ensembles. Lavry's music has been widely performed and has been awarded distinguished prizes. His First and Second Symphonies have been dedicated respectively to the heroes of the Warsaw Ghetto and the Israel War of Liberation. His *Dan Hashomer* (1944–1945) was the first Palestinian opera in Hebrew to receive a stage performance in the country, and his *Shir Hashirim* was the first Hebrew oratorio. His works include four symphonies, five symphonic poems, two operas, four oratorios, two cantatas, two piano concertos, a violin concerto, chamber music, theater and ballet music, and many songs.

LEAGUE OF COMPOSERS IN ISRAEL. Organization, with a membership of approximately 150, established in 1953 with the objectives of assisting the composer in his endeavors, encouraging creative talent, and developing in the public a consciousness of original musical creativity. The league may be credited with helping to set the stage for the establishment of other important musical organizations such as the Israel Music Institute, the Israel Music Centre, and the Chamber Ensemble. It sponsors the annual Israel Music Weeks (starting with the eve of Hanukkah), during which concerts of orchestral, chamber, choral, and folk music are presented. During this time the league holds the Samuel Lieberson Prize Contest and publishes a booklet containing recent programs, a bibliography of current works, and essays on Israeli music. During the summer months a composers workshop is held in which composer, performing artist, and audience participate. The league is the Israeli section of the International Society for Contemporary Music (ISCM).

LEHAZKIR. Expression, occurring in psalm headings 38:1 and 70:1, meaning "in remembrance." That the psalm was chanted at the bringing of the *azkarah* (part of the sacrifice) is suggested by a verse in Leviticus 2:2, "and the priest shall make the memorial-part [*azkaratah*] thereof smoke upon the altar."[1] There is an implication that the word means that the psalm was sung at the sacrificial rites of the *azkarah*, and probably indicates a mode of temple song or chant, in a verse in I Chronicles (16:4): "And he appointed certain of the Levites to minister before the ark of the Lord, and to celebrate [*lehazkir*] and to thank and praise the Lord." Ibn-Ezra and R. David Kimchi render the word by "tune" or "melody type" (to which the psalm was set).[2]

[1]Wilhelm Gesenius, *Hebräisches und aramäisches Wörterbuch*, Leipzig, 1921; A. Cohen (ed.), *The Psalms*, The Soncino Press, London, 1960, p. 117.
[2]Loc. cit.

LEKHA DODI. Popular hymn, the title of which, borrowed from the Song of Songs 7:12, means "Come, My Friend." It was composed by the Kabbalist Rabbi Solomon Alkabetz (1505–1584) of Safed in 1529 (according to others, 1571). Signing his name in the form of an acrostic at the beginning of each stanza (SHeLoMoH HaLeVI), he based his theme of welcoming the Sabbath bride on the Talmud, which relates that Rabbi Hanina and Rabbi Yannai robed themselves and exclaimed on Fridays at sunset respectively: "Come and let us go forth to welcome the queen Sabbath" and "Come, O bride, come, O bride!"[1] Serving as the climax of KABBALAT SHABBAT, the hymn was accepted by all Jewish communities and became

*) Diese,wie die 2.Weise werden auch in den sogenannten **3** Wochen (vom 17.Tage in Tamus bis Tischoh B'aw) gesungen.

Figure 28a. [Abraham Baer, *Baal T'fillah*]

a favorite text for *hazzanim* (cantors) and synagogal composers. In Ashkenazic synagogues it is generally chanted in the ADOSHEM MALAKH MODE. In German communities the melody was varied for special Sabbaths (e.g., Shabbat Teshuvah, Sefirah, and Hazon (*see* ELI TZIYON; *see* Fig. 28a). Eastern European *hazzanim* utilize minor for two stanzas, *Mikdash Melekh* and *Lo Tevoshi*. Hassidim most often employ a *niggun* (melody) with active rhythmic patterns or with figures that are strongly accented, and they generally change the melody and mood for the stanza *Lo Tevoshi*. Sephardic congregations chant the hymn to an old Moorish melody (*see* Fig. 28b). A modern setting for full chorus of mixed voices and cantor

LEKAH DODI (Moorish Chant)

Figure 28*b.* [*The Jewish Encyclopedia*, Funk and Wagnalls Company]

with organ accompaniment is Opus 90 by Mario CASTELNUOVO-TEDESCO, *Lecho Dodi*, written in 1936 at the request of the Great Synagogue in Amsterdam (for an *a cappella* male chorus) and first performed in the United States at the Park Avenue Synagogue in 1943.[2]

[1]Shab. 119a.
[2]Cf. *Synagogue Music by Contemporary Composers*, G. Schirmer, Inc., New York, pp. 82-110.

LEONI (YIGDAL). Name of a melody associated in English hymnals with Thomas Olivers's hymn "The God of Abraham, Praise." The tune, originally created by HAZZAN Meyer Leoni (Meier Leon, Myer Lyon, Leon Singer; c. 1740-1800) for the closing hymn "Yigdal" in the Friday evening service, made such a great impression upon the Wesleyan minister Olivers that he decided to write a hymn to its tune and have it sung by Christian congregations. It was adopted about 1770 and enjoyed extraordinary popularity; the thirtieth edition appeared in 1799. The melody somehow found its way into a chorale by Sir Michael Costa (1810-1884),

Figure 29. [Abraham Baer, *Baal T'fillah*]

"O Make a Joyful Noise," in his oratorio *Eli*, written in 1855.[1] Abraham Zvi IDELSOHN traced the "Leoni" tune (*see* Fig. 29) to an old folk motive prevalent in Jewish, Spanish-Basque, and Slavic song.[2] *See* HATIKVAH.

[1]Max Spicker (ed.), G. Schirmer, Inc., New York, pp. 109–110, corale no. 22.
[2]*Thesaurus of Hebrew-Oriental Melodies*, Leipzig, 1932, vol. VI, p. xxv, and vol. VIII, pp. xviii. xix, *Jewish Music*, Tudor Publishing Company, New York, 1944, pp. 220–225.

LERN-STEIGER. Chant (lit. "study mode") used by students when studying the Talmud or reciting parts that have been included in the service, or both. The melody stays close to the tonic triad of the minor (*see* Fig. 30*a*) or major scales (*see* Fig. 30*b*). The frequent repetition of the same tone gives the chant a meditative quality. The major *lern-steiger* closely resembles the sounds produced by the SHOFAR. *See also* ME'INYANA MELODIES.

Figure 30*a*.

Figure 30*b*. [Abraham Baer, *Baal T'fillah*]

LEVENSON, BORIS (1884–1947). Composer and conductor. Born in Bessarabia, he studied at the St. Petersburg Conservatory and came under the tutelage of Glazunov and Rimski-Korsakov. Prior to settling in the United States in 1921, he conducted operatic and symphonic music in St. Petersburg and Moscow. He composed many works, including the following on Jewish subjects: *Palestine; a Hebrew Suite, Hebrew Fantasy*, and *Fantasy on Two Hebrew Themes*. The last-mentioned was presented by the New York Philharmonic Orchestra in 1936. Levenson also made several arrangements for Jewish songs.

LEVENSTEIN (LEVINSOHN), YOEL DAVID. *See* LEWENSOHN, YOEL DAVID.

LEVITES. Descendants of Levi, the third son of Jacob and Leah (Gen. 29:34).

They formed a sacred caste in ancient Israel charged with guarding the Temple service and with supervising its musical activity. A Levite in the time of DAVID was both a porter and musician.[1]

The tribe of Levi was put in charge of the Sanctuary as a reward for its fidelity and zeal in not having shared in the sin of the golden calf.[2] Their very name,[3] which comes from the Hebrew *lavah*, meaning "to join," "be connected," "cling to," is regarded as an omen that they will cleave to the service of the Lord.[4] The Zohar asks: "Why were the Levites selected to sing in the Temple?" And answers: "Because the name Levi means cleaving. The soul of him who heard their singing at once cleaved to God."[5] According to the Talmud their musical performance manifested itself in a divine sound. The Levites started playing and addressed all Israel with high voice *(kol ram):* "You should not read *kol ram*, but *kekolo shel ram*, like the voice of the High One."[6]

In Temple days Levitical schools of music were responsible for vocal and instrumental music education. A training period of five years, beginning at the age of twenty-five, was required for Levitical work;[7] another verse states that Levites were able to begin their duties when they were thirty years old.[8] Thus between the ages of twenty-five and thirty the Levite was devoted to study.[9] A chorister participated in active duty until he was fifty;[10] he was then disqualified from the heavy task of shouldering the various parts of the tabernacle. He was permitted, however, to continue singing.[11] With the decline of his vocal ability the chorister was no longer allowed to serve in the Temple choir.[12]

See also CHOIR; DUKHAN; WUNDERKIND.

[1] I Chron. 15:18, 20, 16:5.
[2] Joseph H. Hertz (ed.). *The Pentateuch and Haftorahs,* London, 1929–1936, Ex. 32:29.
[3] Numb. 18:2, 4.
[4] William Smith, *Dictionary of the Bible,* Boston, 1883, vol. II, p. 1640, s.v. *Levites.*
[5] ii, 19a.
[6] Jer. Sot. VII:2 (21c).
[7] Numb. 8:24.
[8] Numb. 4:47.
[9] Hul. 24a; Tos. Shek. III, 16.
[10] Ibid., 25.
[11] Cf. Rashi, ibid.
[12] Hul. 24a.

LEVY, ISRAEL. See LOVY, ISRAEL.

LEWANDOWSKI, LOUIS (1821–1894). Composer, music director, and teacher who brought a semblance of organization into the music of the Jewish community of Berlin in the nineteenth century. Lewandowski was born in Wreschen (Września), in the province of Poznań. He and his four brothers accompanied their father as "singers" during the services. After his mother's death and because of extreme poverty, he left for Berlin at the age of twelve and became a *singerel* (singer) for Cantor Ascher Lion (1776–1863). With the aid of Alexander Mendeissohn, a cousin of Felix Mendelssohn, Lewandowski received a thorough musical training. He was the first Jew to be admitted to the Berlin Academy of Arts, where he distinguished himself as a musician and studied with Professors Rungenhagen and Grell. In 1844 the Berlin Jewish Community invited him to organize a choir and serve as its director. Lewandowski is first in the history of the synagogue to hold the office of choirmaster, which heretofore was exclusively in the hands of the cantor. His artistic development took an extraordinary turn when Cantor Abraham J. Lichtenstein (1806–1880)

Louis Lewandowski. [*The Jewish Encyclopedia,* Funk and Wagnalls Company]

succeeded Cantor Lion in 1845. Lichtenstein inspired Lewandowski to arrange synagogue song for four-part choral singing. Furthermore, Lewandowski notated cantorial recitatives in a simple and profoundly religious manner so that they could be rendered easily by all. In 1864 he was invited to become choir director of the New Synagogue in Berlin, where he was given the opportunity to create a complete service with ORGAN accompaniment. There he realized his full powers. The culmination of his career came with the publishing of his *Kol Rinnah* (1871), for solo and two-part voice for Sabbath, festivals, and High Holy Days, and his two-volume *Todah Wesimrah* (1876–1882), for four-part choir, congregational singing, and solo pieces with organ accompaniment for the entire yearly cycle. Among his other works are forty psalms for solo, chorus, and organ; symphonies; overtures; cantatas; and songs. During his career Lewandowski was employed as music educator in the Jewish Free School and Jewish Teachers Seminary in Berlin and was responsible for founding the Institute for Aged and Indigent Musicians. He was honored by the Jewish community of Germany as well as by the German government. In 1866 the title of Royal Musical Director was bestowed upon him. Like Salomon SULZER, revered by the community of Vienna, Lewandowski, a generation later, gained a reputation as a respected and influential synagogue composer in Berlin. His music was adopted throughout the world and is still widely used today.

LEWENSOHN (LEVINSOHN, LEVENSTEIN), YOEL DAVID (1816–1850). Cantor and composer, nicknamed *Vilner Ba'alhabessil* ("little householder of Vilna"); sometimes the surname Strashunsky is appended to his name because of his marriage, at the age of thirteen, to the daughter of the wealthy philanthropist Mordecai Strashun. Born into a musical family in Liepāja, Latvia, where his father, Hirsch Bochur Levi, was HAZZAN, Lewensohn showed unusual musical talent at an early age. In 1826 his father was appointed cantor in Vilna, and Lewensohn often chanted parts of the service. He took over his father's post in 1830, the year his father died, and his fame as a cantor and choir leader soon spread throughout Lithuania and Poland. In 1839 he began formal music studies with Stanisław Moniuszko, and in 1841, upon the suggestion of his teacher, he went to Warsaw, leaving his post and family behind. He continued his musical

Yoel David Lewensohn. [*The History of Hazanuth,* Jewish Ministers Cantors Association of America, New York]

studies with Moniuszko and gave several concerts in Poland. In 1849 he severed all ties with his family; his personal life became unhappy, and he was eventually admitted to an asylum, where he died. Lewensohn became a legendary figure. Numerous newspaper articles, a four-act play (by Mark Arnstein), and a movie (featuring Moyshe Oysher) have been produced, based on the fragmentary facts of his life. Several of his compositions were left in manuscript form, three selections of which (nos. 243, 244, 245) have been printed in Volume VIII of the *Thesaurus of Hebrew-Oriental Melodies* by Abraham Zvi IDELSOHN.

LIFSHITZ, SOLOMON (1675–1758). Early German cantor and writer born in Fürth. The son of Cantor Moses Lifshitz (1652–1731), he acquired a thorough training in liturgical music. In addition, he studied at the yeshivah of David Oppenheim in Nikolsburg, where he also learned *shehitah* (the skill of ritual slaughterer). He practiced the profession of *hazzan-shohet* and teacher in a small town and later became *hazzan* in Prague (c. 1709), Frankfurt, and, finally, Metz (1715). He is known for his volume *Te'udat Shelomo* (1718), which records synagogue musical practices of his time, suggests conduct for the cantor, and contains personal reminiscences.

LOEWENSTEIN, HERBERT. *See* AVENARY, HANOCH.

LOVY (LEVY, LOWY), ISRAEL (1773–1832). Cantor-composer who attracted much attention for his phenomenal voice and for his introduction of four-part choral singing into the synagogue of Paris. Born near Danzig, he settled with his family in Glogau, Germany (Głogów, Poland), where he received a Talmudic and secular education. He acquired his early musical experience as a chorister in the choir of Yitzhak Hazzan, cantor of Glogau. Lovy traveled as an itinerant cantor throughout Central Europe and came in contact with some of the leading cantors of his day. In 1799 he settled in Fürth and continued his studies in piano, violin, and violoncello while familiarizing himself with the music of Haydn, Mozart, and other composers. He sang in Fürth and Nürnberg; prior to Lovy, Jews had not been permitted to give public concerts in these cities. During this period, too, he became proficient in Hebrew, French, and Italian and acquired a thorough knowledge of Hebrew literature. After 1806 Lovy left Fürth and served as a cantor in Mayence (Mainz; 1807–1810) and later in Strasbourg (1810–1818). In 1818 Lovy was called to serve the

Jewish community of Paris, and in 1822, when the synagogue on Rue Notre-Dame-de-Nazareth was completed and dedicated, Lovy organized his first four-part choir, for which he composed a service for the entire yearly cycle. Until this time synagogue music had been sung by the traditional HAZZAN-BASS-SINGER trio. (In Paris the spelling of his name was changed from Lowy to Lovy, to conform to French pronunciation.) His tunes and musical creations were popularized throughout Paris and were known in areas as far distant as Poland. After his death his family printed a number of his selections under the title *Chants religieux* (1862). Lovy is not universally regarded as the innovator of four-part singing in the synagogue because, according to Abraham Zvi IDELSOHN, his work was not traditional but was entirely new. Salomon SULZER, Samuel NAUMBOURG, and Louis LEWANDOWSKI are credited with this accomplishment.

Leo Low.

LOW, LEO (1878–1962). Choral director and composer who did much to raise the artistic standards of, and increase interest in, Jewish music in Poland and the United States. Born in Volkovysk, Grodno Province, he received his early musical education singing in the choirs of Cantors Noah Zaludkovski of Lida and Jacob Berman of Białystok. In 1899 he graduated from the Warsaw Conservatory and for the next few years was employed as *Kappelmeister* of a military orchestra and as conductor of Jewish and non-Jewish operettas. From 1902 to 1908 he served as synagogue choir leader in Vilna and Bucharest. In 1908 he became choir director of the Tlomacki Synagogue of Warsaw, where Gershon Sirota served as cantor. During this period, too, Low was appointed conductor of the Hazomir Choral Society and pioneered for the advancement of Jewish folk song and liturgical music. He wrote articles in the local newspapers defending Jewish music as an art form and was supported by such poets as Y. L. Peretz. He was accompanist to Gershon Sirota in the United States in 1913 and to Mordecai Hirschman in 1920. He was instrumental in organizing and conducting various choral groups such as the Choral Society of Paterson, N.J., and the National Workers Farband Choir in New York City. He also held the post of choirmaster at Temple Beth-El of Brooklyn and at other synagogues in the United States. From 1932 to 1938 he lived in Palestine, where he led a choral group called Tel Aviv. Low's musical compositions include many choral settings for the liturgy in the yearly cycle as well as arrangements of Jewish folk songs. His large Jewish secular works include *Rhapsodie Chasidic* (1929) and a cantata,

Rosh Hashanah L'Ilanoth (1940; words by Yehoash). Among his liturgical settings *Uvashofar Gadol* is the most popular. His song "Mir Trogen a Gesang" (based on a Hebrew text, *Zamru Achim*, by Jacob Fichman) became Hazomir's anthem in Warsaw. His arrangements of such folk tunes as "A Dudule" (*see* DUDULE, A) and "A Chasen'dl oif Shabbos" are included in the repertoire of current concert artists.

LÖWENSTAMM, MAX (MORDECAI) G. (1814–1881). Cantor-composer born in Třebíč, Moravia. Löwenstamm studied with Salomon SULZER and served as cantor in Prague (1840–1842), Pest (1842–1847), and Munich 1847–1881). During his lifetime he became popular and strove to improve the musical standards of synagogue song. He wrote many choral compositions for the synagogue. His *S'miroth l'El Chaj-Synagogengesänge* (1882; 2d ed., 1900) was published posthumously by his son Franz Joseph Löwenstamm.

LOWY, ISRAEL. *See* LOVY, ISRAEL.

MA'ARIV. *See* ARVIT.

MA'AVIR SIDRAH. Practice of reviewing the weekly portion or section of the Pentateuch that is read publicly in the synagogue on Sabbath morning. *Ma'avir sidrah* is in compliance with the dictum that "a man should always complete his *parashoth* [*sidrah* and *parashah* are used interchangeably] together with the congregation, reading twice the Hebrew text and once the [Aramaic] Targum . . . for if one completes his *parashoth* together with the congregation, his days and years are prolonged."[1] The individual does this by cantillating the verse twice according to the melody of the TE'AMIM and then chanting in similar cantillatory style the Targum Onkeles (an ancient translation of the Bible into the Aramaic vernacular then spoken by the Jews and ascribed to Onkeles, the Proselyte of the first century). In ancient days every person called up to the Torah (*see* ALIYAH) read his own portion. Probably in order to prepare properly for the public reading, worshipers adopted the custom of reviewing the *sidrah* with its Aramaic translation well in advance.[2] The practice of reviewing the weekly portion may also have resulted from the prolonged service brought about by the universal acceptance of the annual cycle of Torah reading; consequently, the office of METURGEMAN, who translated the Torah reading into the vernacular, was discontinued. Instead, the worshiper was directed to prepare for the service before attending, thus giving rise to the practice of *ma'avir sidrah*.[3] Some say that the time to be *ma'avir sidrah* is early Sabbath morning,[4] whereas others say Friday afternoon, prior to the MINHAH service.[5]

[1]Ber. 8a, b.
[2]Y. Vainstein, *The Cycle of the Jewish Year*, Jerusalem, 1953, pp. 38, 39.
[3]A. E. Millgram, *Jewish Worship*, Jewish Publication Society of America, Philadelphia, 1971, p. 182.
[4]*Kol Bo*, chap. 37; *Rokeach*, chap. 53.
[5]*Shibolei ha-Leket*, chap. 75.

MA'AYANI, AMI (1936–). Israeli-born composer. He studied composition with Paul BEN-HAIM and conducting with Eytan Lustig. In the United States he furthered his musical studies at Columbia University. Ma'ayani is a leading figure in the musical activities of the LEAGUE OF COMPOSERS IN ISRAEL. His compositions won much recognition for him in both Israel and Europe, notably the Engel Prize of the municipality of Tel Aviv in 1960 for his Concerto for Harp and Orchestra. He wrote orchestral works, chamber music, ballet music, and an opera-oratorio. Of note are *Cantillations*, a work for symphony orchestra; *Maqamat*, a solo for harp; *Songs of Solomon*, a work for strings; *Regalim (Festivals)*, a work (1966) for soprano (or tenor) and symphony orchestra; and *Qumran* (1971), a symphonic metaphor.

MAFTIRIM. *See* TOMEKHIM.

MAGEN AVOT MODE. Mode named after the prayer in the Friday evening service that contains the archetype of this mode. One of the three principal modes (*see* ADOSHEM MALAKH MODE and AHAVAH RABBAH MODE) of the synagogue liturgy, the *Magen Avot* has roots in the concluding phrase of each section of the Pentateuch (F E D A—F F G D) and is identical with the aeolian minor scale (D E F G A B♭ C D). According to the Sages, its melody represents a "sweet tune"[1] possibly expressed in the characteristics of hope and thanksgiving, calmness and serenity. Abraham Zvi IDELSOHN regards the *Magen Avot* mode "as an artificial term which was coined as a collective noun for a group of minor modes."[2] Isadore FREED considers the mode relatively "pure" and the hybrids as "combined" modes.[3] In addition to its liturgical usage, it is also closely associated with the LERNSTEIGER and with Jewish folk music. *See also* MODES, SYNAGOGAL.

[1]*Hamanhig*, Berlin, 1855, p. 24.
[2]*Thesaurus of Hebrew-Oriental Melodies*, Leipzig, 1933, vol. VII, p. 23.
[3]*Harmonizing the Jewish Modes*, Hebrew Union College–Jewish Institute of Religion, New York, 1958, p. 44.

MAGREFAH. Type of ORGAN identified with the HYDRAULIS used in the Sanctuary by ancient Israel about the beginning of the Common Era. It consisted of ten holes, each of which produced ten different kinds of sound, the whole capable of producing a hundred different sounds. Its length (or width?) and height were one cubit each; from it protruded a handle that had ten holes. Each hole produced a hundred different sounds; thus the instrument could produce 1,000 kinds of sounds.[1] Its main function was to call the priests and LEVITES to their specific duties. It was shaped like a shovel, with a tone so loud and penetrating that it was heard as far as Jericho.[2] According to Rabbi Abraham ben David,[3] it was called *magrefah*, meaning "spade" or "shovel," for, just as a shovel gathers together all the wheat, so does this instrument join many different tones.[4] When accompaniment was needed, only specific tones were played. However, when the priests and Levites were summoned for Temple duty, all of its tones were sounded. Consequently, the statement in the Mishnah that "one took the shovel and threw it between the porch and the altar," means that all the tones were "thrown out," thereby producing a tremendous noise. When the *magrefah* was used as a noisemaking signal instrument, its handle served as a device for pumping the air for the instrument. When the Mishnah speaks of "throwing" the *magrefah*, the reference is probably to the swinging motion of the handle in the direction between the porch and altar.[5] *Tosafot* comments that there were two species of *magrefot*, one an altar-cleaning implement used like a rake, the other for music making.[6] Other interpretations and translations for *magrefah* are "hand drum" or "kettledrum";[7] "a fork," signifying an instrument so named because of the similarity of the outline of its upright pipes to the prongs of a fork;[8] "a sort of tympanum";[9] and "a signal gong."[10]

[1]Ar. 10b, 11a.
[2]Mish. Tam. III, V, 6.
[3]Talmudic commentator of the twelfth century, known as RABaD.
[4]Commentary of RABaD on Mish. Tam. III.
[5]Joseph Yasser, "The Magrepha of the Herodian Temple: A Five-fold Hypothesis,"

Journal of the American Musicological Society, vol. 13, 1960, pp. 24–42.
[6]Ar. 10b.
[7]A. F. Pfeiffer, *Über die Musik der alten Hebräer*, Erlangen, 1779, p. 52.
[8]John Stainer, *The Music of the Bible*, rev. by F. W. Galpin, London, 1914, p. 120.
[9]Marcus Jastrow, *Dictionary*, London, 1903, vol. II, p. 730, s. v. *magrefah.*
[10]Cf. Herbert Danby's translation of the Mishnah (ibid.), 1933, p. 587, note 10.

MAH-YAFIT. Initial words, meaning "How beautiful art thou" (Song of Songs 7:7), of a table hymn in acrostic form sung on Friday evening. Attributed to Mordecai b. Yitzhak Kimchi (c. 1290), it was sung in Poland to a melody of German origin. Figure 31*a* is Maier Kohn's version (1870); Fig. 31*b* is another version; and Fig. 31*c* is the tune adopted for a German

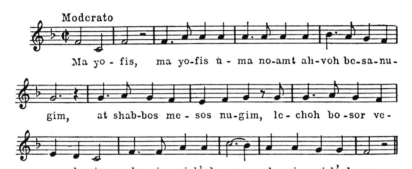

Figure 31*a*. [Abraham Zvi Idelsohn, *Jewish Music in Its Historical Development*, Holt, Rinehart, and Winston]

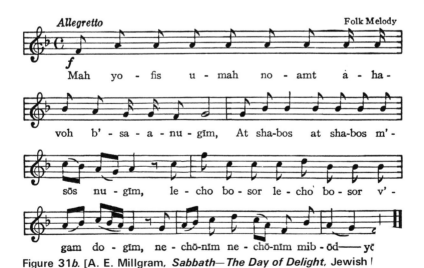

Figure 31*b*. [A. E. Millgram, *Sabbath—The Day of Delight*, Jewish lication Society of America]

Figure 31c.

Sabbath table hymn called "Sei gegrüsst" (Be Greeted) by Rabbi Leopold Stein of Frankfurt, written in the middle of the nineteenth century.[1] In the seventeenth, eighteenth, and nineteenth centuries Polish landowners urged their Jewish tenants to sing the *Majufes* (Judeo-Polish pronunciation) at their wild orgies, accompanied by dances and comical gestures. Concerning the introduction of this Hebraic phrase into the popular melodies of gentile neighbors, Frédéric Chopin wrote "Poor Polish airs! you do not in the least suspect how you will be interlarded with *Majufes.*"[2] Those Jews who flattered their Polish landlords and condescended to sing the *Mah-Yafit* tune were called *Mah-Yafit Yid* or *Mayafisnik.* The appellation eventually referred to all Jews who generally did not maintain their dignity and self-respect as Jews. *See also* ZEMIROT.

[1] Abraham Baer, *Baal T'fillah*, Göteborg, 1877, p. 105, no. 417.
[2] Frederick Niecks, *Frédéric Chopin as Man and Musician*, Novello Ewer and Company, London and New York, 1888, vol. I, p. 183.

MAHARIL. *See* MOLIN, JACOB.

MAHLER-KALKSTEIN, MENAHEM. *See* AVIDOM, MENAHEM.

MAHOL (pl. *meholot*). Term appearing numerous times in Scripture.[1] Scholars differ as to whether it is a dance or a musical instrument used for accompanying the dance. The Septuagint, the Authorized Version, Buber, Kautzsch, and others translate it as "dance," derived from *hul*, meaning "to turn," and thus denoting a kind of "round dance." Ibn-Ezra, Rashi, Mendelssohn, and others believe it to be a musical instrument, such as a pipe (a flute) having holes, from *halal*, "to be pierced or hollow." Reference to an instrument is evident in the Haggadic-Midrashic work *Pirke de-Rabbi Eliezer*, which comments on Exodus 15:20 and asks, "And where did they get *tuppim* and *meholot* in the desert?" Furthermore, it is probable that the flute was utilized especially for dancing since it was a practice to use these two instruments as accompaniment for festivities.[2] The *Shiltay-Haggiborim*[3] describes *mahol* as a cylindrical frame with tinkling metal plates pivoted at intervals in the rim on wires, similar to the tambourine. It is also described as a circular instrument with a bar, passing from one side to the other, to which several loose rings are affixed. The performer holds the instrument by the handle, shakes or waves it, and thus produces

The *mahol* illustrated as a percussion instrument. [Shaul Shaffer, *Hashir Shebamikdash*, Yefey Nof, Jerusalem]

a loud, merry sound. *See also* AL-MAHALAT; EL-HANEHILOT; HALIL.

[1]E.g., Ex. 15:20; Judg. 11:34, 21:21; Jer. 31:4, 13; ps. 150:4.
[2]John Stainer, *The Music of the Bible*, London, 1914, pp. 110, 111.
[3]Chap. 5, pp. 33, 34.

MAHZOR. Word (lit. "astronomical" or "yearly cycle") denoting the prayer book designed for the festival and High Holy Day ritual according to the Ashkenazim. Sephardim refer to the festival prayer book as *mo'adim*, and to the High Holy Day prayer books as Ros-Asana and Kipur books. Originally the term *mahzor* was used for collections of prayers for the entire year. The *mahzor* evolved along with the large number of hymns and religious poems (*see* PIYYUT) composed beginning in the early centuries of the Common Era to about the sixteenth century as the book embodying these creations in addition to the fixed formulas of prayer. In this way it differs from the SIDDUR. Many of these hymns and poems were written by synagogal poets who themselves served as *shelihay tzibbur* (*see* SHELIAH TZIBBUR). For example, the *hazzan-payyetan* (cantor-poet) R. Eleazar Kallir (c. eighth century) reputedly wrote about 200 liturgical poems. The earliest known *mahzor* is *Mahzor Yannai*, a poetical Midrash on the Torah. Some scholars are of the opinion that Yannai flourished about the year 700; others place him about the year 400. The *mahzor* that became the basis for the Ashkenazic ritual was called *Mahzor Vitry* and was written by Simhah ben Samuel (d. 1105) of Vitry, France, a pupil of Rashi. The oldest European *mahzor* is the *Mahzor Romaniya*, also known as *Hazzaniyya shel Romaniya* or *Grigos* (edited by Elijah b. Benjamin Ha-Levi, Venice-Constantinople, 1573–1576). The oldest printed *mahzor* (by Marrano Jews) dates from 1475 and is now housed in the library of the Jewish Theological Seminary in New York City.

MAILAMM. Society founded in 1932 (the name is an acronym formed from the first letters of Makhon Aretz Israeli La-Mada'ey ha Musika) in the United States with chapters in New York City, Los Angeles, and Perth Amboy, N.J., whose objective was to assist the Palestine Institute of Musical Sciences (established 1929). Among its founders were Joseph ACHRON, Abraham Wolf BINDER, Solomon ROSOWSKY, Lazare SAMINSKY, Joseph YASSER, and Miriam Zunser. In 1934 Mailamm became affiliated with the Hebrew University in Jerusalem. In addition to creating a musical bond between Palestine and the Diaspora, the organization undertook to establish a research department and laboratory at the Hebrew University to study Biblical CANTILLATION, to organize the Mailamm Library, and to record sacred chants and folk music. In the United States the society encouraged Jewish creativity in music and presented concerts and lectures by leading composers. Mailamm was dissolved in 1939 and gave rise to the JEWISH MUSIC FORUM.

MAJUFES. *See* MAH-YAFIT.

MAKHELAH. *See* CHOIR.

MAKRI (PROMPTER). One who prompts the BA'AL TOKE'AH by chanting the name of each blast of the SHOFAR on the High Holy Days. The rabbi or an erudite congregant, familiar with the proper procedure, is chosen for this task so that the *ba'al toke'ah* avoids error in the prescribed order and number of sounds. The practice itself goes back to Temple days.[1] The musical notation of the *makri's* declamations can be found in Fig. 38*b*.

[1]Ta'an. 16b.

MANN AUDITORIUM. *See* FREDERICK R. MANN AUDITORIUM.

MAOZ TZUR. Hymn (lit. Fortress Rock) composed for Hanukkah in the thirteenth century by Mordecai ben Isaac Halevy,[1] who wove his name in acrostic form in the initial letters of the five stanzas of the poem. Its melody (*see* Fig. 32*a*) has been a tradition among Western Jewry since the sixteenth century and is also popular among Jews of Eastern Europe and modern Israel. The first part of the melody, known to Jews in Germany by 1450, is an adaptation of an old German folk song, "So weiss ich eins, das mich erfreut, das pluemlein auff preiter heyde" (So now I know one thing which gives me joy, a flower on the wide heath). The middle part of the melody (measures 5–8) is similar to a popular German battle song, "Benzenauer," which was sung in 1504. The folk song and the battle song, according to Abraham Zvi IDELSOHN, were fused into one and adapted for "Maoz Tzur." The opening bars of the melody were adapted by Martin Luther for the opening of his church chorale "Nun freut euch, lieben Christen g'mein" (Now rejoice all you dear Christians together). Johann Sebastian Bach also wrote a four-part setting of the same chorale.[2] Hanoch AVENARY found that the opening phrase of "Maoz Tzur" can be found in several fifteenth- and sixteenth-century *cantionales* in Central Europe. It was a common practice in church music, especially Protestant chorales, to adapt German folk song, and Luther probably heard the tune in Bohemian countries.[3] The tune was also adapted and printed for the first time in London (1815) by Isaac Nathan to the poem "On Jordan's Banks" from Lord Byron's *Hebrew Melodies* (*see* HEBREW MELODY). Another well-known melody associated with "Maoz Tzur" is the one set by Benedetto Marcello (1686–1739), identified as *Ebrei tedeschi* in his ESTRO POETICO-ARMONICO (Venice, 1724–1727) and sung in the seventeenth and eighteenth centuries by Jews of German origin who settled in Italy (*see* Fig. 32*b*).

Figure 32*a*.

Mo - oz tzur y' - shu - o - si____ l' - cho - no - e l'- sha -
ti - kon bes t' - fi - lo - si____ v' - shom - to - do n'- za -

be - ach l'- es to - chin mat - be - ach mi -
be - ach

tzor____ ham - na - be____ ach oz - eg - mor b' -

shir miz - mor cha - nu - kas___ ha - miz - be - ach

Figure 32b.

The earlier, so-called traditional "Maoz Tzur" found its way into the daily and supplementary prayers recited during Hanukkah, namely, in the ADON OLAM hymn,[4] *Hodu* and *Ana* of *Hallel*,[5] the blessings for the kindling of the candles,[6] *Hanerot Hallalu*,[7] *Bime Matisyahu*,[8] and *Yahrkaddish* recited on Simhat Torah.[9] It is generally referred to in these settings as ALTE MELODIE.

[1]Perhaps the same as the author of MAH-YAFIT.
[2]Cf. *Johann Sebastian Bach, 371, Four-Part Chorales*, Associated Music Publishers, New York, p. 82, no. 183.
[3]"Neimah Maos-Tzur," *Tatzlil*, Haifa, 1967, pp. 125–128.
[4]Cf. Fabian Ogutsch, *Der Frankfurter Kantor*, Frankfurt am Main, 1930, p. 102.
[5]Cf. Abraham Baer, *Baal T'fillah*, Göteborg, 1877, p. 53, no. 171; Hirsch Weintraub, *Schire Beth Hashem*, Leipzig, 1901, part 1, p. 53, no. 63.
[6]Baer, op. cit., p. 57, no. 187:3.W.
[7]Cf. Aaron Friedmann, *Schir Lisch'laumau*, Berlin, 1901, p. 61, no. 84.·
[8]Baer, op. cit., pp. 133–134, no. 568.
[9]Cf. Ogutsch, op. cit., p. 39, no. 106; A. J. Weisgal, *Shirei Hayyim Ve-Emunah*, Baltimore, 1950, p. 113.

MAPAKH (⌐). Accent sign meaning "reversed," found in the printed verses of the Bible. Its name is probably derived from the shape of an "inverted" SHOFAR, and thus the accent mark is sometimes called *shofar hafukh* or *mehupakh*. Its musical declamation is described as *yored ve'oleh vegam mitaleh* (descending and then ascending);[1] hence the name mirrors the melody. Having the same appearance as the YETIV, it differs in that it follows the vowel sign of the letter and is placed on the accented syllable of a word, on its last or penultimate syllable. It is a conjunctive (*see* CONJUNCTIVES) sign and is followed by a PASHTA (e.g., Gen. 1:5). *See also* TE'AMIM.

[1]Aaron ben Asher, *Dikduke ha-Te'amim*, ed. by S. Baer and H. L. Strack, Leipzig, 1879, p. 19.
[2]William Wickes, *A Treatise on the Accentuation of the Prose Books of the Old Testament*, Clarendon Press, Oxford, 1887, p. 24.

MAQĀM (pl. *maqamât*). Term originally designating the stage or rostrum set apart for singers who performed before the caliph. The term *maqām* designates a tune based on a "melody type," or a melodic pattern abstracted from the modal melody. Each *maqām* is authoritative and tradition-bound. The singer may use embellishments but may never deviate from the modal pattern of melody, characterized by certain turns, moods, and pitches in the Oriental system of *maqamât*. Israel NAJARA is said to have arranged his DIWAN (songbook) according to twelve *maqamât*. For a thorough exposition of the *maqamât see* the *Thesaurus of Hebrew-Oriental Melodies* by Abraham Zvi IDELSOHN (vol. IV, introduction to chap. 4). *See also* LAHAN; NIGGUN.

Jacob Samuel Maragowsky.

MARAGOWSKY, JACOB SAMUEL (1856–1943). Eastern European cantor-composer and choral director popularly called Zeidel Rovner. Zeidel is the diminutive for the Yiddish *zeida,* meaning "grandfather" (for whom he was nicknamed), and Rovner is for the city of Rovno, Russia, where he was greatly admired. Born in Radomysl, the son of a merchant, he displayed a gift for singing and appeared at Hassidic gatherings. After his father's death his mother wanted him to become a rabbi. When the Hassidic rabbi of Makaryev, Yaakov Yitzhak Twersky, heard Zeidel sing, he was greatly impressed. Although the boy was only seventeen years old, the rabbi ordered him to lead the congregation in prayer during the High Holy Days. Despite his unwillingness to serve as a cantor, Maragowsky led the High Holy Day services for five consecutive years in Kiev; during the remainder of the year he was busily engaged as a merchant. The rabbi later persuaded him to give up the business world to devote full time to the cantorate. He studied for a short time in Kiev with the violinist Aaron Moshe Padhutzer. Even though he had very little formal musical schooling, he achieved great fame as a cantor-composer and conductor. In 1881 he was appointed cantor in the city of Zaslavl. Subsequently he occupied positions in Rovno (1882–1884), Kishinev (1884–1896), Berdichev (1896–1903). London (1903–1904), and Lemberg (Lvov; 1904–1911); in 1911 he returned to Rovno, where he served for three years. In 1914 he emigrated to the United States and officiated mainly on holidays in New York City. He wrote voluminously. Among his published compositions are *Tisborach* (1874), *Haleluyah* (1897), *Uhawti* (1899), *Halelu*, and *Kinos* (1922). Several of these works, as well as other, unpublished compositions, were written for chorus and orchestra and intended to be performed at concerts featuring liturgical music. His works are still widely performed; the congregational setting of *Beh Ana,*[1] attributed to him, has become a favorite the world over. Many manuscripts of his compositions are housed at the Cantorial Training Institute library at Yeshiva University.

[1]Macy Nulman, *Sabbath Chants,* Yeshiva University, New York, 1959, p. 30.

MARKOF. Musical term mentioned in Mishnah Kelim XV:6 and XVI:7. Several meanings are given: (1) a musical instrument made of cedarwood;[1] (2) a wooden musical toy horse;[2] (3) "a musical instrument made stationary" (comp. *arkof*) or an instrument used for accompaniment of songs;[3] (4) the bridge on any of the string instruments (mod. Heb.).[4]

[1]Obadiah Bertinoro, loc. cit.
[2]*The Babylonian Talmud, Seder Tohoroth, The Mishnahs*, The Soncino Press, London, 1935–1952, pp. 76, 79.
[3]Marcus Jastrow, *Dictionary*, London, 1903, vol. II, p. 844, s.v. *markof*.
[4]David Ettinger, *Hebrew Pictorial Dictionary*, Dvir Publishers, Tel Aviv, 1953, pp. 164–165.

MARSCHALLIK. Term used in the Middle Ages for the wedding jester to whom the role of master of ceremonies was entrusted. In Nathan (Nata) Hannover's dictionary the word *marshallis* is rendered *buffon, buffone,* and *scurra* (Lat.).[1] Other duties probably included improvising wedding songs, often in verse or rhymed lines. The term has no connection with the Hebrew *mashal* ("proverb" or "anecdote") and is derived from the old German *marschalk* or *marshall* ("highest royal servant"). In all probability the term was taken over for the Jewish master of ceremonies and the diminutive ending was added for a satirical twist.[2] With the various governmental edicts and decrees limiting expenditures for the Jewish wedding and reducing it to a family affair rather than a community festivity, the BADHAN succeeded the *marschallik* in the seventeenth century and assumed some of his functions.[3]

[1]*Safah Berurah*, Prague, 1660.
[2]Israel Abrahams, *Jewish Life in the Middle Ages*, Atheneum Publishers, New York, 1969, p. 198; *The Jewish Encyclopedia*, vol. II, p. 427; *The Universal Jewish Encyclopedia*, vol. 7, p. 379.
[3]Philip and Hanna Goodman, *The History of Jewish Marriage*, Jewish Publication Society of America, Philadelphia, 1965, pp. 106, 107.

MASHROKITA. Musical instrument mentioned in Daniel 3:5, 7, 10, 15, designating a wind instrument in the form of a pipe, at times made up of a great number of pipes.[1] The word can be traced to the Hebrew verb *sharak*, "to hiss" or "to whistle." It has been described by different writers as: (1) syrinx (panpipe),[2] (2) flute,[3] (3) double flute,[4] (4) UGAB,[5] (5) double oboe.[6] In modern Hebrew, the word *mashrokit* signifies a whistle.[7] *See also* SHARKUKITAH.

[1]According to the author of *Shiltay-Haggiborim*.
[2]First by Greek translators; later, by A. F. Pfeiffer, J. N. Forkel, and Wilhelm Nowack.
[3]K.J.V.; Vulgate; John Wycliffe.
[4]A. W. Ambros, *Musikgeschichte*, Breslau, 1862–1887, vol. I, p. 209.
[5]Johann Jahn, *Biblical Archaeology*, New York, 1853, p. 101.
[6]Curt Sachs, *The History of Musical Instruments*, W. W. Norton & Company, New York, 1940, p. 83.
[7]David Ettinger, *Hebrew Pictorial Dictionary*, Dvir Publishers, Tel Aviv, 1953, pp. 164–166, no. 21.

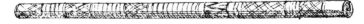

מ שׁ ר ו ק י ת א

A *mashrokita.* [Shaul Shaffer, *Hashir Shebamikdash*, Yefey Nof, Jerusalem]

MASKHIL. Word, the meaning of which is obscure, that appears in the title of thirteen psalms[1] and once in the text itself.[2] Biblical commentators have conjectured that it is: (1) A musical term denoting a melody requiring great skill in its execution. This interpretation is supported by a phrase appearing in psalm 47:8, "Sing ye praises in a skillful song."[3] (2) A direction to the singers indicating the mode in which to sing.[4] (3) "Instruction," as in psalm 32:8 (*askhilkha*), "I will instruct thee." In the margin of the Authorized Version "to give instruction" and "giving instruction" are used. (4) "A meditation," from *haskhel*, "to reason," "meditate";[5] (5) "wise" (Job 22:2), "prudent" (Prov. 19:14), "expert" (Jer. 30:9), and "skillful" (Dan. 1:4).[6]

[1]Pss. 32, 42, 44, 45, 52–55, 74, 78, 88, 89, 142.
[2]Ps. 47:8.
[3]*Metzudat David*, ad loc.; A. Cohen (ed.), *The Psalms*, The Soncino Press, London, 1960, p. 92, footnote 1.
[4]Compare *maskhil* with other musical terms alluded to in psalm headings; e.g., ps. 38:1.
[5]Eric Werner, "Music in the Bible," *The Interpreter's Dictionary of the Bible*, Abingdon Press, Nashville, Tenn., 1962, p. 459.
[6]Cf. A. V.

MATHIL. Officiant (lit. "beginner") who chants the beginning of the service, that is, the *Berakhot* (Blessings) and *Pesukay Dezimrah* (Verses of Song) on Sabbath and holidays. Usually a layman of the congregation who is proficient in the texts and melodies is chosen to serve in this capacity. He may continue chanting the SHAHARIT service proper, or he may be relieved by a BA'AL SHAHARIT.

MATZLAYL. *See* TUNING FORK.

MÉDITATION HÉBRAÏQUE. Work for cello and piano composed in 1925 by Ernest BLOCH.

MEGILLOT, THE FIVE. Name (lit. "the five scrolls") given to a group of scrolls that are chanted in the synagogue during five different seasons, as follows: Song of Songs on Passover, Ruth on the Feast of Weeks, Lamentations on the fast of the Ninth of Ab, Ecclesiastes on the Feast of Tabernacles, and Esther on Purim. In the Ashkenazic tradition the CANTILLATION for the reading of the scrolls of Song of Songs, Ruth, and Ecclesiastes is the same. Lamentations and Esther each has its own musical system of interpretation of the TE'AMIM.[1] Of the five scrolls, Esther is the only one actually called *Megillah*.[2] It is read by the READER in a colorful manner in order to arouse the gratitude of the worshipers for the miracles wrought by God. Distinctive melodies, changes in tempo and dynamic levels, and various stylistic directions are used for certain verses in order to highlight the events of the *Megillah*.[3] The GROGGER is sounded at every mention of Haman's name.

[1]Cf. Abraham Z. Idelsohn, *The Jewish Song Book*, ed. by B. J. Cohon, Publications for Judaism, Cincinnati, 1951, pp. 500–503.
[2]B.B. 14b.
[3]Cf. "Musikalische Traditionen bei Vorlesung der Megillah," *Allgemeine Zeitung des Judentums*, Berlin, 1891; A. Weil, *A Practical Manual on the Scroll of Esther*, London, 1961.

MEHUTANIM TANZ. *See* FRAILACH.

ME'INYANA MELODIES. Term (lit. "from the same subject or theme") used by early *hazzanim* (cantors) of Oriental and Ashkenazic origin for the procedure of chanting a preceding or following passage, or both, of a major prayer in the same mode of that major prayer. For example, in the Yemenite tradition, on Friday evening psalm 92 is sung in the Mishnah mode (*see* Fig. 33a) because it follows immediately after a section of the Mishnah. In similar manner, psalm 150, which serves as an introduction to the ARVIT service on the first evening of Passover, is also sung in this mode since the HAGGADAH is chanted in the Mishnah mode.[1] The term is also applied to

Figure 33a.

Figure 33b.

the practice of introducing into a liturgical recital a bit of the melody from the traditional music of another service that has a similar textual meaning or sentiment. For instance, during the Three Weeks, representative themes from *Beleyl Ze Yivkeyun* (*see* KINOT) were used for *Velirushalayim Irkha* of the *Amidah* (standing prayer; *see* Fig. 33b).

The term *me'inyana* probably originated in rabbinic literature, namely the Talmud,[2] and in the *Baraita d'Rabbi Ishmael*, which constitutes the introduction to the Sifra (the Talmudic exposition of the Scripture).[3]

[1]Abraham Z. Idelsohn, *Thesaurus of Hebrew-Oriental Melodies*, 1925, vol. I, pp. 17, 30.
[2]San. 86a.
[3]No. 12.

MEKONENET. Title (from *kinah*, meaning "lamentation" or "dirge") bestowed upon a professional dirge singer, or "mourning woman." The mere fact that the verses say ". . . send for the women skilled in lament. . . ."[1] and . . . "teach your daughters wailing, and every one her neighbor lamentation"[2] attests to the need for both training and skill in this profession.[3] In ancient days a husband had to provide for all expenses of his wife's funeral, and even the poorest man in Israel had to hire at least two flute players and one wailing woman for the funeral.[4] If they were unavailable locally, they had to be brought from other places.[5]

The characteristics of the *mekonenet*'s songs were (1) a range from a dirge or wail to an elegy; (2) use of hand clapping; (3) RESPONSORIAL and unison singing; and (4) accompaniment of drums or clappers.[6] Eventually the *hesped* (eulogy or funeral oration) became the established custom at funerals in place of the mourning woman's chants and instrument playing.[7]

[1]Jer. 9:16.
[2]Ibid., 9:19.
[3]Amos 5:16.
[4]Mish., Ket. IV:4; Ket. 48a.
[5]Jer. Ber. III:1, 5b.
[6]M.K. 28b; Kel. XV:6, XVI:7.
[7]Ber. 62a.

MELISMA. Style used in setting the text of a chant with numerous notes to one syllable, as opposed to a syllabic treatment in which only one note is set to a syllable. The melisma differs, too, from COLORATURA in being expressive in character, whereas coloratura is a virtuoso-like device. In Hebrew melisma is referred to as *leha'arikh be-niggun* ("to extend the tune") or *limeshokh niggunim* or *niggunim arukhim* (long tunes). Melismata are found in such prayers as *Avot, Vehakohanim,* and KOL NIDRE for the High Holy Days.

Rabbi Jacob Joseph (d. 1769) of Polonnoye comments that the HAZZAN at one time prolonged the service with melismatic treatment of the text in order to have proper *kavanah* (inner disposition or concentration) for certain words and letters in the texts.[1] Earlier, Rabbi Jacob MOLIN (the Maharil) was known for extending the tune at the word *atah* ("Thou") in order to give a marked melodic expression of *kavanah*.[2] The ornamental melisma is characteristic of Oriental and Eastern European HAZZANUT and mystical prayer song. In Western *hazzanut* a syllabic treatment is generally employed.

[1]*Toledot Ya'akob Yosef, Parshat Tzav,* Międzybórz and Korets, 1780.
[2]*Sefer Maharil,* 56a.

MENA'ANE'IM. Term (lit. "shaken instrument" or "rattler," from the root *nu'a,* "to shake" or "to quiver") mentioned only once, in II Samuel 6:5, describing the transport of the Ark by DAVID to Jerusalem. The Vulgate and modern translators render it by sistra (pl.). The *sistrum* (sing.), a kind of metal rattle, consisted of a horseshoe-shaped frame attached to a handle with crossbars upon which hung metallic rings that produced tones when the instrument was shaken. Recent archaeological excavations have indicated that sistra existed in such places as Ur, Kish, and Sumer. *See also* REVI'IT.

An iron *sistrum* of the Byzantine period. The handle is missing. [Haifa Music Museum and Amli Library]

MENAGGEN. (1) Minstrel; in Biblical days an appellation for a musician who played a stringed instrument. A well-known minstrel was King DAVID, who played for Saul.[1] (2) In modern usage the term is loosely applied to musicians who are scholarly in the field of music and music composition. *See also* NIGGUN.

[1]I. Sam. 16:16, 18:10, 19:9.

MERKHA (⌐). Accent mark, meaning "lengthener," that occurs in the printed Bible. It is so named because it "lengthens," or prolongs, the word to the DISJUNCTIVE in the verse, which is usually a TIPKHA or SILLUK (e.g., Gen. 1:1). The absence of a feeling of repose during CANTILLATION is felt in the melody proper. According to AARON BEN ASHER, the *merkha* is joined to its partner with a long tone.[1] *See also* TE'AMIM.

[1]*Dikduke ha-Te'amim*, ed. by S. Baer and H. L. Strack, Leipzig, 1879, p. 19.

MERKHA-KEFULAH (⌐). Rare accent mark, translated as a "double MERKHA," that appears in the printed text of Scripture. It is found fourteen times in the twenty-one books: eight times in verses not cantillated at public readings (I Kings 10:3, 20:29; Ezek. 14:4; Hab. 1:3; Ezra 7:25; Neh. 3:38; and II Chron. 9:2, 20:30) and six times in portions read in the service of the synagogue (Gen. 27:25; Ex. 5:15; Lev. 10:1; Numb. 14:3, 32:42, and in the *Haftarah,* a Prophetical reading from Zech. 3:2 cantillated on Sabbath Beha'alotkha and Sabbath Hanukkah). This sign is invariably preceded by a DARGA and followed by a TIPKHA. William Wickes describes it "as a reduced or impoverished TEVIR" and quotes Kimchi, although disagreeing with him, that "its melody was like a *tevir.*"[1] According to Solomon ROSOWSKY the musical rendering for the *merkha-kefulah* and *tevir* are not the same.[2] Recent research has revealed that, whenever this rare accent was used, the Masoretes were generally alluding to a Haggadic tale found in the Midrash.[3] *See also* TE'AMIM.

[1]*A Treatise on the Accentuation of the Prose Books of the Old Testament,* Clarendon Press, Oxford, 1887, pp. 25, 91, 92.
[2]*The Cantillation of the Bible,* The Reconstructionist Press, New York, 1957, pp. 351, 363.
[3]Cf. David Weissberg, "The Rare Accents of the Twenty-one Books," *Jewish Quarterly Review,* vols. LVI, LVII, LVIII, 1966.

MESAYIM. *See* TOMEKHIM.

MESHORERIM (sing. *meshorer*). Hebrew word meaning "singers." (1) In Biblical days, a term reserved for the LEVITES, who were privileged to participate as Temple singers and instrumentalists. In I Chronicles 15:16–22 a detailed account is given of the various participants and groups under the leadership of HEMAN, ASAPH, and JEDUTHUN. Each leader was responsible for a large number of Levitical musicians; for example, Asaph's choristers numbered 128.[1] The chronicler describing the inauguration of the Temple of Jerusalem by King Solomon tells that special robes were worn by the Temple *meshorer.*[2] In addition, numerous non-Levitical singers and musicians participated in the singing and playing.[3] (2) A group constituting a synagogue choir that originated with the HAZZAN-BASS-SINGER trio of the seventeenth century and existed in Eastern Europe until the latter part of the nineteenth century. To become a *meshorer,* one had to possess certain qualities such as a good voice and a retentive memory. Since Jewish music was not yet written down, the HAZZAN, who was usually illiterate, became dependent upon the memory of the singers for remembering tunes or obtaining new ones. A *meshorer* who had accumulated a large repertoire was much sought after. However, as soon as the *hazzan* learned and incorporated these tunes into his own repertoire, the *meshorer* was often dismissed. *Meshorerim* received money when they sang at weddings and at various holidays throughout the year. They were usually fed by members of the community, visiting a different family on different days of the week. Eliakum ZUNSER writes in his autobiography that in 1853 in the city of Bobruisk, Russia, *Hazzan* Reb Joel I. Humener engaged him to sing as a *meshorer* for the High Holy Days. As payment he received 2 rubles, board at the house of the president of the synagogue, and permission to sleep regularly on a bench in the synagogue.[4] A noted *meshorer* in Jewish life was Shabbethai Bass (1641–1718), author of *Sifte Yeshenim* (1680), who was engaged in the Altneuschule of Prague. A chorister who excelled and eventually became a *hazzan* himself was dignified with the appellation *hameshorer hagadol* ("the great singer"). In his collection of synagogue song manuscripts (1791) Aaron BEER refers to Juda Elias of Hannover and R. Moshe Pan (Peine) of Hildesheim by this designation. Rabbis often complained bitterly about the unseemly personal behavior of *meshorerim* and their improper manner of singing synagogue prayers.[5] In Sephardic congregations the *meshorer* has never had an important function, for the *hazzan* leads the congregation, which participates throughout the reading of the service.

[1]Ezra 2:41.
[2]II Chron. 5:12.
[3]I Chron. 13:8, 15:28.
[4]"How I Wrote My Songs," in L. W. Schwartz (ed.), *Memoirs of My People,* Jewish Publication Society of America, Philadelphia, 1945, p. 221.
[5]Cf. Rabbi Isaiah Horowitz, *Shnei Luhot ha-Brit,* Amsterdam, 1698, p. 253b; *The Jewish Encyclopedia,* vol. IV, p. 41, vol. VI, p. 286.

METURGEMAN (TURGEMAN, METURGAM). Officiant (lit. "interpreter" or "translator") who translates the Hebrew Scripture into the vernacular. During the fifth century B.C.E. religious instruction was conducted by LEVITES.[1] With the cessation of the Levites as teachers, and with Hebrew less understood by the masses (exact time unknown), the office of *meturgeman* was instituted. By the first century in Palestine it was customary for the public reading of the Pentateuch in Hebrew by the READER to be followed by a translation by the *meturgeman* in Aramaic. The Pentateuchal lesson was translated verse by verse; the Prophets, three verses at a time. The *meturgeman* stood near the reader, who cantillated Scripture according to the Masoretic accents,[2] and translated the text orally into the vernacular.[3] The *meturgeman* was forbidden to raise his voice higher than that of the reader. Conversely, if the *meturgeman* was unable to speak as loudly as the reader, the reader was supposed to moderate his voice.[4] That the *meturgeman* utilized musical declamation in his recital is evidenced by the fact that in early days a singsong utterance, or a type of "singing to speech," was utilized for all public recitation of sacred texts. The tradition of accompanying the reading of the Torah with a translation into the vernacular has been preserved by Jews of Yemen to the present day. Whereas the Torah text is cantillated according to the TE'AMIM, the Targum is chanted by a minor to a tune that varies slightly according to the length of the sentences.[5] The office of the *meturgeman* was discontinued with the universal acceptance of the annual cycle of Torah reading into the synagogue. In its place every Jew is required to be MA'AVIR SIDRAH.[6]

[1]Neh. 8:7–9.
[2]Meg. 32a; Rabbenu Asher b. Yehiel's commentary to Ned. 37b.
[3]Jer. Meg. 84.
[4]Ber. 55b.
[5]Johanna Spector, "Nushaoth in the Near East." *Proceedings of the Eighth Annual Conference-Convention,* Cantors Assembly of America, 1955, p. 36.

[6]A. E. Millgram, *Jewish Worship,* Jewish Publication Society of America, Philadelphia, 1971, p. 182.

METZILOT. *See* BELLS.

METZILTAYIM. *See* CYMBALS.

MEZAMMRIM. *See* TOMEKHIM.

MI-KHAMOKHA. (1) Initial words ("Who is like unto Thee?") of a response in the ARVIT and SHAHARIT services, borrowed from Exodus 15:11. During weekday services its mode of chant is derived from that of the neighboring portions of the service. For special Sabbaths and holidays it became customary, particularly in Western European congregations, to utilize representative themes or special holiday melodies. Thus, for example, on Hanukkah the MAOZ TZUR tune is used; on Passover the *Addir Hu* tune is sung; and on Pentecost the AKDAMUT melody is employed.[1] (2) A work (the title of which is *Mi Chomocho-Israel*) for four-part chorus of mixed voices and tenor or baritone solo with organ accompaniment by Roy Harris (1898–).[2]

[1]Cf. Abraham Baer, *Baal T'fillah,* 2d ed., Göteborg, 1883, pp. 99, 166, 167, 217.
[2]*Synagogue Music by Contemporary Composers,* G. Schirmer, Inc., New York, pp. 207–226.

MI SHEBERAH (AB HORAHAMIM) MODE. Mode whose name is derived from the prayers of MUSAF, with which the READER introduces the mode into the Sabbath morning service. The technical musical name is Ukrainian-Dorian; the Arabs call it *Neuter;* and the Greeks call it *Nahawand.* This mode, according to Abraham Zvi IDELSOHN, is constructed as follows: D E F G♯ A B C. It is characterized by the inclusion of an augmented fourth degree in the lower tetrachord (G♯) and consists of seven tones only (heptachord). Since there are songs that end on the second degree of the scale (E), this mode may be considered identical with the AHAVAH RABBAH MODE. However, the two modes differ in their distinctive melodic and modulatory possibilities.[1] Isadore FREED considers the arrangement of this scale a "combined mode" having a complete octave and characterized by the augmented fourth degree. The upper tetrachord may, however, have either a raised sixth and a lowered seventh (A B C D) or a lowered sixth and a raised seventh (A B♭ C♯ D).[2] Earlier cantor-theorists had different arrangements for this mode. According to Pinchos MINKOWSKY, its construction is D E F G A B♭ C♯ D ascending and D C B♮ A G♯ F E D descending. The arrangement given by Aaron FRIEDMANN is as follows: D E F G♯ A B♭ C D.

This mode is also used for chanting various Sabbath, festival, and High Holy Day texts and in Jewish folk song. *See also* VOLLECH.

[1]Cf. *Jewish Music,* Tudor Publishing Company, New York, 1944, pp. 184, 185.
[2]*Harmonizing the Jewish Modes,* Hebrew Union College–Jewish Institute of Religion, New York, 1958, p. 45.

MICHAEL COLLECTION OF JEWISH MUSIC. *See* JAKOB MICHAEL COLLECTION OF JEWISH MUSIC.

MIKHTAM. Word, whose meaning is uncertain, that appears in the heading of six psalms.[1] Various interpretations are given by rabbinic and Biblical commentators: (1) An adjective used (cf. ps. 45:10) to describe these six psalms, which were as precious to DAVID as fine gold, from the root *ketem,* meaning "gold."[2] The Authorized Version has the marginal notation "golden psalm," whereas the Geneva Version uses "a certain tune." (2) A noted song, or a song engraved as a monumental inscription, from the *niphal* form of *ketem*, meaning "stain";[3] thus a "marked song."[4] (3) Perhaps a designation of a song accompanied by bass instruments, like "the cymbals of trumpet sound" in psalm 150:5. This interpretation comes from *katam*, meaning "to conceal," "dark," "hidden" (cf. *taman, atam*), the allusion thus being to this instrument of plaintive character, which was fitting for the six psalms bearing the title *mikhtam*.[5] (4) A secret song first included by the compiler of the Psalter, from the Arabic *mâktum*. meaning "hidden" or "secret."[6] (5) A percussion instrument, possibly the tambourine or cymbal, from the Babylonian noun *naktamu*, signifying a "metal cover [for a vessel]."[7]

[1]Pss. 16, 56–60.
[2]Ibn-Ezra; David Kimchi; *Metzudat Tziyon*, commentary to ps. 16:1.
[3]Cf. Jer. 2:22.
[4]J. D. Michaelis, *Supplement to Hebrew Lexicons*, 1784–1792, no. 1242.
[5]G. H. A. Ewald, *Jahrbücher der biblischen Wissenschaft*, 1849–1865, vol. 8, p. 68.
[6]F. Hitzig, *Die Psalmen übersetzt und ausgelegt*, Leipzig, 1863, p. 80.
[7]S. H. Langdon, "Babylonian and Hebrew Musical Terms," *Journal of the Royal Asiatic Society*, part II, London, April, 1921, p. 184.

Darius Milhaud.

MILHAUD, DARIUS (1892–1974). French composer born in Aix-en-Provence and considered a leading figure among a group of composers known as Les Six (The Six). As a student at the Paris Conservatory, where he studied with D'Indy, Gédalge, and Widor, Milhaud distinguished himself by winning prizes in violin playing, counterpoint, and fugue. In Paris he was a member of the Superior Council for Radio Broadcasts and also served as a member of the advisory boards of the Opéra Comique and the Paris Conservatory. He visited the United States in 1923, and in 1940 he was appointed to the music faculty at Mills College in Oakland, Calif. Milhaud was a descendant of a distinguished Jewish family. His father and grandfather played an important role in the synagogue and community life in Aix-en-Provence. His grandfather, Joseph Milhaud, was the author of several religious volumes. Among Milhaud's copious writings, encompassing every musical form, are works very much influenced by his Jewish ancestry, for example, *Chants populaires hébraïques* (1925), *Poèmes juifs* (1916), *Liturgie comtadine; Cinq chants de Rosch Haschanah* (1934), *Borechu* (1944), SHEMA YISRAEL (1944), and SERVICE SACRÉ (1947). In 1952 Milhaud was commissioned by the Israeli government to write an opera marking the three-thousandth anniversary of the city of Jerusalem. His opera *David* (libretto by Armand Lunel), depicting King DAVID as statesman, general, poet, and musician, was first performed in Jerusalem in 1954. Milhaud's other works that were premiered at Israeli festivals were *Bar Mitzva Cantata*, in 1961; *Ode to Jerusalem*, in 1973; and *Ani Ma'amin (A Son Lost and Found Again)*, based on a text by Elie Wiesel, in 1974.

Moses Michael Milner. [Albert Weisser, *The Renaissance of Jewish Music,* Bloch Publishing Company, Inc.]

MILNER, MOSES MICHAEL (c. 1886–1952). Composer, conductor, and accompanist who contributed greatly to the Jewish musical renaissance in the early twentieth century in Russia. Born in Rokitno, Milner (his original surname was Melnikoff) sang as a chorister first with Nisson SPIVAK (some authors say Jacob Samuel MARAGOWSKY) and later with Abraham Dzimitrovsky at the Brodsky Synagogue in Kiev. For a while he attended the Kiev Conservatory, and in 1907 he was admitted to the St. Petersburg Conservatory, from which he graduated in 1915. Under the influence of Susman Kisselgof, Milner became affiliated with the SOCIETY FOR JEWISH FOLK MUSIC, which later published several of his works. Milner's best-known creations are *Unsane Tokef* (1913), a liturgical work for cantor and choir, and a song, "In Cheder" (1914). Both works were popular and are still performed. His compositions include choral and orchestral works, operas, piano pieces, songs, and incidental theater music.

MIN HAMMETZAR (PSALM 118). (1) Musical setting for solo and chorus (Hebrew text) by Jacques Halévy (1799–1862), appearing in Volume I of *Zemirot Yisrael* (1847) by Samuel NAUMBOURG; (2) work written in the electronic medium in 1971 by Joseph TAL.

MINHAH. Second of the three daily services in the liturgy, recited in the afternoon and traditionally attributed to the patriarch Isaac.[1] The term literally means "gift"[2] or "tribute"[3] and is applied to the cereal portion of the regular sacrifice (*tamid*) offered in the Temple both in the morning and afternoon. After some time it was restricted to the afternoon because of Elijah's victory over the priests of Baal at Carmel, which occurred in the afternoon.[4]

The structure for the weekday service is as follows: *Ashre,* followed by Half-KADDISH (recited by the READER); *Amidah,* repeated aloud by the reader, including the *Kedushah* when there is a quorum of ten (*minyan*); the short *Tahnun* according to some rites (except on Fridays), followed by Kaddish; *Alenu* followed by the mourners' Kaddish. The texts for Sabbath, festival, and High Holy Days vary. *Minhah* on weekdays is chanted either in the pentatonic or *Selihah* mode; on Sabbath, festival, or High Holy Days special, characteristic prayer patterns are utilized within the designated modes for each of these services. On Sabbaths and fast days a portion of the Pentateuch is cantillated before the *Amidah.* The reading on the Sabbath consists of the first section (*parshah*) of the portion (*sidrah*) for the following week. On fast days the section called *Vayehal* (Ex. 32:11–14 and 34:1–10) is read. According to the Ashkenazic ritual, the last clause of Exodus 32:12 and 34:6–7 (up to the word *venake*) and the last clause in 34:9 are chanted in the Pentateuchal mode of the High Holy Days by the reader and congregation. The Pentateuchal reading on fast days is followed by the *Haftarah* taken from the Book of Isaiah (55–56).

[1]Gen. 24:63; Ber. 26b.
[2]Gen. 32:19.
[3]Judg. 3:15.
[4]I Kings 18:36.

Pinchos Minkowsky. [*The History of Hazanuth,* Jewish Ministers Cantors Association of America, New York]

MINKOWSKY, PINCHOS (PHINEAS) (1859–1924). Russian cantor, scholar, and author. Minkowsky was born into a musical and scholarly family in Belaya Tserkov, Ukraine, and in his youth sang in his father's choir. He approached his Talmudic studies with great diligence, and his father wanted him to become a rabbi. Young Pinchos eventually combined music and Jewish learning as his lifework. By 1875 Minkowsky had become the cantor in his native town. His cantorial and musical studies commenced under the tutelage of Nisson SPIVAK and continued later with David NOWAKOWSKY in harmony, Victor Ratikansky in voice, and Robert Fuchs in counterpoint and composition. Minkowsky served as cantor in Kishinev (1878), Kherson (1880–1884), Odessa (1884; c. 1890–1920), and New York (1884–1889). In Odessa he served as president of the musical organization Hazomir, and in the United States as honorary president of the Jewish Ministers Cantors Association of America (*see* CANTORIAL ORGANIZATIONS). His scholarly contributions to Jewish music are evidenced by his numerous articles and essays in Hebrew, Yiddish, and German in various periodicals and journals. He also wrote the important works *Die Entwicklung der synagogalen Liturgie bis nach der Reformation des 19. Jahrhunderts* (1902) and *Moderne Liturgie in undzere Sinagogn in Rusland* (2 vols., 1910). Many of his synagogue compositions have remained in manuscript form. His setting of Hayyim Nahman Bialik's poem "Shabbat Hamalkah" (Sabbath Queen) is a popular song.[1]

[1]*The Jewish Center Songster,* ed. by B. Carp, National Jewish Welfare Board, New York, 1949, p. 6.

MINNIM. Term (lit. "divided out") that is mentioned in psalm 150:4,[1] referring to stringed instruments whose strings are arranged in a graded order.[2] According to the Talmud, strings were made of sheep gut only. Specifically, strings of the NEBEL were made of the "entrails" (*mayav*); those of the KINNOR were made of the "chitterlings" (*bene mayav*).[3] Much disputation is recorded concerning the repair of a string (*nimma,* sing.; *nimmin,* pl.) broken on the Sabbath in Temple days.[4]

The word *minnim* is rendered in the Targum Jonathan by *halilim* (*see* HALIL). More recently, an instrument, the lute, has been proposed as a possible rendering for *minnim*. In modern-day Hebrew, the term for strings is *maytarim* (sing. *maytar*).

[1]Cf. ps. 45:9.
[2]John Stainer, *The Music of the Bible*, London, 1914, pp. 47, 83.
[3]Kin. 25a.
[4]Erub. 102a, 103a.

MISSINAI TUNES. Expression (lit. "tunes from Mount Sinai") used interchangeably with SCARBOVA, meaning "as if handed down from Mount Sinai" and first used in connection with Biblical CANTILLATION.[1] The term was applied to a corpus of Ashkenazic fixed synagogue melodies and chants that originated in southwestern Germany from the eleventh to the fifteenth century. To this corpus of melodies belong tunes for the High Holy Days and festivals, namely, the setting of BAREKHU (ARVIT for the High Holy Days), *Hamelekh*, *Abot*, *Alenu*, KOL NIDRE, *Vehakohanim*, and KADDISH (before MUSAF for the High Holy Days, NE'ILAH, and for the Dew, or *Tal*, and Rain, or *Geshem*, prayers).

The motive for fixing these chants in this manner was the decline in the fourteenth century of spiritual life among Ashkenazic Jewry. In order to preserve their heritage, Rabbi Jacob MOLIN (known as the Maharil), the renowned rabbinic authority of his time, codified the synagogue ritual and gave sanction to the old existing prayer chants. He himself traveled extensively and served as READER, thus establishing the customs of German Jewry and influencing the NUSAH of the prayer service. His ruling, obligatory to this day, states that local custom and universal Jewish traditional melodies not be changed.[2] So far-reaching was his influence that the melodies are sometimes referred to as "tunes of our Rabbi Maharil."

The basis for unifying synagogue prayer chants, so that each community utilizes the same time-honored melodies for the High Holy Days and festivals, goes back to the expulsion from Spain (1492). Ritual and custom were observed in secret hiding places (i.e., caves, forests), and the fixed melodies of that period would often serve as a means of recognizing one's fellow. As a result, the tunes awakened much emotion and devotional prayer.[3] The suffering of these Jews no doubt manifested itself in the *Missinai* tunes of Ashkenazic Jewry.

[1]R. Judah he-Hassid, *Sefer Hassidim*, ed. by J. Wistinezki and Jacob Freimann, 2d ed., 1924, p. 817.
[2]*Orah Hayyim*, 619.
[3]Abraham Eliezer Hirshowitz, *Sefer Minhage Yeshurun*, 2d ed., Vilna, 1899, p. 39(77).

MITZVAH TANZ. Devotional DANCE associated with a religious *mitzvah* (commandment). Since rejoicing at weddings is considered a *mitzvah*, or good deed, the bride dances with male guests; she and her partner each hold the end of a kerchief. No prearranged melody or practiced steps or forms are necessary for this dance.

MIZMOR (ZEMER, ZIMRAH). Term having various meanings and mentioned fifty-seven times in the Book of Psalms. (1) "Praise";[1] Targum Onkeles renders *zimrat*, which is cognate to *mizmor*, as "my praise."[2] (2) "Psalm"; the Septuagint, Vulgate, and others translate it by the Greek *psalmos* (*psalmus*), thus indicating a poem or hymn sung with instrumental accompaniment, probably a stringed instrument plucked with the fingers. Two expressions are used for playing on strings: *zamar*, "to pluck," and *naggan*, "to strike."[3] (3) "Lyric song."[4] (4) "A paragraph," indicating a new beginning.[5] (5) "Chant"; R. Akiba said, "Chant it every day, chant it every day."[6] A system of chanting was used in Talmudic days for study and to aid the memory. (6) "Melody" or "tune"; *zemer* is interpreted as being the tune or melody itself (i.e., "the joyous singing of the human soul") rather than the chanted word (SHIR). The Talmud differentiates between the psalm headings *leDavid Mizmor* and *Mizmor leDavid*. The former intimates that the *Shekhinah* (Divine Presence) rested upon DAVID and he then uttered that song; the latter, that he first uttered that particular song and then the *Shekhinah* rested upon him.[7] The interpretation of *zemer* as "tune," or "melody," is derived from these two psalm headings, in which an expression of feeling and emotion through melody makes the Divine Presence felt.[8] (7) "Choice fruits" (e.g., *mizimrat ha'aretz*) or "courage" (e.g., *azi vezimrat kah*), denoting by means of mystical interpretation that "singing" (*zimrah*) is a medium of power and choice produce in prayer.[9] (8) "To trim" or "prune," from *lo tizmor*, "thou shalt not prune,"[10] homiletically interpreted that the psalms are often called *mizmorim* (pl. of *mizmor*) because, just as pruning removes the chaff and improves the vine so that it can grow choice produce, so the recitation of ZEMIROT prior to prayer removes all obstacles and sins so that God accepts our prayers.[11]

[1]Pes. 117a.
[2]Ex. 15:2.
[3]Carl Heinrich Cornill, *Music in the Old Testament,* The Open Court Publishing Company, Chicago, 1909, p. 11.
[4]G. H. A. Ewald's commentary on the Psalms.
[5]E. G. Hirsch, *The Jewish Encyclopedia,* vol. X, p. 248.
[6]Sanh. 99a, b.
[7]Pes. 117a.
[8]Interpretation of Rabbi Samson Raphael Hirsch.
[9]I. Miron, *Profile of Israeli Music Today,* National Jewish Welfare Board, New York, 1964, p. 2.
[10]Lev. 25:4.
[11]Yitzhak Abuhav, *Menorat Hama'or,* fifteenth century.

MODES, SYNAGOGAL (also known as STEIGER or GUST). Melodic structure of synagogue chants based on the organization of tonal relationships into a series of scales. These prayer modes consist of combinations of melodic patterns within a given scale called NUSAH. Named according to the prayers at which the READER intones these modes, they are the ADOSHEM MALAKH MODE, AHAVAH RABBAH MODE, MAGEN AVOT MODE, MI SHEBERAH MODE, YEKUM PURKAN MODE, and YISHTABAH MODE. Abraham Zvi IDELSOHN added the *Selihah* and *Vidui* modes.

Various attempts have been made to bring a musical system into synagogue song. Hirsch WEINTRAUB and Samuel NAUMBOURG attempted to compare certain prayer chants with the church modes. Probably the first to name the synagogue modes was Cantor Isaac LACHMANN, and in his article "Unsere synagogale national Musik" (1880) in *Der Jüdische Kantor* he mentions the current names of the synagogue modes. A larger work organizing the modes, "Die Tonarten des traditionellen Synagogengesanges," by Joseph SINGER, appeared in 1886. Baruch Joseph Cohon, continuing in the footsteps of his teacher Abraham Zvi Idelsohn, wrote "The Structure of the Synagogue Prayer-Chant" (1950) in the *Journal of the American Musicological Society*. Other theories and studies on the modes were made by Cantor Leib Glantz in "The Musical Basis of Nusach Hatefillah," Joseph YASSER in "The Structural Aspect of Jewish Modality," and Isadore FREED in *Harmonizing the Jewish Modes*.

The prayer modes differ from one another not only in their scale construction but also in their particular liturgical function. The *Adoshem Malakh* mode stands for praise and exaltation and is sung in a majestic manner; the *Ahavah Rabbah* is plaintive and, paradoxically, at times jovial; the *Magen Avot* is sung in a relaxed and peaceful manner, expressing faith, hope, and thanksgiving. The rest of these modes are considered "combined" modes, varying in mood and character. The *Adoshem Malakh* and *Magen Avot* modes can be traced to the cantillations of the Bible. The *Ahavah Rabbah* mode, however, has no Biblical origin. According to some authorities, it derives from the Khazar tribes of the Caspian Sea region who were converted to Judaism in the eighth century. They probably sang in this mode, which gradually infiltrated into Jewish liturgical usage.[1] Others believe that the mode was probably introduced into the synagogue through Turkish and Arabic influences in the fourteenth century.[2] Its use of the augmented second between the second and third degrees, and sometimes between the sixth and seventh degrees, makes it akin to the gypsy scale and the Arabic Hedjaz mode. The Eastern European HAZZAN (namely in Hungary, Poland, southern Russia, and the Ukraine) popularized this mode, and it became a vehicle for inner expression of pain, love, and joy for the Jew. The prayer modes are part of liturgical chant as well as folk song.

[1]Isadore Freed, *Harmonizing the Jewish Modes,* Hebrew Union College–Jewish Institute of Religion, New York, 1958, p. 17.

[2]Eric Werner, *In the Choir Loft,* Union of American Hebrew Congregations, New York, 1957, p. 19; Abraham Z. Idelsohn, *Jewish Music,* Tudor Publishing Company, New York, 1944, pp. 84–89.

MOLIN (MÖLLN, MOELLIN), JACOB (c. 1365–1427). German rabbinic authority referred to as the Maharil (an acronym formed from Morenu Harav Rabbi Yaakov Levi) and also called Mahari Segal and Mahari Molin, greatly responsible for unifying synagogue ritual and its music, whose advice and teachings were sought by Ashkenazic Jewry. A disciple of his father and later of Meir Ha-Levi and Shalom ben Isaac of Austria, he became known for his expertise in Jewish law and was among the first to bear the title *morenu* ("our teacher"). Born in Mainz, Molin lived during the Hussite Wars, when turmoil and disorganization existed among Jewry. With his pious and warm personality, he was able to exert a profound influence upon religion, and upon Jewish life in general, in the home, synagogue, and community. The usages of Molin's religious practices were compiled about 1450 by his pupil Rabbi Eliezer b. Jacob, known as Zalman of St. Goar, in the work *Minhagim Sefer Maharil*, first printed in Sabbioneta, Italy, in 1556. Molin considered it a duty for the rabbi as well as the cantor to officiate at services and functioned as READER during the High Holy Days and festivals. According to tradition he "composed" (or sanctioned) numerous synagogal melodies *(Nigguney Maharil)* and set certain standards and practices for music in the synagogue and community. For example, he popularized the singing of the fixed tune for the *Hamelekh* during SHAHARIT of the High Holy Days. Beginning with a melismatic chant in pianissimo he gradually increased in dynamics and ended with *Hamelekh* in fortissimo.[1] Molin also considered instrumental music essential at wedding festivals. When local governments restricted music for Jews at weddings in certain districts or on certain days, Molin had the wedding party removed to another district.[2] Tradition in synagogue song meant so much to him that he ruled that, in addition to obedience to time-honored observances, local custom and universal

Jewish traditional melodies should not be changed.[3] His work is replete with descriptions of musical practices in the synagogue and community that became the guiding light for all of Ashkenazic Jewry. It is no wonder that Israel Abrahams described Molin as "the forerunner of a whole class of clerical musicians."[4]

[1] Cf. *Maharil, Rosh Hashanah,* Warsaw, 1874, 38b.
[2] Cf. *Maharil, Eruve Hatzerot,* 30b.
[3] Cf. R. Moses Isserles, *Orah Hayyim* 619.
[4] *Jewish Life in the Middle Ages,* Atheneum Publishers, New York, 1969, p. 255.

MOMBACH, ISRAEL LAZARUS (1813–1880). English choir director, composer, and teacher, Born in Pfungstadt, he began his musical studies in 1828 with Enoch Eliasson of London. Mombach became a chorister with Simon Ascher (1841–1870) of the Great Synagogue of London and later became choir director there. During fifty-two years of service he was held in great esteem. Mombach strove to improve the musical service of the synagogue and was influential throughout England. He taught HAZZANUT at Jews' College and taught singing to the senior pupils of the Sabbath classes of the Association for Religious Instruction. He conducted concerts at the Jewish Workingmen's Club and served as a member of the Committee for the Diffusion of Religious Knowledge. Mombach's music was widely accepted and performed in the German synagogues of England and the English colonies. With the exception of those selections written in the traditional modes, most of his settings are a blend of the popular German and English folk song. In 1881 his opus *Ne'im Zemirot Yisrael (The Sacred Musical Compositions of I. L. Mombach)* for the entire yearly cycle was published.

MUNAH (⌐⌐). Graphic sign, meaning "resting" or "sustained," placed below words in the printed Bible.[1] It is invariably the most extensively utilized of the CONJUNCTIVES by the Masoretes. Its melody is not fixed and depends on the DISJUNCTIVES it serves.[2]

Early writers called it SHOFAR, because of its appearance. Although one graphic form is used for the sign, a distinction is made between a *shofar munah* ("sustained" note), *shofar ilui* ("ascending" note), and *shofar mekharbeyl* ("ornamental" note), depending on the disjunctive it precedes.[3] William Wickes suggests that the use of the same graphic sign for three different melodies could be related to the three sounds designated for the *shofar* (i.e., *tekiah, shevarim, teruah*), even though the *shofar* melodies are not the same.[4] He concludes that presently one melody is in use in spite of the threefold distinction.[5] The latter statement would seem incorrect in that cantillators and notators of the ready-made motives do differentiate as to melodic pattern for the symbol *munah.*[6] *See also* TE'AMIM.

[1] E.g., Gen. 1:1.
[2] Cf. Solomon Rosowsky, *The Cantillation of the Bible,* The Reconstructionist Press, New York, 1957, pp. 665, 666; P. Spiro, *Haftarah Chanting,* Jewish Education Committee Press, New York, 1964, p. 42.
[3] Cf. Wolf Heidenheim, *Sefer Mishpetey ha-Te'amim,* Rödelheim, 1808, p. 6b.
[4] *A Treatise on the Accentuation of the Prose Books of the Old Testament,* Clarendon Press, Oxford, 1887, p. 23.
[5] Ibid., note 59.
[6] Cf. Abraham Z. Idelsohn, *The Jewish Song Book,* ed. by B. J. Cohon, Publications for Judaism, Cincinnati, 1951, pp. 488–491; Joseph H. Hertz (ed.), *The Pentateuch and Haftorahs,* London, 1929–1936, vol. II, pp. 972, 973.

MUNAH LEGARMEH (⌐|). Accent mark, meaning "independent MUNAH," occurring in the printed text of Scripture and representing the musical notes in the intonation and the grammatical relationship between the words of the verse.[1] Its graphic form is a combination of two accent marks, a *munah* under the word and a PSIK following it. Generally, these accents appear separately, but when they appear together, they take on the specific grammatical meaning of the *munah legarmeh* (which is considered a *mafsik katan*, a "petty lord"), with its own disjunctive (*see* DISJUNCTIVES) melody. *See also* TE'AMIM.

[1]E.g., Numb. 31:52.

MUSAF. Hebrew term meaning "addition," designating the additional service recited on Sabbaths and holidays in lieu of the additional sacrifice offered in Temple days in accordance with Numbers 28–29.[1] The main feature of the liturgy is its *Amidah* (standing prayer), whose structure includes seven benedictions on Sabbath, festivals, and Yom Kippur, and nine on Rosh Hashanah. The PRECENTOR who leads in this service is known as the BA'AL MUSAF. His office is of significance, particularly during the High Holy Day season, and has influenced the quantity of musical settings and the elaborate style in which this service is chanted. Of great significance is the SHOFAR ritual, which, after the Bar Kokhba rebellion, was shifted from the early part of the Rosh Hashanah service to the *Musaf* service. In the *Musaf* the shofar is blown after each of its three special prayer units, namely, *Malkhuyot, Zikhronot,* and *Shofrot* as well as prior to and after the service proper.

[1]Ber. 26b. Cf. also Yom. 33a; Suk. 53a.

MUSICAL INSTRUMENTS. *See* INSTRUMENTS, MUSICAL.

MUSICOLOGY (Ger. *Musikwissenschaft*). Term used since about the early twentieth century to express a scholarly, systematized study of music in contrast to composition and performance. Although Johann Nikolaus Forkel (1749–1818) in *Allgemeine Geschichte der Musik* (1788–1801) and *Allgemeine Literatur der Musik* (1792) lists many treatises and dissertations on Hebrew music published up to 1788, it was not until Eduard BIRNBAUM that Jewish musicology got under way. He is known for assembling a vast collection of Jewish music and Jewish music literature that is now housed in the library of the Hebrew Union College in Cincinnati. He published about forty learned studies and articles on Jewish music. Although there were other pioneers in Jewish musicology in the United States (Alois KAISER and William SPARGER), Birnbaum's work became the model for a number of Jewish musical researchers, in particular, Abraham Zvi IDEL-SOHN, whose ten-volume THESAURUS OF HEBREW-ORIENTAL MELODIES and *Jewish Music in Its Historical Development* have become the treatises upon which many Jewish musicological works are based. Drawing on a number of fields of knowledge such as history, ethnography, language, acoustics, and paleography, these studies have achieved the acceptance of Jewish musicology itself as well as its acceptance into general music. Since Idelsohn, other musicologists have dealt with the many facets of Jewish musicology, including Israel ADLER, Hanoch AVENARY, Bathja BAYER, Edith GERSON-KIWI, Robert LACHMANN, Johanna SPECTOR, Eric WERNER, and Joseph YASSER.

In Israel, musicological research was instituted at the Jewish Music Research Centre (1965) and the Israel Center for Electronic Music (1960) at the Hebrew University of Jerusalem; at Tel Aviv University (1966); and at Bar-Ilan University (1970). Musicology has also become established at the Israel Institute for Sacred Music in Jerusalem.

MUTZNAFIM. *See* TOMEKHIM.

NADEL, ARNO (1878—c. 1943). Poet, composer, arranger, and writer who propagated and popularized Jewish music in the twentieth century. He went to Königsberg in 1890 from his native city, Vilna, and studied under Eduard BIRNBAUM and Robert Schwalm. From 1895 to 1900 he was a pupil at the Jewish Teachers Training College in Berlin and studied music with Ludwig Mendelssohn and Max Löwengard. In Berlin his interests expanded, and he was active as a music critic for several newspapers, conductor of a choir and musical supervisor in the Berlin Jewish Community, and poet and painter. He devoted much time to studying and researching synagogue and folk music. He is renowned for making known the music of, and producing a study of, an early (1744) collection of synagogue melodies that he called *The Hanoverian Compendium.* Nadel's works include *Jontefflieder* (1919), twenty-two Jewish festival songs (published in ten parts), *Jüdische Volkslieder* (2 vols., 1920 and 1923), and numerous unpublished hymns and choral and instrumental compositions.

NAJARA (NADJARA), ISRAEL (c. 1555 – c. 1628). Prolific poet and HAZZAN, the first to publish a DIWAN for the Jewish communities in the Orient. Born in Safed (or, according to some writers, in Damascus), son of Rabbi Moses Najara, he belonged to the Kabbalistic school. He became a recognized scholar, served for a while as *hazzan* in Damascus (c. 1579) and, during the latter part of his life, was rabbi in Gaza. He composed many religious poems, 108 of which were incorporated into his *diwan, Zemirot Yisrael* (1st ed., Safed, 1587; 2d ed., Venice, 1599 – 1600; and 3d ed., Belgrade, 1837), arranged according to the Arabic *diwan.* The 1599 edition, which appeared under the same title, was an extended collection containing 347 poems. Most of the rhymes and melodies are Arabic, Greek, Turkish, or Spanish in origin, with the intention, as Najara states in his preface, of turning Jewish youth from profane songs. Many of his poems have been taken into the rituals used by Jews in other countries. As late as 1858 a collection called *Pizmonim,* culled from old manuscripts, was published. The most popular of his hymns, which is sung on the Sabbath by Jews of all countries and is printed in all prayer books, is his Aramaic "Yah Ribbon Alam" (God of the World). Najara's signature appears in the initials of the five stanzas of this hymn.

NARDI (NARUDETZKY), NAHUM (1901 –   ). Composer, pianist, and accompanist. Although Nardi was born in Kiev, Russia, and was educated in the conservatories of Kiev (1919), Warsaw (1921), and Vienna (1922), he is considered an Israeli composer because he settled in Israel in 1923 and his music became integrated into the cultural and daily life of the nation. He discovered and trained a generation of Israeli singers whom he imbued with the spirit of his songs, which are filled with Jewish-Oriental flavor. Among the many Yemenite singers with whom he gave concerts in the 1930s in Europe, the United States, and Canada was Bracha Zefira. Nardi's musical works include several hundred songs, many of which are considered folk songs, for example, "Shir Ha'avodah" (words by Natan Alterman) and "Kemah Min Hasak." He also wrote orchestral works, chamber music, and theater music. He was awarded the Alkoni Prize in 1957 and the Engel Prize in 1958.

NATIONAL JEWISH MUSIC COUNCIL. Body with an affiliated membership of as many as sixty-five organizations established in 1944 by the National Jewish Welfare Board of New York to develop and perpetuate interest and activity in Jewish music. Pioneers in the council's activities were Bernard Carp, Ethel Cohen, Gershon EPHROS, Leah Jaffa (Rosenbluth), David Putterman, Joseph YASSER, and many others. In addition to sponsoring numerous publications on Jewish music, it proclaims the annual Jewish Music Festival, whose main function is to promote performance of and participation in Jewish music as well as to provide motivation for the composition of Jewish music.

Sergiu Natra. [Israel Music Institute, Tel Aviv]

NATRA, SERGIU (1924–). Romanian-born composer and teacher who settled in Israel in 1961. In Bucharest, his native city, he studied composition with Leon Klepper at the Bucharest National Conservatory. Natra's works include a symphony, chamber music for various combinations of instruments, choral music, piano pieces, and ballet music. Among his compositions inspired by the Bible are his *Song of Deborah* (1967), for mezzo-soprano and chamber orchestra, and *Dedication* (1972), two poems for mezzo-soprano and orchestra.

NAUMBOURG, SAMUEL (1815–1880). Cantor-composer and scholar who rejuvenated synagogue song in Paris according to modern musical practices. Born in Dennelohe, Bavaria, into a family of cantors, Naumbourg not surprisingly exhibited musical talent at an early age. He received his musical and cantorial training in Munich with M. Roder and Cantor Maier Kohn. After holding the office of *hazzan-shohet* (cantor–ritual slaughterer) in Besançon and choirmaster in the synagogue of Strasbourg, he was invited to officiate at the Great Synagogue in Paris. There he met (1843) Jacques Halévy, with whose assistance he exerted strong influences on synagogal musical practices. The French government commissioned him to arrange a service to be introduced into all French synagogues, and his work resulted in his earning the title of chief cantor of Paris (1845). Naumbourg, an enormously enthusiastic individual, had close contact

Samuel Naumbourg.

with the leading musicians of his time. Included in his three-volume opus *Zemirot Yisrael* (vols. I and II, 1847; vol. III, 1857) are, in addition to his own compositions, works and adaptations by Halévy and Meyerbeer and three compositions dedicated to Rossini. His scholarship and interest in the revival of Jewish music and research are evidenced in his introductory essay to his *Agudath Schirim* (1874) and in his work in reediting, with Vincent d'Indy as collaborator, Rossi's HASHIRIM ASHER LISHLOMO (1876). Naumbourg was held in great esteem by the Paris community and was appointed professor of liturgical music at the Séminaire Israélite. Prior to his death he was elected *officier de l'Académie*.

NEBEL (pl. *nebalim*). Stringed instrument, mentioned twenty-seven times in the Bible, whose exact identification remains uncertain. Some vocalize the *nun* with a *segol*, but Kimchi marks it with a *tsereh*.[1] The *nebel* was an instrument played predominantly at religious services.[2] However, Biblical passages mention it as being associated with secular events such as banquets and luxurious indulgences.[3] In Temple days the minimum number of *nebalim* in use was two, and the maximum six.[4] Mention is also made of a case in which it was kept.[5]

The different views given by scholars and Biblical commentators as to its meaning are: (1) Flavius Josephus regards the KINNOR and the *nebel* as identical instruments, the former having ten strings and played with a plectrum, the latter having twelve strings and played with the fingers.[6] The Jerusalem Talmud is also of the opinion that the *nebel* and *kinnor* are the same, except that the former has more strings.[7] The Babylonian Talmud[8] also agrees that *nebel* and *kinnor* are identical, and, corroborating this view, Rabbenu Gershon comments that, since the verse reads *bekinnor benebel asor*[9] and does not use the conjunction "and" between *kinnor* and *nebel*, it can be inferred that the instruments are the same. Without giving the exact number of strings. Rashi remarks that the *nebel* had more strings than the *kinnor*.[10] The Mishnah mentions that the entrails of a beast are used for the strings of the *nebel* and *kinnor*. The strings of the *nebel* were thicker than those of the *kinnor*.[11] It is evident too that the tone of the *nebel* was louder than that of the *kinnor*;[12] thus possibly the *nebel* was a larger and lower-pitched instrument. (2) According to the Septuagint and Vulgate, the *nebel* is a harp. This meaning is suggested by the numerous renderings of *nebel* in these works by the Greek *psaltêrion* and Latin *psalterium* (*see* PSANTERIN).[13] (3) The King James Version translates it by both PSALTERY and viol. (4) Ibn-Ezra comments that the *nebel* had ten holes, thus possibly considering it to be a wind instrument in the form of a pipe.[14] (5) It is possible that it denotes a kind of bagpipe, since *nebel* in Hebrew also means a "wine bottle" or "skin."[15] The Jerusalem Talmud suggests that the instrument was called *nebel* because of its untanned skin.[16] (6) Abraham Portaleone identifies it with the lute called *liuto chitarronato* (Ger. *Mandoline*),

Bronze coin from the Bar Kokhba period (C.E. 132–135), showing a six-stringed *nebel.* [Haifa Music Museum and Amli Library]

which had thirteen strings that were struck with a quill.[17] (7) Bathja Bayer, with archaeological and pictorial evidence that is not, however, entirely conclusive, points out that the *nebel* of the Biblical and Second Temple period was a lyre-type instrument.[18] *See also* MINNIM.

[1]Cf. *Minhat Shai,* commentary to ps. 150:3.
[2]I Sam. 10:5; II Sam. 6:5; pss. 92:3, 150:3.
[3]Isa. 5:12, 14:11, 22:24; Amos 5:23, 6:5.
[4]Ar. 10a.
[5]Mish., Kel. XVI:7.
[6]*Antiquities of the Jews,* VII, 12, 3.
[7]Suk. V, 55c, bottom.
[8]Ar. 13b.
[9]Ps. 33:2.
[10]Isa. 5:12.
[11]Kin. III:6.
[12]Ar. II:6.
[13]Curt Sachs, *The History of Musical Instruments,* W. W. Norton & Company, Inc., New York, 1940, pp. 115, 116.
[14]Cf. pss. 33:2, 150:3.
[15]Cf. William Smith, *Dictionary of the Bible,* Boston, 1883, vol. III, p. 2629.
[16]Suk., loc. cit.
[17]*Shilte ha-Gibborim,* Mantua, 1612, chap. 5.
[18]"The Biblical Nebel," *Yuval,* Magnes Press, Hebrew University, Jerusalem, 1968, pp. 89–131.

NEGGINOT. Term mentioned numerous times in the Bible in its various forms.[1] Its different meanings are: (1) A general term by which all stringed instruments are described, derived from *naggan,* meaning "to strike" (*see* MIZMOR). The sound of stringed instruments was produced either by striking the strings with a plectrum held in the right hand or by plucking them with the bare fingers. In the Book of Psalms, players of stringed instruments are called *noggnim.*[2] Furthermore, the terms *negginot, sheminit,* and KINNOR all refer to the same instrument—the first, to the mode of playing it; the second, to its compass; and the third, to its specific designation.[3] (2) Probably a melody expressly adapted for stringed instruments.[4] (3) A satirical type of song.[5] (4) "Melody," or "chant," from the Hebrew NIGGUN. (5) A term used for the musical accent signs in Biblical CANTILLATION as well as for the punctuation of the text (TE'AMIM) and known also as *ta'ame hanegginot.* According to Rashi, the term *negginot* is synonymous with *te'amim.*[6]

[1]Pss. 4, 6, 54, 55, 61, 67, 69:13, 76, 77:7; Lam. 3:14, 5:14; Isa. 38:20; Hab. 3:19.
[2]Ps. 68:26.
[3]John Jebb, quoted by John Stainer in *The Music of the Bible,* London, 1914, p. 81.
[4]According to G. H. A. Ewald.
[5]Ps. 69:13; Lam. 3:14.
[6]Meg. 3a.

NE'ILAH. Hebrew word meaning "closing," designating the fifth and final service of Yom Kippur (Day of Atonement). Its full name, as given in the Mishnah, is *Ne'ilat She'arim* ("closing of the gates").[1] This phrase, which brought about much controversy, was interpreted by Rabbi Abba to mean the "closing of the gates of heaven" but, according to Rabbi Yohanan, meant "closing of the gates of the Temple."[2] The former opinion was adopted: "And now that our Temple is in ruins, and the habitation of our glory is taken, we direct our hearts to heaven, praying that before the heavenly Temple is closed, prayers may enter in on high and be accepted with compassion and favor."[3]

The *Ne'ilah* texts and melodies have been designed to move the congregant at the climax of the day to many moods: mercy, forgiveness, confession, praise, hope, confidence, and jubilation. Perhaps in no service of the yearly cycle do the *nushaot* (prayer patterns; *see* NUSAH) and melodies change so frequently. This is done purposely, so that the faintness of fasting will not detract the worshiper from his prayer recitals and, furthermore, so that he will be stirred to still greater devotion in this closing hour of the day. Francis Lyon COHEN notes that "the traditional intonations of the *Ne'ilah* are well calculated to excite the emotions of the worshiper."[4]

Of special significance is the fixed melody for the *Ne'ilah* KADDISH, also employed in the opening passage of the *Amidah* (standing prayer). Many of the prayer patterns that accompany the *piyyutim* (poems) and SELIHOT that follow are fixed tunes (e.g., *Petah lanu sha'ar, Zekhor berit, Merubim tzarhey amekha*), and cantors are known for employing infinite variations of musical expression in the two special prayers, *Atah noten yad* and *Atah hivdalta*. The *Ne'ilah* service is brought to a close with three declarations of faith recited alternately by the READER and by the congregants, who respond vigorously. The three proclamations are SHEMA YISRAEL, recited once; *Barukh Shem*, recited three times; and "The Lord is God" (known as *Shemot*, "sacred names"), recited seven times. The full Kaddish and *tekiah* blast on the SHOFAR, interpolated before *titkabel*, conclude the service. This concluding Kaddish should be chanted, according to Rabbi Jacob I. Emden (1697–1776) and others, in a melody that expresses both fervent rejoicing and profound emotion. In doing so, "we are confident of God's compassion, and that our prayers have been accepted by him."[5] The final outcry by the congregation is *Leshanah haba'ah Birushalayim* ("Next year in Jerusalem"). In some congregations this phrase is said three times, and in Israel the word *habenuyah* is added at the end, thus, "Next year in Jerusalem, rebuilt!"

Prevailing customs for the *Ne'ilah* service are: the Ark is open during the entire service; the congregation stands; and the service is chanted by either the rabbi or a prominent lay member of the community. Today, it is most often chanted by the CANTOR.

[1] Ta'an. 26a.
[2] Jer. Ber. IV, 1; Ta'an. 7c.
[3] S. Y. Agnon, *Yamim Noraim*, Schocken Publishing House, Ltd., Tel Aviv, 1956, p. 362.
[4] *The Jewish Encyclopedia*, vol. IX, p. 215.
[5] S. Y. Agnon, op. cit., p. 368.

NE'IM ZEMIROT YISRA'EL. (1) Title (lit. "Sweet Singer of Israel") bestowed by Scripture upon King DAVID for his poetic and musical talents;[1] (2) title given to the READER of the Torah in Sephardic congregations; (3) caption used in various publicity announcements describing the cantor's rendition in the Eastern European Ashkenazic synagogue.

[1] II Sam. 23:1.

NE'IMOT. (1) Name (from the singular *ne'imah*, meaning "sweetness" or "tunefulness') given to the Masoretic accents. Adding melody to the reading of Scripture creates a pleasant impression, and Talmudic sages comment that one who reads Scripture without melody *(ne'imah)*, as indicated by the singing accents, shows disregard for the Scripture and its laws.[1] *See also* ACCENTS, BIBLICAL; CANTILLATION; NEGGINOT; NEUMES; TE'AMIM; TROP. (2) Term closely associated with song and poetry, as in NE'IM ZEMIROT YISRA'EL. (3) Term signifying praise, as *zemirot* and *tishbahot*, one of three such words in the prayer *Le'El barukh ne'imot yitenu.*[2]

[1]Meg. 32a.
[2]Cf. *Siddur Otzar Hatefillot; Abudraham*, quoted in Etz Yosef commentary.

NEKABEKHA. Word (from the Heb. *nakab*, "to pierce," "bore," "perforate") appearing in Ezekiel 28:13 and rendered as a musical instrument having many holes.[1] Some interpret it as signifying a flutelike instrument or double pipe.[2] J. D. Eisenstein asserts that the Prophet purposely used this general appellation because of the different modes of expression (i.e., joy or sorrow) that these perforated wind instruments *(halilim)* were able to convey, depending upon the number of holes.[3]

[1]Cf. David Kimchi; *Metzudat Tziyon*, ad. loc.
[2]Cf. John Stainer, *The Music of the Bible*, London, 1914, p. 104; Alfred Sendrey, *Music in Ancient Israel*, Philosophical Library, Inc., New York, 1969, pp. 317ff.
[3]*Ozar Yisrael*, New York, 1907–1913, vol. X, p. 110.

NEUMES. Type of musical shorthand (from the Gr. *neuma*, "sign") used by the church (c. 680–1000), whose early notation was depicted by points, commas, hooks, and the like above the text. These signs served as "reminders" for the directional flow of the melody. In their primitive stage, the *neumes* are similar to the accent signs used in Hebrew CANTILLATION derived from a type of "gesture" notation called CHIRONOMY. The Greek term *neuma* is etymologically related to the Hebrew term *ne'imah* (pl. NE'IMOT), meaning "sweet" or "pleasing."[1] This is not, however, entirely conclusive.[2]

[1]H. Reimann, *Handbuch der Musikgeschichte*, Leipzig, 1923.
[2]Cf. Eric Werner, *The Sacred Bridge*, Columbia University Press, New York, 1960, pp. 110, 125, note 30.

NIGGUN (pl. *niggunim*). (1) Tune or "melody type." Jewish melodies are often based on melody types, for example, *gemara niggun* (the chant used by students when studying the Talmud) or Sabbath or Yom Tov (holiday) *niggun*. These melody types are real melodies, or their variations, or contrafact *(see* CONTRAFACTUM) melodies. For example, a popular contrafact melody of the Middle Ages, first mentioned by Jacob MOLIN,[1] was the Judeo-German *Akedah* poem, also referred to as *Jüdischer Stamm* (the initial words of the poem). When its melody was used for another text, the indication would read *be-niggun Akedah*, that is, "to be sung to the *Akedah* tune." Similar tunes adapted to various texts were the *niggunim* of the *Shmuel Buch* and *Baba-Buch*. The actual melodies cannot be ascertained and are probably lost. (2) A tune or melody, often without words, sung by Hassidim *(see* HASSIDIC SONG). (3) The second movement of the BAAL SHEM suite by Ernest BLOCH. (4) The verb *naggan*, meaning "to strike," is an expression for playing upon strings. One who is musically schooled and composes vocal or instrumental music is called *menaggen, ba'al menaggen*, or *yodea naggan*.

[1]*Sefer Maharil*, 49b.

NIKATMON (NIKTIMON). Term (from the root *ankitmin*) appearing in Mishnah Kelim XV:6 and meaning an artificial arm or leg. Thus, according to R. Obadiah Bertinoro, R. Asher b. Yehiel (Rosh), and others, it refers to a musical instrument resembling a wooden leg.[1] Curt Sachs suggests that "it might refer to those typical Egyptian clappers of wood or ivory which were carved to form a human arm with the hand and which were exclusively played by women; or to the boot-shaped clappers of the Greeks."[2]

[1]Ad loc.
[2]Cf. *The History of Musical Instruments*, W. W. Norton & Company, Inc., New York, 1940, p. 109.

NIMMIN. *See* MINNIM.

NOTATION, MUSICAL. The writing and printing of visual symbols that make possible the reproduction of musical sounds. The oldest form of

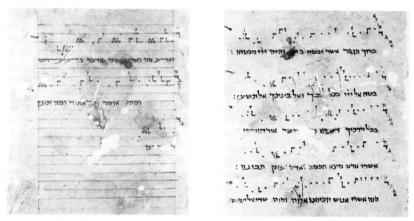

Cambridge Collection fragment containing five verses from the Bible and a portion of *piyyut* with neumatic notation by Obadiah the Norman Proselyte. [University Library, Cambridge, England]

The musical equivalents of the *te'amim* of the Pentateuch according to Johannes Böschenstein, in Johann Reuchlin, *De accentibus et orthographia Hebraeorum libri tres.* [Hebrew Union College Library]

Facsimile of page 1 (Tenore) of Solomon Rossi, *Hashirim Asher Lishlomo.*
[Hebrew Union College Library]

notation is the TE'AMIM, first used during the period from C.E. 500 to 800. Although different systems of notation had existed, the Palestinian or Tiberian symbols, devised by AARON BEN ASHER and made up of hooks, dots, and dashes placed above and sometimes below the consonants, became the standard code for melodizing in all Jewish communities. Prior to Asher, Ben Naphtali of Babylonia had devised a system of notation by placing letters above the consonants; for example, the letter *zayin* denoted the *zakef* ("raising") and the letter *yud* stood for *yetiv* ("staying"). In general the *te'amim* indicate a rough form of melodic contour and are only an aid to the memory of the conventional groups of notes out of which all Biblical CANTILLATION is composed. The oldest notations of synagogal chant discovered to date are those of the twelfth century, of Obadiah the Norman Proselyte (c. 1103 – c. 1150), discovered in the Cairo Genizah about 1920 by Elkan Nathan Adler. Reflecting in part a Near Eastern tradition, the manuscript, written in neumatic notation, contains three liturgical chants: *Mi'al har horev*, a eulogy to Moses; *Wa'eda'mah*, of which only the conclusion has been preserved; and *Baruk haggever*. The earliest printed Jewish music, by the Catholic priest and Hebraist Johannes Böschenstein (1472 – 1536; sometimes spelled Boeschenstain or Boeschenstein), in the Hebrew grammar *De accentibus et orthographia Hebraeorum libri tres* (Haguenau, 1518), by Johann Reuchlin (1455 – 1522), is the representation of the notes for the signs employed in Biblical cantillation in the Ashkenazic tradition. Among other humanists and scholars who copied these notations were Athanasius Kircher of Rome in his *Musurgia universalis* in 1650.

The first printed example of synagogue song, which appeared in Venice in 1623, was written by Solomon ROSSI and is called HASHIRIM ASHER LISHLOMO (CANTIQUES DE SOLOMON ROSSI). Another early work utilizing Hebrew themes is Benedetto Marcello's ESTRO POETICO-ARMONICO, PARAFRASI SOPRA LI SALMI, printed in Venice between 1724 and 1727. An important collection of early synagogue melodies dating from 1744 is *The Hanoverian Compendium*, containing 302 textless but named melodies. Although synagogue song has an ancient oral tradition, the move toward providing a modern printed repertory did not begin until about 1840. It was only in the early nineteenth century that cantor-composers showed signs of musical knowledge and capabilities of notating or composing (e.g., Aaron BEER). The first modern collection of traditional synagogue song is the *Münchener Gesänge*, published in 1839 by Maier Kohn (1802 – 1875). Among the pioneers who compiled, arranged, composed, and printed works on a large scale were Salomon SULZER in Vienna, Louis LEWANDOWSKI in Berlin, Samuel NAUMBOURG in Paris, Hirsch WEINTRAUB in Königsberg, Moritz DEUTSCH in Breslau, and Israel Lazarus MOMBACH in London. Printing of music was undertaken mostly by synagogue composers of Central and Western Europe. The reason may have been their cultural environment and high standards of musicianship, as well as the fact that in these localities they were able to bear the costly process of music printing because of the munificence of a patron or other wealthy individual.

The oldest printed collection of Jewish folk song, dating back to 1727, was published in Fürth by Elhanan Henle Kirchhan (Kirchhain) and entitled *Simhat Hannefesh* (Delight of the Soul). From its contents a vivid idea of the religio-ethical part which music played in the leisure life of the Jew can be gained. It is not until 1908 that Jewish music printing was begun on a large scale, under the auspices of the SOCIETY FOR JEWISH FOLK MUSIC.

NOWAKOWSKY, DAVID (1848 – 1921). Russian synagogue choirmaster, composer, and teacher. Born in Malin (a small village near Kiev), Russia, he sang as chorister for ten years at the CHOR-SCHUL in Berdichev, and during this period he studied harmony, counterpoint, and composition.

David Nowakowsky.

An important event in his career occurred about 1870, when he was appointed choirmaster and associate cantor (*see* HAZZAN) of the Odessa Synagogue, known as the Broder-Schul. Serving for a half-century under Cantors Nissan BLUMENTHAL and Pinchos MINKOWSKY, Nowakowsky became known in Russia and throughout Europe. In the early part of his career he was unable to create for the synagogue as he would have liked because of a personality clash with Cantor Blumenthal. After Blumenthal retired in 1891 and was replaced by Minkowsky, Nowakowsky began to realize his full power as a synagogue conductor and composer. Both men joined in working for the dignity and purity of synagogue song and attracted numerous musicians and dignitaries to the synagogue service. In addition to his synagogue duties Nowakowsky served for more than thirty years as musical director of the Odessa Orphan Asylum and taught music at various schools. His fame today rests chiefly on his choral compositions, many of which have remained in manuscript form. Those in print are *Shire David—Kabbalath Shabbat* and *Shire David—Tefilot Neilah* (1895).

NUSAH. Term (Aramaic pl. *nushaot;* Heb. pl. *nusahim*) derived from the Hebrew root *sah,* signifying "to tear away" or "remove."[1] (1) In regard to the prayer service, it signifies a pattern or an established form of a text. When a text was removed or copied, that text or copy became known as *nusah.* Hence, forms of texts in prayer books belonging to different rites (e.g., *nusah Ashkenaz, nusah Sefard, nusah Ari*) are known as *nusah hatefilah.* (2) The word also signifies a melodic pattern or prayer mode, similar to the Oriental MAQĀM, governing the traditional chanting of the prayer texts. The melodies of prayers were transmitted informally from generation to generation. In this manner they were collated into a body called *nusah.* Although the term itself in its musical connotation may not have existed prior to the mid-1800s, chanting the prayers according to their given melodic patterns and modes was traditional and obligatory.[2] *Nusah* is a vehicle of almost every prayer within the synagogue service. Its general characteristics are: the motives have no fixed rhythm or meter; the motives are subject to repetition and omission and may generally be altered and varied according to the preference of the READER; it affords opportunity for IMPROVISATION.

[1] Prov. 15:25.
[2] *Orah Hayyim* 619.

OBERKANTOR. German term meaning "chief cantor," from *ober* (higher or upper) and *Kantor* (cantor or singer), the counterpart of *Oberrabbiner* (chief rabbi). In the preface to *Der Frankfurter Kantor*, by Fabian OGUTSCH, J. B. Levy refers to Cantor Ogutsch as an *Oberkantor* and translates it by the Hebrew phrase *hazzan elyon*. Similarly, in a biography of Joseph ROSEN-BLATT, his son Rabbi Samuel Rosenblatt makes mention of the fact that the Hamburg community regarded his father as an *Oberkantor*.[1] Most often when the congregation employed an *Oberkantor* they also employed a *hazzan sheni* (*see* HAZZAN), or, as Rabbi Rosenblatt calls him, an *Unter-kantor*.[2]

[1] Cf. *Yossele Rosenblatt: A Biography*, Farrar, Straus & Cudahy, Inc., New York, 1954, p. 73.
[2] Loc. cit.

ODYSSÉE D'UNE RACE, L'. Symphonic poem dedicated to the State of Israel by Heitor Villa-Lobos (1887–1959). The work was first performed in 1954 by the ISRAEL PHILHARMONIC ORCHESTRA at the International Festival for Contemporary Music in Haifa.

OGUTSCH, FABIAN (1845–1922). Cantor-composer. Born in Podberezye (Paberžé), Vilna Province, Lithuania, he attracted attention when he was a child by his sweet voice and musical ability. Ogutsch received his vocal and cantorial training with Russian cantors and later studied harmony and composition in Frankfurt am Main, Germany. His early positions as cantor were in Koschmin (Koźmin, 1875–1877), Schwerin (Skwierzyna, 1877–1880), and Ostrów Wielkopolski (1880–1883). In 1883 he was appointed chief cantor of the synagogue on the Börneplatz, in Frankfurt am Main, where he served with great distinction for thirty-eight years. He composed numerous choral settings for cantor and choir and is best known for his volume *Der Frankfurter Kantor* (1930; compiled by J. B. Levy), which is of lasting value for research and scientific study of southern German HAZ-ZANUT.

ORGAD (BUSCHEL), BEN-ZION (1926–   ). Israeli composer and educator. Orgad emigrated to Palestine from his native Essen, Germany, in 1933. He received his early general education at the Herzliah in Tel Aviv. In 1947 he graduated from the Israel Academy of Music in Jerusalem and later earned a degree in musicology from Brandeis University in the United States (1961). His principal teachers were Kinori, Rudolf Berg-man, Paul BEN-HAIM, and Joseph TAL in Israel, and Aaron Copland and Irving Fine in the United States. As an educator he attained the position of supervisor of music education in the Ministry of Education and Cul-

Ben-Zion Orgad. [Israel Music Institute, Tel Aviv]

ture. One of his earliest and best-known works is his *Hatsvi Israel* (1949), a symphony in two movements for baritone solo and orchestra. Later works characterized by Hebraic content are *Mizmorim* (1966–1968), a cantata on Psalms, and *A Tale of a Pipe* (1971) for soloists, female choir, and nineteen instruments (according to text by S. Y. Agnon and the prayers for the Day of Atonement). He wrote numerous orchestral and vocal works, chamber music, and pieces for various instrumental combinations.

ORGAN. Instrument probably used in Temple days and known in the Talmud as the MAGREFAH.[1] After the destruction of the Temple (C.E. 70), as a sign of national mourning instrumental music was no longer allowed in divine services and was used only on certain festal occasions (e.g., weddings). The organ in Jewish history has been considered a "Christian instrument" because it was the principal instrument in the church from the beginning of the second millennium. Protest arose over its use in the synagogue because it is forbidden to imitate practices that are typical of the religious rituals of non-Jews.[2] As early as the twelfth century, however, records show that a pipe organ was played in a Baghdad synagogue on weekdays. In Prague, beginning in 1594, the organ was used before welcoming the Sabbath, reflecting the custom of greeting the Sabbath as a "bride" with the festive hymn LEKHA DODI. In any event, the playing of music had to be concluded a half hour before sunset.[3]

Only in the nineteenth century did the "organ-synagogue" become a controversial issue between the Reform and Orthodox movements. In 1810 Israel Jacobson (1768–1828) installed an organ in his boys' school in Seesen, Germany. In 1815, in Berlin, he used organ music in private services held in his home. This aroused great indignation and opposition on the part of the rabbinic scholars of the time, and this house of worship was closed later that year by King Frederick William III. In 1818 the Hamburg community introduced the organ. This time it was played by a non-Jewish organist, and its use was established in the Reform Temple; the practice soon spread throughout Reform synagogues and some Conservative congregations in Western Europe and the United States. In the United States an organ was first installed in 1841 in Temple Beth Elohim of Charleston, S.C., and in 1847 in Temple Emanu-El in New York. An abundance of music has been published for the instrument as well as for cantor and choir with organ accompaniment. Orthodox practice does not permit the use of any musical instruments in divine service on Sabbath and holidays.[4] The playing of the organ is questionable even during the weekdays[5] but is permitted at weddings. Among the Sephardic community the organ is completely alien. According to the late Sephardi Chief Rabbi of Israel, Rabbi Ben-Zion Meir Hay Uzziel, "It is both an obligation and a *mitzvah* [religious precept] to eliminate it from the House of the Lord."[6] *See* IN-STRUMENTS, MUSICAL.

[1]Ar. 10b, 11a.
[2]Cf. Maimonides, *Hilkhot Avodah Zarah*, XI, I; R. Zvi Hayut, *Minhat Kena'ot*, p. 5; R. Samson Raphael Hirsch, *Commentary on the Pentateuch*, 1867–1878, Lev. 18:3.
[3]David Tzvi Hoffman, *Sefer Melamed Leho'il*, Frankfurt am Main, 1925, p. 12.
[4]Maimonides, *Yad, Shabbat* 23:4; *Orah Hayyim*, 338, 339.
[5]Hoffman, op. cit.
[6]*Talpioth*, vol. III, pamphlets 3 and 4.

OVAYR LIFNAY HATAYVAH. Expression (lit. "passes before the Ark"), used interchangeably with YORAYD LIFNAY HATAYVAH in the Talmud,[1] describing the action of the PRECENTOR and the position he took when praying. Various interpretations, however, are given for the word *ovayr:* (1) "Passing"; thus "he who passes before the Ark" signifies rising from one's seat and stepping up to the Ark containing the Torahs in order to recite specifically the loud *tefilah* (*Amidah*).[2] (2) "Transmits"; the preference for the word *ovayr* rather than *omayd* ("stands") may be due to the fact that, by serving as an exemplary religious representative, the READER becomes an influential "medium" through whose devotional chant many influences are transmitted.[3] (3) "Repeats"; a reference to the reader who appeared before the Ark in order to repeat the *Amidah* prayer aloud for the congregation.[4]

[1]Ber. Mish. v:4.
[2]Ismar Elbogen, "Studies in the Jewish Liturgy," *Jewish Quarterly Review*, vol. 19, 1907.
[3]*Ahavat Shalom, Parshat Ve'ethanan.*
[4]Eliezer Levi, *Yesodot Hatefillah*, Tel Aviv, 1952, pp. 88, 106.

OVERTURE ON HEBREW THEMES. Opus 34, scored for clarinet, string quartet, and piano, written (1919) by Sergei Prokofiev in New York and inspired by folk themes given to him by Simeon BELLISON. The clarinet does a solo dance representing the KLEZMER of Eastern Europe; the cello takes up the theme from the Yiddish folk song "Zeit Gezunter Heyt, Meyne Liebe Eltern."

P

PA'AMONIM. *See* BELLS.

PANDURAH. Name of a musical instrument[1] described in various ways: (1) A pandean pipe," or panpipe, that is, a primitive wind instrument played by shepherds. The Greeks called it *syrinx*.[2] (2) A small, stringed, lutelike instrument derived most probably from the Sumerian *pan-tur*, "bow-small" (i.e., small bow).[3] (3) A guitarlike instrument.[4]

[1]Cf. Jer. B.B. VII, end, 15d; B.K. X, end, 7c.
[2]Marcus Jastrow, *Dictionary*, London, 1903, vol. II, p. 1186.
[3]Curt Sachs, *The History of Musical Instruments*, W. W. Norton & Company, Inc., New York, 1940, pp. 82, 137.
[4]Cf. F. W. Galpin, supplementary notes to John Stainer, *The Music of the Bible*, London, 1914, pp. 27, 46.

Oedoen Partos. [Israel Music Institute, Tel Aviv]

PARTOS, OEDOEN (1907–   ). Hungarian-born composer, teacher, and virtuoso violinist. Educated in Budapest, where he studied the viola with Jenő Hubay and composition with Zoltán Kodály, Partos served as concertmaster of various orchestras in Switzerland, Germany, and Budapest and appeared as a guest soloist throughout Europe. Partos went to Palestine in 1938 as principal violinist of the Palestine Philharmonic Orchestra and served as leader of its viola section until 1956. He absorbed Jewish-Oriental flavor from his experience in arranging songs in various settings for Bracha Zefira and was among the first of a group to compose in the Eastern-Mediterranean style. In 1951 he accepted the position of director of the Israel Academy of Music, Tel Aviv, and in 1961 was appointed an associate professor at Tel Aviv University. Favoring string instruments, which focus upon the solo performer, Partos became known as Israel's foremost concerto composer. His musical compositions include concerti, chamber music, choral works, a cantata, and songs. His work for viola and orchestra, *Yizkor* (1946), a memorial to the Jewish victims of the Nazi holocaust, won the Engel Prize in 1948. Among his well-known songs of Jewish folk melodies from Yemen, Persia, and Spain is his *Five Israeli Songs* (1966) for mezzo-soprano (or baritone) and chamber orchestra to Biblical and miscellaneous poetry. His *Metamorphoses* (1971), for piano, and *Three Fantasies* (1972), for two violins in the thirty-one-tone system, were commissioned by various foundations.

PASHTA (֝). Accent sign, meaning "stretching" or "extending," used in Biblical CANTILLATION and referring either to the chironomic gesture of the extended finger or hand that indicates an ascending tone (*see* CHIRONOMY) or the melody itself that is "stretched out in length." Designated by the same symbol as the KADMA, it is a postpositive accent mark; that is, it is always placed over the last letter of the word (e.g., Gen. 32:18). William Wickes suggests that it is placed in the postpositive position "to distinguish it from AZLA, with the same form."[1] Often two *pashtas* may appear over one word; the one at the right indicates the syllable to be stressed, the one to the left is the "name sign" (e.g., Gen. 1:2). *See also* TE'AMIM.

[1]*A Treatise on the Accentuation of the Prose Books of the Old Testament*, Clarendon Press, Oxford, 1887, p. 19.

PATCH TANZ. DANCE (lit. "clap dance") of Eastern European origin. In a slow duple meter, it is part of the Jewish wedding. While dancing in a circle, the participants stop at certain intervals to clap their hands in a given measure. Foot stamping is sometimes simultaneous or is substituted for hand clapping.

PAZER (֝). Name of an accent mark (*see* ACCENTS, BIBLICAL), meaning "dispersed," placed above the word in the printed text of the Bible[1] and possessing the highest rank of pausal power in the category called *shelishim* (counts; *see* DISJUNCTIVES). Its name is actually a description of its melodic pattern, and its melody, according to AARON BEN ASHER, "ascends and returns in a scattered manner."[2] William Wickes associates its musical rendering with a musical ornament called a trill.[3] Two or three *pazers* may appear in one verse,[4] and as many as eight in succession.[5] *See also* KARNE-FARAH; TE'AMIM.

[1]E.g., Gen. 1:21.
[2]*Dikduke ha-Te'amim*, ed. by S. Baer and H. L. Strack, Leipzig, 1879, p. 18.
[3]*A Treatise on the Accentuation of the Prose Books of the Old Testament*, Clarendon Press, Oxford, 1887, p. 21.
[4]Numb. 11:26.
[5]I Chron. 15:18.

PHONOGRAPH RECORD. Disk, usually measuring 7, 10, or 12 inches in diameter, in whose grooves sound tracks have been engraved. Liturgical, Hassidic, art music, folk, theater, and children's songs make up current discography listings. Of these recordings, liturgical disks were among the earliest made. Thomas Edison, who built the first phonograph in 1877, took a graph of the voice of Cantor Joseph ROSENBLATT in his laboratory in Menlo Park and found that it had the largest range of any previously recorded voice.[1] Among the first to reproduce his voice on a disk was Cantor Gershon Sirota, who in 1902 recorded *Umipene Hata'enu* for the Gramophone Typewriter Company. Recordings were soon popularized by Joseph Rosenblatt, Mordecai Hershman, and Zavel Kwartin. Pinchos MINKOWSKY protested vehemently against those cantors who recorded their voices because they disregarded the sanctity of the synagogue prayers (i.e., sanctity of place and sanctity of time).[2] In agreement with Minkowsky were Boruch Leib ROSOWSKY[3] and Abraham Moshe BERNSTEIN.[4] Despite this controversy, cantors continued to record their voices. From 1906 to 1921 Abraham Zvi IDELSOHN, using phonograph apparatus made available to him by the Imperial Academy of Science in Vienna, set out to collect Jewish-Oriental song. His transcriptions of these phonographed melodies are invaluable and fill five volumes of his THESAURUS OF HEBREW-ORIENTAL MELODIES. A collection of about 4,000 phonograph records, covering a sixty-year period, by more than 400 Jewish singers, instrumentalists, and performing groups and from many parts of the world—Russia, Poland, Hungary, Israel, and the Middle East—is now part of the Rodgers and Hammerstein Archives of Recorded Sound, housed in the New York Public Library at Lincoln Center in New York City. More than 15,000 items are now housed in the National Sound Archives in the Jewish National and University Library in Jerusalem. Since 1964 the recordings made and collected by Idelsohn, Robert LACHMANN, and Johanna SPECTOR have been incorporated into the archives and augmented by recent recording techniques (e.g., magnetic tape). An important collection of Jewish music on records and tapes is in the archives of Edith GERSON-KIWI. Fortunately, many early-twentieth-century cantorial and Yiddish 78-rpm records have been transferred to long-playing disks, thereby preserving folklore and making possible musical enjoyment and education.

[1]Samuel Rosenblatt, *Yossele Rosenblatt: A Biography*, Farrar, Straus & Cudahy, Inc., New York. 1954, p. 160.

[2]Cf. *Moderne Liturgie in undzere Sinagogn in Rusland*, Odessa, 1910, vol. I.

[3]I. Shalita, *Encyclopedia of Music: A Biographical Dictionary of Jewish and World Musicians*, 1959, pp. 556, 557.

[4]Issachar Fater, *Yiddishe Musik in Poilen*, World Federation of Polish Jews, Tel Aviv, 1970, p. 66.

PHRYGUSH. *See* AHAVAH RABBAH MODE.

PILDERWASSER, JOSHUA SAMUEL. *See* WEISSER, JOSHUA SAMUEL.

PIYYUT (pl. *piyyutim*). Term, from the Greek *poietes* (poet), denoting a form of poetic composition created from about the sixth century on for synagogue use. The composition of these prayer-poems reached its peak during the eleventh and twelfth centuries and continued into the sixteenth century. They greatly appealed to the masses because of the composition of their texts and the airs from which they were inseparable.

The Targum Yerushalmi[1] translates the verb *naggen* (sing) as *payyet* and applies it to all types of poetic texts and their songs. Saadiah Gaon described the art of *piyyut* composition by the term HAZZANUT, and the texts were often referred to by the composer's name; for example, Yannai's poems were known as *Hazzanut Yannai*. A twelfth-century observer relates that when the leader of prayer began to recite the poetry and its tunes (*hazzanya*), the entire congregation joined in.[2] The poet-cantor, who often was a rabbi, chanted his own prayer-poems when he officiated. The inclusion of *piyyut* in the obligatory prayers was the result of the hostile edict of Emperor Justinian I (C.E. 553), which prohibited reading, study, and teaching of rabbinic lore and the recital of the SHEMA and *tefilah*. The *piyyutim* became so exaggerated by the eleventh century that such authorities as Hai Gaon, Judah ben Barzillai, and Maimonides made protests against their introduction and recital. In spite of this, the composition and use of these prayer-poems and melodies continued and were sanctioned by such Sages as Rashi and Rabbenu Tam. The ruling is still that any departure from local custom in the selection of *piyyutim* and the traditional tunes is wrong.[3]

The earliest known poets (*payyetanim*) were Yose ben Yose (called *ha-yatom;* 6th cent.), Yannai (c. 650), and Eleazar Kallir (c. 700). According to Israel Davidson, there are 2,843 *payyetanim* and a total of 35,200 religious and secular Hebrew poems.[4]

The creation of *piyyut* had the following effect upon synagogue music: (1) Secular tunes and rhythms were adapted, possibly influenced by troubadours and minnesingers. (2) Because of the new poetic devices used (i.e., rhyme, fixed number of syllables, refrains, involved stanzas, various uses of initial letters of words, and acrostics), *piyyut* stimulated the singing of a more intricate type of music. (3) The new liturgical poetry gave rise to a professional leader of the service, called the HAZZAN, since the untrained lay precentor was unable to fulfill this task. (4) Refrains and responsive chanting eventually led to CONGREGATIONAL SINGING. (5) *Hazzanim* vied for each other's prayer-poems and were known for snatching a tune from or exchanging a melody with a colleague. (6) The more attractive services gave incentive and stimulation to the worshiper. (7) The congregants were fascinated with the poetry and new songs of the poet-cantor, and a kind of "worship-entertainment" resulted.

[1]II Kings 3:15.
[2]Ismar Elbogen, *Der jüdische Gottesdienst in seiner geschichtlichen Entwicklung,* J. Kauffmann Verlag, Frankfurt am Main, 1924, pp. 284, 285.
[3]*Shulhan Arukh, Orah Hayyim* 619.
[4]*Thesaurus of Medieval Hebrew Poetry,* Jewish Theological Seminary, New York, 1924–1933; supplements, to 1937.

PIZMON (pl. *pizmonim, pizmonot*). Term originally synonymous with PIYYUT but later used to designate a rhymed poem or hymn in the liturgy (mainly in the penitential prayers, e.g., SELIHOT) arranged in strophic form with a refrain for congregational response. The following interpretations are offered as to the origin and meaning of the word: (1) "psalm," from the Greek *psalmos,* which is cognate to *pizmon;*[1] (2) "to respond in a loud voice," a Targum rendering for *vaya'an* in Job 3:1 (Dr. E. Munk comments that "we can find no such rendering in the *Targumim* known to us today"[2]); (3) possibly the initial letters used in the phrase *piyyut zeh mehadrin: meshubah ve'osin negginah,* meaning "this piyyut is adorned: it is praiseworthy and accompanied with music";[3] (4) "lamentation," from the Aramaic *pazam;* (5) "treasure," from the Hebrew *paz;* (6) "embroidery," from the French *passementerie* or German *Posament;* (7) "to speak or sing in one's turn."[4]

General characteristics of the *pizmon* are as follows: It has no more than four lines to a stanza; its melody is often set rhythmically; and frequently, a traditional melody is used, as in "Zekhor Berit" and "Yisrael Nosha." Numerous ZEMIROT texts that are sung at the Sabbath meal also have four rhymed lines to the stanza with a refrain (e.g., "Tzur Mishelo," "Yom Ze Mekhubad") and are called *pizmonim.*

[1]*The Jewish Encyclopedia,* vol. X, s.v. *pizmon;* Ismar Elbogen, *Toldot Hatefillah Veha'avodah Beyisrael,* 1924, p. 125.
[2]*Abudraham,* 1341; *Sefer Ta'ame Haminhagim,* sec. on Rosh Hashanah, 689; Elie Munk, *The World of Prayer,* Philipp Feldheim, Inc., New York, 1963, p. 321.
[3]Munk, op. cit.
[4]Marcus Jastrow, *Dictionary,* London, 1903, vol. II, p. 1150, s.v. *pezeym.*

POLATSHIK, SENDER (1786–1869). Cantor of the early nineteenth centurn, born in Gąbin, Poland, and popularly called "Sender Minsker."

He derived his nickname from the city of Minsk, where he served as cantor for forty-seven years. Prior to this, he was employed in the nearby townlet of Mir. Polatshik sang as a chorister in the choir of Nahum Leib Weintraub (brother of Salomon WEINTRAUB) in Berdichev. Polatshik's individual style of rendition, called "Sender's STEIGER," was impromptu, and although he stripped the chants of their ornaments, he had the power to raise the feelings of his worshipers with his powerful bass-baritone voice. He had no musical schooling and rehearsed his singers orally, thus placing upon them the burden of memorizing their parts. He left many disciples, among them Boruch KARLINER, Yisroelke Suvalker, and Leyzerki Lodger.

POLNISCH (POLISH). Term used by German Jews to describe the florid and embellished style of synagogue music as sung by Eastern European cantors. Numerous chants in this character are marked with the letters P.W. (*polnische Weise*) or M.P. (*minhag Poland*) in a work by Abraham BAER, *Baal T'fillah* (e.g., p. 258, no. 1165). *See also* BA'AL TEFILAH.

POUGATCHOV, EMANUEL. *See* AMIRAN, EMANUEL.

PRECENTOR. Title (lit. "to sing before," from the Latin *prae*, "before," and *canere*, "to sing," that is, "to lead in the singing") used for the SHELIAH TZIBBUR or HAZZAN who serves as the congregation's representative leader in the service through his prayerful chants. The term, first applied to the principal director of the singing or musical portions of the service in the cathedral or cathedral church, was used in Germany and England in public documents pertaining to the *hazzan*.[1]

[1]H. G. P. Gengler, *Deutsche Stadtrechts-alterthümer*, A. Deichert, Erlangen, Germany, 1882, p. 104.

PROBE. German word, meaning an audition or rehearsal, often used in conjunction with musical activity. *See also* REPETIZI'E.

PROMPTER. *See* MAKRI.

PROPHETS, THE. Second violin concerto by Mario CASTELNUOVO-TEDESCO, written in 1931 and first performed in New York in 1933 with the New York Philharmonic under the direction of Arturo Toscanini with Jascha Heifetz as soloist. The work (dedicated to and commissioned by Heifetz), in three movements, characterizes the three prophets Isaiah, Jeremiah, and Elijah and is partly based on Jewish Italian melodies from the collection of Federico CONSOLO.

PSALM 92 (TOB LEHODOT). Choral composition to the original Hebrew text composed by Franz Schubert (1797–1828) and scored for baritone solo and mixed chorus. Written in July 1827 under the guidance of a friend, the celebrated cantor-composer Salomon SULZER of Vienna, the work later appeared in Sulzer's *Schir Zion* (1840). Schubert had been deeply moved when he heard his *Lied* "Der Wanderer" sung and interpreted by Sulzer, who was famed as a singer and interpreter of Schubert *Lieder*. In appreciation Schubert composed *Psalm 92*. Its first public performance was on May 12, 1904, in the large hall of the Musikverein with Joseph Sulzer (son of Salomon Sulzer) as conductor of two Vienna synagogue choirs and Cantors Bela Gutmann and Don Fuchs as soloists. The work was also presented on the London symphony concert stage, with George Henschel (1850–1934) as conductor.

PSALM 118. *See* MIN HAMMETZAR.

PSALMODY. Practice of psalm singing, first introduced by King DAVID in Temple days. The Book of Psalms, regarded as the richest collection of religious poetry, was chanted by the LEVITES, and when the synagogue became the spiritual home of the Jew, many of the psalms were incorporated into the services. Among the numerous psalms included are the *shir shel yom* ("the psalm of the day"), recited at the close of each morning service of the week;[1] the *Hallel*,[2] chanted on the festivals of Passover, Pentecost, and Tabernacles; and the fifteen pilgrimage psalms, SHIR HAMA'ALOT ("a song of ascents"), chanted on Sabbath afternoons.[3] Many psalms have titles that in Temple days most probably indicated which tune should be used or, in some instances, which instrument should be played for accompaniment. The psalmodic solo, the RESPONSORIAL and ANTIPHONAL SINGING styles, and the psalm modes have also been preserved in the synagogue service, especially in Sephardic and Oriental communities. *See also* PSALMS, BOOK OF; PSALTER.

[1]Pss. 24, 48, 82, 94, 81, 93, 92.
[2]Pss. 113–118.
[3]Pss. 120–134.

PSALMS, BOOK OF. Title (from the Gr. *psalmos*, from *psallein*, to play instrumental music and to sing to musical accompaniment) of a collection of 150 hymns of praise. The Hebrew title is *Sefer Tehillim* or, as contracted, *Tillim*, and in Pesahim 117*a* it is referred to as *Tilli*. The Hebrew name is derived from the singular *tehillah*, "praise," which is found in the superscription of only one psalm (145:1). The entire book is called *Tehillim* ("praises") because it was the manual of the Temple service of song in which praise was the leading feature. *Sefer Tehillim*, which is the first of the Ketuvim (Hagiographa), consists of 150 psalms. Traditionally, King DAVID is regarded as the composer, for he completed and arranged the entire work.[1] In addition to being chief editor, he is identified as the founder and legislator of the Temple PSALMODY. The psalms are divided into five books. "Moses gave [Israel] the five books of the Torah, and to correspond with them David gave them the *Sefer Tehillim* in which there are also five books."[2] Numerous psalm headings give directions as to which instruments should be used for accompaniment or, in some instances, what tune should be employed (e.g., AL-HAGITTIT or AL-MAHALAT). The psalms were sung and accompanied by the LEVITES, who were divided into three groups, corresponding to David's three singing directors, ASAPH, HEMAN, and JEDUTHUN. Levitical singing was an essential feature and an indispensable part of the sacrifice; "instrumental music was merely to sweeten the tone."[3] The printed Book of Psalms is one of three books having their own system of accentuation (*see* TA'AME EMET). The Masoretes (beginning about C.E. 500), no longer familiar with the older musical school, which identified the tune or instrumental accompaniment of the psalm by its superscription, had to employ a written accentual system for the CANTILLATION of the psalm, perhaps based on scale forms of the ancient tradition.[4] In the course of time the intonation of these signs has been lost among the Ashkenazim, but not among Syrians and Sephardim, possibly because the Ashkenazic congregation favored a specific chant in each successive verse, with melodic definiteness and individuality that were easily remembered, as compared with a continuous, demanding, and pointed cantillation varied from verse to verse. Presently this mode of chant is utilized with certain fixed motives or tunes for psalms recited during the High Holy Days (e.g., SHIR HAMA'ALOT, *Ledavid Mizmor*). Others maintain that the accentuation of the Psalter has no musical meaning and that the psalms were chanted either as RECITATIVE or in a free, hymnological manner.[5] The significance of the Book of Psalms, and of Temple psalm singing, to general music lies in the influence both exerted indirectly through Catholic chant. Abraham Zvi IDELSOHN found melodic patterns and exact counterparts of several Gregorian melodies in remote Jewish congregations of the Middle East who had never come in contact with other Jews of Palestine or the Diaspora after the destruction of the First Temple (597 B.C.E.).[6] The Book of Psalms has always served as an inspiration to many composers and as the basis for their works, even up to the twentieth century (e.g., Bernstein, Schönberg, Stravinsky). The first Jew to pioneer in choral psalm writing was Solomon ROSSI. *See also* PSALMODY; PSALTER.

[1]B.B. 14b.
[2]*Midrash Tehillim,* chap. i.
[3]Ar. 11a; Suk. 50b, 51a.
[4]Cf. *The Jewish Encyclopedia,* vol. III, p. 539.
[5]Hanoch Avenary, *Studies in the Hebrew, Syrian and Greek Liturgical Recitative,* Israel Music Institute, Tel Aviv, 1963, pp. 22, 23.
[6]Cf. Curt Sachs, *The Rise of Music in the Ancient World, East and West,* W. W. Norton & Company, Inc., New York, 1943, p. 79; A. Einstein, *A Short History of Music,* Vintage Books, Inc., New York, 1955, p. 14; Eric Werner, *The Sacred Bridge,* Columbia University Press, New York, 1959, p. xiii.

PSALTER. English word, designating the Book of Psalms (*see* PSALMS, BOOK OF), derived from the Greek *psaltêrion* or Latin *psalterium* (Heb. NEBEL; Eng. psaltery), the instrument that accompanied the collection of songs themselves. In ecclesiastical Latin, the term *psallere* means "to sing the Psalms of David." *See also* PSALTERY; PSANTERIN.

PSALTERY. Term signifying an ancient stringed instrument, often used as a translation of NEBEL. Structurally, it consisted of strings, plucked with the fingers or with a plectrum, and sounding board. *See also* PSALTER; PSANTERIN.

PSANTERIN. Ancient stringed instrument mentioned in Daniel 3:5, 7, 10, 15. Various translations are: (1) PSALTERY or dulcimer;[1] (2) a vertical angular harp;[2] (3) NEBEL.

[1]John Stainer, *The Music of the Bible,* London, 1914, p. 73; K.J.V. gives only "psaltery" as its translation.

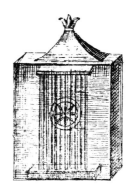

A *psanterin.* **[Shaul Shaffer,** *Hashir Shebamikdash,* **Yefey Nof, Jerusalem]**

פסנתרין

²Curt Sachs, *The History of Musical Instruments*, W. W. Norton & Company, Inc., New York, 1940, p. 83.

PSIK (⌐—). Short perpendicular line placed between two words in the printed text of the Bible with the purpose of separation by a slight pause, that is, temporarily interrupting the flow of the melody.[1] The graphic sign, meaning "interrupter," or "cutting off," has no musical value and properly speaking is not one of the TE'AMIM. Its acceptance came later, since its presence depends upon the fixing of the other signs.[2] It does, however, take on a distinct melody of its own when it is associated with the MUNAH; this combination is called MUNAH LEGARMEH.

[1]Gen. 1:5.
[2]William Wickes, *A Treatise on the Accentuation of the Prose Books of the Old Testament*, Clarendon Press, Oxford, 1887, p. 122, no. 5.

PURIM-SPIELE. Folk dramas (lit. "Purim plays") presented at Purim. The dramatization of the story of Purim dates back to the ninth and tenth centuries and continued throughout the Middle Ages in Germany. The Purim-Spiele proper appeared in the early eighteenth century. Examples of such early plays are *An Ahasuerus Play with Lamentations* (Frankfurt am Main, 1708), *Ahasuerus Spiel* (Amsterdam, 1718), and *Akta Esther mit Achaschwerosch* (performed in 1720). The title page of the last says that "it was acted in Prague in a regular theater, with trumpets and other musical instruments." Although music was banned for Jews as a sign of national mourning, it was permitted at Purim. In these productions the actors were the *badhanim* (*see* BADHAN) or *leitzim* (jesters) and sometimes local Talmudic students, who were often accomplished musicians. Instrumental music was supplied by *klezmorim* (*see* KLEZMER) and singing by MESHORERIM. These plays were never complete without the inclusion of singing and playing of "Shoshanat Ya'akob" (Lily of Jacob), a PIYYUT taken from the ritual. The Purim-Spiele, with their wealth of songs, duets, and choruses, had a great influence on the creation of the Jewish theater, founded by Abraham GOLDFADEN. *See also* YIDDISH THEATER MUSIC.

R

RABINOVITCH, ISRAEL (1894–1963). Editor and writer on Jewish music. Born in Byteń, in the province of Grodno, Russia, the son of a KLEZMER, he grew up in a musical atmosphere, playing in a *klezmer* band at the age of eleven. After his arrival in Montreal in 1911, he continued his musical

Israel Rabinovitch.

studies. He played the violin in the orchestra of the Young Men's Hebrew Association, was first president of the Jewish Music Council of Montreal, and served as editor of the *Canadian Jewish Eagle* (*Canader Adler*). His work *Of Jewish Music—Ancient and Modern* (1952), expanded from his Yiddish volume *Musik bei Yidden* (1940), is a contribution to Jewish music study.

RABINOVITZ, MENASHE, *See* RAVINA, MENASHE.

RACHEM. Title (lit. "have mercy") of a plaintive Hebrew-Yiddish song by Mana-Zucca, Opus 60, No. 1 (lyrics by Max S. Brown), made popular about 1919 by Cantor Joseph ROSENBLATT. The song has been orchestrated and set for a three-part chorus of women's voices. English and Italian versions of the original text have also appeared.

RAVINA (RABINOVITZ), MENASHE (1899–1968). Musicologist, pedagogue, critic, and composer. Born in the Ukraine, Ravina came from a musical family and spent much of his early life in the heder, yeshivah, and Gymnasium. After studying in conservatories in Leipzig, Berlin, and Dresden, he decided to go to Palestine in 1924. By the following year he was involved in numerous activities—he served as a leader of community singing at the weekly Oneg Shabbat gatherings in Tel Aviv (with the support of Hayyim Nahman Bialik), an organizer of the first Choir Convention, a music critic of the daily newspaper *Davar,* and a music teacher in several schools in the country. He served as a representative to the International Music Congress in Prague (1936) and was an active participant in the LEAGUE OF COMPOSERS IN ISRAEL and National Council for Music. His musicological research led to lectures and numerous articles in Israeli and foreign periodicals and encyclopedias. Among his well-known studies are *Organum and the Samaritans* (1963) and *Milon Lemuzikah* (Music Dictionary). He composed several piano pieces and is mainly known for writing folk songs and children's songs ("Tu B'Shvat," "Ha'aviv," "Ale Givah," and many others).

RAV'S NIGGUN, THE (DEM REBBEN'S NIGGUN). Wordless tune attributed to Rabbi Shneor Zalman (1747–1813) of Lyady, founder of the Hassidic movement called HaBaD (*see* Fig. 34). It is said to have been composed in 1799 during the rabbi's imprisonment in the fortress of St.

Figure 34. [Abraham Zvi Idelsohn, *Manual of Musical Illustrations,* Hebrew Union College]

Petersburg. The melody is currently sung on the nineteenth of the Jewish month of Kislev, the anniversary of the day of his release from prison; the beginning of the month (Rosh Hodesh) of Elul; and at weddings, circumcisions, and other major events. The tune, "composed" in the AHAVAH RABBAH MODE, contains four parts or sections corresponding to the four steps for the elevation of the soul. Its objective is to aid the soul to become a disembodied spirit and to elevate it by stages from the lowest to the highest spiritual regions. Part 1 is called *hishtapkhut hanefesh*, the outpouring of the soul; part 2, *hitorerut*, spiritual awakening; part 3, *hitpa'alut* and *deveykut*, excitation of feeling and communion; and part 4, *hitpashtut hagashmiyut*, disembodying of the soul. The tune is also interpreted as giving expression to the four realms of the universe: *briah*, creation of minerals; *yetzirah*, creation of living beings; *asiyah*, creation of man; and *atzilut*, emanation. Thus the melody is sometimes referred to as the tune of the four phases, or "gates." Another explanation is that each of the sections corresponds to the Tetragrammaton.

READER. General appellation for the functionary who cantillates the Scriptural portion or leads the congregation in prayer, or both. The term is often interpolated between the phrases of the Hebrew text in the SIDDUR as an indication to begin chanting.[1]

The Reform movement minimized the flowery, embellished style and manner of chant of the HAZZAN and introduced Christian singers and an ORGAN. According to Pinchos MINKOWSKY, these practices were instrumental in the usage of the name reader instead of *hazzan*. It is also possible that the name may have been borrowed from the Spanish and Portuguese tradition, in which the act of praying is called *rezar* ("reading") and in which the "Sephardi *hazzan* simply reads the appointed prayers in a slow, methodical, measured voice and tempo."[2] Furthermore, in some communities the *hazzan's* duties also included the reading of Scripture (*kore*) in addition to leading the prayers,[3] and thus the English name reader may have become an all-inclusive term for this office.

[1]Cf. P. Birnbaum, *Prayer Book for Sabbath and Festivals*, Hebrew Publishing Company, New York, 1950.
[2]H. P. Salomon, "Sephardi Terminology," *The American Sephardi*, Yeshiva University, 1971, pp. 63, 64.
[3]Meg. 25b; Tos. Meg. III, 13; A. Büchler, "The Reading of the Law and Prophets in a Triennial Cycle," *Jewish Quarterly Review*, vol. 5, pp. 18, 93.

REBBEN'S NIGGUN, DEM. *See* RAV'S NIGGUN, THE.

RECITATIVE. Term (from the Lat. *recitare*, meaning "to recite") used for a vocal style in opera, oratorio, or cantata and applied to the cantor's free chant of synagogue prayers halfway between recitation and song, emphasizing the natural inflections of speech. The recitative in general music history developed in the latter part of the sixteenth century, but this type of speech melody existed among the Jewish people from earliest times. The expression describing Levitical chanting in the Temple is *vedibru haleviyim beshir*,[1] literally, "the Levites spoke in song," thus signifying the rendition of a vocal passage in a manner approaching speech. The HAZZAN, who later emerged as the leader in prayer, continued to chant the texts in recitative style. Simple chants, encompassing a small range, were used for weekday services, and a more elaborate and embellished chant was eventually chosen for the Sabbath and holidays. A combination of both religious and popular forces led to the flowery recitative that inspired *hazzanim* on the Sabbath and holidays. Whereas on the one hand they sought to enhance and beautify the service by utilizing existing Oriental influences, worldly musical influences, such as opera and oratorio, infiltrated Jewish ghetto life, and a decorative and flowery type of recitative heretofore unknown in synagogue song evolved. In recent years, however, synagogue music has undergone a metamorphosis in that these vocal displays no longer have a place in synagogue life. Congregational participation, the deemphasis of cantorial virtuosity, and a desire for decorum dictated this change. Gershon EPHROS[2] differentiates between four types of recitatives: (1) the *parlando* recitative, having its roots in the basic NUSAH *hatefilah* (traditional prayer chants); (2) the *tefilah*-developed recitative, the somewhat more elaborate recitative intended for medium voice and good hazzanic COLORATURA; (3) the virtuoso recitative, a kind of rendition that requires an exceptional voice capable of singing rapid runs, trills, and light ornaments; and (4) the accompanied recitative, in which the voice part recites and the choir or instrument, or instruments, insert their illustrative harmonic commentary. The last category is further subdivided for the purpose of service or the concert stage. *See also* DITTY; IMPROVISATION.

[1]Tam. 33b.
[2]"Recitatives for the Cantor, Old and New," *Proceedings*, Cantors' Assembly and Department of Music of the United Synagogue of America, 1953, p. 45.

REHASH. Acronym formed from the first letters of three Hebrew titles, *rav* (rabbi), HAZZAN (cantor), and *shammash* (sexton). The term was the technical designation used as early as the thirteenth century for the fees and gifts given to the three religious functionaries for their participation in wedding ceremonies.[1] Possibly, the expression is hinted at in psalm 45:2 (*Rohash libi davar tov*, "My heart overflowed with goodly matter"); the psalm itself is known as a "royal marriage song."[2]

The revenue received from weddings by the rabbi, cantor, and *shamosh* was in proportion to the dowry given to the groom, and the *hazzan* and *shamosh* derived almost all their income from these wedding allocations. In 1623 the Lithuanian Council ordered that even though the rabbi did not require fees from couples on relief, the cantor and *shammash* should receive the customary wedding fee.[3] Of the three, the role of the cantor as officiant at weddings is the earliest and dates back to the tenth century.[4]

[1]Isaac b. Moses, *Or Zarua* I, no. 113.
[2]Abraham Eliezer Hirshowitz, *Otzar Shalem Leminhagey Yisrael*, Pardes Publishing House, Inc., New York, 1963, p. 50.
[3]Cf. S. W. Baron, *The Jewish Community*, Jewish Publication Society of America, Philadelphia, 1942, vol. II, pp. 83, 118, 119.
[4]Israel Abrahams, *Jewish Life in the Middle Ages*, New York, 1896, p. 200.

REPETIZI'E. Yiddish word, meaning rehearsal. *See also* PROBE.

RESPONSES. Answers or refrains given by the congregation to the utterances of the officiant, including such acclamations as AMEN, ANENU, HALLELUYAH, and HOSHA NA. Generally, the chant or melody used for the reply or refrain echoes that of the officiant. With the development of the institution of the modern CHOIR, a complete corpus of choral responses and refrains was set down by Salomon SULZER of Vienna in his *Schir Zion*. An important collection of chants and responses for the Ashkenazic congregation and choir is the *Baal T'fillah* by Abraham BAER (*see* BA'AL TEFILAH). Responses of the Sephardic and Oriental congregations are given in Isaac Levy's four-volume *Antología de Liturgia Judeo-Española.* *See also* CONGREGATIONAL SINGING; MI-KHAMOKHA.

RESPONSORIAL. Pertaining to alternation between a leader and a chorus. An early example of responsorial chant is *The Shirah* in Exodus 15:1–18 (*see* SHIRAH, THE). Responsorial psalmody is described in the Mishnah[1] and has been preserved in the synagogue service. It was also employed at weddings[2] and at funerals.[3] *See* ANTIPHONAL SINGING.

[1]Suk. III:11; Sot. V:4.
[2]Ber 31a; Ket. 16b, 17a.
[3]M.K. 28b; Meg. 3b.

REVI'I (REVI'A) (⌐—). Aramaic name for a sign placed above the word in the accentuated version of the Bible[1] and translated by numerous scholars as "square," from its four-square shape. William Wickes defines it as "resting," or "sustained" (see the Targum translation of the word *rovetz* in Ex. 23:5), referring to the pause, or character, of the melody. He states also that it is an ordinary point, like a *holam* or a *hirik*, and is not square, as mistakenly claimed by editors of printed texts.[2] Wickes's explanation can be supported by the Hebrew term *meyushav*, meaning "settled," "at ease," which also refers to this accent.[3] Scholars also debate about its pausal power. Some accord it the rank "king"; others, "duke" (*see* DISJUNCTIVES). Solomon ROSOWSKY considers it last in power among the "kings."[4] *See also* TE'AMIM.

[1]Cf. Gen. 1:2.
[2]*A Treatise on the Accentuation of the Prose Books of the Old Testament,* Clarendon Press, Oxford, 1887, pp. 18, 19.
[3]Wolf Heidenheim, *Sefer Mishpetey ha-Te'amim,* Rödelheim, 1808, p. 6a.
[4]*The Cantillation of the Bible,* The Reconstructionist Press, New York, 1957, p. 10.

REVI'IT (REVI'IN). Name of a musical instrument and a rendering for MENA'ANE'IM.[1] The Mishnah[2] makes mention of *revi'it shel alit,* translated as "the clappers of a wailing woman" (MEKONENET).[3]

[1]Targum in II Sam: 6:5.
[2]Kel. XVI:7.
[3]Commentary of Maimonides, ad loc.; *The Babylonian Talmud, Seder Tohoroth, The Mishnahs,* The Soncino Press, London, 1935–1952, pp. 79, 80.

RIKKUD. Hebrew word for DANCE, designating a special dance that became a joyous expression[1] of the Hassidim and is prompted by an intriguing tune, often called a *rikkud'l,* sung with great gusto. It is characteristically danced in a circle, the dancers' feet moving in a leaping manner (cf. *rakkdu* in ps. 114:4) and with gesticulative expression. So much spiritual importance is attributed to the *rikkud* that a special prayer is often recited before the dance.[2] Judah Ha-Levi (1075–1141) wrote in his *Kuzari,* "and if thy joy lead thee so far as to sing and dance [*el haniggun veharikkud*], it becomes worship and a bond of union between thee and the Divine influence."[3]

[1]Eccl. 3:4.
[2]Menashe Unger, *Reb Yisroel Baal-Shem-Tov,* Farlag "Hassidut," New York, 1963, p. 292.
[3]Tr. by R. Yehudah ibn-Tibbon and ed. by A. Zifroni, Schocken Press, Jerusalem and Tel Aviv, 1968, part II, p. 109, paragraph 50.

RINAH. One of ten expressions referring to prayer.[1] Among the various meanings found in verses of Scripture are: (1) "Entreaty," found in Jeremiah 7:16: "Lift up in their behalf neither entreaty nor prayer." (2) "Song," in I Kings 8:28: "To hearken unto the song and unto the prayer."

The Sages comment on this verse: "Where there is song, there shall be prayer."[2] (3) "Joy," as in psalm 126:5: "They that sow in tears shall reap in joy ["cries of joy"]." (4) "Shout," or sing aloud. Since *rinah* often occurs in combination with the word *patzah*, as in psalm 98:4 and Isaiah 14:7, 54:1, 44:23, 52:9, 49:13, and 55:12, meaning "bursting forth," it would thus indicate an expression of powerful emotion. (5) "Complain," as in Lamentations 2:19: "Arise, complain [cry out] in the night." (6) "Exultation," based on Zephaniah 3:17: "He will exult over thee with song."

[1]*Devarim Rabba* 80:2.
[2]Ber. 6a.

Joseph Rosenblatt.

ROSENBLATT, JOSEPH (1882–1933). Cantor who became a legend in Jewish life. Born in Belaya Tserkov, in the Ukraine, young "Yossele" gained a remarkable insight into liturgical music by assisting his father at services in the synagogue. The family later moved to Sadgora, Bukovina, a town known for its Hassidic environment, and there he spent his most formative and impressionable years. Rosenblatt served as cantor and gave concerts in Czernowitz (Chernovtsy), Munkács (Mukachevo), Pressburg (Bratislava), and Hamburg. Upon his arrival in the United States in 1912, he accepted a position as cantor in the First Hungarian Congregation, Ohab Zedek, in New York City. In 1917 he refused an invitation to appear with the Chicago Opera Company on the grounds that opera was not compatible with traditional Jewish principles. Rosenblatt made his debut at Carnegie Hall (1918) and established himself in the concert field. In 1920, at the request of the RCA Manufacturing Company, he recorded about eighty selections of liturgical chant and Jewish folk song; he also made recordings for the Edison Company of Vienna and Columbia Records (*see* PHONOGRAPH RECORD). Rosenblatt's sentiments for the land of Israel manifested themselves in a film called *The Dream of My People* (1933), in which he chanted Jewry's ancient prayers of longing and yearning for Zion. Several books containing his settings of recitatives and choral compositions have been published; the best known is *Tefiloth Josef* (1927). He is also known for his choral settings *Psalm 113* (1921), dedicated to Warren G. Harding; *Psalm 114* (1922); and *Uvnucho Yomar*. The unusual quality and range of his voice, as well as his devoutness and idealism, made him world-famous. A biography, *Yossele Rosenblatt*, was published (1954) by his son Samuel Rosenblatt.

ROSENHAUPT, MORITZ (1841–1900). Cantor-composer. He studied with his father in his birthplace near Kassel, Germany, and later was apprenticed to Cantor Karl Loewe in Strasbourg. In 1861 he was appointed cantor and teacher at Cochem on the Mosel, and in 1864 he was called to a similar position in Speyer, where he became a pupil of Professor Wiss and Dr. Benz and studied harmony, counterpoint, and orchestration. In 1881 he succeeded Cantor Joseph Singer in Nürnberg and served with great distinction until his death. Rosenhaupt was the author of a three-volume work, *Schire Ohel Yaakov, Gottesdienstliche Gesänge für Israeliten,* consisting of the Friday evening service (vol. I, 1879), Sabbath morning service (vol. II, 1887), and weekday service (vol. III, 1895). He also wrote overtures, choral compositions, a concerto, organ and piano pieces, and Hebrew and German songs.

Boruch Leib Rosowsky.

ROSOWSKY, BORUCH LEIB (1841–1919). Cantor-composer and teacher who was active in Riga, Latvia. Born in Naliboki, a village in White Russia, he studied the Bible and Talmud first with his father and later at the yeshivah of Mir, Poland. At an early age Rosowsky showed an unusual talent for music. However, he did not receive formal instruction until he was twenty-six years old, when he enrolled at the St. Petersburg Conservatory on the recommendation of Anton Rubinstein. After a three-year stay, he became an apprentice to Salomon SULZER of Vienna and Hirsch WEINTRAUB in Königsberg, completely imitating the latter's style. In 1871 he was called to the Great Synagogue in Riga, where he served as cantor for forty-eight years. Among the numerous cantors, musicians, and singers who were his choristers and students were Solomon Golub, Hermann Jadlowker, and Joseph Schwarz. Rosowsky wrote a number of works for the synagogue, the most important of which is his two-volume *Shirei Thefiloh* (1924), edited by his son Solomon ROSOWSKY.

Solomon Rosowsky.

ROSOWSKY, SOLOMON (1878–1962). Composer, teacher, and musicologist. The son of Boruch Leib ROSOWSKY of Riga, Latvia, he inherited from his father the feeling for the melos of the synagogue. Rosowsky, educated at the St. Petersburg Conservatory, began to study music only after his graduation from the University of Kiev, where he received a law degree. Among his teachers was Rimski-Korsakov, who gave him, and other Jewish students, encouragement to create a Jewish national music. As a result, Rosowsky, with several other musicians, organized the SOCIETY FOR JEWISH FOLK MUSIC. Upon completion of his studies at the conservatory in 1911, he gave concerts and was music editor and critic for the St. Petersburg daily *Dyen* and wrote occasionally for *Novy Voskhod* and *Rasviet*. In 1918 he became music director of the Jewish Art Theater. Rosowsky returned to Riga in 1920 and founded the first conservatory of Jewish music, called the Jewish Conservatory. After a five-year stay, he left for Palestine and continued his activities in composition, teaching, and research in Jewish music. He also carried out research and lectured in the United States, England, and France on Biblical CANTILLATION and in 1947 settled in New York, where he taught at the New School for Social Research and at the Cantors Institute of the Jewish Theological Seminary. His magnum opus, *The Cantillation of the Bible: Five Books of Moses*, was published in 1957. He wrote orchestral works, chamber music, choral works, piano solos, songs, incidental music, and theatrical music.

ROSSI, SOLOMON (c. 1570–c. 1630). Italian musician also known as Solomone (Salamone) de Rossi (of the Red Ones), the name being derived from the Hebrew Shelomo Min-ha-Adomim, who was employed from about 1587 to about 1628 at the court of the dukes of Gonzaga of Mantua and became the first Jewish composer of European renown. It is believed that Rossi was a descendant of an ancient aristocratic Mantuan family that had been brought as captives from Jerusalem to Rome by Titus. The son of Azarya de Rossi (c. 1514–1578), a Jewish scholar, Solomon always affixed to his name the word "Ebreo" (the Hebrew) and was permitted to walk about (c. 1606) without the yellow badge that other Jews of Mantua were compelled to wear. During his career at the court he served as viol player, singer, violinist, conductor, and composer. Like Claudio Monteverdi (1567–1643), he was an innovator in musical thought and technique. Both Monteverdi and Rossi contributed music to the comedy *L'idropica* (the former wrote the prologue, and the latter the first of four intermezzi) and the sacred play *Maddalena*. Rossi's sister, Madama Europa, is known to have participated in the premiere (Mantua, 1608) of Monteverdi's opera *Arianna*, a historic musical event of the day. Rossi wrote thirteen books of compositions (1589–1628). He is credited with being the first to write trio sonatas, apply the principles of monodic song to instrumental music, and develop the form and technique of variation. Spurred by Leone da Modena, chief rabbi of the republic of Venice, Rossi composed a work for the synagogue of Mantua's Jewish community, HASHIRIM ASHER LISH-LOMO (1623; *Cantiques de Solomon Rossi*), thus introducing choral art music into the synagogue. Rossi's secular compositions establish him as the forerunner of the baroque style in both vocal and instrumental music. Although his synagogal compositions were sung for a very brief time, his idea of introducing elaborate music into the synagogue service was perpetuated in the nineteenth century in Germany as well as in communities in Central Europe. Currently his compositions are performed predominantly outside the synagogue by choruses throughout the world, and several have been recorded.

ROTHMULLER, ARON MARKO (1908–   ). Yugoslavian-born singer, composer, and author. When he was four years old, his family moved from their native town to Zagreb. There he attended the high school of the Academy of Music and soon developed an absorbing interest in Jewish folk song. He furthered his musical education at the Vienna Conservatory (1928 and 1932), studying under Alban Berg and Franz Steiner. His operatic career brought him to Hamburg (1932), Zagreb (1932–1934), Zurich (1935–1947), Vienna (the State Opera; 1946), and London (the New London Opera Company; 1947). A devotee of Jewish music from his youth, he founded in Zagreb (1932) and cofounded in Zurich (1941) a society for the advancement of Jewish music called Omanut. Rothmuller's works include chamber music for various combinations of instruments, choral music, and songs of Sephardic and Ashkenazic origin. His literary work *The Music of the Jews* (1954), which was first published in German (*Die Musik der Juden;* 1951), traces the development of Jewish music from early times to the present.

ROZHINKES MIT MANDLEN. Popular Yiddish folk song from *Shulamit,* an operetta by Abraham GOLDFADEN, which was first performed in Nikolayev, Russia, about 1880. Although the operetta was performed also in the Polish, German, and Hungarian languages. "Rozhinkes mit Mandlen" (Raisins and Almonds) with its Yiddish text became the most popular lullaby throughout Eastern Europe. The opening of this folk song is very similar to the PASHTA–ZAKEF KATAN note grouping in the CANTILLATION of Song of Songs (*Shir Hashirim*). Numerous settings of the melody have been made, and the song is popular among vocal and instrumental artists of the concert stage.

Ruth Rubin.

RUBIN, RUTH (1906–   ). Researcher, author, and singer. Born in Khotin, Bessarabia, she was taken at an early age to Montreal, Canada, where for more than two decades she devoted herself to the study and research of the secular Yiddish folk songs of Eastern Europe. In addition to recording Yiddish folk songs, she performed in lecture-recitals in many countries. She contributed numerous articles, in both English and Yiddish, to various journals and periodicals and is best known for her books *A Treasury of Jewish Folksong* (1950) and *Voices of a People: The Story of Yiddish Folksong* (1963).[1] The Ruth Rubin Archives of Jewish Song, established in 1967, is housed at the Haifa Music Museum and Library.

[1]McGraw-Hill, New York, 2d ed., 1973.

Joseph Rumshinsky.

RUMSHINSKY, JOSEPH (1881–1956). Composer and conductor of YID-DISH THEATER MUSIC. Born in Vilna, Rumshinsky grew up in a musical environment; his father occasionally led the services in the synagogue and his mother led the women in singing songs she had heard the BADHAN sing. Young Yoshtchikel, as he was called, was admitted as a chorister in the choir of Cantor Cohen of the Vilna synagogue. At an early age he studied piano, theory, and harmony. Although he was very young, he led synagogue choirs and is known to have conducted the choir for Cantor Solomon Rozumni. He came in contact with and sought the advice of Abraham Moshe BERNSTEIN, Joseph ALTSHUL, and Jacob Berman. He also met Esther Rachel Kaminski, who introduced him to the Yiddish theater. In 1899 he traveled to Łódź, Poland, where he organized and conducted the Hazomir Choral Society, which paved the way for the establishment of other such groups and for bringing Yiddish folk music to the masses. From Poland he journeyed to London, and in 1904 he arrived in the United States. For a short while he taught piano, arranged and composed music, and led synagogue choirs; eventually, however, he became the leading creator of Jewish operetta in New York. Rumshinsky composed more than a hundred operettas for Yiddish theater, among which are *Dem Rebbens Niggun, Tzubrochene Fiedele,* and *Shir Hashirim.* He also wrote a two-act opera, *Ruth.* As occupied as he was with Yiddish theater, he never neglected liturgical music and continued to conduct synagogue choirs and the choral ensemble of the Jewish Ministers Cantors Association of America. For the latter organization he composed several liturgical works, among them, his cantata *Az Yashir.* He wrote numerous songs, contributed articles to newspapers, and wrote an autobiography, *Klangen fun Mein Leben* (1944).

SABKHA. Stringed instrument mentioned in Daniel 3:5, 7, 10, and 15. It is generally translated by "trigon" (a lyre-like instrument), and corresponds to the Greek *sambyke* and the Latin *sambuca*. John Stainer identifies the *sabkha* with a triangular harp,[1] and Curt Sachs with a horizontal angular harp (i.e., the body and neck form an angle, and the strings are in a horizontal position).[2]

[1] *The Music of the Bible*, London, 1914, p. 73.
[2] *The History of Musical Instruments*, W. W. Norton & Company, Inc., New York, 1940, pp. 83, 84.

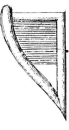

A *sabkha*. [Shaul Shaffer, *Hashir Shebamikdash*, Yefey Nof, Jerusalem]

שבכא

SACRED SERVICE. *See* AVODATH HAKODESH.

SACRED SERVICE FOR THE SABBATH EVE. Work written by Mario CASTELNUOVO-TEDESCO in 1943 for cantor solo (baritone), four-part mixed chorus, and organ.

SAGERIN (ZUGERIN, FORZUGERIN, FORLEINER). Name, from the German *sagen*, meaning "to say," for a woman who acted as a prayer leader or recited prayers aloud in a monotonous, wailing croon for her companions who lacked reading ability.[1] This practice developed because girls were not instructed in Hebrew, according to the Talmudic statement "Whoever teaches his daughter Torah [Law] teaches her obscenity."[2] In the Middle Ages women were known to have conducted separate services in communities such as Worms and Nürnberg. Since the synagogue in Worms had no gallery for women, a *sagerin* became a necessity. Among the texts read aloud by the *sagerin* were the *Tehinot* (Supplications), written for worship in the vernacular of the locality. The *sagerin* also served as prayer leader for other gatherings of women. A noted *sagerin* in the thirteenth century in Worms was Urania (d. 1275), daughter of the chief cantor of the synagogue. The epitaph on her tombstone reads: "This headstone commemorates the eminent and excellent lady Urania, the daughter of R. Abraham, who was chief of the synagogue singers. His prayer for his people rose up unto glory. And as to her, she, too, with sweet tunefulness, officiated before the female worshipers to whom she sang the hymnal portions. In devout service her memory shall be preserved."[3]

[1]Ber. 45b; Ar. 3a.
[2]Sot. 20a. Cf. Rashi, Sot. 21b.
[3]Israel Abrahams, *Jewish Life in the Middle Ages*, Atheneum Publishers, New York, 1969, p. 26.

SALESKI, GDAL (1888–1966). Russian-born cello virtuoso, composer, and lecturer who brought to light in his writings the musicians of Jewish descent active in art music. As a child he sang in the choir of Abraham Dzimitrovsky in the local synagogue of his native Kiev. At the age of fourteen he was admitted to the Kiev Imperial Music School, where he studied the cello. Because of the frequent pogroms in Russia, the family started out for the United States but managed to travel only as far as Leipzig. Saleski received a scholarship to the Leipzig Conservatory, where he studied the cello with Julius Klengel and graduated in 1911 with the Mendelssohn Prize. He later returned to Russia and at the St. Petersburg Conservatory attended chamber music classes and studied the cello and composition. He appeared as first cellist with various symphonic orchestras and gave solo recitals in European cities. He participated with many artists in touring Russia and giving concerts for the SOCIETY FOR JEWISH FOLK MUSIC. Upon his arrival in the United States in 1921, Saleski played the cello with leading orchestras, participated in chamber music concerts, and gave numerous lecture-recitals. From 1933 to 1937 he played with the Radio City Music Hall Orchestra and subsequently became a member of the NBC Symphony Orchestra under the baton of Arturo Toscanini. He was an active member of the JEWISH MUSIC FORUM, to which he presented a scholarly paper[1] and which he served as treasurer (1948–1949). Saleski made a number of transcriptions of compositions by outstanding composers and wrote works for cello and strings. He is best known for his literary achievements, for example, *Famous Musicians of a Wandering Race* (1927) and *Famous Musicians of Jewish Origin* (1949).

[1]"Famous Music Interpreters of Jewish Descent," *Jewish Music Forum Bulletin*, vols. VII, VIII, 1946 and 1947, pp. 38–40.

Lazare Saminsky. [ASCAP]

SAMINSKY, LAZARE (1882–1959). Composer, conductor, lecturer, and writer. Born near Odessa, Russia, he studied with Rimski-Korsakov, Liadov, and Tcherepnin at the St. Petersburg Conservatory, from which he graduated in 1910. While attending the conservatory, he studied mathematics at St. Petersburg University, where he directed one of his own works and also conducted the university choir and orchestra. His enthusiasm for Jewish music manifested itself when he participated in founding the SOCIETY FOR JEWISH FOLK MUSIC and, in 1920, organized a chapter in London. Until his arrival in the United States in December 1920, he served as an assistant editor of a Russian newspaper, conducted at concerts in Tiflis and in London, lectured on general and Jewish music in Jerusalem, Jaffa, Oxford, and Liverpool, and traveled extensively while carrying out research in Oriental music. In 1924 Saminsky was appointed music director of Temple Emanu-El of New York City. He organized the League of Composers (1924) and the Three Choir Festival (1936). Saminsky was always devoted to the cause of the Jewish composer and in 1945 presented a paper called "Creative Allegiance of the Modern Jewish Composer" before the JEWISH MUSIC FORUM.[1] Saminsky wrote numerous works, including symphonies, choral compositions, chamber music, operas, and song cycles. Many of them are rooted in the Jewish idiom, for example, *Lament of Rachel* (1913; rev. 1920), *Chassidic Suite* (1923), *Jephtha's Daughter* (1928), and *Sabbath Evening Service* (1926; 3d ed., 1947). His *Music of the Ghetto and the Bible* (1934) is a noteworthy contribution to Jewish music literature.

[1] *Jewish Music Forum Bulletin*, vols. VII, VIII, 1946 and 1947, pp. 3-5.

SAMUEL GOLDENBERG AND SCHMUYLE. One of ten sections in the program pieces of *Pictures at an Exhibition* by Modest Moussorgsky (Musorgski). This section describes a dialogue between a rich Jew and a poor Jew. The work, composed in 1874 for the piano, was later orchestrated by Maurice Ravel.

SANGMEISTER. Word used in the Nürnberg documents of the Middle Ages for HAZZAN.[1] Dr. S. Ochser mentions a Moses Sangmeister (1461) among the religious functionaries of Nürnberg;[2] most probably, the title had become part of his name.

[1] Cf. M. Stern, *Die israelitsche Bevölkerung der deutschen Städte*, vol. III, *Nürnberg im Mittelalter*, 1896, p. 93.
[2] *The Jewish Encyclopedia*, vol. IX, p. 361, s.v. *Nuremberg*.

SCARBOVA. Term, used interchangeably with MISSINAI TUNES, referring to a body of melodies in the Ashkenazic rite that are not to be changed. Dictionaries give "antique" or "old" as its general meaning.[1] Such adjectives as "commonplace," "trite," and "stock" have also been given.[2] In Jewish music, the term has been interpreted as "holy," from the Latin *sacra*.[3] Thus, *scarbova niggunim* embody a corpus of "holy" tunes that set the specific atmosphere and solemnity of the holiday or occasion. More recently, however, the meaning of the term has been revised to "official melodies," from the Polish *skarb*, "treasure"; thus, from treasure, "official."[4]

[1] Alexander Harkavy, *Complete Dictionary*, Hebrew Publishing Company, New York, 1898, p. 222.
[2] Uriel Weinreich, *Modern English-Yiddish, Yiddish-English Dictionary*, YIVO and McGraw-Hill Book Company, New York, 1968, p. 515.
[3] Abraham Z. Idelsohn, *Jewish Music*, Tudor Publishing Company, New York, 1944, p. 136.
[4] Hanoch Avenary, "The Musical Vocabulary of Ashkenazic Hazanim," *Studies in Biblical and Jewish Folklore*, Indiana University Press, Bloomington, 1960, pp. 194, 195.

SCHALIT, HEINRICH (1886-   ). Composer, musical director, and organist. Born in Vienna to a scholarly family, Schalit attended the State Academy of Music in Vienna, studied composition with Robert Fuchs, and graduated in 1906. He was appointed (1927) organist of the Great Synagogue in Munich, and in 1933, when he was forced by the Nazi government to leave Germany, he accepted the post of musical director at the Great Synagogue in Rome, where he remained until 1939. Forced

Heinrich Schalit.

to leave Italy by decree of the government, Schalit emigrated to the United States in 1940 and held positions in Rochester, N.Y., Providence, R.I., Hollywood, Calif., and Denver, Colo. As a composer, Schalit began writing works of Jewish content about 1914. Hebrew poetry became his source of inspiration, and he wrote several song cycles to texts by Judah Ha-Levi that had been translated into German. Among his liturgical works are *Sabbath Eve Liturgy* (1959), *Sabbath Morning Liturgy* (1952), and *Seven Sacred Songs* (1953). He also wrote a suite for string orchestra and a work for organ.

SCHELOMO. Hebrew rhapsody by Ernest BLOCH, composed in 1916 for cello and orchestra.

SCHLESINGER, SIGMUND (1835–1906). Choir director and organist, among the first to exert a strong influence on the musical practices of the Reform synagogue in the United States in the nineteenth century. He was born in Württemberg, Germany, received his musical education in Munich, and emigrated to the United States in 1860. From 1863 to 1903 he was choir director and organist at Congregation Sha'arey Shamayim in Mobile, Ala. He is known for arranging musical services for the *Union Prayer Book.*

Boruch Schorr.

SCHORR, BORUCH (1823–1904). Chief cantor of the Great Synagogue of Lemberg (Lvov), noted for his opus *N'ginoth Baruch Schorr,* edited by his son Israel Schorr in 1906 (reissued in 1928). Schorr first attracted attention when he sang at Hassidic gatherings as a child in Lemberg, his native city. Bezalel SCHULSINGER, who was touring in Lemberg, was very much impressed when he heard Boruch sing. Schulsinger persuaded Boruch's parents to permit the boy to join his choir. After singing with Schulsinger for two years, Schorr became a chorister with Yeruchom BLINDMAN. His career as a cantor began in Khotin, Bessarabia (1846–1848). Subsequently he held positions in Kamenets Podolski (1848–1850), Iaşi (1851–1854), Budapest (1855–1859), Lemberg (1859–1890; 1896–1904), and New

York (1891–1896). Schorr, a versatile composer, wrote an operetta, *Samson*, which was performed in 1890 at a Yiddish theater in Lemberg. As the curtain came down, he was called to take a bow onstage with the leading soprano singer. When the religious community heard of such undignified conduct, it immediately, and with the sanction of Rabbi Isaac Aaron Ettinger, suspended him from his office for four weeks. Schorr, offended by this decision, left for New York, where he served at the Attorney Street Synagogue for five years. The Lemberg community, remembering Schorr's improvisations and choral compositions, which explored new regions of expression while arousing the feelings of the worshipers, longed for their cantor and invited him to return. He received an overwhelming welcome when he returned to Lemberg in 1896, and he remained there until he died while officiating on the last day of Passover. During this period Schorr wrote, in addition to his musical compositions, his volumes *B'chor Schorr*, a commentary on the Pentateuch, and *Yisron L'chochmah*, a commentary on Ecclesiastes.

SCHULKLOPFER (SCHULKLOPPER). Name derived from *schul*, the Judeo-German designation for synagogue, and *klopfen*, "knock," that is applied to the *shammash* (beadle) who daily (except for the Ninth of Ab) summoned the congregation to services, announced the arrival of the Sabbath, awakened the congregants to the SELIHOT services, and made announcements of public festivities and of lost or stolen articles. He announced his arrival by knocking at the door or window with a fixed number of taps,[1] using a special mallet (except on Sabbath, when he used his fist) and a unique chant.[2] The title itself dates back to the year 1225,[3] but the office is much older and originated in the second century, when the *hazzan ha-kenesset* (*see* HAZZAN) was responsible for these duties.[4] In certain localities he was called *schulbruffer*,[5] and in larger communities he assisted the *shammash*.[6] For example, in 1719 in Fürth the community, consisting of 400 families, was permitted to employ a *schulklopfer* in addition to a CANTOR and gravedigger.

Among the exhortations chanted by the beadle-*schulklopfer* were *Shtet uf* [*kinder*] *le'avodat Habore*, "Wake up [children] for the service of the Creator," *Shtet uf zu Selihot*, "Wake up for the *Selihot* service," or "Israel, O holy folk, awake, arouse yourselves, and rise to the service of the Creator." The announcements of the beadle-*schulkopfer* disappeared from Eastern European communities by the early 1900s. The singsong phrases, as probably utilized by the *schulklopfer*, are still, however, recalled by present-day synagogue worshipers (*see* Fig. 35a).[7] In Sephardic and Orien-

Figure 35a.

tal communities a *shammash* would summon each person by name to attend the *Selihot* service.[8] Figure 35b shows two texts and melodies that were used in these communities. The cantor and congregation would

לְךָ אֲדֹנָי הַצְּדָקָה וְלָנוּ בֹּשֶׁת הַפָּנִים

קוּם קְרָא בְתַחֲנוּנִים	מַה־לְּךָ נִרְדָּם	בֶּן־אָדָם
מֵאֲדוֹן הָאֲדוֹנִים	דְּרֹשׁ סְלִיחָה	שְׁפֹךְ שִׂיחָה
בְּטֶרֶם יָמִים פּוֹנִים	וְאַל־תְּאַחַר	רְחַץ וּטְהַר
לִפְנֵי שׁוֹכֵן מְעוֹנִים	רוּץ לְעֶזְרָה	וּמַהֲרָה
בְּרַח וּפַחֵד מֵאֲסוֹנִים	וְגַם רֶשַׁע	וּמִפְשַׁע
יִשְׂרָאֵל נֶאֱמָנִים	שִׁמְךָ יוֹדְעֵי	אָנָּא שְׁעֵה

Figure 35*b*. [Isaac Levy, *Antología de liturgia Judeo-Española,* Jerusalem]

actually begin the *Selihot* service with the idea of "awakening to the service of the Creator."

[1]Cf. *The Jewish Encyclopedia,* vol. XI, p. 114.

[2]S. W. Baron, *The Jewish Community,* Jewish Publication Society of America, Philadelphia, 1942, vol. II, p. 106.

[3]Cf. Israel Abrahams, *Jewish Life in the Middle Ages,* Atheneum Publishers, New York, 1969, p. 56, note 4.

[4]Jer. Bez., chap. 5; Meg., chap. 3.

[5]H. Dicker, *Die Geschichte der Juden in Ulm,* Rottweil, 1937, p. 104.

[6]M. Güdemann, *Die Geschichte des Erziehungswesens und der Kultur des abendländischen Juden während des Mittelalters und der neueren Zeit,* Vienna, 1888, vol. III, p. 95.

[7]Notated according to an oral rendition by the late Rabbi Hyman M. Friedman, who came from a small town near Vilna.

[8]P. Goodman, *The Rosh Hashanah Anthology,* Jewish Publication Society of America, Philadelphia, 1970, p. 300.

SCHULSINGER, BEZALEL (c. 1790–1860). Noted cantor of the early nineteenth century with whom many *hazzanim* (cantors; *see* HAZZAN) served as "singers" (choristers). Popularly called "Bezalel Odesser," he served for about thirty-five years as *stadt hazzan* (*see* HAZZAN, STADT) in Odessa. Schulsinger was a native of Galicia (or Podolia), and late in life he emigrated to Jerusalem, where he died. His style of chant became known for its simplicity and constantly renewed charm. He lacked theoretical musical knowledge, but his choral compositions were notated and copied by those of his students who had technical musical training. Recently several of his recitatives were published in the *Cantorial Anthology* by Gershon EPHROS (vol. II, *Yom Kippur,* pp. 289–292).

SCHULSINGER. Name used for HAZZAN in some German documents.[1]

[1]Cf. *The Jewish Encyclopedia,* vol. VII, s.v. *Judenschule.*

SECOND SYMPHONY. Work (op. 36) in four movements by Paul BEN-HAIM completed in 1945. The music undertakes to describe the landscape of Israel and, in the composer's words, depicts a "symphony of light." The first movement represents morning; the second, evening; the third, night; and the fourth, day. The work has a pastoral quality throughout, utilizes elements of Jewish-Oriental song, and represents a synthesis of European and Eastern art. Its premiere performance was in 1948 with the ISRAEL PHILHARMONIC ORCHESTRA, under the baton of George Singer. The symphony was awarded the Engel Prize.

Sholom Secunda.

SECUNDA, SHOLOM (1894-1974). Composer, conductor, and lecturer, born in Aleksandriya, in the southern Ukraine. Secunda emigrated to the United States in 1908. In New York City he attended Cooper Union, Columbia University, and the Institute of Music and Art. In his early youth he sang as a synagogue chorister and in 1914 produced his first musical play (in collaboration with Solomon Shmulevich) at the Oden Yiddish Theater. His musical activities branched out, and he served as musical director and composer at many Yiddish theaters, as lecturer in various institutions of higher learning, as synagogue choral conductor, and as music critic for the *Jewish Daily Forward*. Secunda is known for writing Yiddish musical plays and operettas, scores for films, oratorios, chamber music, liturgical works, and folk songs. Especially popular are his songs "Bei Mir Bist Du Sheyn," "Dos Yiddishe Lied," and "Dona, Dona."

SEFARDI, YEHIEL NAHMANI. *See* CONSOLO, FEDERICO.

SEGOL (⁞‒). Accent mark in the printed book of Scripture, meaning "bunch" or "cluster of dots,"[1] and so named for its similarity to the vowel sign *segol*. The *segol* consists of three dots to show that it is a relatively greater pausal accent than the ZAKEF KATAN with its two dots, which in turn is greater than REVI'I, which has only one dot.[2] The sign always appears over the last letter of the word (postpositive) but not necessarily over the accented syllable so that the dots will not be confused with others that appear above the word. In words having penultimate accents, the *segol* appears twice; the sign to the left is the name sign, and the sign to the right indicates the accented syllable. It is generally preceded by the ZARKA,[3] and occasionally a MUNAH is found between the *zarka* and the *segol*.[4] Melodically, the *segol* resembles the ETNAHTA, for it draws out the last note, but to a lesser degree, leading to a semicadence. *See also* TE'AMIM.

[1]Compare *eshkol* in Numb. 13:23.
[2]William Wickes, *A Treatise on the Accentuation of the Prose Books of the Old Testament*, Clarendon Press, Oxford, 1887, p. 17.
[3]E.g., Gen. 4:16.
[4]E.g., ibid., 24:15.

SELAH. Word in the Book of Psalms (*see* PSALMS, BOOK OF) occurring seventy-one times in thirty-nine psalms and three times in Habakkuk (3:3, 9, and 13). It appears either at the end of a psalm (e.g., ps. 3:9) or in the middle of a psalm, in which case it is placed at the end of a clause (e.g., ps. 57:4). Its meaning has been variously interpreted by scholars and remains doubtful. Several commentators have given no musical meaning to the word and have interpreted it as "forever," derived from the word *le'almin* or *lealmo*, by which the Targum renders *selah*.[1] Ibn-Ezra is of the opinion that it is a word of emphasis, meaning "so it is," "thus," or "and the matter is true and right," interpreting psalm 81:8, "I proved thee at the waters of Meribah *selah*" to mean "I proved thee at the waters of Meribah so it is [*emet*]."[2] Others are of the opinion that it stands for an affirmation, like AMEN and *shalom*, or an exclamation like HALLELUYAH, found at the end of Scriptural writings. However, because thirty-one of the thirty-nine psalms that contain the word *selah* have the word LAMENATZE'AH in their headings, as well as other musical connotations such as NEGGINOT, MIZMOR, and AL-ALAMOT, many authorities believe that it has a musical meaning.

(1) The Septuagint translates it by *diapsalma*, a term as obscure as *selah*. Some explanations given are a silence or pause in the psalm, an instrumental interlude, a change of meter at places marked by the term, and a change of choir, that is, an indication of which section of the psalm was to be sung by another choir (*see* ANTIPHONAL SINGING). (2) David Kimchi is of the opinion that *selah* signifies a raising of the voice, denoting a fortissimo, from *salal*, "to raise," the final letter, *h*, being paragogic. G. H. A. Ewald interprets this to mean an interruption in the singing when the priests raised their trumpets and cymbals and with strong tones marked the words just spoken, while the singers' voices stopped or became hushed. (3) *Selah* is possibly an acronym from the initial letters of *siman leshanot hakol*, "sign to change the voice," or *sov lema'alah ha-shar*, "go back to the beginning, O singer," that is, *da capo*.[3] It has also been suggested that *selah* is equivalent to a *ritornello* ("little return"), that the verses in which *selah* occurs were repeated either by another choir or by the instruments.[4] (4) *Selah* may also be an indication of dynamics, "to lower the voice" (p., pp.), from *salah*, "to lay low." (5) *Selah* may possibly denote a drum in the shape of a basket, from the Hebrew *sal*, meaning "basket." When struck, this "basket-drum" indicated either a change of melody or a cessation of the psalm.[5]

In 1951 a cantorial school was founded in Tel Aviv, Israel, called Selah, an acronym derived from the initial letters of Seminar Lepituah Ha-Hazzanut (lit. Seminary for the Development of Cantorial Music). It was established under the sponsorship of the cultural division of the Hapoel Hamizrachi and later became part of the school known as Bilu.

[1] Erub. 54a.
[2] Ps. 3:3.
[3] J. G. Eichhorn, *Allgemeine Bibliothek der biblischen Literatur*, Leipzig, 1787–1801, vol. V, p. 545.
[4] Cf. John Stainer, *The Music of the Bible*, London, 1879, p. 82.
[5] J. Steinberg, *Mishpat Ha'urim*, Vilna, 1902, p. 581.

SELIHOT. Penitential prayers (from *selah*, "to forgive"). Originally recited only on Yom Kippur, since the Middle Ages they have been recited also prior to the morning prayer during Aseret Yeme Teshuvah (the penitential season) as well as after the morning prayer on certain fast days. In the *Selihot* literature the dominant refrain is the "Thirteen Attributes of Mercy."[1] With the great suffering of Israel that took place between the tenth and seventeenth centuries, the *Selihot* literature increased and included numerous poetic compositions describing the misery and hopes of the people.

A special *Selihah* mode, with major and minor characteristics, is prevalent in the chant of the penitential prayers. The minor characteristics are basically similar to the Prophetic and psalm modes; the major characteristics are used mainly at the closing of a prayer (e.g., *Kel Melekh Yoshev*). The free improvisation of the *piyyutim* (poems) influenced cantors of Eastern European countries to employ the emotional AHAVAH RABBAH MODE as well. It is a practice that the cantor who officiates during the High Holy Day period also officiates on the first day of the penitential prayers. In a way, this is to do away with the notion that he who takes a fee for his services during the holiday sees no blessing from that fee: if he officiates on the first day of the *Selihot*, his fee becomes inclusive.[2] Another musical custom connected with the *Selihot* is the three-time knock on every door or window given by the SCHULKLOPFER, who announces in a chantlike manner, "Israel, O holy folk, awake, arouse yourselves, and rise to the service of the Creator." In Yemen it is the practice to blow the SHOFAR during the recitation of the "Thirteen Attributes of Mercy" in addition to the usual blasts after the morning service.[3]

[1] R.H. 17b.
[2] Reubin Margoliot, *Nefesh Hayyah*, Lwów, 1934.
[3] S. Y. Agnon, *Days of Awe*, Schocken Books, Inc., New York, 1948, pp. 32, 35.

Alfred Sendrey.

SENDREY, ALFRED (1884–). Conductor, composer, and teacher, noted as a bibliographer and musicologist of Jewish music. Sendrey began his musical education in his native Budapest, Hungary, where he graduated from the Royal Academy of Music. He continued the study of musicology at Leipzig University, where he received a doctor of philosophy degree. As an opera conductor, Sendrey traveled extensively and held leading positions in Germany and the United States. From 1924 to 1932 he conducted the Leipzig Symphony Orchestra and was music director of the Mid-German Radio Station. In 1933 he went to France and was appointed musical adviser to the French State Broadcasting System in Paris, a post he held for seven years. In 1940 he settled in the United States and taught at the Young Men's Hebrew Association in New York, the Westlake College of Music, and the University of Judaism in Los Angeles. In 1967 the University of Judaism conferred upon him the degree of doctor of humane letters. Sendrey stands out for his *Bibliography of Jewish Music* (1951), a corpus of almost 10,000 titles with a foreword by Curt Sachs. The work opens up new vistas in Jewish MUSICOLOGY and history and is invaluable for Jewish music research. He also wrote *David's Harp* (1964; with Mildred Norton), *Music in Ancient Israel* (1969), and *The Music of the*

Jews in the Diaspora (1970). Among his compositions are several orchestral and choral works and miscellaneous pieces for various instruments.

SERVICE SACRÉ (POUR LE SAMEDI MATIN AVEC PRIÈRES ADDI-TIONELLES POUR LE VENDREDI SOIR). Sacred service (for the Sabbath morning with additional prayers for Friday night), composed by Darius MILHAUD, for baritone solo, READER, mixed choir and orchestra, or organ. The work, composed at the request of Mrs. E. S. Heller (following the suggestion of Cantor Reuben R. Rinder) in 1947 for Temple Emanuel in San Francisco, was first performed on May 18, 1949.

SETER (STAROMINSKY), MORDECAI (1916–   ). Israeli composer and teacher. He was born in Novorossisk, Russia, and in 1926 was taken to Palestine, where, at an early age, he gained a knowledge of music by studying piano with Jacob WEINBERG, Mrs. Rivkah Burstein-Arbor, and Arie Abileah. At the age of sixteen he enrolled at the École Normale, where he spent several years working with Nadia Boulanger, Lazare Lévy, and Igor Stravinsky and became thoroughly grounded in professional musicianship. After he returned to Palestine in 1937, he came under the influence of Joachim STUTSCHEWSKY, who persuaded him to study and familiarize himself with Jewish music. He absorbed the characteristics of Jewish music, which later appeared in his own compositions. In Israel he became active as an independent composer and as a teacher at the Israel Academy of Music. Among his best-known compositions are *Sabbath Cantata* (1940) for soloists, mixed choir, and string orchestra (or organ), *Ricercar* (1956) for violin, viola, violoncello, and string ensemble, *Midnight Vigil* (1961), an oratorio for tenor, mixed choir, and orchestra, and *Festivals* (1964) for mixed choir. His works won for him the Engel Prize of the municipality of Tel Aviv (1945 and 1954), the ACUM Prize (1958), the Prix d'Italia (1962), and the Israel Prize (1965).

SHABBAT SHIRAH. *See* SHIRAH, THE.

SHAHARIT. Morning service (Heb. *Tefillat Shaharit,* Aramaic *Tzeloso Detzafra*), from *shahar* (morning or down). Its origin is attributed to the patriarch Abraham,[1] and it is sometimes referred to in rabbinic literature as *Tefillah shel Yotzer,* from the first blessing in the *Shaharit* proper, *Yotzer Or* ("Creator of Light"). The basic structure consists mainly of the SHEMA and its benedictions and the *Amidah.* Other sections that were incorporated into the *Shaharit* service are: *Birkhot Hashahar* (Morning Blessings), *Pesukay Dezimrah* (Verses of Song), *Tahanun* (Supplication), and Torah reading with variations in accordance with the day of the week and holidays. Each section has its particular musical mode of chant. On weekdays it is chanted in a musically elevated speech or declamation. On the Sabbath and holidays a higher pitch level, with wider intervals, is used in order to express jubilation. The officiant for this service on the High Holy Days is called BA'AL SHAHARIT. *See also* ARVIT; MATHIL; MINHAH; MUSAF.

[1]Cf. Gen. 22:3; Ber. 26b.

SHALISHIM. Term, mentioned only once in I Samuel 18:6, whose meaning has been the object of conjecture and speculation by Biblical commentators and scholars. (1) The Septuagint translates it by "cymbals." Rashi (quoting the Targum Jonathan) and R. David Kimchi have the same view. (2) The Vulgate gives *sistra* as its meaning. (3) The marginal notation in the Authorized Version translates it as "three-stringed instruments," from the root *shalosh,* "three." Thus, some Biblical commentators have suggested "tri-

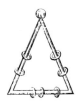

The *shalishim* as described under (4). [Shaul Shaffer, *Hashir Shebamikdash,* Yefey Nof, Jerusalem]

angular harps" or "three-stringed lutes." (4) The word has been defined as triangles, as suggested by the root *shalosh.* The instrument is a steel rod bent into an equilateral triangle, suspended on a thread, and struck with a metal stick. (5) It has been defined as a dance, according to R. Yosef b. Shimon Kara, made up of three rows (i.e., two outer rows and one inner row).[1] According to Curt Sachs, it is a dance with "three" (participants), such as the Roman tripudium of the priests of Mars, the old German *Treialtrei,* and the Austrian *Dreysteyrer.* He believes that *shalishim* has no reference to a musical instrument because the word *besimhah* comes between the words *shalishim* and *tupim* (musical instruments), and "poets and chroniclers never separate coherent notions."[2] (6) F. W. Galpin interprets it to mean a three-stringed instrument, probably the long-necked guitar, or tamboura.[3] (7) Some scholars render it "noble songs" (cf. the word *shalishim* in Prov. 22:20).

[1] Ad. loc.
[2] *The History of Musical Instruments,* W. W. Norton & Company, New York, 1940, p. 123.
[3] Cf. John Stainer, *The Music of the Bible,* rev. by F.W. Galpin, London, 1914, p. 190.

SHALSHELET ($\sum$). Hebrew term for an accent mark, meaning literally "chain"; that is, its name and symbol characteristically represent its chainlike melody as utilized in Biblical CANTILLATION. The most melismatic of all the TE'AMIM, it occurs only seven times in the Bible (Gen. 19:16, 24:12, and 39:8; Lev. 8:23; Isa. 13:8; Amos 1:2; and Ezra 5:15), excluding the books of Job, Proverbs, and Psalms. It has been suggested that, according to Midrashic interpretation, whenever this rare accent mark occurs, the element of "hesitation," "reticence," "repetition," or "vacillation" is present.[1]

[1] David Weissberg, "The Rare Accents of the Twenty-one Books," *Jewish Quarterly Review,* vol. LVI, April 1966, p. 334.

SHARKUKITAH. Term used in the Jerusalem Talmud[1] and translated as "whistle" or "shepherd's pipe" (from *sherak,* "to whistle").[2] *See also* MASHROKITA.

[1] Kid. I, 60b, top.
[2] Marcus Jastow, *Dictionary,* London, 1903, vol. II, p. 1634.

SHELIAH TZIBBUR. All-embracing name, meaning "messenger," "emissary," or "delegate" of the congregation, that is applied to the person who recites the prayers aloud before the congregation. He is also known as *SHaTZ,* an acronym derived from the initial letters of the two words. After Temple sacrifices were replaced by prayer (based on Hos. 14:3), the role of the priest, who had been delegated to bless the Jewish people and offer their sacrifices, was taken over by the *sheliah tzibbur,* who serves as the religious functionary who leads the congregation in prayer. This title, known as early as a century before the Common Era, became synonymous with HAZZAN about the sixth century, and the terms are presently used interchangeably.[1]

As worship became part of daily conduct, it became incumbent upon each individual to pray thrice daily. The duty of the *shatz* was to clear from obligation one who was unlettered or unfamiliar with the prayers, as well as one who was familiar with them (i.e., if the individual accidentally omitted something).[2] Thus, the repetition by the READER of the *Amidah* (prayer of benedictions recited in a standing position) is termed *hazarat ha-shatz*. The essential qualifications of the *shatz* are a sweet voice, knowledge of the prayer chants, exemplary piety, and an ability to minister to the congregation.[3] The *Pesikta de Rav Kahana* relates: "It is written 'honour the Lord with thy wealth [*behonkha*].'[4] Do not read *behonkha* but *bigronkha* [with your throat]. Should you have a pleasant voice and be in the synagogue, arise and honour the Lord with your voice."[5] In Talmudic days this post was honorary, and the liturgy was intoned in an informal way. Sages such as R. Akiba, R. Elazar, Rav, and R. Hiyya b. Ada served in this capacity. In the medieval period the word *shatz* was often appended to the reader's first name; for example, Meir ben Isaac of Orléans, author of AKDAMUT, was called R. Meir Shatz. The Almighty Himself is likened to a *sheliah tzibbur*,[6] thus indicating the high status of this office. *See also* CANTOR; PRECENTOR.

[1]Sof. X. 4; R. Hayyim Joseph David Azulai, *Birkei Yosef, Orah Hayyim*, 181; *Pirke de-Rabbi Eliezer*, chaps. 12, 16.
[2]R.H. 34b.
[3]Ta'an. 16a.
[4]Prov. 3:9.
[5]25,2.
[6]R.H. 17b.

SHEMA YISRAEL. (1) Initial words ("Hear O Israel") of a declaration of faith that is a central section of the liturgy[1] and from time immemorial has been on the lips of Jewish martyrs. Figure 36 demonstrates special musical settings that have become traditional when taking out the Torah on Sabbath and festival (Fig. 36*a*) and High Holy Days (Fig. 36*b*). (2) Setting by Darius MILHAUD scored for four-part chorus of mixed voices, tenor or baritone solo, and organ.[2]

[1]Deut. 6:4; Ber. 61b.
[2]*Synagogue Music by Contemporary Composers*, G. Schirmer, Inc., New York, pp. 194–197.

Figure 36*a*.

Figure 36*b*.

SHER (SHERELE). Russian dance (lit. "scissors") in moderate duple meter, at one time prevalent among Jews of Eastern Europe and now found in Israel and the Diaspora. The *sher* was a favorite of the tailors' guild, and in its execution the dance describes a pair of shears and the threading of a needle. It is generally performed at weddings and similar joyous occasions.

SHERIFF, NOAM (1935–   ). Israeli-born composer and educator. His principal teachers were Paul BEN-HAIM and Boris Blacher in composition and Igor Markevitch in conducting. He founded a symphony orchestra at the Hebrew University in Jerusalem, appeared as a conductor with the ISRAEL PHILHARMONIC ORCHESTRA (IPO), the Kol Yisrael symphonic and light orchestras, and the Israel Defense Army Orchestra, and was a professor of orchestration at the Academy of Music in Jerusalem. Sheriff first drew attention as a composer when his *Festival Prelude* was given its premiere performance (1957) by the Israel Philharmonic Orchestra under the baton of Leonard Bernstein. He won the IPO Prize for this work and again in 1960 for his *Song of Degrees* for orchestra. Among his other works are *Ashrei* (1961) for alto, flute, two harps, and tom-toms, *Israel Suite* (1965) for symphony orchestra, and *Chaconne* (1967) for orchestra. His works were performed in Israel and abroad, and he also wrote for the theater and for films.

SHESTAPOL. WOLF (c. 1832–1872). Eastern European cantor-composer, popularly called Velvele Chersoner. He served as STADT HAZZAN (*see* HAZZAN, STADT) in Kherson (Cherson), where he established a synagogue musical service according to CHOR-SCHUL practices. Shestapol, born in Skvira, southwest of Kiev, sang at the age of eight as a chorister in his father's choir in Odessa and later with Bezalel SCHULSINGER. At the age of twelve he was already composing synagogue music. Among the cantors of his day he was considered unusual in that he was able to read music fluently. Nissan BLUMENTHAL, his teacher and mentor, recommended him to the Kherson community, and in 1843 he was appointed permanent cantor there. Shestapol felt the need to further his musical and cantorial knowledge and was sent, at the expense of the Kherson community, to Salomon SULZER in Vienna to study the music and practice of the modern *chor-shul*. He later returned to Kherson, where his musical creations and service became a model for almost all congregations in Russia. A prolific composer, Shestapol left a great number of compositions in manuscript form; several have been arranged in the *Cantorial Anthology* by Gershon EPHROS.[1] His settings with songlike character, which have become popular and are sung throughout the world, are his KADDISH for the High Holy Days (especially the melody beginning with the words *behayekhon* and *le'ela*)[2] and *Adoshem Zekharanu*.[3]

[1]E.g., *M'chalkel Chayim*, no. 4, Bloch Publishing Company, Inc., New York, 1940, p. 51.
[2]I. Goldfarb and S. E. Goldfarb, *Synagogue Melodies for the High Holy Days*, Brooklyn, N.Y., 1926, pp. 32, 33.
[3]M. Nathanson, *Manginoth Shireynu*, Hebrew Publishing Company, New York, 1939, p. 49.

SHIDAH VESHIDOT. Obscure phrase cited in Ecclesiastes 2:8 whose meaning has been variously interpreted: (1) David Kimchi comments: "Its explanation, according to the Geonim, is an instrument of music which was found in the time of the existence of the Temple."[1] (2) The phrase is derived from the Arabic verb *shada*, "to sing sweetly [a song]" or "to chant a poem."[2] According to Avraham Kahana, it is possibly an elucidation of the previous phrase in the same verse, *veta'anugot bene* *ha'adam* ("and the delights of the sons of men").[3] (3) Song and melody that accompany a game of capturing a woman.[4] (4) Dancers, both male and female.[5] (5) According to the Talmud, in Babylon it is translated as male and female demons; in Palestine it means carriages.[6]

[1]*Sefer Hasharashim*, Venice, 1546–1548, s.v. *shadad.*
[2]*Hava Arabic-English Dictionary*, Catholic Press, Beirut, 1915.
[3]*Torah Nevi'im Uketuvim im Perush Madai*, Hotzo'at-Mekorot, Tel Aviv, 1929, pp. 161, 162.
[4]J. Steinberg, *Mishpat Ha'urim*, Vilna, 1902.
[5]*Mahzor Kol Bo; Bet Yisrael.*
[6]Git. 68a.

SHIGGAYON. Word used in psalm 7:1 and occurring in Habakkuk 3:1 but with a different spelling (*shiggyonot*). The several musical interpretations are: (1) a musical instrument;[1] (2) a "melody type";[2] (3) a dithyrambic song of impassioned character, the meaning being deduced from the intransitive verb *shagah*, to "rave," "swerve," "stagger";[3] (4) the same as HIGGAYON.[4]

[1]Cf. Rashi, ad loc.
[2]Cf. David Kimchi; Ibn-Ezra, ad loc.
[3]Wilhelm Gesenius, *A Hebrew and English Lexicon of the Old Testament*, Boston, 1906, p. 993.
[4]H. Hupfeld, *Die Psalmen, übersetzt und ausgelegt*, 1855–1862, i, 109, 199.

SHILOAH, AMNON (1928–   ). Israeli musicologist. Born in Lanús, Argentina, Shiloah settled in Palestine in 1941. From 1933 to 1941 he studied at the Alliance Israélite in Damascus and later completed his general and musical education in Jerusalem at the Hebrew University and the Academy of Music. From 1954 to 1958 he studied in Paris at the National Conservatory and the Sorbonne, obtaining certificates from both schools, and in 1963 the Sorbonne conferred upon him a doctorate in musicology. Between 1953 and 1965 Shiloah sojourned in Israel and Paris, carrying on a variety of musical activities. In Israel he was a member of the Kol Yisrael Orchestra, presented radio programs on musical subjects, was a music critic for a newspaper, and lectured on Oriental music at the Hebrew University. In France he served as a tutor at the École Nationale des Langues Orientales and lectured at the ethnomusicological department of the Musicology Institute, at the Musée Guimet, and on French radio. In 1968 Shiloah was visiting lecturer at the University of Illinois, and from 1969 to 1971 he served as director of the Jewish Music Research Centre and vice-chairman of the Israeli Musicological Association. In 1971 he became chairman of the department of musicology at the Hebrew University of Jerusalem. Shiloah wrote numerous essays on the music of the Oriental communities, including *La musique dans le monde arabe et juif* (1965), *Rôle et fonction de la musique orientale* (1967), and *Kitvei ha-yehudim b-hokmat ha-musiqa* (1968). Of particular significance is his preparation of a recording, *Morasha-Heritage*, of the authentic songs of the various Jewish communities in Israel; the songs were sung by informants, and Shiloah supplied a commentary (Eng., Fr., Heb.).

SHIR or SHIRAH (pl. *shirim* or *shirot*). Song, hymn, or poem. Rabbinic literature records ten *shirot:*[1] (1) Psalm 92, uttered by Adam on the first Sabbath of creation, when the Sabbath protected and saved his life; (2) "Song of the Red Sea," upon the exodus of the Jews from Egypt;[2] (3) "Then sang Israel this song," celebrating the appearance of the well in the desert;[3] (4) "Farewell Song," sung by Moses before his death;[4] (5)

"Then spoke Joshua to the Lord," when the sun stood still and the moon stayed until the people avenged themselves upon their enemies;[5] (6) "Then sang Deborah and Barak," on the occasion of victory in war;[6] (7) "And Hannah prayed, and said," giving thanks to the Lord for giving her a son;[7] (8) "And David spoke unto the Lord the words of this song," on the occasion when the Lord saved him from his enemies and from the hand of Saul;[8] (9) "The Song of Songs," first of the five scrolls incorporated into the Ketuvim (Hagiographa); and (10) the final song which will be uttered when the Messiah will come and Jerusalem will be restored. The Baal Haturim[9] does not mention the song of Adam as one of the ten songs. Instead, he cites Hezekiah's song proclaiming God for all kingdoms of the earth.[10]

Thirty psalms are designated as *shir*, one of ten synonyms of praise by which they were uttered[11] and probably indicating that they were actually sung. As to the difference between *shir* and MIZMOR, there are various schools of thought: (1) *Shir* signifies a song of gratitude or thanksgiving uttered by the voice alone, whereas *mizmor* is a song intended for musical performance with instrumental accompaniment. As to the words *shir* and *mizmor* appearing in the same superscription,[12] Solomon Buber interprets this to mean that the psalm was accompanied by choral singing.[13] Ibn-Ezra comments that there is no differentiation between the phrase *mizmor shir* and *shir mizmor*. (2) Without elucidation Emil G. Hirsch translates *shir* as "song," probably suggesting that the psalm was actually sung in the Temple and that *mizmor* denotes a "paragraph," hence a new beginning.[14] (3) According to Samson Raphael Hirsch, *shir* denotes the chanting of the words in a song, whereas *mizmor* is primarily the singing of a melody or tune.[15] Since the Hebrew language does not differentiate between these two concepts, the form of the verb "to sing" is employed in both. Distinction is made, however, between *shir*, the masculine form, and *shirah*, the feminine. The Midrash Rabba states: "All the songs that have heretofore been composed [i.e., in Scripture] are of the feminine gender, but the song of the future . . . will be of the masculine gender," thus referring to *shir hadash*, "a new song."[16]

[1]*Mishle Yehoshu'a*, Yiddish homily in *Mahzor Kol Bo*, sec. on *Song of Songs*.
[2]Ex. 15:1–18.
[3]Numb. 21:17.
[4]Deut. 32:1.
[5]Josh. 10:12.
[6]Judg. 5:1.
[7]I Sam. 2:1.
[8]II Sam. 22:1.
[9]Ex. 15:1.
[10]II Kings 19:15.
[11]Pes. 117a.
[12]E.g., ps. 48:1 and twelve other psalms.
[13]*Midrash Tehillim*, Vilna, 1891, XXIV:7, p. 204.
[14]*The Jewish Encyclopedia*, vol. X, p. 248.
[15]Cf. *The Psalms*, New York, 1960.
[16]Isa. 42:10.

SHIR HAMA'ALOT. Superscription (lit. "a song of ascents or degrees") in fifteen psalms[1] whose meaning has been variously interpreted: (1) The Mishnah maintains that the "ascents" or "degrees" allude to the fifteen steps in the Temple that led from the Court of the Women to the Court of the Israelites. On each step, one of the fifteen psalms was chanted by the LEVITES to the accompaniment of various musical instruments on the festival of Sukkot (Feast of Tabernacles) during the ceremony of the Feast of Water Drawing (*see* WATER DRAWING, FEAST OF).[2] (2) Some scholars explain the fifteen psalms as compositions sung on the return from Babylon to Jerusalem or when the pilgrims ascended Mount Zion on the three festivals. (3) Possibly, the word is derived from the poetical construction of some of the psalms; that is, the concluding words of one sentence are often repeated at the beginning of the next verse,[3] for example,

I will lift up mine eyes unto the mountains
From whence shall my help come?
My help cometh from the Lord[4] . . .

As a remembrance of the Temple ritual, and as an expression of hope for the restoration of Israel, the *Shir Hama'alot* psalms are recited after the Sabbath MINHAH service starting with the first Sabbath after Sukkot.

[1] Pss. 120–134.
[2] Mid. 11:5; Suk. V:4; Suk. 51a, b.
[3] Wilhelm Gesenius, *Hebräisches und chaldäisches Handwörterbuch über das Alte Testament*, Leipzig, 1915, p. 446.
[4] Ps. 121:1–2.

SHIRAH, THE. Name, meaning "The Song," applied in Jewish literature to the song chanted by Moses and the children of Israel at the Red Sea (Ex. 15:1–18). The early song of victory and praise opens with the words *Az Yashir Moshe* (Then sang Moses) and is known also as *Shirat Hayam*, "Song of the Sea," "Song of the Red Sea," or "The Song of Moses." The form of its chant was RESPONSORIAL; Moses led the men, and his sister Miriam led the women.[1] In Temple days the LEVITES chanted the *Az Yashir* during the Sabbath afternoon sacrifice.[2] Eventually it became the closing paragraph of *Pesukay Dezimrah* (Verses of Song) of the daily SHAHARIT service, in keeping with the precept that the people remember their deliverance from Egypt.[3] The Sabbath on which the portion of the Torah is read in the synagogue is called Shabbat Shirah (Sabbath of Song), and during its recitation the congregation stands. In the Torah scroll the verses are metrically arranged in thirty lines like "bricks in a wall."[4] The READER is not strictly bound to the system of CANTILLATION used in reading the Pentateuch. Figure 37a is the Ashkenazic Eastern European tradition. The

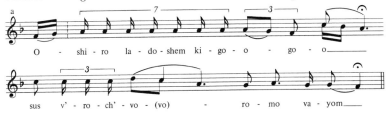

O - shi - ro la - do - shem ki - go - o - go - o.
sus v' - ro - ch' - vo - (vo) - ro - mo va - yom

Figure 37a.

O. o - sham - nu
Cha - zak cha - zak v' - nis - cha - zek

Figure 37b.

Figure 37c–e.

opening phrase resembles the *Ashamnu* prayer of Yom Kippur, and the SILLUK clause is identical to the melody used at the conclusion of each of the Five Books of Moses (*see* Fig. 37b). In the Ashkenazic tradition, different customs have arisen as to which verses are chanted with this special tune. Some chant the *Shirah* with the regular TROP system, making a change and using the special *Shirah* melody only in the verses in which God's name is mentioned. In other locales (e.g., Poland, Galicia) each sentence is rendered with this special melody. Figure 37c is the melody in use on Shabbat Shirah in Spanish-Portuguese communities. It differs from Fig. 37d, an ancient Sabbath morning tune sung during the service proper. Figure 37e is of Yemenite tradition.

[1] Sot. 30b; Rashi, Ex. 15:21.
[2] R.H. 31a.
[3] *Hamanhig* I:24; *Abudraham,* "Seder Shaharit shel Hol."
[4] Meg. 16b refers to the form as *ariah al gabe leveynah* (a half brick over a whole brick) *u-leveynah al gabe ariah* (and a whole brick over a half brick). Cf. Shab. 103b; Sof., chaps. XII, XIII.
[5] J. L. Ne'eman, *Tseliley Hammiqra,* Tel Aviv, 1955, vol. I, p. 131.

SHKUDER, YISROEL YA'AKOB (1804–c. 1846). Famous itinerant cantor of the nineteenth century. Born in Lithuania, he sang with Bezalel SCHUL-SINGER. He died in Vilna, shortly after officiating in that city in honor of a visit by Sir Moses Montefiore. His *Bemotzoe Menuha* for choir, notated in a single-voice line, appeared in the THESAURUS OF HEBREW-ORIENTAL MELODIES (vol. VIII, no. 242) by Abraham Zvi IDELSOHN.

SHOFAR. Ancient wind instrument (lit. "ram's horn") preserved to the present day in the Jewish ritual. The term is variously translated as "trumpet,"[1] "cornet,"[2] "horn" (*see* KEREN), "wild goat's horn," and "clarion." It is used, as described in the Bible, at the giving of the Torah,[3] for announcing the "Year of the Jubilee,"[4] for purposes of war,[5] for religious ceremonials,[6] to warn of approaching danger,[7] to call the people together on a solemn fast day,[8] and as an accompaniment to a song of praise.[9] The blowing of the *shofar* on Rosh Hashanah (New Year) is based on the command in Leviticus 23:24 and Numbers 29:1. Although the Bible makes mention of a *teruah* (discussed below) without clearly mentioning the *shofar* as the instrument to be used, its use is deduced by comparison with Leviticus 25:9, in which the *shofar teruah* is mentioned in connection with the "Jubilee Year." The *shofar* is blown also at the close of the Yom Kippur service, every morning after the SHAHARIT service throughout the Jewish month of Elul,[10] and, according to the ritual of the Sephardim, on Hoshana Rabbah (seventh day of the Feast of Tabernacles). It was also sounded for announcing the Sabbath,[11] in excommunication ceremonies,[12] and at funerals.[13] As a sign of final redemption the Jewish people await the blowing of the *shofar* by the prophet Elijah (*Shofar shel Mashiah*), as based on Isaiah 27:13. Recently a cornerstone made of limestone with the

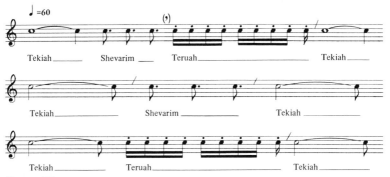

Figure 38a.

Figure 38b. [J. Heller, Kol T'hilloh]

inscription *Lebeyt Hatekiyah* ("To [or belonging to] the place of the blowing of the *shofar*"), followed by the first two letters of another word, *lamed* and *heh*, was found on the Herodian pavement at the foot of the Wall in Jerusalem, where it had fallen when the Temple was destroyed. The *shofar* blast, which probably sounded from the rampart or tower, signaled the approach and the close of the Sabbath during the days of the Second Temple.

The *shofar*, approximately 10 or 12 inches long, is turned up at the bell. Sound is produced through the vibrations of a column of air which is set in motion by the breath of the BA'AL TOKE'AH. In the Temple its mouthpiece was covered with either gold or silver (depending upon the occasion of its use, i.e., Rosh Hashanah or fast days), but after the destruction of the Temple (C.E. 70), no decorations were permitted. A ram's horn is specifically selected on Rosh Hashanah in order to call to mind the *Akedah* (binding of Isaac), when Abraham offered up a ram in place of his son.[14]

Figure 38c. [Salomon Sulzer, *Schir Zion*]

Figure 38d. [M. Wodak, *Hamnazeach*]

SHOFAR-CALLS

Figure 38e, f. [*The Jewish Encyclopedia,* vol. XI, Funk and Wagnalls Company]

    Three different sounds or blasts are blown on the *shofar*. They are *tekiah* (lit. "blast"), a sustained tone; *shevarim* (lit. "breaks"), three disconnected or broken sounds; and *teruah* (lit. "din"), a succession of nine staccato tones or a quavering sound that has been compared to the wailing of someone in distress. The final *tekiah* of each of the four series prescribed, known as *tekiah gedolah* (the great blast), is a prolonged *tekiah* (*see* Fig. 38*a−f* for the variety of sounds that are produced in several different communities and rites). The use of a series of symbols, such as

Teḳi'ah   Teru'ah   Shebarim   Teḳi'ah

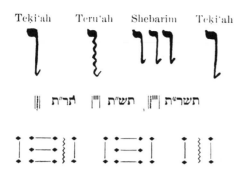

(top) The Parma notation as reproduced in Salomon Sulzer's *Schir Zion.* (center) Graphic signs found in R. Amram's *siddur.* (bottom) Graphic signs found in Saadiah Gaon's *siddur.*

Shofrot of various forms and lengths: without a mouthpiece (upper), with a silver mouthpiece (center), with a gold mouthpiece (bottom). [Haifa Music Museum and Amli Library]

Stone with a built-in niche into which the inscription *Lebeyt Hatekiyah* was cut, indicating the place where the *shofar* was blown. [Israel Exploration Society, Jerusalem]

strokes of particular length and shape representing the duration and outline for the *shofar* calls, appeared in a thirteenth-century Hebrew manuscript called the Codex Adler.[15] Such graphic signs can also be found in a fourteenth-century manuscript, Codex Shem,[16] and in R. Amram's SIDDUR.[17] Salomon SULZER reproduced in his *Schir Zion*[18] the Parma notation of the *shofar* calls, called *Simani Noti* in the Codex Shem, and applies the term *quilisma* (from the Greek *kulisma*, meaning "roll") to the *teruah* sound of the *shofar*. He maintains that it represents a trill and not the rapid tone repetition that is generally used. (Cf. Fig. 38c for Sulzer's interpretation of the *shofar* sounds as they appear in the Parma notation.)

The appellation for the sounds is *tekiot* or *kolot*. The Rosh Hashanah service includes a total of 100 sounds executed according to a particular scheme.[19] Rabbinic authority does not stress the exact pitch, timbre, or intensity of the *tekiot*. All sounds produced by the *shofar* are acceptable, that is, "kosher";[20] however, the duration of each unit of sound is prescribed by law.[21]

[1] A.V.
[2] K.J.V.
[3] Ex. 19:16–19.
[4] Lev. 25:9.
[5] Jer. 4:5, 19.
[6] I Chron. 15:28.
[7] Ez. 33:4–5.
[8] Ps. 81:4.
[9] Ps. 98:6.
[10] Except on the day preceding Rosh Hashanah. Cf. *Orah Hayyim* 581.
[11] Shab. 35b.
[12] Sanh. 7b; Rashi, ad loc.
[13] M.K. 27b.
[14] Gen. 22:13; R.H. 16a.
[15] Library, Jewish Theological Seminary, New York, no. 932, fol. 216.
[16] Parma Library, no. 74.
[17] Warsaw, 1865, p. 45b.
[18] C. 1840, p. 257, no. 344.
[19] R. A. L. Rubenstein, *Companion to the Mahzor*, 1957, pp. 43, 44.
[20] *Orah Hayyim* 586, 6.
[21] Ibid., 590, 3.

SHTEL Vocal presentation without words, serving as a prelude or introduction to a prayer and sung by a superior chorister[1] or by the cantor himself.[2] This melody is generally extemporized and free-flowing rather than composed.

[1] Cf. Abraham Z. Idelsohn, *Jewish Music*, Tudor Publishing Company, New York, 1944, p. 302.
[2] Cf. Abraham M. Bernstein, *Musikalisher Pinkas*, Vilna, 1927, p. xv.

SHTEYGER. *See* STEIGER.

SHTUBEN-TROP. *See* STUBEN-TROP.

SIDDUR. Name (Heb. "order") given to the prayer book used in the synagogue and home for weekdays and Sabbaths. Sephardic and German Jews refer to this compilation as *tefilah* ("prayer"), and Yemenite Jews call it *tiklal* or *taklal* ("all-containing"). In ancient days writing down prayers was banned by rabbinic authority,[1] and the HAZZAN recited the prayers from memory. Consequently, he had to put himself in the proper frame of mind and prepare the order of his prayers.[2] The worshipers either knew the recitals by heart or repeated them after the *hazzan*. With the lifting of the ban (ninth and tenth centuries) on writing down the prayers of the synagogue, they were finally standardized, and the unity of tradition was safeguarded. With the invention of the printing press in the fifteenth century, publishers, according to Leopold Zunz, began to assume a function previously discharged by the *hazzan*. The order of the prayers became standardized, as did their customs, thus leading to a decline in the role of the *hazzan*. Zunz maintains that this decline was evident only in the Ashkenazic tradition, in which the *hazzan* had formerly repeated the *tefilah* aloud in order to enable the illiterate or those who did not possess a *siddur* to fulfill their obligation by answering AMEN. In the Sephardic, Oriental, and Italian congregations, however, the *hazzan*'s position has been retained, for he recites the prayers aloud, word by word, while the worshipers pray silently along with him and sometimes respond to his chant.[3] From the Middle Ages on, the Law has required that the *hazzan* not read from memory if a printed *siddur* is before him, for he may err.[4] For this reason, a special, clearly printed *siddur* was very often placed on the desk used by the READER, and in some communities this *siddur* was printed on parchment.[5]

The first edited compilation of the prayers and ritual was the *siddur* of Rav Amram, written about C.E. 875 by disciples of Amram Gaon. Another edition, which paved the way for future compilers, was Saddiah Gaon's *siddur*, issued about C.E. 892. The first printed prayer book appeared in Rome on April 7, 1486.

[1]Git. 60b; Tos. Shab. 13:4.
[2]R.H. 34b.
[3]*Der Ritus des synagogalen Gottesdienstes geschichtlich entwickelt*, Berlin, 1859, p. 145.
[4]*Orah Hayyim* 53:51.
[5]R. A. Katz, *Leket Hakemah Hahadash*, London, 1961, p. 110.

SIENA PIANO. *See* IMMORTAL PIANO, THE.

SILLUK (⊤). (1) Accent mark (lit. "cessation," "close," or "final") placed under the word in the printed Bible at the end of every verse. Another term used for the final accent of the verse is *sof pasuk* (lit. "end of a sentence"), which is represented by two points (:) similar to the colon mark. It serves as the main guide for the READER in separating the verses from one another and is not actually considered one of the TE'AMIM.[1] (2) An expression referring to the final *piyyutim* (poems) that serve as the last stanzas of the Kerobah cycle in the liturgy, leading to the *Kedushah* prayer, for example, *Unesaneh tokef*, an outstanding poem in the High Holy Day liturgy of the Ashkenazic rite.

[1]Wolf Heidenheim, *Sefer Mishpetey ha-Te'amim*, Rödelheim, 1808, p. 6; William Wickes, *A Treatise on the Accentuation of the Prose Books of the Old Testament*, Clarendon Press, Oxford, 1887, p. 16.

SIMHAT BET HASHO'EVAH. *See* WATER DRAWING, FEAST OF.

SINGER, JOSEPH (1841–1911). Cantor and writer, among the first to approach synagogue prayer chant on a scientific basis. The son of a cantor, Singer began to prepare for his profession in his early youth by singing in his father's choir in his native town in Hungary. He entered the teachers' institute in Trnava, Slovakia, from which he graduated in 1860, and later studied at the conservatory in Prague. In 1866 he was appointed cantor in Beuthen (Bytom), and in 1874 he was called to serve in Nürnberg. When Salomon SULZER retired from active service in 1881, Singer succeeded him as chief cantor of the Seitenstettengasse Temple in Vienna. During his thirty years of service to the Viennese community, Singer also became well known for his concerts and as a singer of oratorio. He wrote numerous choral settings for the synagogue. His outstanding achievement, however, is his monograph "Die Tonarten des traditionellen Synagogen-Gesanges" (1886), in which he systematized the traditional prayer modes. His numerous articles and essays in *Der Jüdische Kantor* (Bromberg, i.e., Bydgoszcz) and in the *Österreichisch-Ungarische Cantoren-Zeitung* (Vienna) reveal him as a true innovator in and investigator of Jewish music.

Ephraim Skliar. [Albert Weisser, *The Modern Renaissance of Jewish Music,* Bloch Publishing Company, Inc.]

SKLIAR, EPHRAIM (1871-?1943). Musician and choral director dedicated to the revival of Jewish music in the early twentieth century in Russia. A native of Timkovichi (a small town near Minsk), Skliar was taken to Slutsk when he was a very young child. There he revealed an unusual talent for music and often led the services in the local synagogue. He went to Poland as an itinerant "singer," and in 1890 he entered the Warsaw Conservatory. Mily Balakirev, who happened to be visiting Poland, took an interest in Skliar and encouraged him to study with Rimski-Korsakov at the St. Petersburg Conservatory, from which he graduated in 1903. Skliar's enthusiasm for Jewish music composition and performance had a lasting effect upon his fellow students and associates. He was among those responsible for the establishment of the SOCIETY FOR JEWISH FOLK MUSIC. In 1902 he organized the Kinor Zion, a group devoted to the writing and performing of Jewish music. He served as the choir director of the St. Petersburg Synagogue and in 1907 was appointed conductor of the Hazomir Choral Society in Łódź. In 1912 he took up permanent residence in Riga, where he was director of the Royal Conservatory, and led synagogal and secular choirs. Skliar wrote numerous choral works and made arrangements of folk and art songs, many of which have remained in manuscript form.

SMOIRA-COHN, MICHAL (1926-   ). Israeli musicologist and teacher. Born in Tel Aviv, she received a musical education at the Israel Academy of Music, from which she graduated in 1946. From 1955 to 1958 she studied at the Musical Research Institute of the University of Uppsala, Sweden. At various times she was associated with the music department of Kol Zion Lagolah (foreign broadcasts), the Jerusalem Conservatory of Music, the Israel Academy of Music, the Rubin Academy of Music, and the University of Tel Aviv. She was editor of *Bat-Kol*, manager of the Haifa Symphony Orchestra, and music critic of the daily newspaper *Ha'Aretz*. In 1968 she became director of music at the Israel Broadcasting Authority. Michal Smoira-Cohn lectured and wrote extensively on various phases of Jewish and general music. She is known for her writings *Folk Song in Israel-An Analysis Attempted* (1963) and *Music-An Historical Introduction* (1966, Heb.).

SOCIETY FOR JEWISH FOLK MUSIC. Society founded in 1908 in St. Petersburg, Russia, with the objective of amassing, arranging, and performing Jewish folk music and bringing it to an artistic level. Rimski-Korsakov reputedly gave the organization its first impetus. The leading spirit of the society was Joel ENGEL, and associated with him were such composers as Joseph ACHRON, Michael Fabianovich GNIESSIN, Alexander Abramovich KREIN, Moses Michael MILNER, Solomon ROSOWSKY, Lazare SAMINSKY, Ephraim SKLIAR, and Jacob WEINBERG. By 1912 membership numbered 389, and a branch had been organized in Moscow. With the advent of World War I, the society's work was curtailed, but its ideas were promulgated in Berlin, Palestine, and the United States.

SOF PASUK. *See* SILLUK.

SPARGER, WILLIAM (1860–1904). Cantor-composer. In addition to serving as cantor of Temple Emanu-El of New York, Sparger was an arranger of synagogue music and one of the earliest to try his hand at Jewish musicology and Jewish music bibliography. With Max SPICKER he wrote (1901) a two-volume work for the Sabbath evening and morning services. He also composed miscellaneous choral works for the various services. His "Introductory Essay on the Liturgical Chant (Chasonuth) of the Synagogue" in *A Collection of the Principal Melodies of the Synagogue* (1893; in collaboration with Alois KAISER) is an important contribution to the development of Jewish musicology. His *Literature on the Music of the Jews: An Attempt at a Bibliography* (1892) shows Sparger as a forerunner in this field.

SPECTOR, JOHANNA (1920–   ). Ethnomusicologist and educator. Born in Libau (Liepāja), Latvia, she emigrated to the United States in 1947. In 1934 she received a diploma from the Staatsakademie für Musik of Vienna; in 1950, a doctor of Hebrew letters degree from the Hebrew Union College–Jewish Institute of Religion in Cincinnati, Ohio; and in 1960, a master of arts degree from Columbia University, New York. As a research fellow at the Hebrew University of Jerusalem (1951–1953 and 1957–1958), she concentrated on the music of the Near East and Middle East as well as on Jewish music. She was active as an educator at the Academy of Music in Jerusalem (1951–1953) and after 1954 at the Jewish Theological Seminary in New York, where in 1962 she founded the department of ethnomusicology. In 1970 she was appointed seminary professor of musicology. She helped found various organizations active in the preservation of the culture of Oriental communities. Jewish musicology was enriched by her archives of about 3,000 tape recordings of Jewish music of the Middle East and Europe. Her private collection of about 8,000 tape recordings includes Arabic, Persian, Turkish, Samaritan, and Indian music as well as the music of the Eastern churches and the Indian-Jewish music of Cochin and Bombay. She also made colorslides and took photographs (about 5,000) of Samaritans, Indian Jews, Yemenite Jews, synagogues around the world, and other such subjects and collected rare Middle Eastern musical instruments. Her essays appeared in numerous books, periodicals, and encyclopedias. Among her more recent writings are "Bridal Songs and Ceremonies from San'a, Yemen" (1960) and "Music of the Jews of Yemen" (1972).

SPICKER, MAX (1858–1912). Conductor and teacher. Born in Königsberg, Germany, he received his musical education at the conservatory in Leipzig. Prior to emigrating to the United States in 1882, he was an orchestra conductor in theaters in Germany. In New York he was conductor of the Beethoven Männerchor, director of the Brooklyn Conservatory, instructor at the National Conservatory, and choirmaster of Temple Emanu-El (1898–1910). Spicker is known for writing *The Synagogal Service* (2 vols., 1901; with William SPARGER), for the Sabbath evening and morning services, and various choral and orchestral works.

Nisson Spivak. [*The History of Hazanuth,* Jewish Ministers Cantors Association of America, New York]

SPIVAK, NISSON (1824–1906). Lithuanian-born cantor, choir director, and composer known as the leading exponent of nineteenth-century Eastern European synagogue song. As a youngster he sang as a chorister with Zalman Konstantiner. Boruch KARLINER, and Yeruchom BLINDMAN. Although he was reputed to have a small, raucous voice (*see* HAZZAN, VOICELESS), he nevertheless occupied prominent posts as a cantor in Belz, Kishinev, and Berdichev. He was nicknamed, and most often called, "Nissi Belzer" and occasionally was referred to as "Nissi Kishinever" or "Nissi Berdichever." He gave numerous concerts and compensated for his vocal deficiencies with his improvisations, melodic themes, and choral arrangements. Spivak, a follower of the Hassidic movement, often visited with Hassidic rabbis (e.g., Davidel of Talno), and he died while on a trip to Sadgora, where he was presenting a concert to the Hassidic rabbi there. His many compositions remained in manuscript form, and various selections have been edited by Gershon EPHROS in his *Cantorial Anthology.*[1]

[1]E.g., vol. 2, Bloch Publishing Company, Inc., New York, 1940, pp. 265–270.

STARK, EDWARD (1863–1918). Cantor-composer. Edward acquired a knowledge of Jewish liturgical music from his father, Joseph Stark, who was cantor in Hohenems, Ichenhausen, and New York. In 1893 he was appointed cantor of Temple Emanuel in San Francisco, where he served until 1913. He is known for arranging musical services for the *Union Prayer Book* for the Sabbath (1909, 1911), New Year (1910), and Day of Atonement (1913). He also wrote services for children and sacred choral works with organ and instrumental accompaniment. Among Stark's literary works are "Music in the House of Worship"[1] and "Die traditionelle Musik des Judentums."[2]

[1]*American Hebrew,* New York, 1896, pp. 325, 326.
[2]*Österreichisch-Ungarische Cantoren-Zeitung,* vol. XXIV, Vienna, 1902.

STAROMINSKY, MORDECAI. *See* SETER, MORDECAI.

STEIGER (SHTEYGER). Judeo-German term, meaning "manner," "way," or "mode," used by Ashkenazic *hazzanim* (cantors) to indicate certain traditional "melody patterns" characterized by their modes, emotional atmosphere, and melodic turns (for example, *Ahavah Rabbah steiger;*

see AHAVAH RABBAH MODE). The term has also been explained as being derived from the German word *steigen,* meaning "to ascend," thus designating certain organized groups of notes in scale formation. *See also* GUST; MODES, SYNAGOGAL.

STERNBERG, ERICH WALTER (1891–). Israeli composer and teacher. Born in Berlin, he studied law at the University of Berlin and received his musical education under Hugo Leichtentritt and Hermann Abert. Jewish subject matter inspired Sternberg long before he settled in Tel Aviv in 1932. In Germany he included in his string quartets a SHEMA YISRAEL prayer melody as well as "Der Parom" (The Ferry), a song by Eliakum ZUNSER. Among his many orchestral and choral works, his theme and variation for orchestra, *The Twelve Tribes of Israel* (1942), and *Yishtabach* (Praise Ye, 1945), set for chorus, haritone solo, and speaker (words by Judah Ha-Levi), are best known. Sternberg received numerous awards and honors, among them the Engel Prize (1940, 1946) and awards from the Federal Republic of Germany and the LEAGUE OF COMPOSERS IN ISRAEL. The municipality of Tel Aviv–Jaffa paid tribute to him on his eightieth birthday with a celebration that took place at the Tel Aviv Museum on June 15, 1971.

STIMMGABEL. *See* TUNING FORK.

STUBEN-TROP (SHTUBEN-TROP). Word, from the German *Stube,* meaning "room," and the Greek *tropos,* meaning "manner" or "mode," referring to the manner or mode of vocal intonation used in the heder[1] when religious literature is studied or recited. It is recorded that on Yom Kippur "the Maharil would cantillate the Biblical reading of SHAHARIT and MINHAH in the manner of the youngsters, called *stuben-trop.*"[2] Since there is no existing musical notation, it is difficult to ascertain how the melody actually sounded. Nevertheless, a number of theories have been offered. The melody may be similar to the special High Holy Day Scrip-

Figure 39. [Abraham Zvi Idelsohn, *The Jewish Song Book*, ed. by B. J. Cohon, Publications for Judaism, Cincinnati]

tural CANTILLATION used today in the Ashkenazic rite. In the Rhine Province this melody was actually called *stuben-trop*[3] (*see* Fig. 39, which shows the system used for this reading). The melody, according to Abraham Berliner, should be called *stufen-trop* (intervals-*trop*) and not *stuben-trop* (chamber-*trop*).[4] The word may also refer to the singsong type of melody used by teachers to introduce the study of AKDAMUT, a practice called an *ausraidenish*, that is, a sort of preliminary exegesis.[5] Its tune is also similar to that of the High Holy Day cantillation used today.

[1] One-room school, usually in the teacher's home or the synagogue.
[2] *Sefer Maharil*, Jerusalem, 1969, p. 49.
[3] Leopold Zunz, *Der Ritus des synagogalen Gottesdienstes geschichtlich entwickelt*, Berlin, 1859.
[4] *Aus dem inneren Leben der deutschen Juden im Mittelalter*, 1871, 2d ed., 1900.
[5] Israel Rabinovitch, *Of Jewish Music*, The Book Center, Montreal, 1952, pp. 113, 114.

STUTSCHEWSKY, JOACHIM (1891–   ). Israeli cellist, educator, and composer known for pioneering in the advancement of Jewish music in Switzerland, Austria, and Israel. Stutschewsky, born in Romny, Russia, came from a musical family. For several generations his ancestors had been itinerant musicians, and his father played in the local orchestra. When he was only five, he began to study the violin and at the age of twelve changed to the cello. After graduating in 1912 from the Leipzig Conservatory, where he had studied the cello with Julius Klengel and musicianship with Emil Pauer, he left in 1914 for Zurich, where, for ten years, he gave concerts and taught the cello. In 1924 he departed for Vienna, joined the Wiener Trio, and continued to give concerts in many large European cities. In Vienna he founded a society for the development of Jewish music and included his own pieces of Jewish content in his concert programs. In 1938 he arrived in Palestine and that year was appointed musical inspector of the General Council of the Jewish Community of Palestine (Vaad Leumi). He continued to propagate Jewish music by organizing concerts at Brenner House in Tel Aviv and encouraging young composers to develop an "Israeli flavor" in their music. Imbued from his early youth with a feeling of Jewish folklore and aware of the potential destruction of European Jewry and its folkways, he began to collect, record, and arrange Hassidic and secular Jewish music. He wrote a variety of articles and books on Jewish music, such as *Musical Folklore of Eastern European Jewry* (1958), *Musicah Yehudit* (1945), and *Haklezmorim* (1959). Among his compositions are a symphonic poem, a suite, cantatas, chamber music for various combinations of instruments, art songs, and folk song arrangements. His six-volume opus, *The Art of Cello Playing*, is used in many schools throughout the world. In 1963 the Violoncello Society of New York presented him with the Piatigorsky Award; in 1970 the Salomon David Steinberg Foundation of Zurich awarded him a special prize in recognition of his achievements; and in 1971, upon the occasion of his eightieth birthday, numerous festive concerts were held in Israel.

SULZER, SALOMON (1804–1890). Cantor-composer, often called the "father of the modern cantorate." He received his name from Sulz, a small Austrian village in which his ancestors had settled temporarily when they were exiled from Hohenems (a town in the province of Vorarlberg, Austria, to the southeast of Lake Constance). In 1748 the family returned from Sulz to Hohenems, and in 1809 they changed their name from Loewy (Levy) to Sulzer. In his early youth he was tutored in synagogue music by Salomon Eichberg (1786–1880), cantor of Hohenems.

Sulzer went to Switzerland to further his studies, first with Cantor Lippmann, and served as an itinerant cantor in Switzerland, Germany, and France. His general musical education was acquired in Karlsruhe, Germany, and in Vienna he studied with Ignaz von Seyfried (a pupil of Haydn and a friend of Mozart and Beethoven), Josef Fischhof, and J. Weigl. In 1820, at the age of sixteen, he returned to Hohenems and served as cantor there until 1825. In 1826 he was called to the post of the Viennese Seitenstettengasse Temple, where for forty-five years he rejuvenated synagogue song and exerted a profound influence on European synagogue music. Cantors and synagogues throughout Europe turned to Sulzer for advice in Jewish music education and on the improvement of the musical service. Blending his cantorial and musical skill almost to perfection, he produced a work of surpassing value, his monumental opus *Schir Zion*. The first volume was published about 1840 and the second about 1866. Thirty-seven compositions were contributed by other composers, including Franz Schubert, Von Seyfried, and Fischhof.

His *Dudaim,* containing responses and short compositions for school and home, was published in 1860. Among many honors, Sulzer received a medal from the Grand Duke of Baden for his *Schir Zion* (1843), a professorship of vocal instruction at the distinguished Vienna Music Society (1845–1848), and the Ottomanic Mejidiye Medal of the Fourth Rank (1864). In 1874 he became a knight of the Order of Franz Josef and was made an "honorable citizen" of Vienna by its mayor. On April 2, 1881, Sulzer bade farewell to his congregation and retired from his office. In the same year he founded the Österreich-Ungarischer Kantorenverein. Assisted by his son Professor Joseph Sulzer, a renowned cellist and director of the combined Vienna synagogue choirs, he devoted his last years to reediting his works. Unfortunately he did not live to see the new editions. His recitatives for the cantor, his congregational responses, and his choral compositions are still sung the world over. His approach to liturgical music has played a conspicuous role in synagogue literature in that he was the first to reconstruct the traditional melodies and responses in accordance with the rules of classical harmony. *See* PSALM 92.

SUMPONYAH. Term used in Daniel 3:5, 10, and 15 and mentioned also in the Mishnah Kelim XI:6. The numerous explanations given for the word are (1) a bagpipe;[1] (2) an "air pipe" or "air passage," derived from the word *simpon,*[2] meaning "a tube";[3] (3) an organ composed of a series of pipes;[4] (4) a lyre;[5] (5) a dulcimer;[6] (6) a drum.[7]

According to Francis W. Galpin and Curt Sachs, *sumponyah* is not the name of an instrument but a word that means "playing together" (from the Greek *symphonia*), a reference to the orchestral performance, or simultaneous sound, of the instruments that are in the verses cited above.[8]

[1]Saadiah Gaon; Abraham Portaleone; Athanasius Kircher; Giulio Bartolocci.
[2]Suk. 36a.
[3]Julius Fürst.
[4]David ibn-Yahia.
[5]Johannes Buxtorf, Jr.
[6]K.J.V.
[7]Hugo Grotius; St. Isidore of Seville.
[8]*The History of Musical Instruments,* W. W. Norton & Company, Inc., New York, 1940, pp. 84, 85.

The *sumponyah* represented as a wind instrument. [Shaul Shaffer, *Hashir Shebamikdash,* Yefey Nof, Jerusalem]

סמפוניא

SURVIVOR FROM WARSAW, A. Work in cantata form for speaker, male chorus, and orchestra, composed by Arnold Schönberg (1874–1951) to his own libretto (in English with German interpolations and the Hebrew prayer SHEMA YISRAEL). Completed in 1947 and first performed in 1948, the opus deals with the atrocities in Warsaw in World War II and describes the battle of the defenders of the Warsaw Ghetto. *See also* DE PROFUNDIS; KOL NIDRE.

T

TA'AM HA'ELYON and TA'AM HATAHTON. Upper (superlinear) and lower (sublinear) position of the TE'AMIM as they appear in the Decalogue in Exodus 20 and Deuteronomy 5. The two sets of *te'amim* affect the syntax as well as the CANTILLATION of these verses. The *ta'am hatahton* separates the First Commandment into five sentences (2–6), whereas the *ta'am ha'elyon* makes it one sentence, beginning with *Onokhi* and ending with *uleshomrey mitzvosoy*. Similar divisions appear in the other Commandments: "Remember the Sabbath," "Thou shalt not kill," "Thou shalt not commit adultery," and so on. The cantillation is also influenced in that different accent marks are used for the *ta'am ha'elyon* and the *ta'am hatahton*, and thus the musical declamation and pausal character are different. William Wickes assigns the *ta'am ha'elyon*, which separates the verses according to the Commandments, to the Oriental communities, where they undoubtedly originated. The *ta'am hatahton*, on the other hand, was introduced by the Palestinians—"breaking up the longer verses, and bringing together the shorter ones; with the view of easing and equalizing the reading."[1] The ruling is that when one reads for himself (MA'AVIR SIDRAH), he uses the *ta'am hatahton*. When the Decalogue is read in public, however, it is cantillated according to the *ta'am ha'elyon*, in much the way it was read and given at Mount Sinai, stressing that the Commandments are ten in number.[2] Rabbi Jacob I. Emden points out that the *ta'am ha'elyon* utilizes accent marks that are more pronounced in character than those used for the *ta'am hatahton*. The accent marks of the *ta'am ha'elyon* are of a higher level of pitch and require strong dynamic levels; those of the *ta'am hatahton*, in contrast, are of lower pitch level and call for a less dynamic level.[3] Thus, when the Decalogue is cantillated in public and especially on Shavuot (Feast of Weeks), which commemorates the giving of the Torah and is identified with the anniversary of the giving of the Decalogue, these verses must be chanted with the "festive melody" (*ta'am ha'elyon*) and not with the "low chant" (*ta'am hatahton*) meant for individual reading.[4]

[1] *A Treatise on the Accentuation of the Prose Books of the Old Testament*, Clarendon Press, Oxford, 1887, pp. 130, 131.
[2] *Orah Hayyim* 141:4, 491:1.
[3] *Luah Eresh*, chap. 462.
[4] Elie Munk, *The World of Prayer*, Philipp Feldheim, Inc., New York, 1963, vol. II, pp. 163, 164.

TA'AME EMET. System of accents employed in the three poetical books of Job, Proverbs, and Psalms. Although these graphic signs are similar to those accents utilized in the remaining twenty-one books (*ta'ame kaf alef*) of the Bible, they have their own distinct names, method of chanting, and functions. The different method of chanting, as well as the shorter verses

in these books, called for a different system of notation.[1] The CANTILLA-
TION generally has been forgotten, for these books were not read in public
service; but Simeon b. Zemah Duran reports that the mode of chant was
retained as late as the fourteenth century.[2] Abraham Zvi IDELSOHN writes
that the melodies have been forgotten only by the Ashkenazim but that
that the Babylonians, Syrians, and Sephardim preserved these modes.
(For the musical notation of the accents of these books *see* Idelsohn's
THESAURUS OF HEBREW-ORIENTAL MELODIES, vol. II, 1923, pp. 13–16).

[1]Cf. M. L. Margolis, "Accents in Hebrew," *The Jewish Encyclopedia*, vol. I, p. 158.
[2]*Magen Avot* 52b.

TA'AME HAMIKRA (TA'AME HANEGGINOT). *See* TE'AMIM.

TABLA. Musical instrument, used especially at public processions,[1] a type of
bell or collection of bells. Rashi translates *hirdolis* (*see* HYDRAULIS) by
tabla.[2] This term, however, does not fit the context in which *hirdolis* is
used.[3] *See also* INBAL; ZOG.

[1]Cf. Sot. 49b; Ber. 57a; Shab. 110a; M.K. 9b.
[2]Ar. 10b.
[3]Cf. Marcus Jastrow, *Dictionary*, London, 1903, vol. I, p. 226, s.v. *gurgana*.

Joseph Tal. [Israel
Music Institute, Tel
Aviv]

TAL (originally GRUENTHAL), JOSEPH (1910–   ). Israeli composer,
pianist, conductor, and teacher. He moved to Berlin from his native
Pniewy (near Poznań), Poland, and assimilated the musical culture of
Germany while studying at the Berlin Academy of Music under Thiessen
and Trapp. He gave concerts in Europe as a pianist and was employed by
a Berlin radio station. In 1934 he arrived in Palestine and joined Kibbutz
Gesher, where he worked for more than a year with his comrades rebuild-
ing the land. In 1937 he joined the faculty of the Academy of Music in
Jerusalem, teaching piano and composition, and was its director from
1948 until 1952. In 1950 the Hebrew University appointed him as its
first lecturer in music, and subsequently he became director of the
Israel Centre for Electronic Music at the campus of the university and
professor of musicology. Tal persevered almost singlehandedly in the
field of electronic music in Israel and exerted a strong influence on
younger musicians. In 1957 he was granted a UNESCO scholarship for
research in electronic music, and in 1971 he was elected a fellow of the
Berlin Academy of Arts and appointed musical director of an international course on contemporary music at the Eduard van Beinum Institute in
the Netherlands. He wrote several books on the theory of music, lectured
at universities in the United States and in music centers of Europe and the
Far East, and participated in various councils and conferences around the
world. His works include operas, an oratorio, symphonies, concerti,

cantatas, chamber music, piano pieces, and ballet music. He has become known for his choreographic poem *Exodus* (1945–1946), First Symphony (1954), Concerto No. 5 for Piano and Electronic Accompaniment (1964), and *Ashmedai* (1970; libretto by Israel Eliraz), an opera based on Talmudic legend and first performed in Hamburg in 1971.

TANBURA. Musical instrument, mentioned in Sotah 49b, to which different meanings are ascribed: (1) tambourine;[1] (2) a long-necked lute or guitar used by Eastern-Mediterranean peoples.[2]

[1]Marcus Jastrow, *Dictionary,* London, 1903, vol. I, p. 540.
[2]F. W. Galpin, supplementary notes to John Stainer, *The Music of the Bible,* London, 1914, pp. 46, 190; Curt Sachs, *The History of Musical Instruments,* W. W. Norton & Company, Inc., New York, 1940, pp. 255, 256.

TANZHAUS. Institution (lit. "dance house") that originated in Germany about the thirteenth century to provide a hall for Jewish weddings and for dancing. Since wedding festivities lasted for a week, and in larger communities weddings were frequent, "the *tanzhaus* must have been in pretty constant occupation by merry parties."[1] Salo W. Baron believes that the name *tanzhaus* is a misnomer in that it was primarily a wedding hall in which mixed dancing almost never occurred except when the bride participated in a ritualistic DANCE (*see* MITZVAH TANZ).[2] Further support to this opinion is given by Moritz Güdemann,[3] Johann Jakob Schudt,[4] and others who state that the *tanzhaus* is identical with the *bet hatunot* (lit. "house of weddings"). As the *tanzhaus* spread to France, Italy, and large cities of Eastern Europe (e.g., Warsaw), it eventually became a public hall for dancing. This development met with much opposition from rabbinical authorities, for, according to Jewish law, mixed dancing is prohibited; rabbis often threatened transgressors with severe penalties.[5] In the nineteenth century the *tanzhaus* sprang up in small towns populated by Jews, and a *tanzmeister* (dance instructor) was imported from the city. The instructions of the dance steps were chanted to lyrics marking the rhythm, thus giving rise to a division of dance songs.[6] Y. L. Cahan holds that many Yiddish love songs and children's rhymes stem from these dance songs.[7]

[1]Israel Abrahams, *Jewish Life in the Middle Ages,* New York, 1896, p. 75.
[2]*The Jewish Community,* Jewish Publication Society of America, Philadelphia, 1942, vol. II, p. 315.
[3]*Die Geschichte des Erziehungswesens und der Kultur der abendländischen Juden während des Mittelalters und der neueren Zeit,* Vienna, 1888, vol. III, p. 138.
[4]*Merkwürdigkeiten,* vol. II, 1714–1718, p. 5.
[5]Cf. *Orhot Tzadikim,* chapter on *simha; Sefer Hassidim* 168:9; *Kol Bo* 66.
[6]Ruth Rubin, *Voices of a People,* New York and London, 1963, pp. 186, 187.
[7]*Studies of Yiddish Folk Creations,* YIVO, New York, 1952, p. 88.

TARHA. *See* TIPKHA.

TE'AMIM. Oldest term (from *ta'am,* meaning "sense," "meaning," or "taste") for Biblical accentuation,[1] also called *ta'ame hamikra* (accents of Biblical verse) or *ta'ame hanegginot* (melodic accents). The phrase "and caused them to understand the reading" in Nehemiah 8:8 denotes the accentuation (*pisuk te'amim*).[2] Rashi comments that the Masoretic notes (NEGGINOT) are also called *te'amim*.[3] Thus the function of the accents is to indicate the intonations and the logical and syntactical importance of the syllables sung to them. Although the Talmud makes mention of Biblical CANTILLATION[4] and teaching of accentuation,[5] nowhere is there a reference to the graphic forms, for they had not been introduced into the printed Biblical text at the time of the composition of the Talmud.

Throughout the ages there have been various opinions concerning the origin of the *te'amim*. Some scholars maintain that the Torah that Moses received on Mount Sinai was furnished with vowel points and accentuation.[6] Others believe that the Torah that Moses received on Mount Sinai did not have the vowel points and accentuation but that he wrote a second Torah exactly like the first and added the vowel points and accentuation.[7] The Sinaitic origin of punctuation was emphatically denied by Mar Natronai II (c. 859), who also prohibited its introduction into the Torah scroll.[8] Another theory is that the *te'amim* were handed down orally from Mount Sinai and that the form of the accents was put down by Ezra and the men of the Great Synagogue about 450 B.C.E.[9] According to Simhah ben Samuel, a pupil of Rashi, the method of chanting the accents was revealed to Moses, and the post-Talmudic Sages were actually responsible

[1]May occur on one word or on hyphenated words. Sing in same manner.

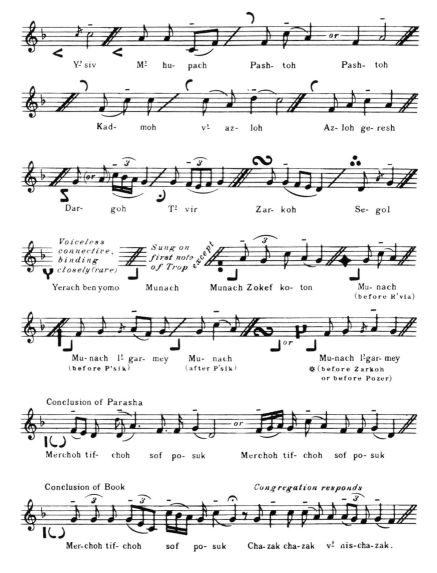

* When two or more successive Munachs precede ∞ or ⱱ ,even the final one is sung "l'garme."

Figure 40a. [Abraham Zvi Idelsohn, *The Jewish Song Book*, ed. by B. J. Cohon, Publications for Judaism, Cincinnati]

for introducing the accent marks.[10] Consequently, the currently accepted view is that the vowels and accents did not exist in the time of the Talmud and that they were probably developed between the sixth and tenth centuries.[11] At the head of the distinguished family of Masoretes and punctuators was AARON BEN ASHER of Tiberias, who is credited with having finally fixed the vowels and accents as they appear in the texts.[12]

There are twenty-eight *te'amim* in the Scriptural text. Of these, fifteen are posted above the word, twelve below, and one in between. They are, in alphabetical order: AZLA, DARGA, ETNAHTA, GERESH, GERSHAYIM, KADMA, KARNE-FARAH, MAPAKH, MERKHA, MERKHA-KEFULAH, MUNAH, MUNAH LEGARMEH, PASHTA, PAZER, PSIK, REVI'I, SEGOL, SHALSHELET, SILLUK (*sof pasuk*), TELISHA-GEDOLAH, TELISHA-KETANAH, TEVIR, TIPKHA, YERAH-BEN-YOMO, YETIV, ZAKEF GADOL, ZAKEF KATAN, and ZARKA. In Fig. 40*a* the tune for each accent mark is notated for the Pentateuch. Figure 40*b* gives a comparative table of the essential motives as they are intoned in various communities throughout the world. Each symbol, which serves as a re-

Figure 40b. [Abraham Zvi Idelsohn, *Manual of Musical Illustrations,* Hebrew Union College]

minder of the melody, is equal to an extended pattern of notes and has six different modes for chanting it, depending upon the occasion of its reading (e.g., Sabbath, High Holy Days, *Megillot*). Figure 40c gives a comparative chart for the *merkha tipkha, merkha sof pasuk* clause in the six systems used in the Eastern European tradition. *See also* ACCENTS, BIBLICAL; BA'AL KOREI; CANTILLATION; CHIRONOMY; CONJUNCTIVES; DISJUNCTIVES; NE'IMOT; NEUMES; STUBEN-TROP; TA'AM HA'ELYON AND TA'AM HATAHTON; TA'AME EMET; TROP.

[1]*The Jewish Encyclopedia,* vol. I, p. 149.

Figure 40c.

[2]Meg. 3a.
[3]Ad loc.
[4]Meg. 32a.
[5]Erub. 21b; Ned. 37a.
[6]Ben Asher, quoted by David Weissberg in "Rare Accents of the Twenty-one Books," *The Jewish Quarterly Review,* vol. LVI, no. 4, April 1966, pp. 330, 331; *The Jewish Encyclopedia,* vol. I, p. 156.
[7]J. D. Eisenstein, *Ozar Yisrael,* New York, 1907–1913, vol. V, p. 29.
[8]Cf. Heinrich Graetz, *Geschichte der Juden von den ältesten Zeiten,* 2d ed., 1863–1891, vol. V, p. 502.
[9]*Kuzari,* sec. 3; Joseph Derenbourg, *Manuel du lecteur,* Paris, 1871, p. 53.
[10]*Mahzor Vitry,* Berlin, 1893, p. 91.
[11]Elijah Levita, *Massoret ha-Massoret,* 1538; S. D. Luzzatto, *Dialogues on the Kabbalah and the Antiquity of Punctuation,* 1852.
[12]William Wickes, *A Treatise on the Accentuation of the Prose Books of the Old Testament,* Clarendon Press, Oxford, 1887, p. 6.

TEHILLIM. *See* PSALMS, BOOK OF.

TEHINNAH. Name (lit. "supplication") of a devotional prayer book for women developed in various vernaculars during the sixteenth century. It was designed primarily for those who could not read Hebrew and wished to express their religious needs on various occasions (e.g., before candle lighting, for family well-being). The vocal intonation of the *tehinnah* recitations was filled with much emotion and expression and caused the women to shed copious tears as they read them. This intonation was generally a dirgelike drone in singsong manner based on the synagogue modes (*see* MODES, SYNAGOGAL). Various *tehinnot* found their way into the SIDDUR and MAHZOR. For a listing of *tehinnot see The Jewish Encyclopedia,* vol. IV, s.v. *Devotional Literature.*

TELISHA-GEDOLAH (___). Accent mark appearing in the printed text of Scripture (e.g., Gen. 1:12). The name means "major drawing out," alluding to its melody and mode of chant. Its correlate is TELISHA-KETANAH. Simhah ben Samuel comments on the various methods of chanting the accents as revealed to Moses, and he notes the "drawing out" of the tune (*talash*).[1] William Wickes states unequivocally that this accent mark is a musical term, from the root *talash*, "to pluck out," "draw out with effort," indicating that it means to "draw out" the voice with a marked effort and impulse.[2]

The *telisha-gedolah* is considered a disjunctive accent (*see* DISJUNC-TIVES) and is listed among the "counts." It appears on the first letter of the word and is one of the six prepositive signs that do not indicate the accented syllable. Generally, accents show the stress in the word in which they occur. However, this is not so in the case of the *telishas*. Wickes,[3] quoting Joseph Derenbourg, explains it as follows: "Grammarians tell us that they were so placed, that they might not be confounded with the circular sign (o), marked over words which are object of a Massoretic note."[4] Wolf Heidenheim notes that although both *telishas* had the same circular form, printed Bibles differentiated between them by turning the *telisha-ketanah* to the right of the reader and the *telisha-gedolah* to his left; that is, the "stem" of the circle was pointed in different directions.[5] When the accented syllable and the sign do not coincide, editors of the printed Bible sometimes double the *telisha-gedolah* sign on one word. When this is done, the sign to the right is the "name sign" and the sign to the left indicates the accented syllable in the word.[6] *See also* TE'AMIM.

[1]*Mahzor Vitry*, Berlin, 1893, p. 91.
[2]*A Treatise on the Accentuation of the Prose Books of the Old Testament*, Clarendon Press, Oxford, 1887, p. 22.
[3]Loc. cit.
[4]*Manuel du lecteur*, Paris, 1871, p. 92.
[5]*Sefer Mishpetey ha-Te'amim*, Rödelheim, 1808, p. 30.
[6]M. Breuer, *Pisuk Te'amim Shebimikra*, 1958, p. 15, note 2.

TELISHA-KETANAH (___). Tropal sign meaning "minor drawing out," posted on the last letter of the word (e.g., Gen. 1:21). Its correlate is *telisha-gedolah*. This conjunctive sign (*see* CONJUNCTIVES) is counted among the postpositives and does not indicate the accented syllable. The reason for the postpositive position of this sign is discussed under TELISHA-GEDOLAH. When the accented syllable and the sign do not coincide, editors of the printed Bible have often doubled the sign. Thus, the one to the left is the "name sign" and the one to the right indicates the syllable to be stressed.[1] In its melodic pattern for the Pentateuch, as in its grammatical division in clauses, the *telisah-ketanah* is semicadential, whereas the *telisah-gedolah* is cadential. *See also* TE'AMIM; YERAH-BEN-YOMO.

[1]M. Breuer, *Pisuk Te'amim Shebamikra*, 1958, p. 42, note 5.

TEN SONGS FROM THE HEBREW. Series of songs by Stefan Wolpe composed between 1936 and 1938 to Hebrew and English texts. They were inspired by the land of Israel and its folklore and were first performed in the United States in 1949 at a concert of the League of Composers in the United States in memory of Paul Rosenfeld.

TEVIR (___). Masoretic sign meaning "broken," placed below the word in the printed Bible (e.g., Gen. 3:12). William Wickes, quoting Joseph Derenbourg's *Manuel du lecteur*,[1] attributes its name to the fact that its melodic contour "breaks the word."[2] *See also* TE'AMIM.

¹Paris, 1871, p. 72.

²*A Treatise on the Accentuation of the Prose Books of the Old Testament*, Clarendon Press, Oxford, 1887, p. 20.

THEATER MUSIC. *See* YIDDISH THEATER MUSIC.

THESAURUS OF HEBREW-ORIENTAL MELODIES. Abraham Zvi IDELSOHN's ten-volume anthology (*Hebräisch-orientalischer Melodienschatz*) of sacred and secular music of various Jewish communities and sects. It is a scientific and historical study, published in Hebrew, German, and English between 1914 and 1933 by Breitkopf and Haertel of Leipzig, Verlag Benjamin Harz of Jerusalem-Berlin-Vienna, and F. Hofmeister of Vienna. The work was subsidized by the Kaiserliche Akademie der Wissenschaften in Vienna, the Gessellschaft zur Förderung der Wissenschaften des Judentums, and the Zunz Foundation in Berlin. The subjects of the ten volumes are: Volume I, Yemenite Jews; Volume II, Babylonian Jews; Volume III, Persian, Bokharan, and Daghestan Jews; Volume IV, Oriental Sephardim; Volume V, Moroccan Jews; Volume VI, German Jews; Volume VII, Jews of southern Germany; Volume VIII, synagogue song of Eastern European Jews; Volume IX, folk songs of Eastern European Jews; Volume X, songs of the Hassidim. The German edition is the only complete one; the English edition has only seven volumes (I, II, VI–X); and the Hebrew edition has only five volumes (I–V).¹ The thesaurus was republished by B. M. Israël of Amsterdam (1965) and the Ktav Publishing House, Inc., in New York City (1973).

¹Cf. I. J. Katz, *Judeo-Spanish Traditional Ballads from Jerusalem*, The Institute of Medieval Music, Ltd., New York, 1972, p. 61.

THREE JEWISH POEMS. Orchestral work by Ernest BLOCH in three sections ("Dance," "Rite," and "Funeral Procession"), composed in 1913 and dedicated to the memory of his father. Its premiere performance was in 1917 at a concert of the Boston Symphony Orchestra.

THREE PSALMS. (1) Setting for psalms 22, 114, and 137 for baritone and orchestra, written by Ernest BLOCH (1912–1914). (2) Setting, by Isadore FREED, for psalms 100, 103, and 121 for mixed voices with or without organ accompaniment. (3) Work, by Paul BEN-HAIM, completed in 1962 and scored for soloists, choir, and orchestra (or organ). The composition in three movements, "Supplication" (ps. 4), "Consolation" (ps. 23), and "Praise" (ps. 147), was commissioned by Congregation Emanuel of San Francisco in honor of Cantor Reuben R. Rinder's fifty-year service to the congregation.

TIKKUN HATZOT. *See* HATZOT.

TIPKHA (⌐⌐). Chironomic sign (e.g., Gen. 1:17) meaning "hand breadth," a manual sign employed in cantillating the Bible. Another name for this graphic sign is *tarha*, meaning "laboring" or "toiling." William Wickes ascribes to its character a slow (*lento*), heavy melody that immediately precedes the cadence at an ETNAHTA or SILLUK. *See also* CHIRONOMY; TE'AMIM.

TOB LEHODOT. *See* PSALM 92.

TOF (pl. *tuppim*). Percussion instrument generally translated as "tympanum," "timbrel," "tambourine," or "tabret." It has been described as a small portable drum that was popular among the Semitic tribes and was made of a wooden hoop, possibly with two membranes,¹ and without jingles or sticks.² The player struck the drumhead with his fingers. From Biblical

תוף הנזכר במשנה   תוף הדומה לספינה

The *tof* according to the Mishnah (left) and the author of *Shiltay-Haggi-borim* (right). [Shaul Shaffer, *Hashir Shebamikdash*, Yefey Nof, Jerusalem]

sources it is evident, too, that it was most often played by women.[3] It almost always appears in connection with the DANCE,[4] for marking the rhythm of the dance, and was not permitted in the Temple ritual. *See also* ERUS.

[1]Based on the Mishnah in Kin. III:6.
[2]Curt Sachs, *The History of Musical Instruments*, W. W. Norton & Company, New York, 1940, pp. 108, 109.
[3]Ex. 15:20; ps. 68:26.
[4]Judg. 11:34; I Sam. 18:6; Jer. 31:4.

TOKE'AH. *See* BA'AL TOKE'AH.

TOMEKHIM (also called *mesayim, mezammrim, mutznafim,* and *maftirim*). Term (lit. "supporters") used as early as the third century C.E. to refer to two helpers or assistants who served as prompters to the READER, who recited the prayers from memory. Since there was a ban on transcribing prayers,[1] the institution of the *tomekhim* was required. No reader was permitted to function unless he had at least one assistant. When two were present, one stood to the reader's right, the other to his left.[2] Even after the basic structure of the prayer book was set,[3] these two "supporters" continued as musical assistants, thus forming the nucleus for the present-day synagogue CHOIR. In Afghanistan synagogues, the *tomekhim,* who are respected laymen, take turns as assistant prayer leaders to the rabbi, who conducts the service during the High Holy Days. In Cochin the worshipers vie for the privilege of assisting the reader in chanting the prayers.[4] *See also* MESHORERIM; SIDDUR.

[1]Shab. 115b.
[2]Sof. XIV:14; Tos. Meg., chap. IV.
[3]Between the sixth and ninth century C.E.
[4]P. Goodman, *The Rosh Hashanah Anthology*, Jewish Publication Society of America, Philadelphia, 1970, pp. 208, 211, 212.

TROP or TROPE. Term (from the Greek *tropos,* meaning "turn," "manner," or "mode") for the graphic signs used in Scriptural CANTILLATION. Each *trop* expresses a ready-made motive; connecting these motives creates a mode. The term, implying a musical style, was used by the Biblical and Talmudic commentator Rashi.[1] Abraham Berliner quotes Rashi (Gen. Rabbah XXXVI) as having explained the phrase *pisuk te'amim* as *tropen.*[2] *See also* ACCENTS, BIBLICAL; NEGGINOT; NE'IMOT; TE'AMIM.

[1]Kid. 71a, *mavli'im oso,* etc.
[2]*Beiträge zur hebräischen Grammatik in Talmud und Midrasch,* 1879, p. 29, note 1.

TRUMPET (Heb. *hatzotzerah*). Wind instrument mentioned twenty-nine times in the Bible and used for calling an assembly, during the journeying of camps, for sounding the alarm of war, and for celebrating the

Reconstruction of a metal trumpet from one depicted on a silver coin of the Bar Kokhba period (C.E. 132–135). [Haifa Music Museum and Amli Library]

sacrifices on festivals and new moons.[1] The Hebrew word *hatzotzerah* is an onomatopoeic construction, possibly from the characteristic sounds produced by the instrument.[2] Moses transmitted the divine command that only priests could blow the two silver trumpets (pl. *hatzotzerot*). They were probably played simultaneously or alternately; in the latter case, either the same note or a different note was used.[3] The *hatzotzerah* sounds were similar in nature to those of the SHOFAR; that is, the *tekiah* and *teruah* blasts were assigned to both. According to some Biblical critics, both instruments belong to the species of KEREN, the general term for a horn.[4] In Solomon's Temple the number of trumpets was increased to 120, and they were used in the orchestra that accompanied songs of thanksgiving and praise.[5] According to Flavius Josephus, the trumpet was a straight tube approximately 2 feet long, somewhat wider than a HALIL (pipe), and broadening gradually in the front into a bell.[6] Trumpets corresponding to the description given by Josephus are depicted on the arch erected in Rome (c. C.E. 80) in honor of the emperor Titus, who, after the destruction of the Temple in Jerusalem, took holy objects, among them the trumpets, to Rome. The shape and form of trumpets thought to have been depicted on Maccabean coins (175–140 B.C.E.) have been recently attributed to the Bar Kokhba coinage (C.E. 132–135).[7]

[1]Numb. 10:1, 2, 9, 10.
[2]Wilhelm Gesenius, *Hebräisches und chaldäisches Handwörterbuch über das Alte Testament,* Leipzig, 1915, p. 255.
[3]Curt Sachs, *The History of Musical Instruments,* W. W. Norton & Company, Inc., New York, 1940, p. 113.
[4]Joel Brill's preface to Moses Mendelssohn's version of the Psalms.
[5]II Chron. 5:12.
[6]*Antiquities of the Jews,* III, 12, 6.
[7]Bathja Bayer, *The Material Relics of Music in Ancient Palestine and Its Environs,* Israel Music Institute, Tel Aviv, 1963, p. 38.

TUNING FORK. Metal rod (Ger. *Kammerton, Stimmgabel;* Heb. *kolan, mazleg lekhivnun, matzlayl*) in the shape of a U at the end a stem, used to check the pitch of instruments and to give the correct pitch to singers. When struck, it produces a certain fixed tone that serves as a pitch standard, for example, A, 440 vibrations per second. Invented in 1711 by John Shore (Handel's trumpeter), the tuning fork was perfected by Rodolphe Koenig of Paris about 1850.

Among cantors it is customary to use the tuning fork to establish the key in which to chant. After striking it, the cantor places it close to his ear, or he may place the stem against his teeth, which act as sound resonators to reinforce the tone. Concerning its use on the Sabbath, many Responsa have been written, pro and con. Several decisions and rulings appear in *Naharay Aparsemon* by Yaakov Tennenbaum, 1898, pp. 26–27, decision 3; *Mishnah Berurah* by Yisrael Meyer Hakohen, 1907, 338:4; *Melamed Lehoil* by David Tzvi Hoffmann, 1926, responsum 63; *Arukh Hashulkhan* by Yehiel Michael Epstein, Vilna, ed. 1923, 338:8; and *Yesodei Yeshurun* by Gedalie Felder, vol. IV, 1962, p. 284.

TURGEMAN. *See* METURGEMAN.

TZILTZELIM. *See* CYMBALS.

UGAB. Instrument mentioned in Genesis 4:21, Job 21:12 and 30:31, and psalm 150:4, apparently used only for personal or informal religious expression. The opinions of ancient and modern commentators are widely divided with regard to the meaning of the word. Various translations given are: (1) "Pipe," denoting a kind of wind instrument and most probably a generic name for a family of wind instruments.[1] In all the above-mentioned sources the Targum Onkeles translates the term by the Aramaic ABUB (pipe). The Authorized Version, too, in the margin of psalm 150:4, translates it by "pipe." (2) "Organ."[2] *Tosafot* also translates *hirdolis* (water organ) by *ugab*.[3] (3) "Pandean pipes" (panpipes) or syrinx.[4] (4) Viola da gamba, a stringed instrument.[5] (5) "Bagpipe,"[6] an instrument that is rendered by SUMPONYAH and, according to some scholars, is identified with the *ugab*.[7] (6) Vertical flute, from *agob*, meaning "lovemaking"; flutes were closely associated with love charms.[8] (Cf. Rashi, Job 21:12.)

[1]Marcus M. Kalisch, *An Historical and Critical Commentary on the Old Testament*, 1858; Curt Sachs, *The History of Musical Instruments*, W. W. Norton & Company, Inc., New York, 1940, p. 106.

[2]Vulgate; A. V.; K.J.V.

[3]Ar. 10b.

[4]Joel Brill, second preface to Moses Mendelssohn's version of the Psalms; *see also* A. F. Pfeiffer; J. N. Forkel; John Stainer.

[5]Abraham Portaleone, *Shilte ha-Gibborim*, Mantua, 1612.

[6]Carl Heinrich Cornill, *Music in the Old Testament*, The Open Court Publishing Company, Chicago, 1909, p. 12.

[7]Ibn-Ezra, commentary to Dan. 3:5.

[8]Sachs, ibid.

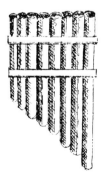

The, *ugab* represented as an instrument with eight reeds. [Shaul Shaffer, *Hashir Shebamikdash*, Yefey Nof, Jerusalem]

VEPRIK (WEPRIK), ALEXANDER (1899–1958). Composer and teacher, born in Łódź, Poland. He received a musical education at the Warsaw Conservatory (1909–1914) and at the Leipzig Conservatory and later attended the Moscow Conservatory, studying under Nikolai Miaskovsky. In 1923 he was appointed to the teaching staff of the conservatory in Moscow. Among his works that were influenced by the Jewish idiom are *Kaddish* (op. 6), for chamber-music group, and his orchestral work *Dances and Songs of the Ghetto* (op. 12), which was introduced by the New York Philharmonic Orchestra under the baton of Arturo Toscanini. He is also known for writing Hebrew and Jewish songs.

VINAVER, CHEMJO (1900–1974). Choral conductor and composer born in Warsaw. A descendant of a Hassidic family, young Chemjo was imbued with HASSIDIC SONG, which he later collected and notated. In the early 1920s he went to Berlin, where he studied music under Siegfried Ochs and others. In 1926 Vinaver gave his first concert, conducting a chorus in Jewish liturgical music at the Berlin Hochschule für Muzik. His performances were soon accepted by the musical public in Berlin and other major German cities. In 1933 Vinaver and his chorus of thirty male voices made their way from Nazi Germany to European countries and Palestine, presenting programs of an entirely Jewish character. In Palestine, Vinaver served for a while as music director of the Habima Theater. After emigrating to the United States in 1938, he continued his choral activities with a group called the Vinaver Choir, and in 1941 he accepted the post of music director of the Society for the Advancement of Judaism in New York City. He later emigrated to Israel. Vinaver is known for *The Seventh Day: A Friday Evening Service* (1946) and for his *Anthology of Jewish Music* (1955).

VIOLIN CONCERTO. Four-movement composition by Ernest BLOCH, first performed in 1938 by Joseph Szigeti and the Cleveland Orchestra and directed by Artur Rodzinski. The five-note motive that is heard at the outset of the work recurs throughout the entire composition and is a characteristic cadence in Hebraic chant.

VIRTUOSO. Performer whose execution displays great technical facility. An early virtuoso singer was Hygros of the tribe of Levi. It is recorded that his brethren, the priests, "staggered backward with a sudden movement" when they heard his voice.[1] He possessed a certain art in "tuning his voice to a trill" and did not wish to teach this technique to others.[2] Vocal virtuosity flourished among *hazzanim* (cantors; *see* HAZZAN), who introduced melismatic ornamentation into their recitatives (*see* RECITATIVE), a style that dominated synagogue song for many years. As for instrumental music, it was not until the early 1800s that the KLEZMER Michael Joseph Gusikow (1806–1837) made a great impression as a virtuoso performer on the straw fiddle (Ger. *Strohfiedel*). After listening to Gusikow at a concert in Leipzig in 1836, Felix Mendelssohn wrote in a letter, "He is quite a phenomenon, a famous fellow, inferior to no virtuoso in the world, both in execution and facility."[3] The nineteenth and twentieth centuries saw many virtuoso performers of Jewish descent such as Mischa Elman (1891–1967), Jascha Heifetz (1901–   ), Heinrich (Henri) Herz (1806–1888), Bronisław Hubermann (1882–1947), Joseph Joachim (1831–1907), Ignaz Moscheles (1794–1870), Isaac Stern (1920–   ), and Sigismund Thalberg (1812–1871). Gdal SALESKI lists the names of conductors, violinists, cellists, pianists, and vocalists in his book *Famous Musicians of Jewish Origin*, writing in his preface: "Without them the musical world would almost be like a night without stars."[4]

[1]Yom. 38b.
[2]Ibid., Mish. III:2.
[3]Cf. Mendelssohn's letters from 1833 to 1847, tr. by Lady Wallace, Boston, 1863, pp. 98–99; *Grove's Dictionary of Music and Musicians*, London, 1898, s.v. *strohfiedel*.
[4]Bloch Publishing Company, Inc., New York, 1949.

VITEBSK. Trio for violin, cello, and piano composed in 1929 by Aaron Copland and dedicated to Roy Harris. The work is based on the Hassidic tune "Mipne Mah" (Why?), which Copland had heard in Solomon Ansky's play *The Dybbuk* (*see* DYBBUK, THE). The tune was popular in Vitebsk, a Russian city in which Ansky had lived.

VOICE IN THE WILDERNESS. Symphonic poem in six sections for orchestra with violoncello obbligato, written by Ernest BLOCH in 1936. The work represents Bloch's expression of Hebrew temperament and spirit, based on the prophetic Biblical phrase "A voice calleth out in the wilderness" (Is. 40:30).

VOLLECH (also *vollechel*, with the endearing diminutive *el*). Style of folk song, either in RECITATIVE or rhythmical manner, that originated in Walachia, in Romania. Its scale is characterized by an augmented fourth degree in the lower tetrachord D E F G♯ A B C D (*see* MI SHEBERAH MODE). Carl Engel maintains that this scale emanated from Asia and appears in folk songs of countries such as Turkey and Hungary, as well as in Transylvania, Moldavia, and Walachia in Romania.[1]

The character of the *vollech* has often been described as free fantasy. The singer or instrumentalist adds all sorts of embellishments and coloraturas ad libitum to the main tune in pastoral fashion. Numerous Hassidic dance melodies and wedding tunes are in *Walachish* style: the melody is left to the fancy of the instrumentalist; the musical accompaniment keeps time. The Walachian tune found its way into almost every religious service of the yearly cycle. Rabbi Israel Baal Shem Tov (1700–1760) explains that the reason for chanting the *Ya'aleh* hymn on Yom Kippur Eve to a Walachian melody (*beniggun valuchu*) was because in Walachia the Jews suffered the greatest cruelties of the tyrants (1456–1462). Because the Walachian Jews never changed their customs, nor denied their God, the people of Israel sing the Walachian tune on their most holy day, Yom Kippur.[2]

[1]*The Music of the Most Ancient Nations,* William Reeves, London, 1864, p. 361.
[2]S. Y. Agnon, *Yamim Noraim,* Schocken Publishing House, Ltd., Tel Aviv, 1956, p. 308.

VORBETER. Term (from the Ger. *vor,* "before," and *beten,* "pray" or "say one's prayers") used in Germany for the HAZZAN.

VORLESER. *See* BA'AL KOREI.

VORSINGER. Term, signifying the HAZZAN, utilized in the Middle Ages in Nürnberg documents.[1] A Wolfel Vorsinger (1425) is mentioned among religious functionaries in Nürnberg;[2] the title had probably become part of his name.

[1]Cf. M. Stern, *Die israelitsche Bevölkerung der deutschen Städte,* vol. III, *Nürnberg im Mittelalter,* 1896, p. 93.
[2]S. Ochser, *The Jewish Encyclopedia,* vol. IX, s.v. *Nuremberg,* p. 361.

WALACHIAN TUNE. *See* VOLLECH.

WASSERZUG, HAYYIM (1822–1882). Cantor-composer known for introducing four-part choral singing in Poland, also called Reb Hayyim Lomzer. Born in Sieradz, Poland, he received a rudimentary knowledge of music from his father, who was the cantor in that city. Later, in Warsaw, he continued his musical education and vocal training under private tutelage. During his lifetime he was cantor in the following cities: Konin (1840), Nowy Dwór (near Warsaw, 1841–1854), and Łomża (1854–1859), in Poland, Vilna (1859–1867), and London (1868–1882). Wasserzug was offered an operatic career with the Italian Opera Company in St. Petersburg but declined because of his devoutness. He impressed Polish cantors with the importance of musical knowledge, thereby incurring great opposition from the Hassidic Jewry in Warsaw. His magnum opus for the synagogue is *Shire Mikdash* (1878).

WATER DRAWING, FEAST OF (SHIMHAT BET HASHO'EVAH). Ceremony in the Temple on Sukkot (Feast of Tabernacles) during which a libation of water was made upon the altar.[1] In describing this celebration the Mishnah states, "He who has not seen the rejoicing at the place of the Water-Drawing has never seen rejoicing in his life."[2] Music and dance played an important role in the festivities, which began on the second evening of the festival and lasted for six nights. Men of piety danced with torches in their hands (a form of juggling)[3] and sang hymns and songs. In a description of this festival, which was celebrated throughout the night, R. Joshua b. Hananya says that songs, music, shouting, clapping the hands, and jumping were all part of the rejoicing.[4] On the steps that lead from the Court of the Men to the Court of the Women, the LEVITES without number sang the "hymns of degrees" (SHIR HAMA'ALOT), fifteen in number (pss. 120–134), corresponding to the number of steps.[5] The most important instrument used for accompanying the singers was the HALIL. Harps, lyres, cymbals, and trumpets were also played. At the Upper Gate stood two priests who sounded the SHOFAR as a signal to proceed to draw the water of libation from the Pool of Siloam (Shiloah). After the destruction of the Temple, the water libation ceremony ceased. It is commemorated throughout the world with singing, dancing, recitation of various psalms, poems, and refreshments. For a description of how the occasion is celebrated in modern times, *see Arugot Habosem* in *Siddur Otzer Hatefilloth* (1914), s.v. *Hilkhot Hag Hasukkot*, vol. II, p. 1172.

[1] Suk. IV:I.
[2] Ibid., V:II.
[3] Ibid., 53a.
[4] Jer. Suk. 55b.
[5] Suk. V:II.

Jacob Weinberg.

WEINBERG, JACOB (1879–1956). Odessa-born composer, teacher, and pianist who is identified as an early proponent of Jewish music. Weinberg's musical training began when he was seventeen, at which time he entered the Moscow Conservatory and studied piano with Igumnoff, composition with Taneyev, and orchestration with Ippolitov-Ivanov. He furthered his studies in piano with Theodor Leschetizky in Vienna and toured Russia as a piano virtuoso and accompanist from 1912 to 1914. In 1915 he was appointed professor of piano and composition at the conservatory in Odessa, where he remained until 1921. Weinberg played a vital part in the activities of the SOCIETY FOR JEWISH FOLK MUSIC of Moscow. In 1923 he emigrated to Palestine and engaged in organizing and establishing the Jewish National Conservatory of Music in Jerusalem. Upon his arrival in the United States in 1928 he taught at the New York College of Music and in 1933 joined the faculty of Hunter College in New York. He served as cofounder of the NATIONAL JEWISH MUSIC COUNCIL and as a member of the governing board of the JEWISH MUSIC FORUM, and was a founder of the Festival of Jewish Arts. Weinberg's compositions include sacred and secular works for chorus, a concerto, chamber music, an opera, and art songs. Both Jewish-Oriental and Eastern European folk influences are evident in many of his creations. The best known are his opera *Hechaluz* (The Pioneer; 1926), *Sabbath Eve Service* (1935), and *Shabbat Ba-Arets* (1938–1939).

Lazar Weiner.

WEINER, LAZAR (1897–   ). Composer, teacher, and choral director. As a child, Weiner was a chorister at the Brodsky Synagogue of Kiev, Russia, his native city, where he also studied the piano. His formal musical training began at the State Conservatory of Music (Kiev) and continued under Robert Russell Bennett, Frederick JACOBI, and Joseph Schillinger in the United States. His musical involvement in the United States, to which he emigrated in 1914, covers a wide range of activity. In 1923 he organized a chorus for the International Ladies Garment Workers Union. Composing, arranging, and programming music of Jewish content for public choral performances became his chief objective. Other endeavors in this period of his life were coaching, piano teaching, and accompanying virtuoso cantors (e.g., Zavel Kwartin, Joseph ROSENBLATT, Gershon Sirota). Weiner became music director of the Central Synagogue of New York City (1930) and of the Workmen's Circle Choir (1931) and later assumed the role of conductor of the Mendelssohn Symphony Orchestra in Brooklyn. His devotion to the advancement of Jewish music manifested itself in his active membership in MAILAMM and the JEWISH MUSIC FORUM. As a composer, Weiner is known for his musical settings for original Yiddish texts or translations into Yiddish. His significant Yiddish works are the cantatas *Legend of Toil* (1933) and *Prologue to the Golem* (1951). His *Shir l'Lel Shabbath* (1948) stands out as his most important liturgical work. The approximately 200 works by Weiner include secular and liturgical choral music, chamber music for various combinations of instruments, songs, and piano solos.

WEINTRAUB, HIRSCH (1811–1881). Cantor-composer and violinist. Son of cantor Salomon WEINTRAUB, Hirsch received early training in music from his experience as a chorister in his father's choir in Dubno, Poland, his native city. He received formal instruction in general music and violin and later studied harmony in Vienna and Berlin, and counterpoint with Eduard de Sobolewski in Königsberg. Weintraub succeeded his father in Dubno after the latter's death in 1829 and remained there until 1834, when he decided to leave to continue his studies and tour with his quartet. For a while he played first violin with the Philharmonic Orchestra in Königsberg. In 1838 the Jewish community of Königsberg appointed him chief cantor. He remained there for the rest of his life and was laden with honors by Emperor William I and the Jewish population. His works include three volumes called *Schire Beth Adonai*, published in 1859. The first two volumes are liturgical choral compositions; the third volume contains chants and settings by his father and is called *Schire Schelomo*.

WEINTRAUB, SALOMON (1781–1829). Cantor and composer. Born in Konstantinovka, Russia, Weintraub, who was nicknamed "Kashtan" (chestnut) because of his reddish hair, became a noted cantor and, through his son, Hirsch WEINTRAUB, is known for his liturgical musical settings. Salomon gained an early knowledge of music from his father, Cantor Shimshon Weintraub, who in his early youth sang for Rabbi Israel Baal Shem Tov.[1] Both Salomon and his brother Nahum Leib were sent to sing with "Kalman the *hazzan*" of Mohilev (Mogilev), who traveled extensively, accompanied by his "singers." When Salomon's voice finally matured, he became an itinerant cantor and formed his own group of "singers." During his career he officiated in Zamość, Tiktin, Lemberg (Lvov), and Brisk (Brest). A significant period in his life was spent in Dubno, Poland, where he was engaged for many years only for the High Holy Days. He also gave concerts and was acclaimed for his rendering of the services with unique IMPROVISATION filled with intricate embellishments. His choral compositions had to be memorized by his choristers because he could neither read nor write music. Weintraub intentionally had his son Hirsch instructed in music so that he could arrange his compositions in order that they would not be lost. His son eventually published them under the title of *Schire Schelomo* (Leipzig, 1859).

[1]Menashe Unger, *Reb Yisroel Baal-Shem-Tov,* Shulsinger Bros., Inc., New York, 1963, p. 279.

WEISE. German word meaning "melody," "tune," or "manner." It was used in nineteenth-century compilations of liturgical music to signify a "melody type" (*see* NUSAH) or a particular melody used in a specific area or tradition. Abraham BAER wrote a work entitled *Baal T'fillah* in which he notated the *Weise* as it was utilized in different traditions (*see* BA'AL TEFILAH).

WEISSER, ALBERT (1920–   ). Composer, musicologist, and teacher. Born in New York City, he was educated at Washington Square College and received a master's degree in music from the Graduate School of Arts and Science of New York University. He taught at the School of American Music in New York (1949–1953) and at Brooklyn College (1958–1967). In 1968 he began to teach at the Jewish Theological Seminary. He also served as musical consultant to YIVO. Among Weisser's compositions of Jewish content are *Anim Smiros* (1953) for cantor, chorus, and organ, *Three Popular Songs after Sholom Aleichem* (1959), and *Elokenu Veloke Avotenu* (1955). His literary contributions are *The Modern Renaissance of Jewish Music* (1954), an account of the development and achievements of Jewish music in Eastern Europe and the United States during the past hundred years or so; *Bibliography of Publications and Other Resources on Jewish Music* (1969); and *Selected Writings and Lectures of Joseph Yasser* (1970).

Joshua Samuel Weisser.

WEISSER (originally PILDERWASSER), JOSHUA SAMUEL (1888–1952). Cantor-composer and teacher. Born in Novaya Ushitsa in the Ukraine, Weisser received his early musical education by studying with several cantors in the Ukraine. In 1909 he was appointed to his first post, in Vinnitsa, where he became a pupil of Eliezer Mordecai GEROVITSCH. After he arrived in the United States in 1914, he served as cantor of the Tiferet Israel, Nahlat Tzvi, and Tremont Talmud Torah synagogues of New York and was general secretary (1923–1924) and president (1939–1940) of the Jewish Ministers Cantors Association of America. He became a prolific writer of the synagogue RECITATIVE and taught prospective cantors. Weisser published books of recitatives for almost every service in the yearly cycle. On two occasions (1937, 1938) he received first prize for his choral compositions in worldwide competitions conducted by *Die Hazzanim-Welt* of Warsaw. His last work for cantor and four-part choir, *Shirei Beth Hakneseth* (vol. I, 1951; vol. II, 1952), is a culmination of his creativity both in Europe and in the United States. He also notated

Hassidic melodies, composed numerous Yiddish songs in folk style, and wrote articles and essays that appeared in various journals and periodicals.

WEPRIK, ALEXANDER. *See* VEPRIK, ALEXANDER.

Eric Werner.

WERNER, ERIC (1901–   ). Musicologist, teacher, composer, and writer. Born near Vienna, he attended the Gymnasium there, then the Universities of Vienna, Graz, Prague, Berlin, Göttingen, and Strasbourg, receiving his doctor of philosophy degree in 1928. Prior to emigrating to the United States in 1938, he held teaching positions in Saarbrücken (1926–1933) and Breslau (1934–1938). In 1939 he was appointed professor of Jewish music and liturgy at the Hebrew Union College–Jewish Institute of Religion in Cincinnati, Ohio, and chairman of its School of Sacred Music in New York in 1951. Subsequently he became consulting professor at Tel Aviv University. Werner, a member of the council of the American Musicological Society and of the American Academy for Jewish Research, received a Guggenheim fellowship in 1957. Werner's musical works include settings for the liturgy of the various services in the yearly cycle, choral compositions, songs, a work for chamber orchestra, a work for organ, and a *Symphony Requiem: Hazkara* (1943). Among his outstanding literary works are *In the Choir Loft* (1957), *The Sacred Bridge* (1959), and *Anthology of Music* (1961). He also contributed numerous articles and essays to the *Musical Quarterly Review* and other publications.

WUNDERKIND. German term (lit. "child wonder") applied to a child who displays a precocious genius, especially in music. Among musicians of Jewish origin who began as child prodigies are composers (e.g., Giacomo Meyerbeer), conductors (e.g., Serge Koussevitzky), and instrumentalists (e.g., Bronisław Hubermann). In synagogue life the *Wunderkind* often appeared as a soloist in the choir or sometimes as the "leader in prayer."[1] His participation in religious services dates back to Temple days, when Levite boys were added to the twelve adult singers in order to "add flavor to the music." These boys were called "tormentors," for they caused embarrassment to the adults because of their sweet voices.[2] In the early nineteenth century, cantors, too, complained about the boy singer (*yingele*) who made a "big hit" with the public[3] and protested that they were deprived of their livelihood by the "child cantor."[4]

[1]Cf. *Orah Hayyim* 53, pertaining to a minor as officiant.
[2]Ar. 13b.
[3]Cf. Samuel Rosenblatt, *Yossele Rosenblatt: A Biography,* Farrar, Straus & Cudahy, Inc., New York, 1954, pp. 325–326.
[4]Joshua Weisser, "Inglach-Hazzanim un Hazzanim Inglach," *Jewish Music Journal,* May–June 1935, no. 2, p. 10.

YAKOVKIN (YAKOVKA) (fl. late 19th cent.). Choir leader of the Shalash-ner synagogue in Odessa, Russia, renowned for writing recitatives (*see* RECITATIVE) and choral compositions. Abraham Zvi IDELSOHN included his *Weshomru* (no. 259), as sung by Gershon Sirota, in his THESAURUS OF HEBREW-ORIENTAL MELODIES (vol. VIII).

YARE'AH-BEN-YOMO. *See* YERAH-BEN-YOMO.

Joseph Yasser.

YASSER, JOSEPH (1893–   ). Musicologist, organist, and teacher. Born in Łódź, Poland, Yasser studied the piano in his early youth with Jacob WEINBERG. He graduated from the State Conservatory of Moscow in 1917, and from 1918 to 1920 he headed its organ department. In Russia he en-joyed great success as an organist, lecturer, and choral conductor. After he arrived in the United States in 1923, he made numerous appearances as an organist and held positions in various temples. From 1929 until his retirement in 1960 he served as organist and choirmaster at Temple Rodeph Sholom in New York City. Yasser was a cofounder of MAILAMM, the JEWISH MUSIC FORUM, the NATIONAL JEWISH MUSIC COUNCIL, and the Jewish Liturgical Music Society of America. In addition, he served as vice-president of the American Library of Musicology, chairman of the New York chapter of the American Musicological Society, vice-president of the World Center for Jewish Music, and a member of the Committee on Studies in Jewish Music of the American Academy for Jewish Research. From 1952 to 1960 he served as faculty member of the Cantors' Institute and Seminary College of Jewish Music of the Jewish Theological Seminary of America. Yasser's attainments in scholarly research were recognized when he published his significant works *A Theory of Evolving Tonality* (1932) and *Medieval Quartal Harmony* (1938), in which he incorporated ideas and concepts that were applied only later to Jewish music studies. In an annotated bibliography of his literary and lecture contributions called *Selected Writings and Lectures of Yoseph Yasser* (1970), there are, among the 147 listings, 64 articles, papers, and lectures devoted to Jewish music.

YEKUM PURKAN MODE. Mode named after the prayer in the Sabbath liturgy that contains its archetype. Cantors usually begin to intone this prayer with the following succession of notes: G C C E C. It is considered by cantor-theorists to belong to the family that includes the ADOSHEM MALAKH MODE (*see* B. J. Cohon's divisions of its motives in "The Structure of the Synagogue Prayer-Chant" in the *Journal of the American Musicological Society,* vol. III, no. 1). According to Pinchos MINKOWSKY[1] and Elias ZALUDKOWSKI,[2] when the *Yekum Purkan* mode is ascending, it is identical with the *Adoshem Malakh* mode (C D E F G A B♭ C); when descending, it includes a lowered sixth degree (C B♭ A G F E♭ D C); thus the mode has a major feeling when ascending and a minor feeling when descending. Cohon, who bases his study on the conclusions of Abraham Zvi IDELSOHN, does not include the minor third when the mode is descending. The interval is possibly used as an occasional variation.

[1]Cf. *Die Entwicklung der synagogalen Liturgie bis nach der Reformation des 19. Jahrhunderts,* Odessa, 1902; J. D. Eisenstein, *Ozar Yisrael,* New York, 1907–1913, vol. IV, p. 263.
[3]Cf. "Unzere Nushaot," *Jewish Music Journal,* 1934, no. 1, p. 6.

YERAH-BEN-YOMO (YARE'AH-BEN-YOMO). Symbol (⎯ᵧ⎯) appearing sixteen times below the word in the printed text of the Bible as a servant (*see* CONJUNCTIVES) to KARNE-FARAH. It originally had a number of names and forms. Because of its original circular form, it was called *galgal* ("wheel") or *agulah* ("round"), and because it was like a small *telisha*, it was also called TELISHA-KETANAH or *telisha ze'irah*. Because the circle was sometimes incomplete and sometimes complete, it was called *yerah-ben-yomo,* meaning "the moon a day old,"[1]

William Wickes states that its melody originally probably resembled that of the *telisha-ketanah,*[2] and it is actually notated so, in various sources, with slight variations.[3] Abraham Zvi IDELSOHN lists its intonation as "voiceless connective, binding closely [rare]."[4] J. L. Ne'eman,[5] quoting Kalonymus b. Judah,[6] states that the melodic contour of the *yerah-ben-yomo* is the same as that of the MUNAH (*shofar yashar*). Ne'eman explains, however, that, whereas the tonal interval of the *munah* is a descending major second (A–G), the *yerah-ben-yomo* is a descending minor second (A♭ –G). See also TE'AMIM.

[1]William Wickes, *A Treatise on the Accentuation of the Prose Books of the Old Testament,* Clarendon Press, Oxford, 1887, p. 26.
[2]Ibid.
[3]E.g., Joseph H. Hertz (ed.), *The Pentateuch and Haftorahs,* London, 1929–1936, vol. II, p. 973.
[4]*The Jewish Song Book,* ed. by B. J. Cohon, Publications for Judaism, Cincinnati, 1951, pp. 489, 491, 503.
[5]*Tseliley Hammiqra,* Tel Aviv, 1955, pp. 94, 122.
[6]*Sha'ar-ba-Ta'amim,* a treatise on the Hebrew accents written as a supplement to Abraham de Balmes's grammar, *M'kneh Abram,* Venice, 1523.

YERUSHALAYIM SHEL ZAHAV. Folk song (lit. "Jerusalem of Gold") by Naomi Shemer, first written for a song festival on May 15, 1967, commemorating Israeli Independence Day. During and after the Six-Day War of June 1967, it became a song of victory.

YETIV (‐‐‐‑<). Accent sign, meaning "staying," "resting," or "pause," in the musical declamation of the Bible (e.g., Gen. 3:11, monosyllable, and Gen. 6:9, disyllable). Its appearance is identical to that of the MAPAKH, and it is always placed under the word, before the first letter. It came into existence when the PASHTA came on a monosyllable or a disyllable word that was penultimate (*milel*) and had no *servus* (*meshoret*) preceding it. It is thus a disjunctive sign (*see* DISJUNCTIVES) with a distinct melody. *See also* TE'AMIM.

YIDDISH THEATER MUSIC. Corpus of operas and operettas. This music received its impetus from Abraham GOLDFADEN, who in 1876 performed with the first professional troupe in a "wine cellar" catering to the Jewish populace. The Jewish State Theater of Bucharest, Romania, officially designated a state theater in 1958, is the descendant of Goldfaden's original Iaşi company. The music, on the whole, flourished on a large scale to about 1940, when production of Yiddish theater slowly dwindled and came to a standstill. Goldfaden was succeeded by composers such as Herman Wohl, Sholom Perlmutter, Louis Friedsell, and Jacob Brody. The last prominent composers of the Yiddish theater were Joseph RUMSHINSKY, Peretz Sandler, Alexander Olshanetsky, Abraham ELLSTEIN, and Sholom SECUNDA.

Yiddish theater music most probably dates back to the Middle Ages (thirteenth century) with the appearance of the BADHAN, who entertained at weddings and other festivities. Although the taste for theatrical amusement was never strongly developed among all Jews, exceptions were made with regard to the PURIM-SPIELE, from which Yiddish theater music evolved. Alfred SENDREY does not attribute much importance to this music, either as folk or art music, yet he admits, "it played a large role in the musical culture of the Jews at the turn of the century" and "it will be of

A performance by the Jewish State Theater of Romania. [Pacific World Artists, Inc., New York]

interest to the historian of civilization and to the investigator in sociology rather than to the musicologist."[1] Albert Weisser also does not have high regard for this music and concludes, "Listening today to the body of music it has produced is an embarrassing and painful experience."[2] Abraham Wolf BINDER considers this music an important factor contributing to the development of modern Jewish music in the United States and abroad.[3] Numerous folk tunes from this body of melodies (e.g., ROZHINKES MIT MANDLEN, "Flaker Faierl," "A Pastuch'l") have remained as genuine Yiddish folk song.

[1]*Bibliography of Jewish Music,* Columbia University Press, New York, 1951, pp. xxi, xxii.
[2]*The Modern Renaissance of Jewish Music,* Bloch Publishing Company, Inc., New York, 1954, p. 156; he has since modified his opinion.
[3]"Jewish Music," in *The Jewish People Past and Present,* Central Yiddish Culture Organization, New York, 1952, vol. III, p. 348.

YIGDAL. *See* LEONI.

YISHTABAH MODE. Mode named after the *Yishtabah* prayer, which is chanted in the SHAHARIT service on Sabbath. It differs in its scale construction and distinctive phrases depending on whether it is used in the Western European or the Eastern European Ashkenazic tradition. Western European Ashkenazim use the AHAVAH RABBAH MODE mixed with the MAGEN AVOT MODE. According to Abraham Zvi IDELSOHN, "some consider it a subdivision of the *Magen Avot steiger . . .;* others take it as a variant of the *Ahavah Rabbah* mode."[1] Eastern European Ashkenazim chant the *Yishtabah* with the aeolian *Magen Avot* when ascending (D E F G A B♭ C D); when descending, they make use of a lower seventh degree, thus creating a half step between the seventh and eighth degrees of the scale (D C B♭ A G F E♭ D). Isadore FREED[2] and Eric WERNER[3] attribute a special coloring to the *Yishtabah* mode. It opens with the aeolian *Magen Avot* mode (e.g., D A G F G A), modulates on the fourth degree to major (e.g., D G A B), and returns to the aeolian *Magen Avot* by using an augmented second interval (e.g., E D C♯ B♭ A G A).

[1]*Thesaurus of Hebrew-Oriental Melodies,* 1933, vol. VII, chap. IV: xxiii. *See also* no. 44; part III, no. 14.
[2]*Harmonizing the Jewish Modes,* Hebrew Union College–Jewish Institute of Religion, New York, 1958, p. 45.
[3]*In the Choir Loft,* Union of American Hebrew Congregations, New York, 1957, p. 24.

YOM KIPPUR KATAN. Fast day (lit. "Little Day of Atonement") observed by pietists on the day preceding Rosh Hodesh (the new month) with the exception of the month of Tishre. Public recital of special penitential prayers and Torah reading are held during the MINHAH service of that day. The institution of this minor Yom Kippur was inaugurated by Moses Cordovero, a sixteenth-century Kabbalist of Safed. From the numerous musical settings for the liturgy[1] and from various recordings,[2] it is evident that cantors were at one time greatly involved in this service. In the minutes of the Anshe Chesed Trustees of Nov. 29, 1849, it is recorded that one of the duties of Cantor Leon Sternberger was "to be in the synagogue on *Yom Kippur Katan* and to read if the Board of Trustees should request him to do so."[3]

[1]Salomon Sulzer, *Schir Zion,* c. 1840, p. 423; A. Goldenberg, *HaHazzan, Yom Kippur Katan,* Berlin, 1913.
[2]E.g., *Ribono Shel Olom,* by Cantors A. Karniol and S. Vigoda.

³Cf. H. B. Grinstein, *The Rise of the Jewish Community of New York,* Jewish Publication Society of America, Philadelphia, 1945, p. 484.

YORAYD LIFNAY HATAYVAH. Phrase (lit. "he who descends before the Ark") used interchangeably in the Talmud[1] with OVAYR LIFNAY HATAYVAH. Rashi comments that the term *yorayd* is used because it is a *mitzvah* (religious precept) to pray from a lower level.[2] In the synagogue the PRECENTOR stood at the reading desk, which was at a lower level than the floor of the congregation,[3] based on the verse "Out of depths have I called Thee, O Lord."[4] The sermon, the reading of the Torah, and the "priestly blessing" took place from the platform. Here the word *aliyah* ("ascend") is utilized in order that the READER, who sat on the platform, not err in assuming that he, too, chants the prayers from the platform.[5] Thus the term *yorayd* was used, possibly designating that the reader left his seat and "went down," for it is indicated that "he should stretch out his legs and go down."[6] This practice was later abolished when the *Shomronim* (Samaritans) made it part of their own religious worship.[7] Yehudah Elbogen maintains that the expression *ovayr* was used in synagogues in Palestine and that *yorayd* was used in Babylonia.[8] However, Eliezer Levi finds no basis for this assumption, for *yorayd* is used in the Mishnah[9] and Sages such as Rabbi Akiba and Rabbi Elazar, who were in Palestine, "went down before the Ark."[10]

[1]Ta'an. Mish. II:2; R.H. 32a.
[2]Cf. Ber. 10b.
[3]*The Babylonian Talmud,* The Soncino Press, London, 1935–1952, Ber. 34a, note 7.
[4]Ps. 130:1.
[5]Jer. Meg. III:1.
[6]Ber. 34a.
[7]R. A. Kon, *Siah Tefilah,* Jerusalem, 1964, p. 48.
[8]*Der jüdische Gottesdienst,* 1913, p. 461.
[9]Ta'an., ibid.
[10]*Yesodot Hatefillah,* Bitan Hassefer, Israel, 1952, p. 88.

YOVAYL. Instrument whose name derives from the Arabic *yovla,* "ram,"[1] meaning "Jubilee horn"; thus an instrument used for the announcement of the "Year of the Jubilee" (*shenat hayovayl*).[2] The *yovayl* probably resembled the KEREN and the SHOFAR, as found in Scripture, *bimshokh bekeren hayovayl,* "when they blow a long blast with the ram's horn,"[3] or *shofrot hayovlim,* "trumpets of ram's horns."[4] The appearance of the word *yovayl* with *keren* and *shofar* means that it is an epithet ascribed to the instrument.[5] There also seems to be a similarity between the name Jubal (the father of all such as handle the KINNOR and UGAB")[6] and *yovayl,* and hence "music."[7]

[1]R.H. 26a.
[2]Lev. 25:9–54.
[3]Josh. 6:5.
[4]Ibid., 6:8.
[5]Salomon Munk, "Palestine," in *L'univers pittoresque,* 1845, p. 456, note *a.* Cf. Mish., Kel. xi:7.
[6]Gen. 4:21.
[7]*The Jewish Encyclopedia,* vol. VII, p. 301.

Z

ZAKEF GADOL (_⸴_). Masoretic symbol, meaning "major raising" or "full, upright," placed above words in the printed Bible.[1] Its name is derived from the "upright" finger, or "raising" of the finger, as employed at one time by the prompter or teacher to remind the READER of the melodic direction (chironomic; see CHIRONOMY). Grammarians place it together with its correlate ZAKEF KATAN in the disjunctive (*see* DISJUNCTIVES) category. The reason for the two forms of *sakef* has been explained as follows: the *zakef* signs generally occur more frequently than any other accent (four or more often appearing in one verse), "and probably on this account were subjected to various musical modifications, with the view of varying the recurring melody." To differentiate musically between these signs, the two points represent the simple sign *sakaf katan* and its simpler melody, and the two points with the upright line, *sakaf gadol,* represent the double *zakef,* which has a fuller, stronger tone. The *zakef gadol* does not in any way represent greater pausal power than the *zakef katan.*[2] The distinct characteristic of this accent in cantillating the Pentateuch is that its upbeat progresses within the interval of a major third in trisyllable *milra* words (e.g., Gen. 4:18) and tetrasyllable *milel* words (e.g., Ex. 32:32). All other accent marks repeat the upbeat note as many times as necessary.[3] *See also* TE'AMIM.

[1]Gen. 1:14.
[2]William Wickes, *A Treatise on the Accentuation of the Prose Books of the Old Testament,* Clarendon Press, Oxford, 1887, p. 18.
[3]Cf. Solomon Rosowsky, *The Cantillation of the Bible,* The Reconstructionist Press, New York, 1957, p. 330.

ZAKEF KATAN (_⸴_). Accent mark meaning "lesser upright" or "minor raising," appearing in the printed Bible.[1] Its derivation and grammatical use are explained under ZAKEF GADOL. This accent, like the SILLUK and ETNAHTA, appears in almost every verse. When the TE'AMIM are divided into groups, the *zakef katan* serves as a "family head"; that is, the other accents gravitate toward it in order to create a pause.[2]

[1]E.g., Gen. 1:2.
[2]Cf. J. L. Ne'eman, *Tseliley Hammiqra,* Tel Aviv, 1955, pp. 20, 21.

ZALUDKOWSKI, ELIAS (c. 1888–1943). Cantor-composer and writer, born in Meitchet, Grodno Province, Poland. His father, Cantor Noah (Lieder) Zaludkowski (1859–1931), gave him a rich Jewish musical culture and the opportunity to study the Talmud and attend the Gymnasium. He studied voice in Milan and graduated in 1909 from the Stern Conservatory in

Berlin. During his career he occupied positions as cantor at the Sinai Synagogue in Warsaw (1912–1914), the Choral Synagogue in Rostov (1914–1921), the Choral Temple in Vilna (1922–1925), the Central Synagogue in Liverpool (1925–1926), Congregation Shaarey Zedek in Detroit (1926–1932), Congregation Shaarey Zedek in New York (1932–1937), and Congregation Beth Sholom in Pittsburgh (1937–1943). He wrote numerous articles, including "Der Matzev fun Hazzanim in America" (1934),[1] "Proyekt tzu Kolonizirin Yiddishe Musiker in Eretz-Yisroel" (1939),[2] and "Unzere Nushaot" (1934).[3] His volume *Kulturträger von der jüdischen Liturgie* (1930), a collection of biographies of cantors and choral directors, is an invaluable contribution to Jewish liturgical music study. Zaludkowski also wrote *Friday Evening Late Service* (1940, 1941) and Hebrew and Yiddish songs.

[1]*Die Hazzanim-Welt*, vol. I, Warsaw.
[2]*Die Hazzanim-Welt*, vol. III, Warsaw.
[3]*Jewish Music Journal*, 1934, no. 1, p. 60.

ZARKA (〰). Accent sign, meaning "scatterer," used in the CANTILLATION of the Bible[1] and possibly referring to the character of the melody symbolized by its graphic form. Its position was made postpositive (i.e., over the last letter of the word) in order to conform with its position in the TA'AME EMET. In the *ta'ame emet* there are two types of *zarkas*, one a conjunctive (*mesharet; see* CONJUNCTIVES) placed at the beginning of a word, the other a disjunctive (*mafsik; see* DISJUNCTIVES) at the end of the word. Thus, because it is also a disjunctive, in the twenty-one books (*ta'ame kal alef*), it retains its position for the sake of conformity.[2] In words having penultimate accents (e.g., Numb. 27:3), two *zarkas* sometimes appear on one word, one in its usual postpositive position and bearing its name sign and the other over the accented syllable to the right.

The term *zarka* also refers to the table that lists the TE'AMIM according to the order of their names and graphic signs (*zarka* is first on the list).[3]

[1]E.g., Gen. 2:23.
[2]Wolf Heidenheim, *Sefer Mishpetey ha-Te'amim*, Rödelheim, 1808, p. 15a.
[3]J. L. Saalschutz, *Von der Form der hebräischen Poesie*, Königsberg, 1825. Cf. Salomon Sulzer, *Schir Zion*, Vienna, 1905, p. 99.

ZEMER. *See* MIZMOR.

ZEMIROT. Word meaning "hymns" or "songs". (1) According to the Sephardim, the word refers to the preliminary section of the SHAHARIT service, which is composed of psalms. Ashkenazim use the term *Pesukay Dezimrah* for this section. (2) Body of poems, sung during the three Sabbath repasts and at the conclusion of the Sabbath, expressing joy for the Sabbath day and extolling God for his excellencies, glories, and gracious acts. Early notices for the singing of *zemirot* are: "It is customary amongst Jews that when they partake of food and drink and rejoice, they sing and give praise to God";[1] and "One should welcome and escort the departure of the Sabbath with song."[2] On Friday evenings in the winter, wrote Israel Abrahams, "the family would remain for hours around the table singing these curious but beautiful hymns."[3]

Zemirot texts developed mainly between the eleventh and sixteenth centuries under the Kabbalistic influences of Rabbi Isaac Luria (c. 1534–1572), known as the Ari (abbrev. for Ashkenazi R. Isaac), and ISRAEL NAJARA.

General characteristics of *zemirot* are: (1) the melodies are usually borrowed from Jewish and non-Jewish folk song; (2) most *zemirot* are metric, utilizing the most common meters—duple, triple, and quadruple; (3) they are sung predominantly in unison, and only on occasion is harmony employed; (4) most of the texts are in acrostic form with recurring refrains (*see* PIZMON); (5) the chief singers are the father and sons. Women join in the refrains or even sing their own *zemirot*.

An early collector of Ashkenazic *zemirot* melodies was Abraham Moshe BERNSTEIN, who notated from oral tradition about 126 tunes for the Sabbath alone in his *Musikalisher Pinkas*. Numerous Sephardic and Oriental *zemirot* melodies were notated by Isaac Levy in his *Antología de liturgia Judeo-Española* (part 1).

[1]*Midrash Rabbah, Shir Hashirim.*
[2]Rabbi Isaiah Horowitz, *Shnei Luhot ha-Brit,* Amsterdam, 1698.
[3]*Jewish Life in the Middle Ages,* Atheneum Publishers, New York, 1969, p. 133.

Zavel Zilberts.

ZILBERTS, ZAVEL (1881–1949). Choral director and composer. He received his early musical education from his father, Cantor Baruch Hirsch of Karlin, near Pinsk, Russia, the city of his birth. At the age of sixteen, after the death of his father, he was invited to lead the services and conduct the synagogue choir. In 1899 he enrolled at the Warsaw Conservatory, from which he graduated in 1903 with great distinction. From 1903 to 1907 he served as musical director and conductor of the Hazomir Choral Society of Łódź, Poland, and from 1907 to 1914 he was choir director at the Moscow Central Synagogue. Later he again accepted the conductorship of the Hazomir Choral Society of Łódź, and in 1920 he emigrated to the United States. In the United States, Zilberts led various synagogue choirs and was active as an organizer and conductor of several choral groups, namely, the Jewish Ministers Cantors Association of America, Workmen's Circle Choir, the Paterson Singing Society, and the Zilberts Choral Society of New York City and Newark. Among his musical compositions are numerous choral settings for Biblical and liturgical texts, folk songs, and cantatas. His setting for *Havdalah* has remained a classic in liturgical music literature. In 1969 the Cantors Assembly of America posthumously published his work *The Complete High Holiday Liturgy for the Hazzan* (transcribed by Moshe Nathanson).

ZIMRAH. *See* MIZMOR.

ZOG (pl. *zogin*). Term, meaning "hood," "shell," or "the body of the bell" (the outer part), that appears in the Mishnah[1] and Talmud.[2] The inner part is called INBAL, and both terms are used by Rashi to describe TABLA.[3]

[1]Naz. VI:I.
[2]Zeb. 88b; B.K. 17b.
[3]Ar. 10b.

ZOGACHTS. Term (from the Ger. *sagen,* "to say") denoting the Eastern European cantor's free IMPROVISATION of synagogue chant. The style is characterized by a highly florid manner of interpreting the RECITATIVE, with embellishments, ornamentations, coloratura, and modulations. The cantor who sings in this manner is called a *zoger* (*zuger*).

ZUGERIN. *See* SAGERIN.

Eliakum Zunser.

ZUNSER, ELIAKUM (1836–1913). Eastern European poet and singer. He is known for his songs that preached nationalism and Zionism, and as a BADHAN he became a legendary figure. The name Zunser was probably derived from Zunse (a small village near Vilna, Lithuania), where his ancestors lived prior to moving to Vilna, where he was born. In his early youth he attended the heder and sang with Cantor Joel Ihumener in Bobruisk. Because of poverty and intolerable and vicious harassment by the Russians, he wandered from city to city and at one time was imprisoned. After his release from prison he journeyed to Kovno (Kaunas), where he took up the occupation of embroidery. In 1861 he abandoned this vocation, returned to Vilna, and decided to become a *badhan.* From 1860 to 1870 his fame grew rapidly throughout Lithuania and in northern Russia, and he became the yardstick by which all members of his profession were measured. He was the first *badhan* to have a rudimentary knowledge of music. By his personal qualities he raised the profession of *badhan* to the dignified level of a singer. His appearances brought him into contact with the elite of Vilna, and he was encouraged to study Hebrew literature and history. His contact with the Hoveve Zion (Lovers of Zion) movement was evidenced in the "return to Zion" theme that began to appear in his songs. In 1889 he toured the United States and in 1908 settled in New York and worked as a printer and publisher. Zunser wrote approximately 600 songs. His first published book was *Shirim Hadashim* (1862), and he is well known for an edition of fifty songs called *Selected Songs of Eliakum Zunser* (1928), with piano accompaniment by William Fichandler, based on notes by Joseph RUMSHINSKY. He also wrote a drama, *Mechirath Yosef* (1868). A biography, *Eliakum Zunser—Poet of His People* (1950), was written by Sol Liptzin.

HIGHLIGHTS IN THE HISTORY
OF JEWISH MUSIC

B.C.E.

726–698   In the Temple service under King Hezekiah the Levites and the priests praise the Lord with *metziltayim* (*see* CYMBALS), *nebalim, kinnorot*, and *hatzotzerot* (*see* TRUMPETS).

627   Jeremiah prophesies the destruction of the Temple. Professional dirge singers are called upon to lament.

586   The Temple is destroyed, and the Jews are exiled from Zion to Babylonia.

538   King Cyrus of Persia conquers Babylon and sets the Jews free to return to Jerusalem and rebuild the Temple; 50,000 Jews return to their homeland while 200 singing men and women accompany the homecoming.

515   The Second Temple is consecrated.

     Ezra reads the Law to the people at Jerusalem and institutes public reading of the Law for the MINHAH service on Sabbath.

444   Nehemiah, together with Ezra, rebuilds the Wall in Jerusalem. Music and song are again heard in full grandeur.

420   Synagogues are established, and the present form of the divine service is introduced by the Sanhedrin.

C.E.

70   With the destruction of the Second Temple by the Romans, all musical activity comes to a standstill for several centuries. As a sign of national mourning instrumental music is prohibited even for religious purposes.

c. 130   Rabbi Akiba b. Joseph, the greatest scholar of his time, stresses vocal intonation for studying the Law. A system of chanting is in use for the study and revision of religious literature (Sanh. 99a).

c. 270   Rabbi Yohanan, a Palestinian scholar, prescribes chant for public recitation of the Bible and study (Meg. 32a).

c. 500   The Biblical accents (*see* ACCENTS, BIBLICAL), the TE'AMIM, are first brought into use by the Masoretes.

     The *payytanim* compose PIYYUT as a liturgical expression, thereby influencing musical practices in the synagogue.

c. 700   The function of the HAZZAN changes from the office of caretaker or beadle to that of READER. He begins to innovate forms of liturgical chant and assumes the responsibility for guarding and preserving the old tradition.

c. 745   Hebrew hymnody reaches its first peak with the poet Eleazar Kallir.

c. 759   Yehudai Gaon of Sura is responsible for standardizing the tradition of synagogal chant. Early *hazzanim* receive this tradition from him.

934   Saadiah Gaon, in the tenth chapter of his *Emunoth Vedeoth*, investigates the influence of music on the soul.

c. 950   AARON BEN ASHER, the last and most eminent Masorete of Tiberias, writes down from oral tradition a complete system of accentuation and vocalization for the Bible (known as the Tiberian system) in accordance with his tradition.

c. 1103–1150   Earliest notation of a Hebrew melody, *Mi al Har Horev*, is written by Obadiah the Norman Proselyte.

1180   Maimonides writes on music in his responsa literature (129, 143).

1421   Rabbi Jacob MOLIN (the Maharil) unifies the Ashkenazic synagogue ritual and liturgy. He strongly influences the chant of the prayer service.

C.E.

1512	Abraham Portaleone writes *Shilte ha-Gibborim*, which deals with Biblical music and musical instruments in an encyclopedic form
1518	Johannes Böschenstein, a monk, prepares for the first time in musical notation the accentuation of the Pentateuch, for Johann Reuchlin's Hebrew grammar *De accentibus et orthographia Hebraeorum libri tres.*
1587	Israel NAJARA publishes a DIWAN called *Zemirot Yisrael*, the first collection of poems printed in the Orient.
1587–1628	Solomon ROSSI is the first Jewish composer of European renown to be employed at the court of the dukes of Gonzaga of Mantua.
1594	The ORGAN is used before welcoming the Sabbath in Prague.
1623	Solomon Rossi publishes HASHIRIM ASHER LISHLOMO, the first printed art music for the synagogue.
1629–1639	Rabbi Leone da Modena founds and directs a Jewish academy of music in the ghetto of Venice.
c. 1700	The HAZZAN-BASS-SINGER institution is inaugurated in Amsterdam by Michael b. Nathan.
1724	Benedetto Marcello, a gentile musician in Venice, is attracted to ancient Hebrew melodies and publishes a collection of psalms, eleven of which are based on existing Jewish themes.
c. 1750	R. Israel Baal Shem Tov, the founder of Hassidism, incorporates music in his teachings, with strong appeal to the masses. The movement gives a fresh start to folk song throughout Eastern Europe.
c. 1765	The Berlin cantor Aaron BEER is one of the first *hazzanim* to acquire musical knowledge. He collects more than 1,200 tunes by contemporary composers.
1815	Israel Jacobson, a reformer of synagogue ritual, introduces the organ in services in Berlin.
	Lord Byron's *Hebrew Melodies* (*see* HEBREW MELODY) are set to music by Isaac Nathan.
1822	Israel LOVY introduces modern four-part choral singing to Paris.
1826	Salomon SULZER of Vienna, called "the father of the modern cantorate," establishes order in synagogue song.
c. 1840	The first volume of Salomon Sulzer's magnum opus, *Schir Zion*, is published. It becomes a model for congregations throughout the world.
1855	A HAZZANUT department is established at Jews' College in London as part of the rabbinical faculty department.
1864	Louis LEWANDOWSKI makes a great contribution to liturgical music with *Kol Rinnah* and *Todah Wesimrah* and is the first in the synagogue to hold the office of choirmaster.
1878	Abraham GOLDFADEN founds the Yiddish theater in Iaşi, Romania. It flourishes in New York until the mid-1900s.
1882	The first Bilu settlers arrive in Palestine. Poetry and music are revived and begin to flourish.
1883	The earliest cantors' organization, called the Österreich-Ungarischer Kantorenverein, is organized in Austria-Hungary.
c. 1893	Early beginnings of Jewish musicology are inaugurated by Eduard BIRNBAUM.

C.E.

1894   The Jewish Ministers Cantors Association of America (Hazzanim Varband) is the first professional cantorial association to be established in the United States.

1899   The first choral society, called Hazomir, flourishes in Łódź, Poland.

1902   The Moscow Quintet for National Jewish Music is founded and subsequently gives concerts of Jewish music throughout Russia under the leadership of Simeon BELLISON.

1908   The SOCIETY FOR JEWISH FOLK MUSIC is established in St. Petersburg.

1910   The Bureau of Jewish Education (New York) stimulates the study of Jewish music by including it in the curriculum for the Hebrew school.

        The Shulamith Music School is organized by Shulamith Ruppin in Palestine.

1911   Platon G. BRUNOFF organizes the Poale Zion Singing Society in the United States.

1914–1933   Abraham Zvi IDELSOHN publishes the ten-volume THESAURUS OF HEBREW-ORIENTAL MELODIES.

1917   The first concert of art music in the Hebraic spirit is given in the United States with the performance of works by Ernest BLOCH.

1923   The Palestine Opera is organized by Mordecai Golinkin.

1924   Joel ENGEL, the "father of Israeli music," is the first to write composed folk songs on the soil of the Holy Land.

1932   MAILAMM (Makhon Aretz Israeli La-Mada'ey ha Musika) is founded.

1933   The Palestine Conservatoire of Music is founded by Emil Hauser. It develops into the Jerusalem Music Academy and the Israel Academy of Music with independent schools in Jerusalem and Tel Aviv, both now known as the Rubin Academy of Music.

1936   Israel's first symphonic orchestra is formed under the name Palestine Philharmonic Orchestra.

1939   The JEWISH MUSIC FORUM is organized as a "society for the advancement of Jewish musical culture."

1939–1940   The first Israeli symphony (*see* FIRST SYMPHONY) is composed by Paul BEN-HAIM.

1944   The NATIONAL JEWISH MUSIC COUNCIL is established on the American scene under the auspices of the National Jewish Welfare Board of New York.

1948   With the establishment of the state of Israel many dispersed communities return to the homeland. As a result, a number of musical traditions are blended.

        The School of Sacred Music of the Hebrew Union College–Jewish Institute of Religion is established.

        The Palestine Philharmonic Orchestra is renamed ISRAEL PHILHARMONIC ORCHESTRA.

1950   The music department of the Israeli Ministry of Education and Culture establishes the Ethnological Institute for Jewish Music.

1951   The music program at Yeshiva University expands into a cantorial workshop.

1952   The Cantors Institute and Seminary College of Jewish Music is founded at the Jewish Theological Seminary of America.

C.E.

The Hebrew Arts School for Music and the Dance is established by the Hebrew Arts Foundation in New York City.

1953   The LEAGUE OF COMPOSERS IN ISRAEL is established.

1954   The cantorial workshop at Yeshiva University becomes the Cantorial Training Institute.

1958   A music department is instituted at Gratz College in Philadelphia.

1960   The National Israeli Song Festival is established by the office of the Prime Minister of Israel.

1961   The Israel Music Institute is founded by the National Council of Culture and Art, the Ministry of Education and Culture, the America-Israel Cultural Foundation, and the League of Composers in Israel.

1965   The Jewish Music Research Centre is established at the Hebrew University of Jerusalem. It is housed in the Jewish National and University Library.

1972   The Israel Music Institute publishes more than 350 works and musicological monographs by Israeli composers and musicologists. In conjunction with the National Council of Culture and Art, it assists in the release of commercial recordings of Israeli music by the Israel branches of CBS and RCA.

The League of Composers in Israel brings Israeli music to countries throughout the world and welcomes immigrant composers as members.

The Jewish Welfare Board's Jewish Music Council and Sephardic Community Activities Program at Yeshiva University launches the 1972 nationwide observance of Jewish Music Month, featuring "The Music of the Sephardic and Oriental Jews."

1973   The Israel Institute for Sacred Music emphasizes "Prayers of Exile and Chants of Redemption" at the Fifteenth Annual Sacred Music Convention.

"Musical Offerings to Israel," in celebration of Israel's twenty-fifth anniversary of statehood, is the theme of the 1973 Jewish Music Festival, sponsored by the Jewish Music Council of the Jewish Welfare Board.